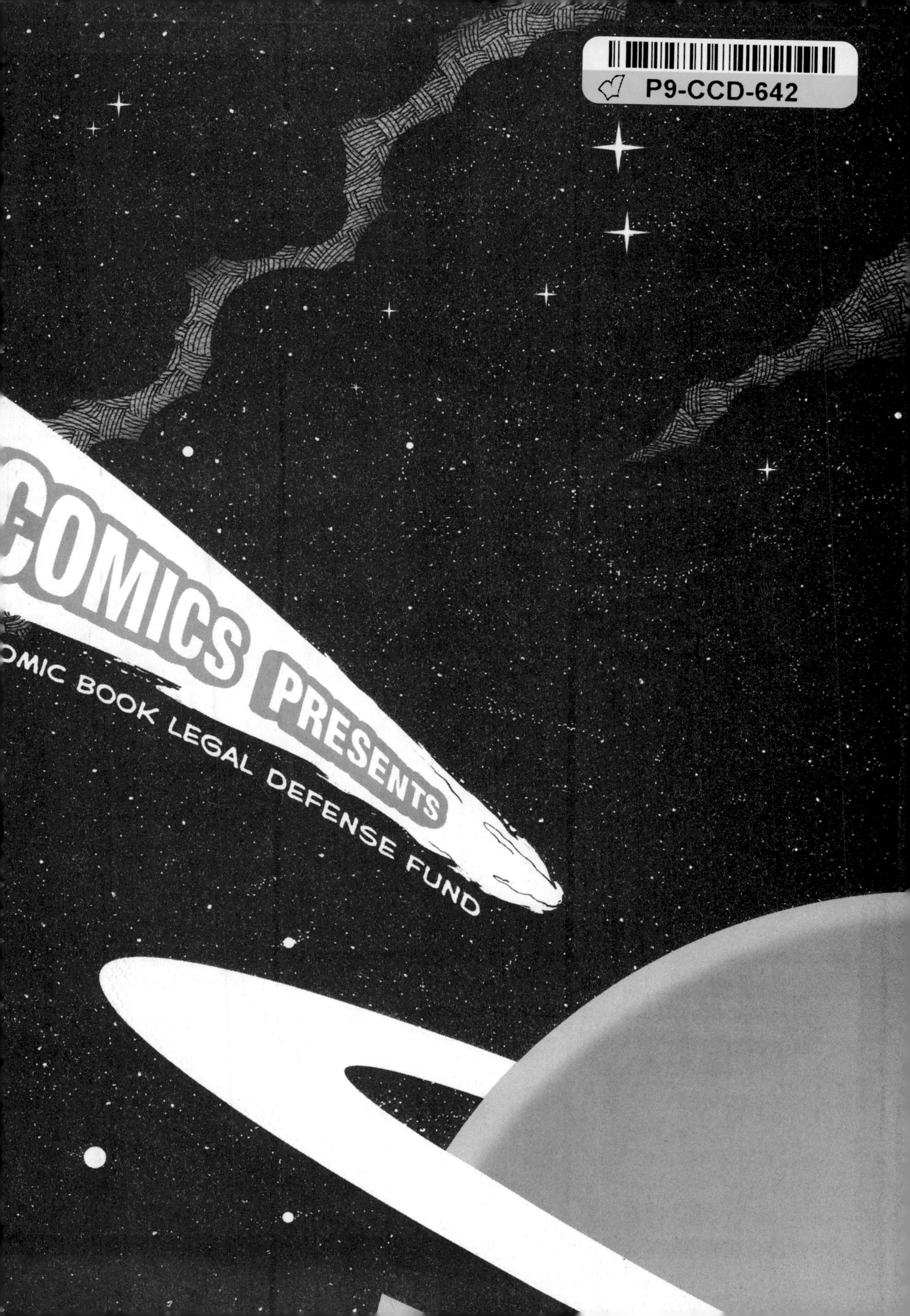
COMICS PRESENTS
OMIC BOOK LEGAL DEFENSE FUND

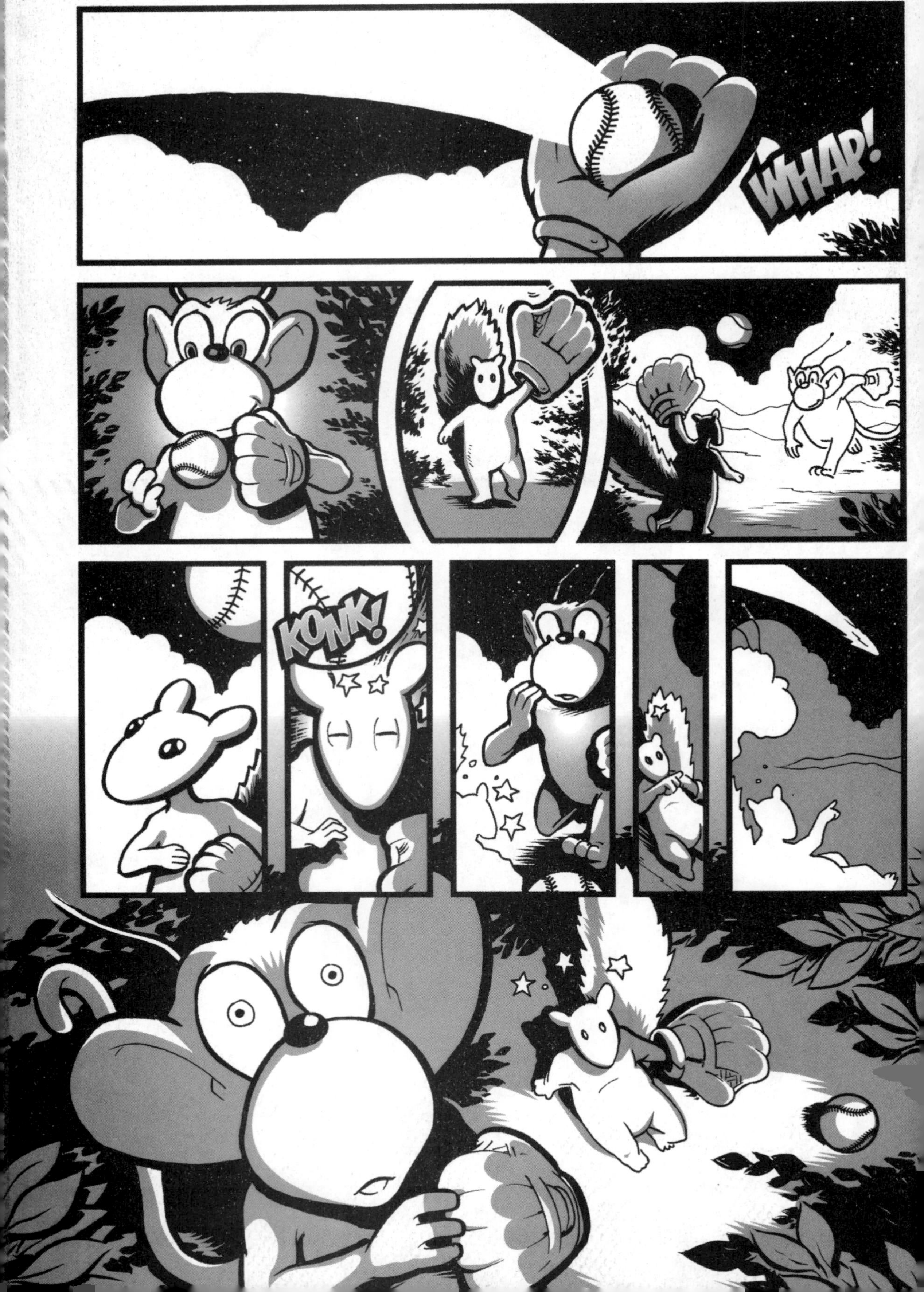
WHAP!
KONK!

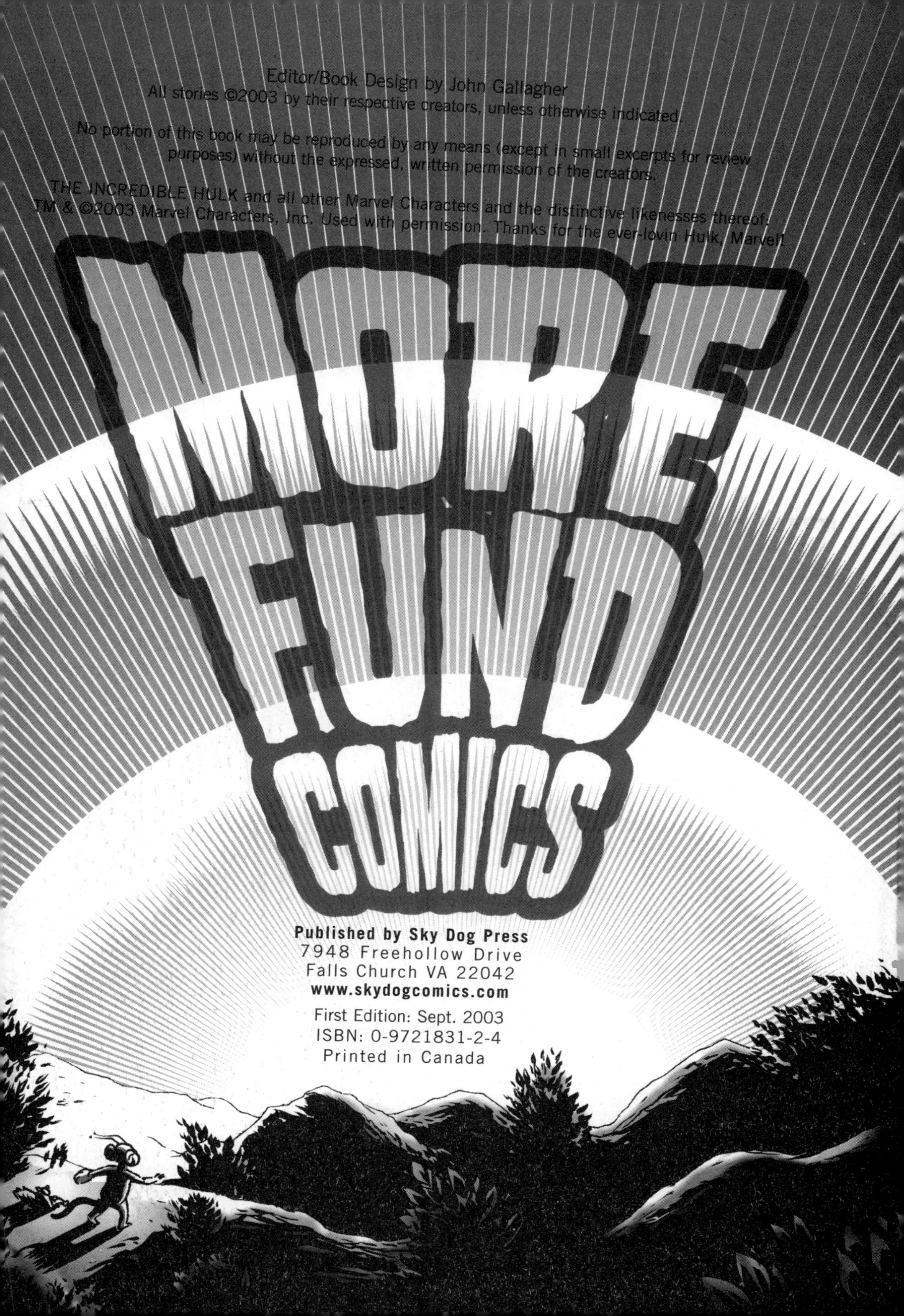

Editor/Book Design by John Gallagher

MORE FUND COMICS

Published by Sky Dog Press
7948 Freehollow Drive
Falls Church VA 22042
www.skydogcomics.com

First Edition: Sept. 2003
ISBN: 0-9721831-2-4
Printed in Canada

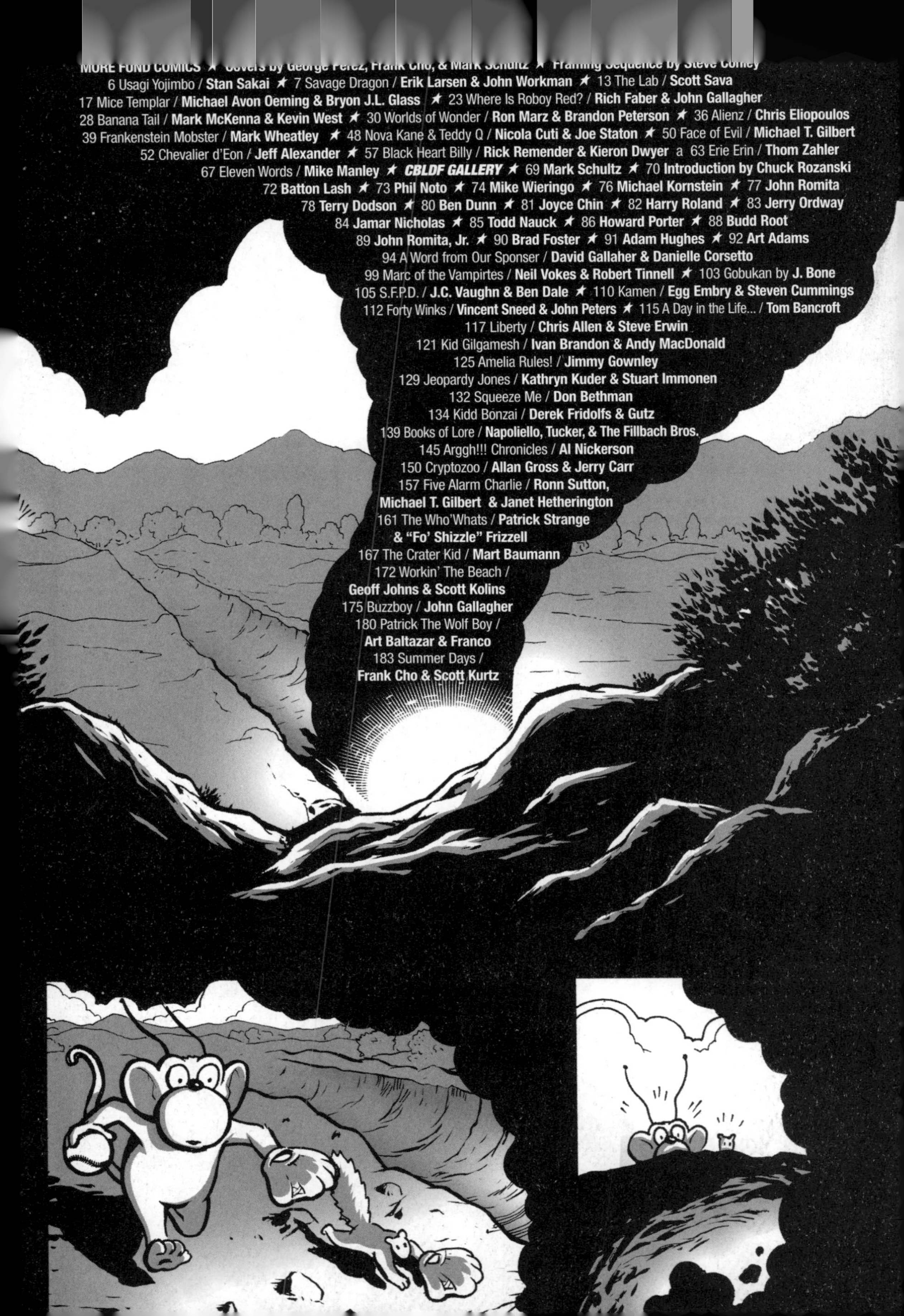

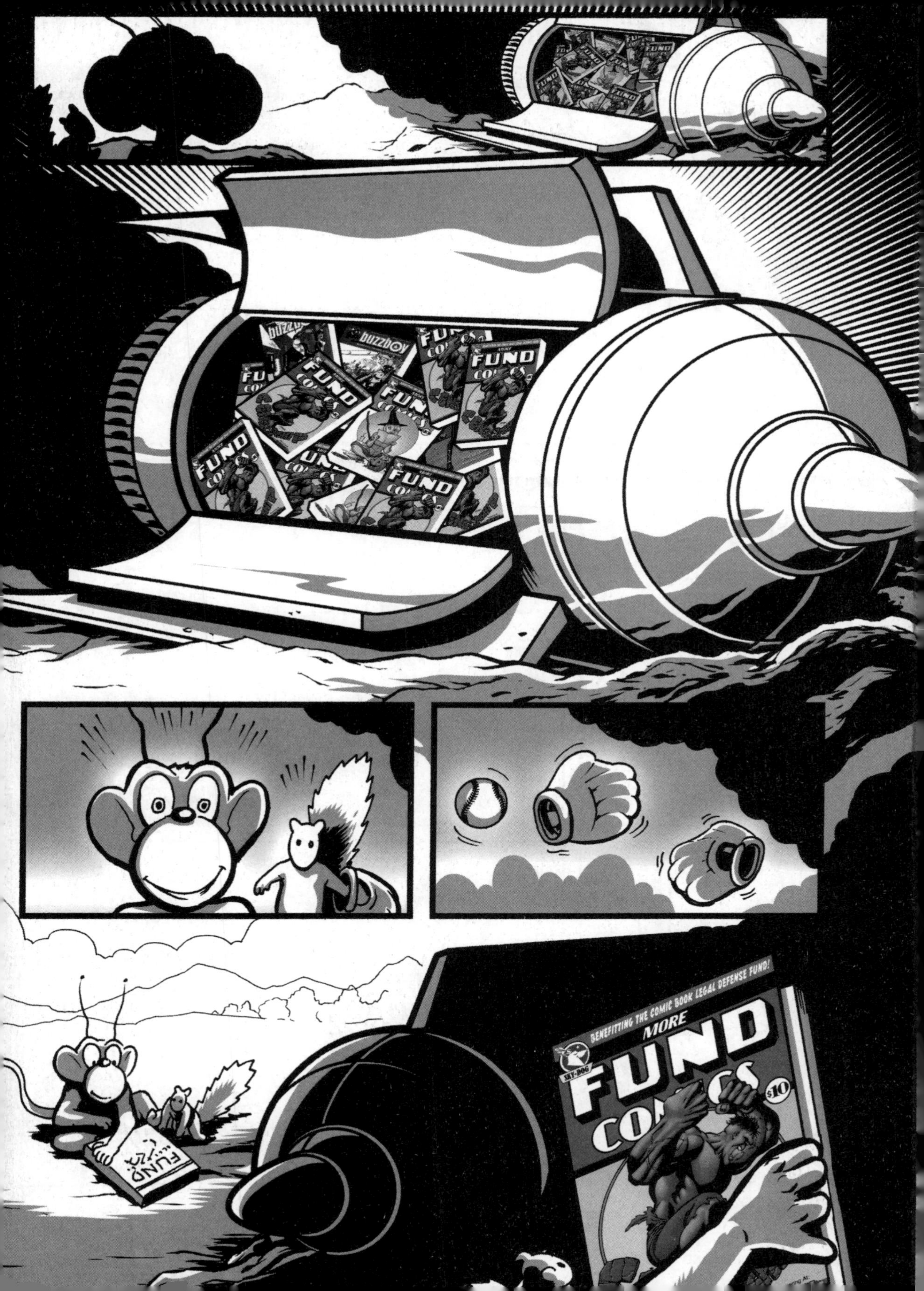
FUND COMICS
BUZZBOY
BENEFITTING THE COMIC BOOK LEGAL DEFENSE FUND!
MORE
FUND
COMICS
$10
SKY-DOG

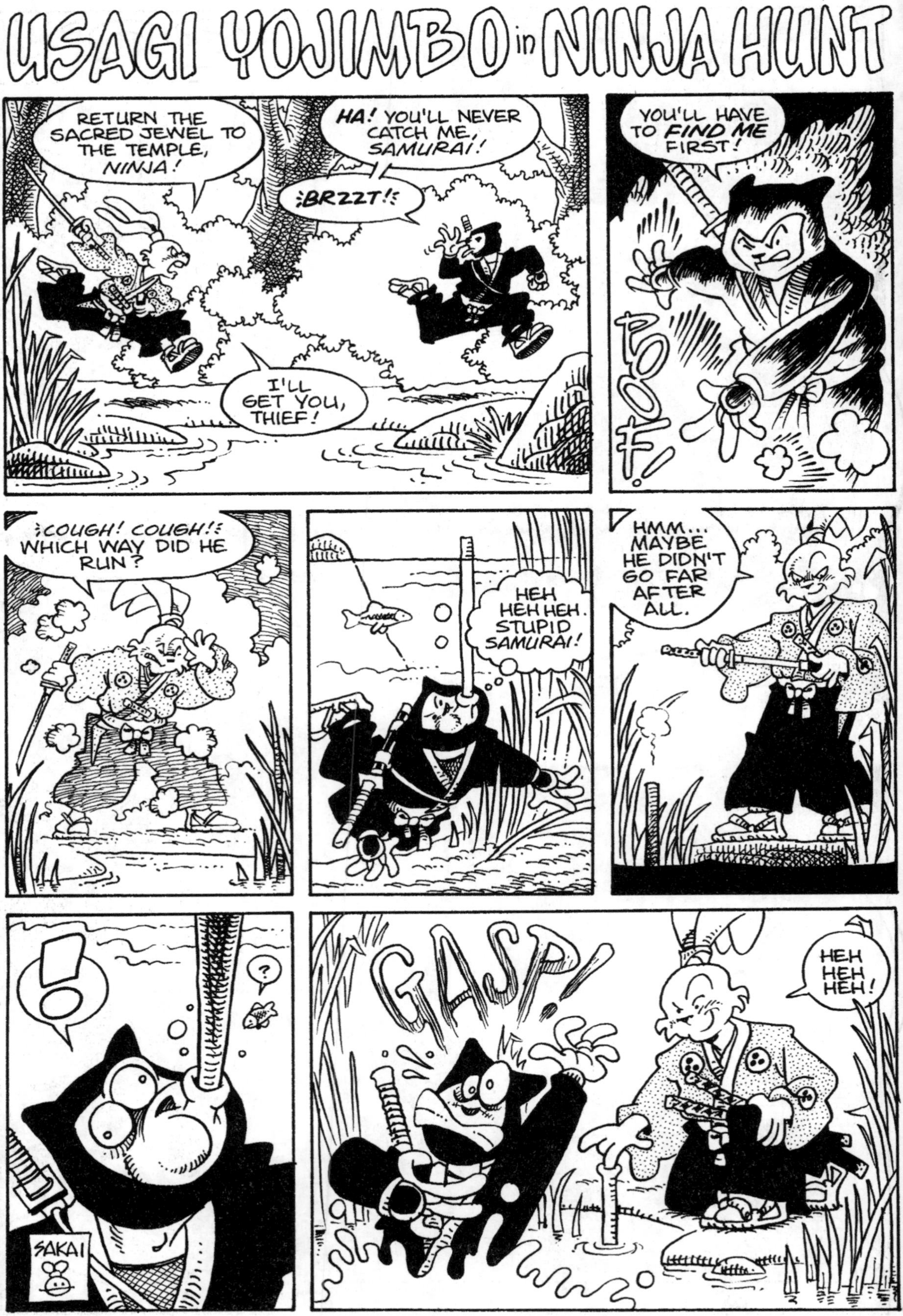
USAGI YOJIMBO in NINJA HUNT
RETURN THE SACRED JEWEL TO THE TEMPLE, NINJA!
HA! YOU'LL NEVER CATCH ME, SAMURAI!
BRZZT!
I'LL GET YOU, THIEF!
YOU'LL HAVE TO FIND ME FIRST!
POOF!
COUGH! COUGH! WHICH WAY DID HE RUN?
HEH HEH HEH. STUPID SAMURAI!
HMM... MAYBE HE DIDN'T GO FAR AFTER ALL.
!
?
GASP!
HEH HEH HEH!
SAKAI

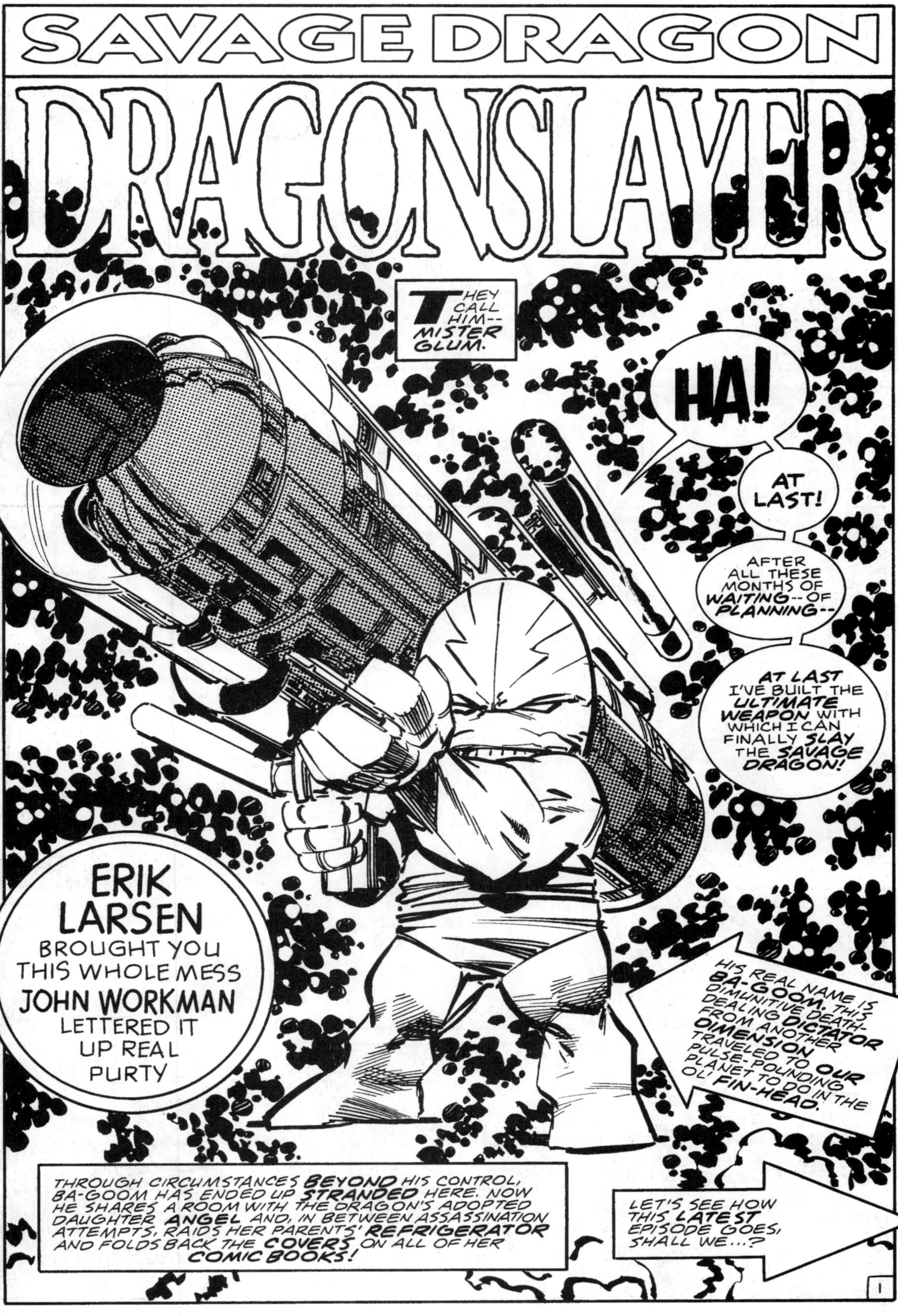
SAVAGE DRAGON
DRAGONSLAYER
THEY CALL HIM--MISTER GLUM.
HA!
AT LAST!
AFTER ALL THESE MONTHS OF WAITING--OF PLANNING--
AT LAST I'VE BUILT THE ULTIMATE WEAPON WITH WHICH I CAN FINALLY SLAY THE SAVAGE DRAGON!
ERIK LARSEN BROUGHT YOU THIS WHOLE MESS JOHN WORKMAN LETTERED IT UP REAL PURTY
HIS REAL NAME IS BA-GOOM. THIS DIMINUTIVE DEATH-DEALING DICTATOR FROM ANOTHER DIMENSION TRAVELED TO OUR PULSE-POUNDING PLANET TO DO IN THE OL' FIN-HEAD.
THROUGH CIRCUMSTANCES BEYOND HIS CONTROL, BA-GOOM HAS ENDED UP STRANDED HERE. NOW HE SHARES A ROOM WITH THE DRAGON'S ADOPTED DAUGHTER ANGEL AND, IN BETWEEN ASSASSINATION ATTEMPTS, RAIDS HER PARENTS' REFRIGERATOR AND FOLDS BACK THE COVERS ON ALL OF HER COMIC BOOKS!
LET'S SEE HOW THIS LATEST EPISODE GOES, SHALL WE...?
1

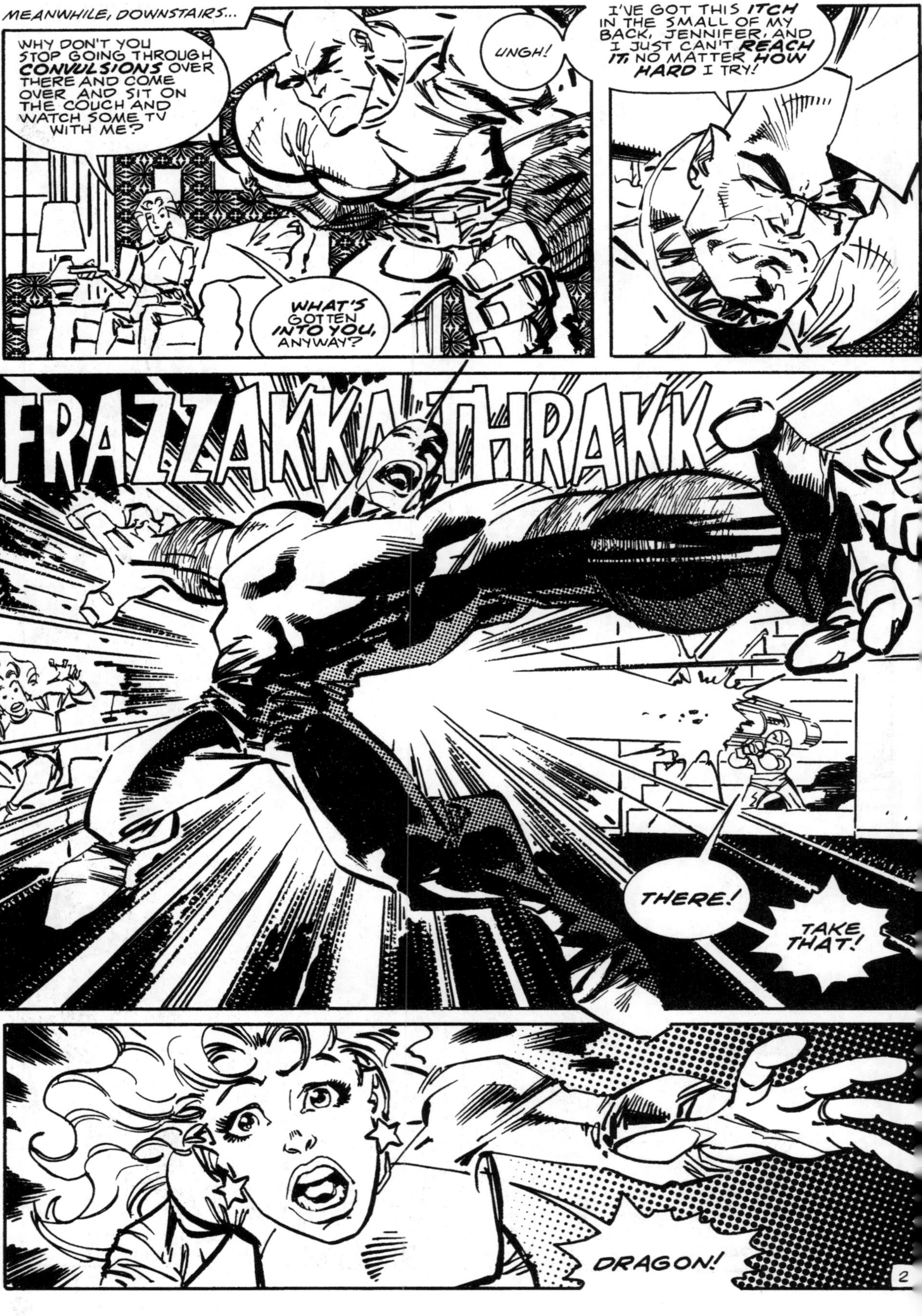

MEANWHILE, DOWNSTAIRS...
WHY DON'T YOU STOP GOING THROUGH CONVULSIONS OVER THERE AND COME OVER AND SIT ON THE COUCH AND WATCH SOME TV WITH ME?
UNGH!
WHAT'S GOTTEN INTO YOU, ANYWAY?
I'VE GOT THIS ITCH IN THE SMALL OF MY BACK, JENNIFER, AND I JUST CAN'T REACH IT, NO MATTER HOW HARD I TRY!
FRAZZAKKATHRAKK
THERE!
TAKE THAT!
DRAGON!

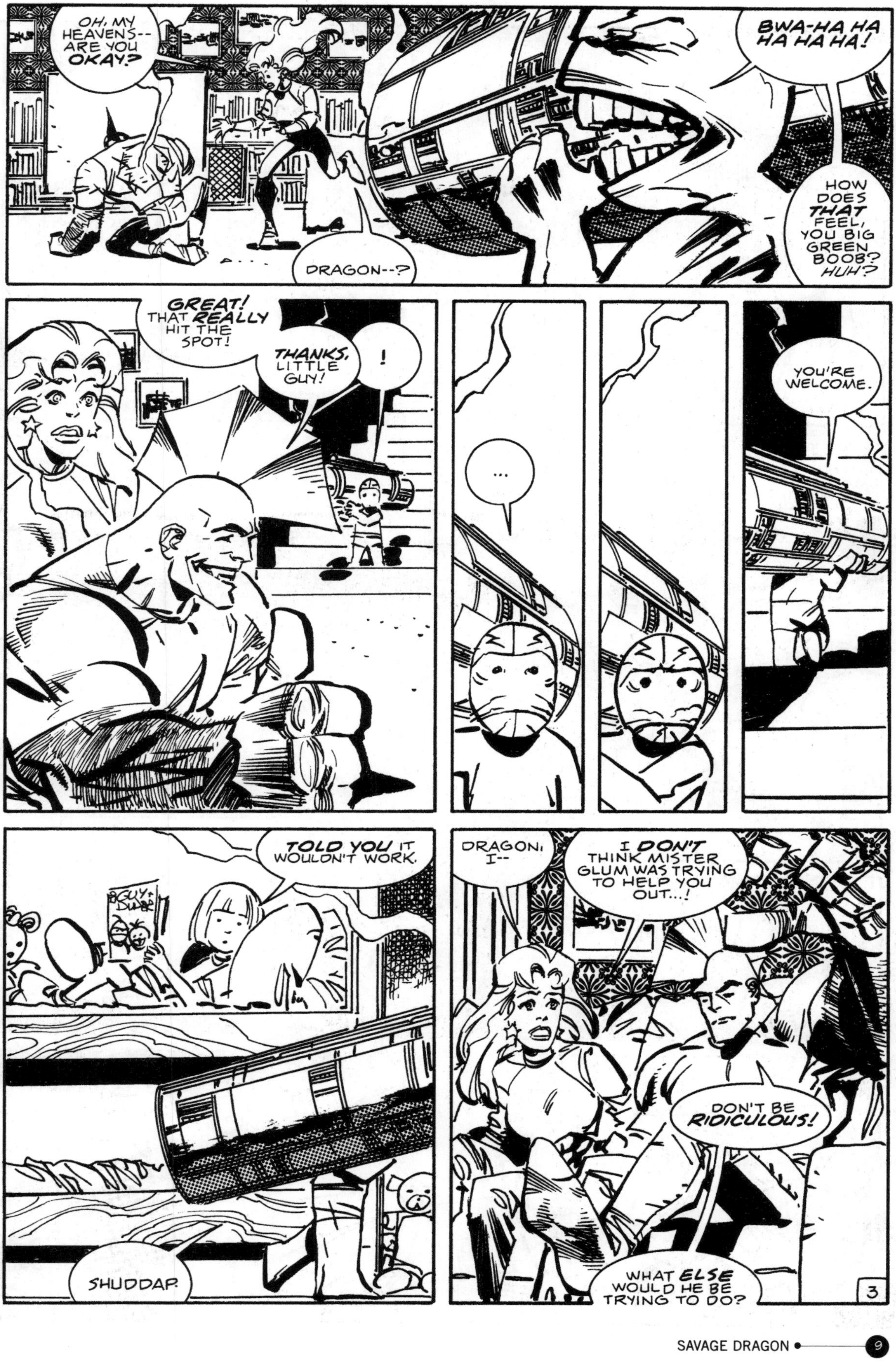

OH, MY HEAVENS-- ARE YOU OKAY?
BWA-HA HA HA HA HA!
HOW DOES THAT FEEL, YOU BIG GREEN BOOB? HUH?
DRAGON--?
GREAT! THAT REALLY HIT THE SPOT!
THANKS, LITTLE GUY!
!
...
YOU'RE WELCOME.
TOLD YOU IT WOULDN'T WORK.
SHUDDAP.
DRAGON, I--
I DON'T THINK MISTER GLUM WAS TRYING TO HELP YOU OUT...!
DON'T BE RIDICULOUS!
WHAT ELSE WOULD HE BE TRYING TO DO?
3

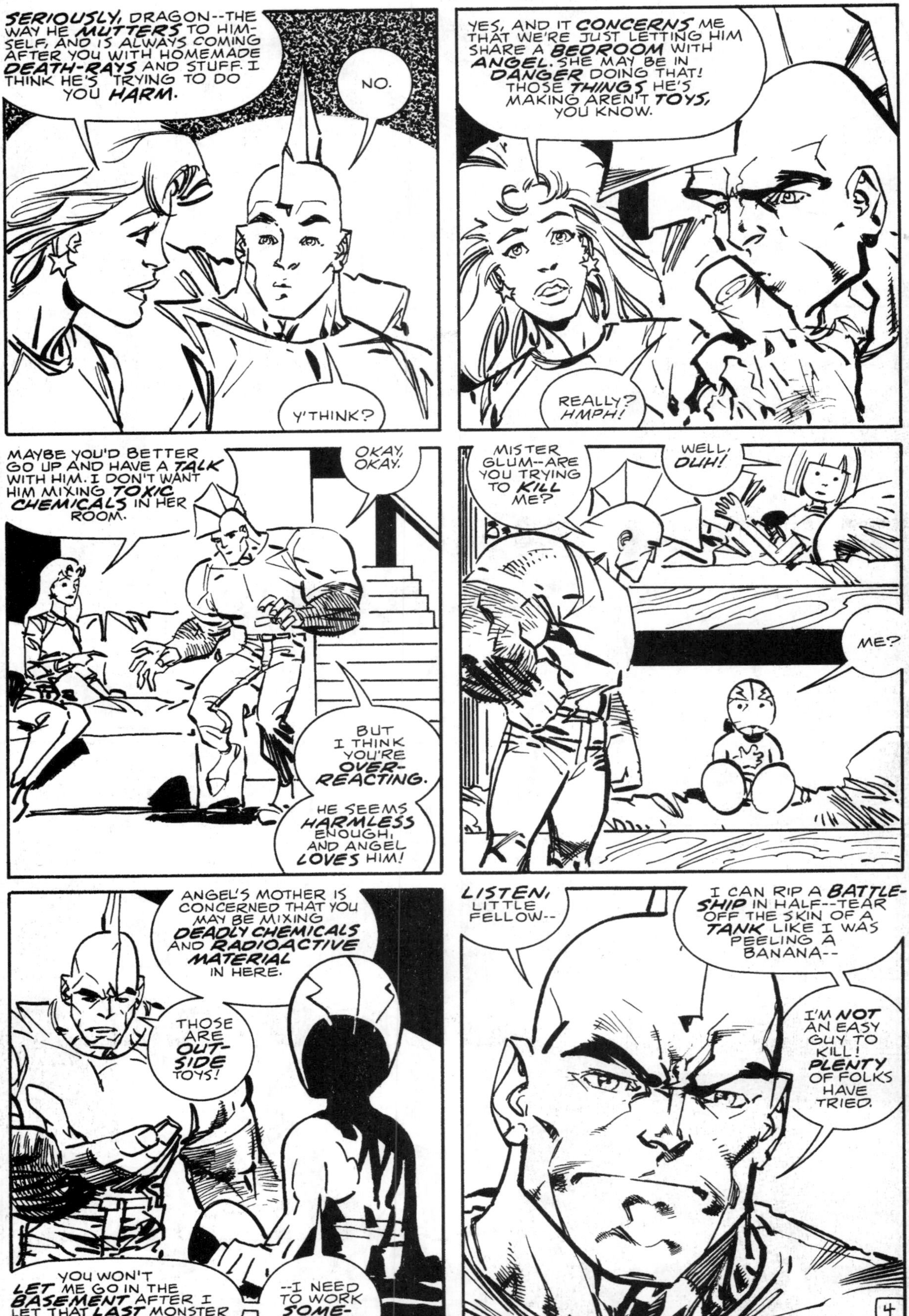
SERIOUSLY, DRAGON--THE WAY HE MUTTERS TO HIMSELF, AND IS ALWAYS COMING AFTER YOU WITH HOMEMADE DEATH-RAYS AND STUFF. I THINK HE'S TRYING TO DO YOU HARM.
NO.
Y'THINK?
YES, AND IT CONCERNS ME THAT WE'RE JUST LETTING HIM SHARE A BEDROOM WITH ANGEL. SHE MAY BE IN DANGER DOING THAT! THOSE THINGS HE'S MAKING AREN'T TOYS, YOU KNOW.
REALLY? HMPH!
MAYBE YOU'D BETTER GO UP AND HAVE A TALK WITH HIM. I DON'T WANT HIM MIXING TOXIC CHEMICALS IN HER ROOM.
OKAY, OKAY.
BUT I THINK YOU'RE OVER-REACTING.
HE SEEMS HARMLESS ENOUGH, AND ANGEL LOVES HIM!
MISTER GLUM--ARE YOU TRYING TO KILL ME?
WELL, DUH!
ME?
ANGEL'S MOTHER IS CONCERNED THAT YOU MAY BE MIXING DEADLY CHEMICALS AND RADIOACTIVE MATERIAL IN HERE.
THOSE ARE OUT-SIDE TOYS!
YOU WON'T LET ME GO IN THE BASEMENT AFTER I LET THAT LAST MONSTER OUT OF DIMENSION-X--
--I NEED TO WORK SOME-WHERE!
LISTEN, LITTLE FELLOW--
I CAN RIP A BATTLE-SHIP IN HALF--TEAR OFF THE SKIN OF A TANK LIKE I WAS PEELING A BANANA--
I'M NOT AN EASY GUY TO KILL! PLENTY OF FOLKS HAVE TRIED.
4

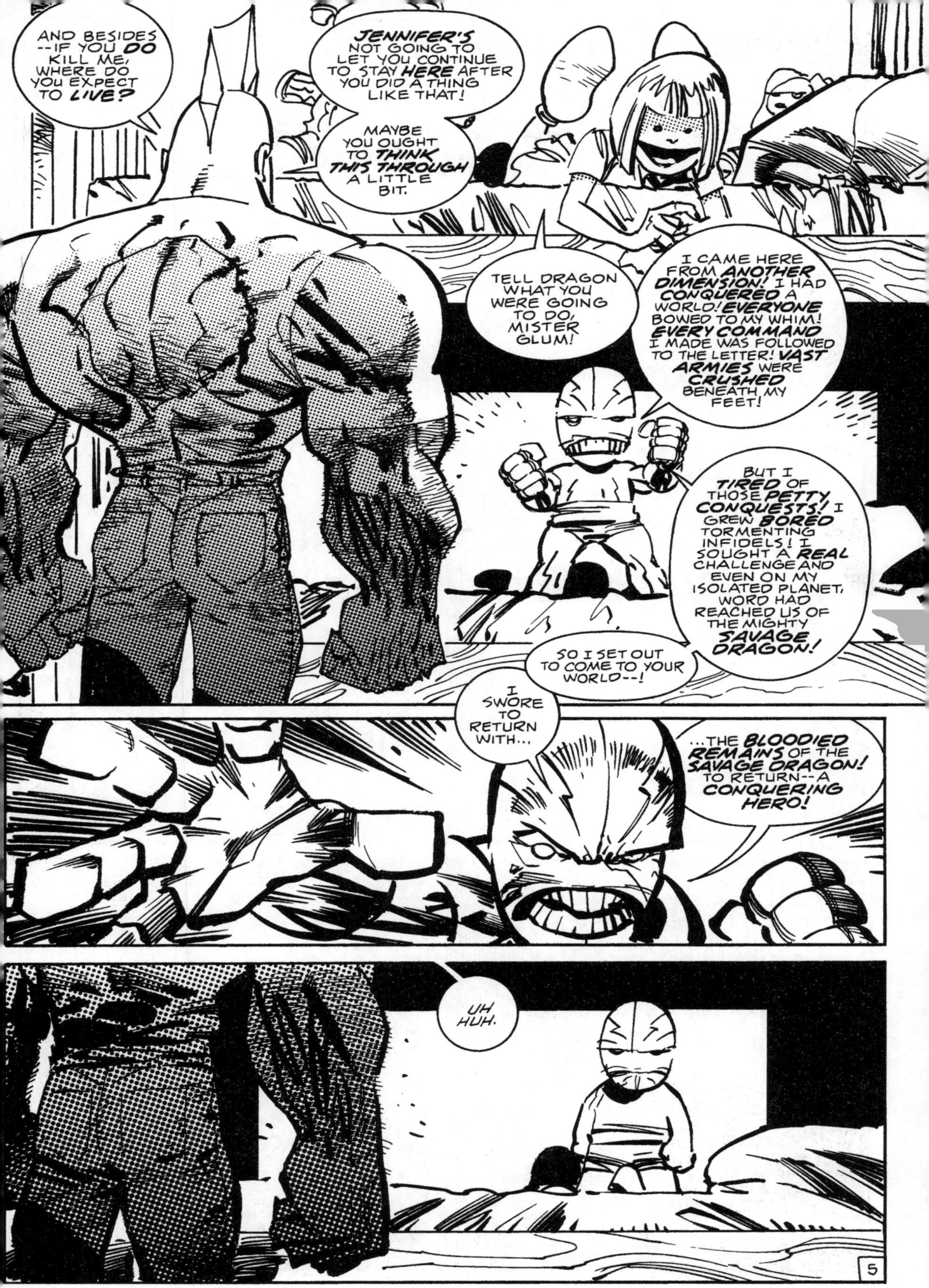
AND BESIDES --IF YOU DO KILL ME, WHERE DO YOU EXPECT TO LIVE?
JENNIFER'S NOT GOING TO LET YOU CONTINUE TO STAY HERE AFTER YOU DID A THING LIKE THAT!
MAYBE YOU OUGHT TO THINK THIS THROUGH A LITTLE BIT.
TELL DRAGON WHAT YOU WERE GOING TO DO, MISTER GLUM!
I CAME HERE FROM ANOTHER DIMENSION! I HAD CONQUERED A WORLD! EVERYONE BOWED TO MY WHIM! EVERY COMMAND I MADE WAS FOLLOWED TO THE LETTER! VAST ARMIES WERE CRUSHED BENEATH MY FEET!
BUT I TIRED OF THOSE PETTY CONQUESTS! I GREW BORED TORMENTING INFIDELS! I SOUGHT A REAL CHALLENGE AND EVEN ON MY ISOLATED PLANET, WORD HAD REACHED US OF THE MIGHTY SAVAGE DRAGON!
SO I SET OUT TO COME TO YOUR WORLD--!
I SWORE TO RETURN WITH...
...THE BLOODIED REMAINS OF THE SAVAGE DRAGON! TO RETURN--A CONQUERING HERO!
UH HUH.
5

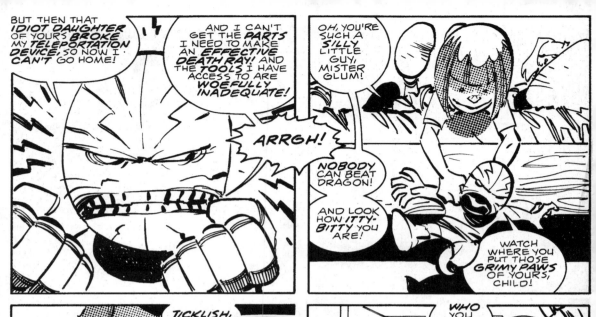

BUT THEN THAT *IDIOT DAUGHTER* OF YOURS *BROKE* MY *TELEPORTATION DEVICE*, SO NOW I CAN'T GO HOME!

AND I CAN'T GET THE *PARTS* I NEED TO MAKE AN *EFFECTIVE DEATH RAY!* AND THE *TOOLS* I HAVE ACCESS TO ARE *WOEFULLY INADEQUATE!*

ARRGH!

OH, YOU'RE SUCH A *SILLY* LITTLE GUY, MISTER GLUM!

NOBODY CAN BEAT DRAGON!

AND LOOK HOW *ITTY-BITTY* YOU ARE!

WATCH WHERE YOU PUT THOSE *GRIMY PAWS* OF YOURS, CHILD!

TICKLISH, TOO!

HE! HE! HE! HO!

WATCH IT!

HEE! HE! HOO!

STOP IT! STOP IT!

WHO YOU GONNA KILL?

WHO YOU GONNA KILL?

UNHAND ME, GIRL!

I *MEAN* IT!

YOU *DON'T* WANT TO GET ME ANGRY!

WELL...?

WHAT DID YOU FIND OUT?

JUST WHAT I THOUGHT.

HE'S *COMPLETELY* HARMLESS!

LOOK FOR *MORE* ADVENTURES OF THE EVER-LOVIN' *DRAGON* FAMILY EVERY MONTH IN THE PAGES OF *SAVAGE DRAGON!* ON SALE WHEREVER BETTER COMICS MAGAZINES ARE SOLD! ASK FOR IT BY NAME!

6

THE LAB BY SCOTT SAVA

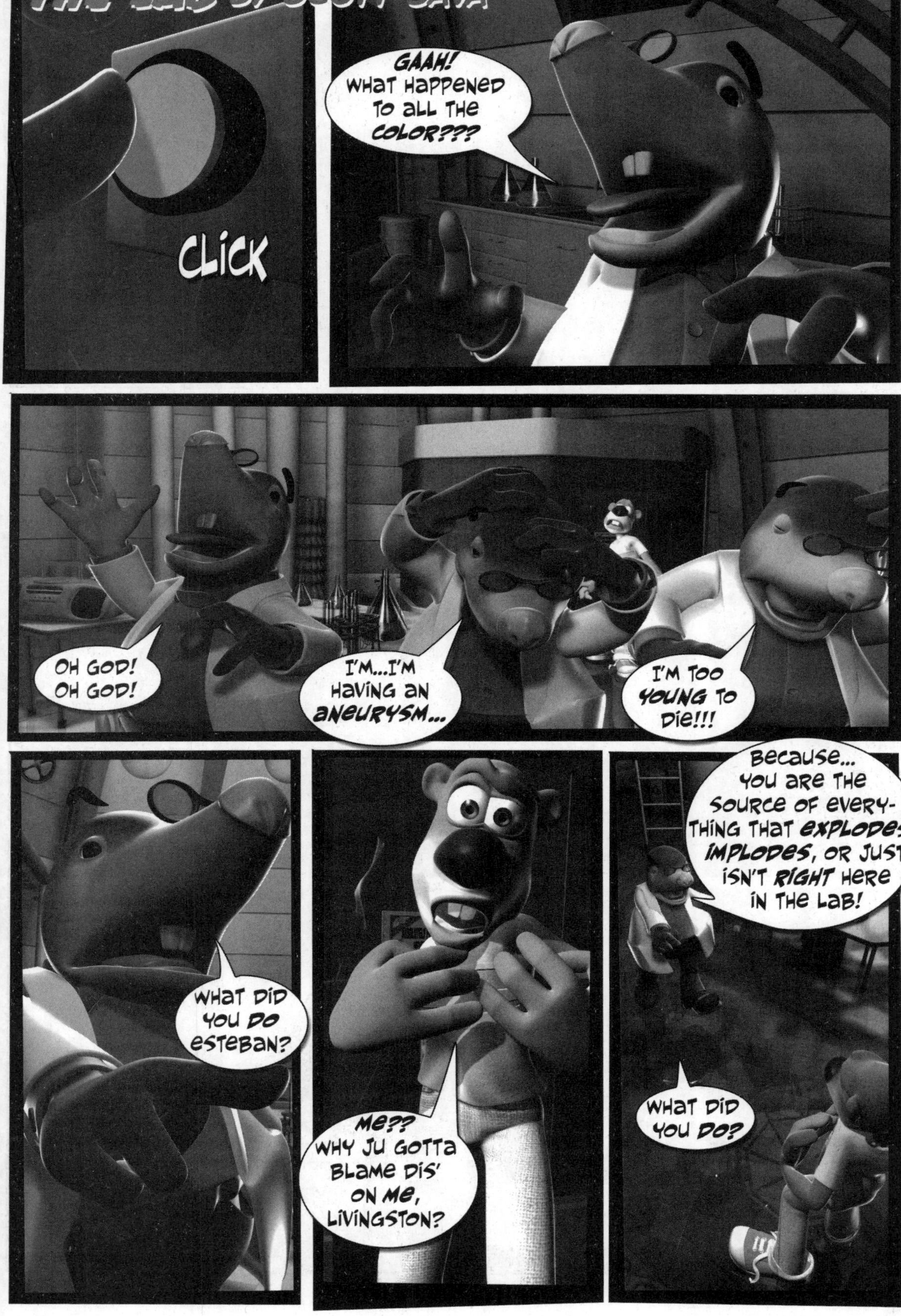
CLICK
GAAH! WHAT HAPPENED TO ALL THE COLOR???
OH GOD! OH GOD!
I'M...I'M HAVING AN ANEURYSM...
I'M TOO YOUNG TO DIE!!!
WHAT DID YOU DO ESTEBAN?
ME?? WHY JU GOTTA BLAME DIS' ON ME, LIVINGSTON?
BECAUSE... YOU ARE THE SOURCE OF EVERY-THING THAT EXPLODES, IMPLODES, OR JUST ISN'T RIGHT HERE IN THE LAB!
WHAT DID YOU DO?

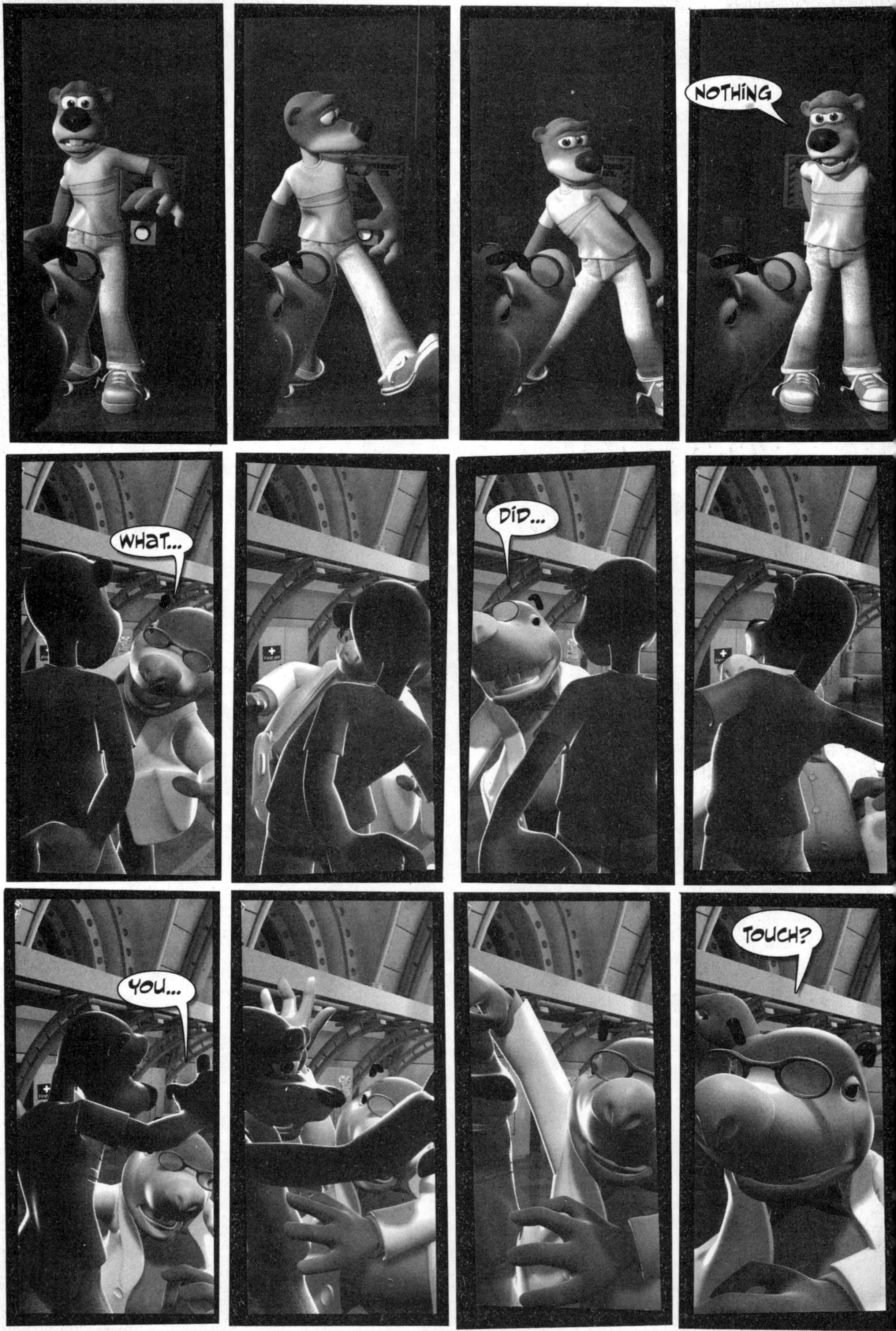
NOTHING
WHAT...
DID...
YOU...
TOUCH?

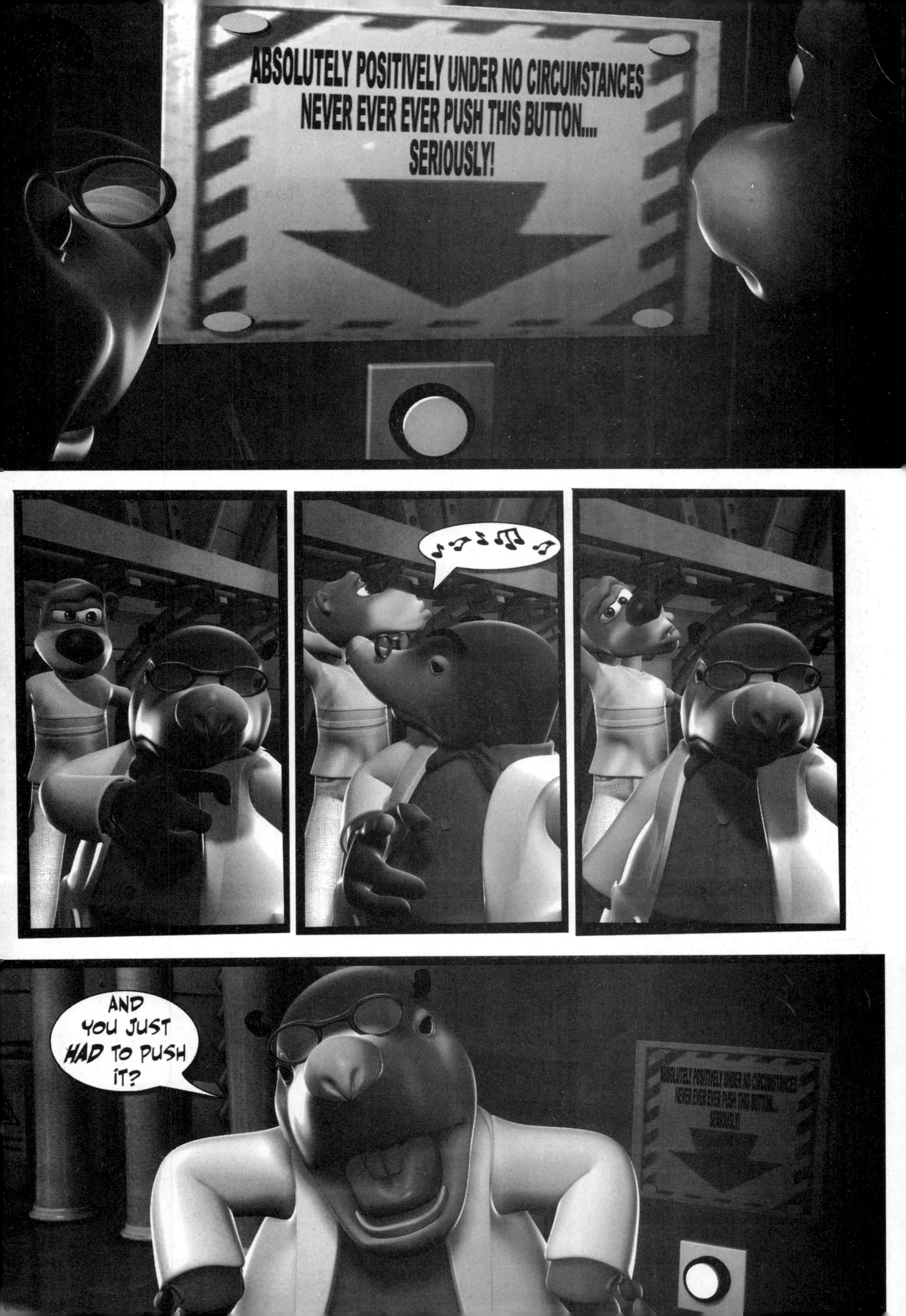
ABSOLUTELY POSITIVELY UNDER NO CIRCUMSTANCES
NEVER EVER EVER PUSH THIS BUTTON....
SERIOUSLY!
AND YOU JUST *HAD* TO PUSH IT?
ABSOLUTELY POSITIVELY UNDER NO CIRCUMSTANCES
NEVER EVER EVER PUSH THIS BUTTON...
SERIOUSLY!

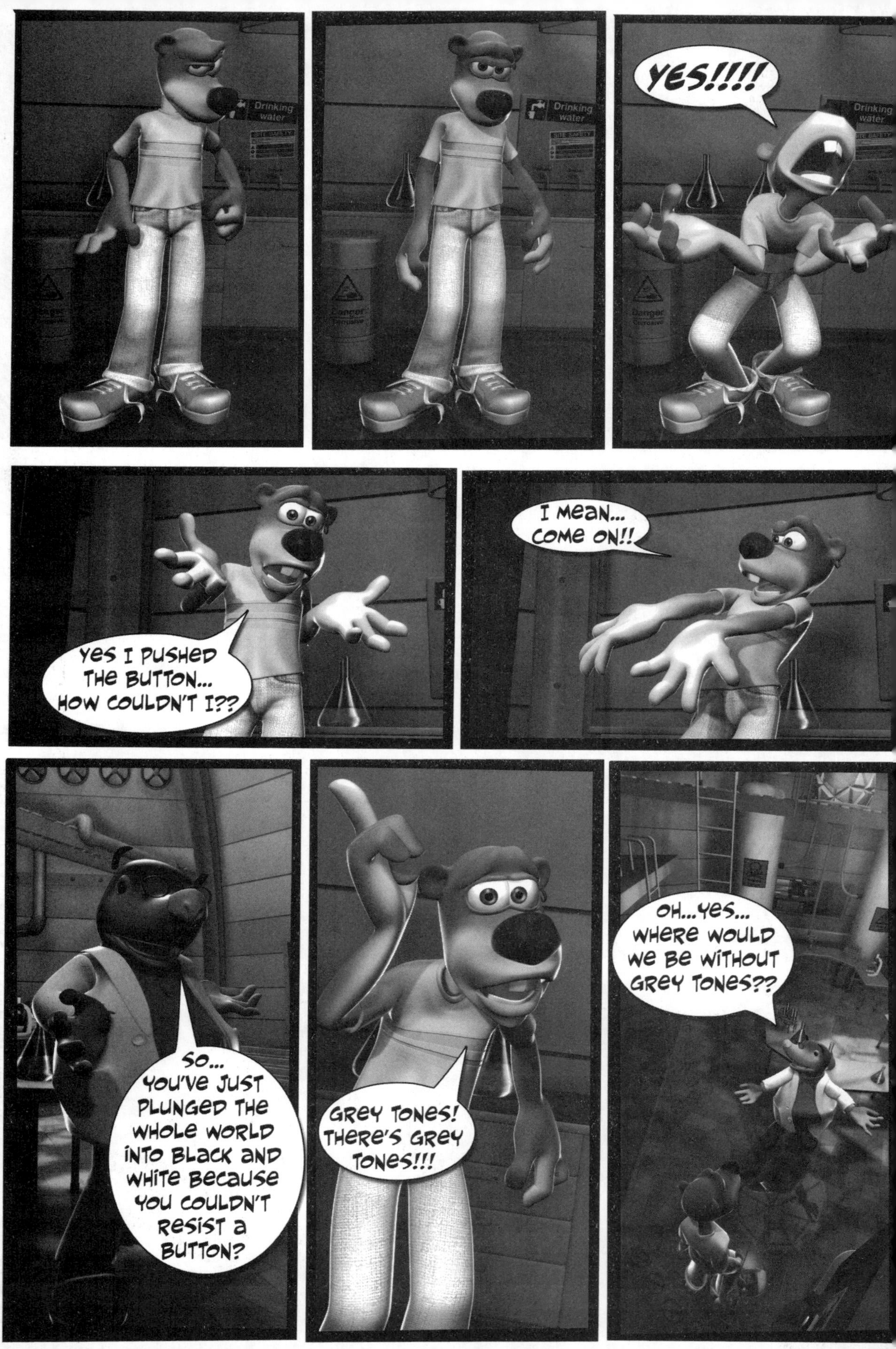
Drinking water
SITE SAFETY
Danger Corrosive
YES!!!!
YES I PUSHED THE BUTTON... HOW COULDN'T I??
I MEAN... COME ON!!
SO... YOU'VE JUST PLUNGED THE WHOLE WORLD INTO BLACK AND WHITE BECAUSE YOU COULDN'T RESIST A BUTTON?
GREY TONES! THERE'S GREY TONES!!!
OH...YES... WHERE WOULD WE BE WITHOUT GREY TONES??

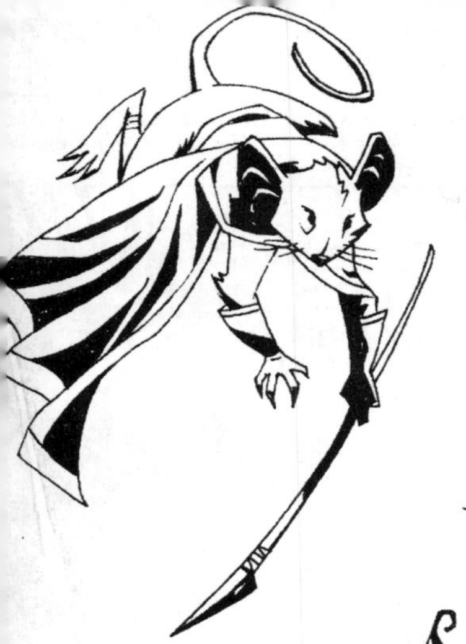

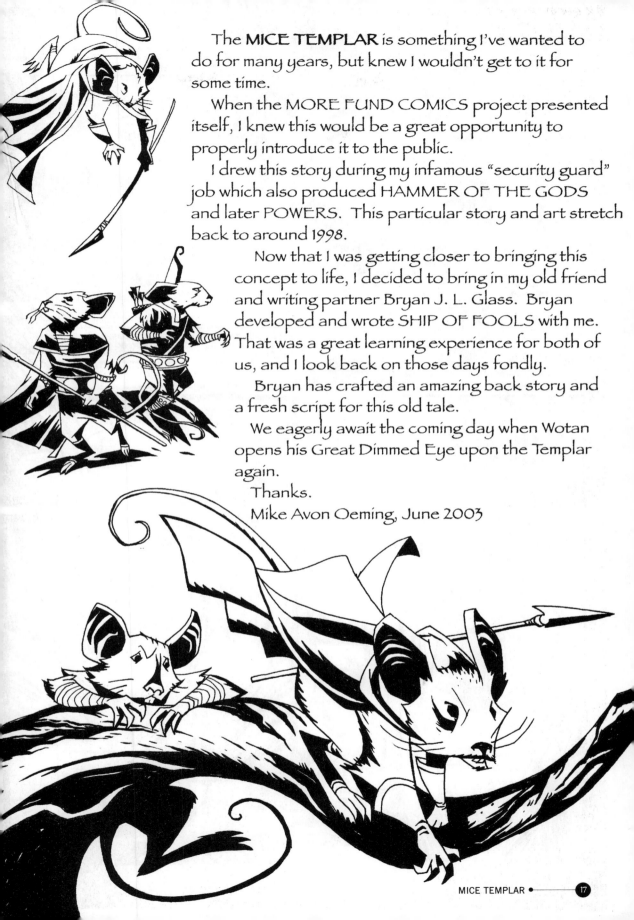

The **MICE TEMPLAR** is something I've wanted to do for many years, but knew I wouldn't get to it for some time.

When the MORE FUND COMICS project presented itself, I knew this would be a great opportunity to properly introduce it to the public.

I drew this story during my infamous "security guard" job which also produced HAMMER OF THE GODS and later POWERS. This particular story and art stretch back to around 1998.

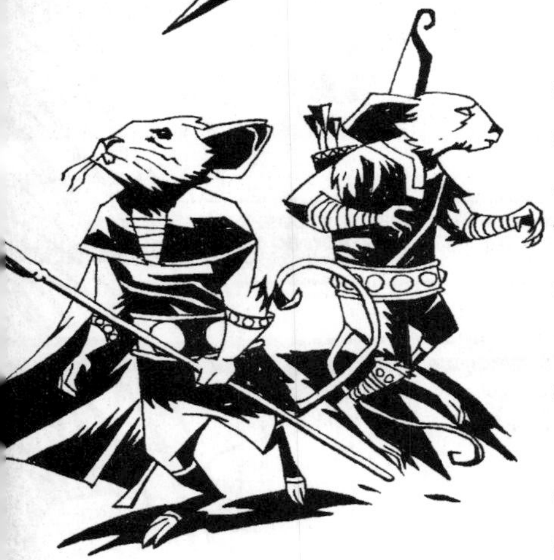

Now that I was getting closer to bringing this concept to life, I decided to bring in my old friend and writing partner Bryan J. L. Glass. Bryan developed and wrote SHIP OF FOOLS with me. That was a great learning experience for both of us, and I look back on those days fondly.

Bryan has crafted an amazing back story and a fresh script for this old tale.

We eagerly await the coming day when Wotan opens his Great Dimmed Eye upon the Templar again.

Thanks.

Mike Avon Oeming, June 2003

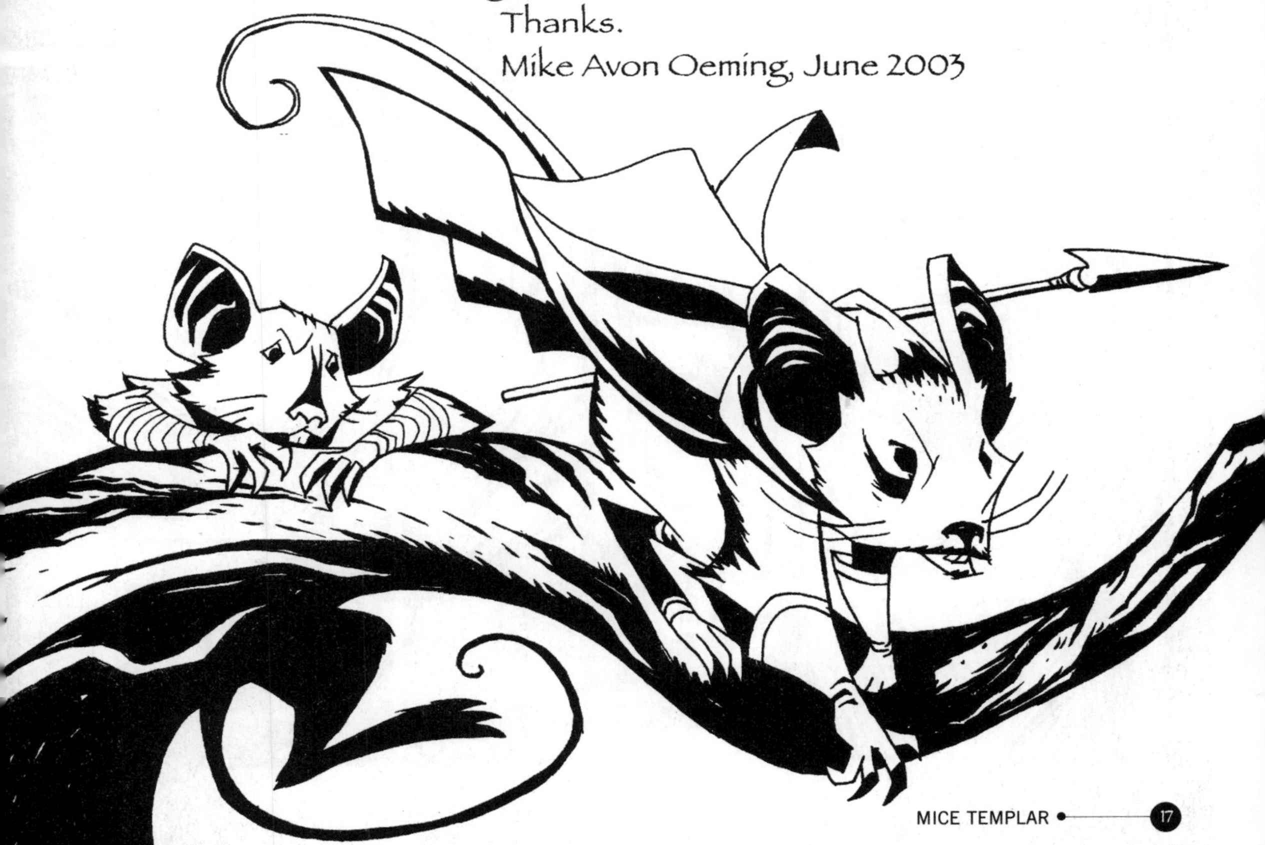

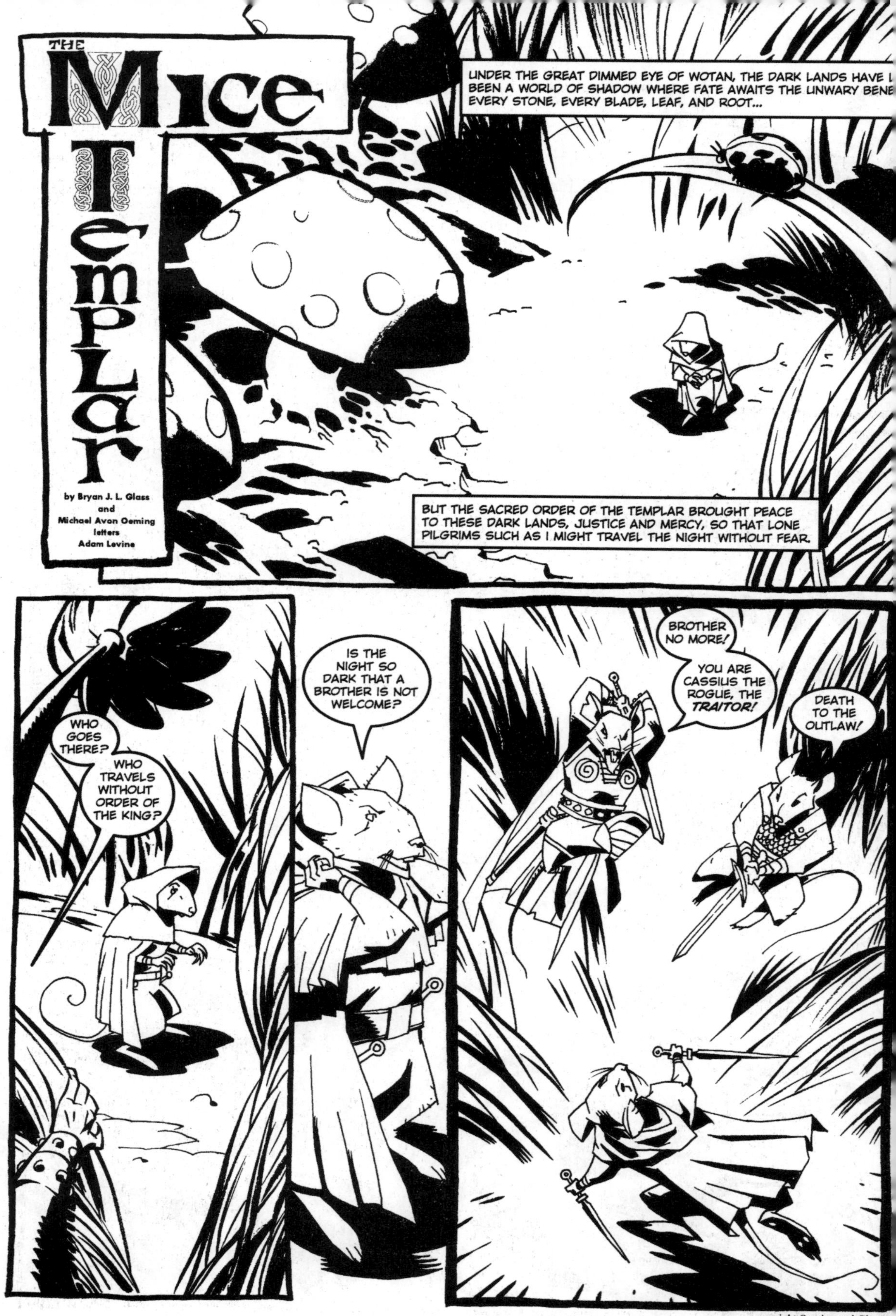
THE Mice Templar
by Bryan J. L. Glass
and
Michael Avon Oeming
letters
Adam Levine
UNDER THE GREAT DIMMED EYE OF WOTAN, THE DARK LANDS HAVE L
BEEN A WORLD OF SHADOW WHERE FATE AWAITS THE UNWARY BENE
EVERY STONE, EVERY BLADE, LEAF, AND ROOT...
BUT THE SACRED ORDER OF THE TEMPLAR BROUGHT PEACE TO THESE DARK LANDS, JUSTICE AND MERCY, SO THAT LONE PILGRIMS SUCH AS I MIGHT TRAVEL THE NIGHT WITHOUT FEAR.
WHO GOES THERE?
WHO TRAVELS WITHOUT ORDER OF THE KING?
IS THE NIGHT SO DARK THAT A BROTHER IS NOT WELCOME?
BROTHER NO MORE!
YOU ARE CASSIUS THE ROGUE, THE *TRAITOR!*
DEATH TO THE OUTLAW!

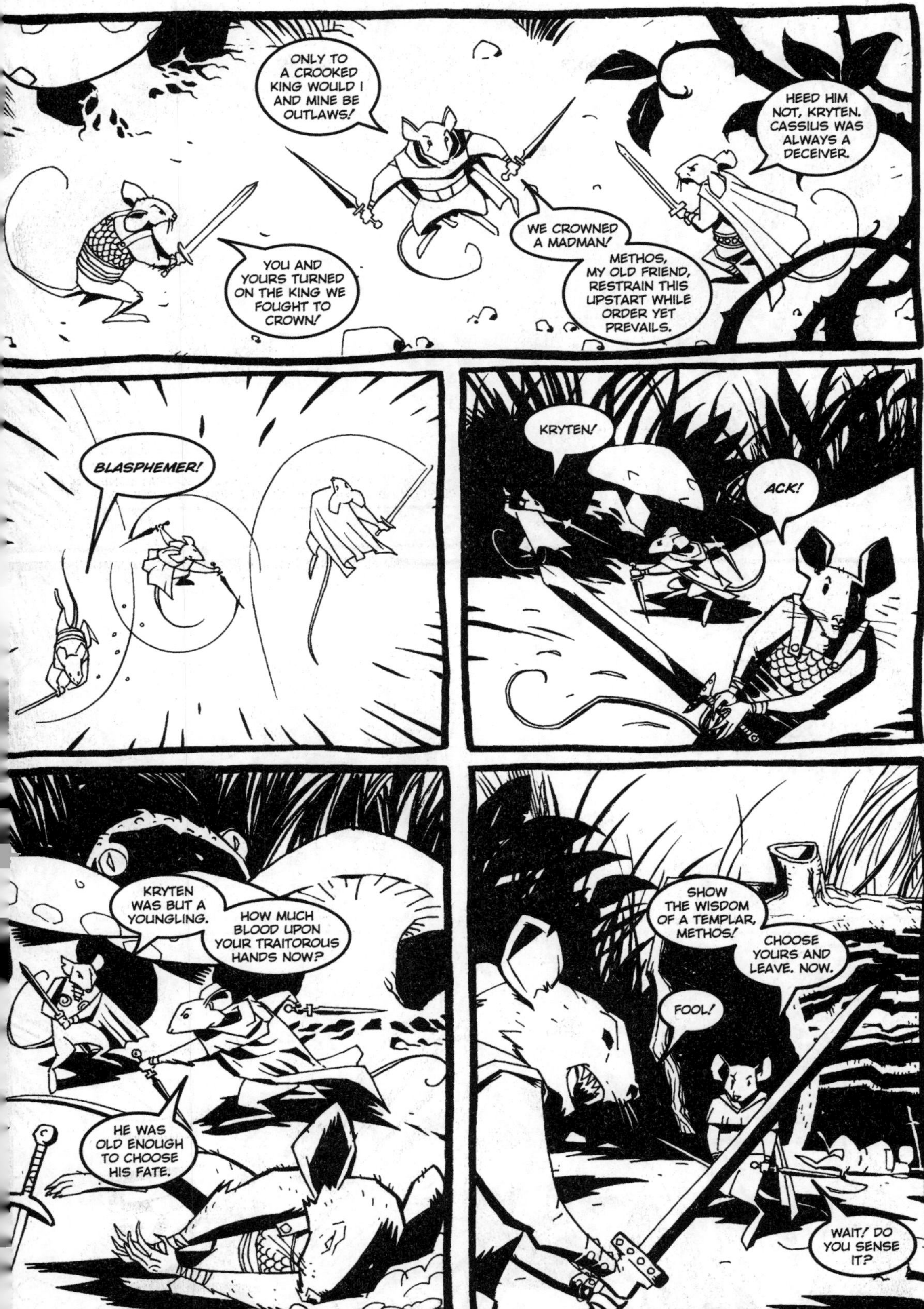
ONLY TO A CROOKED KING WOULD I AND MINE BE OUTLAWS!
HEED HIM NOT, KRYTEN. CASSIUS WAS ALWAYS A DECEIVER.
YOU AND YOURS TURNED ON THE KING WE FOUGHT TO CROWN!
WE CROWNED A MADMAN!
METHOS, MY OLD FRIEND, RESTRAIN THIS UPSTART WHILE ORDER YET PREVAILS.
BLASPHEMER!
KRYTEN!
ACK!
KRYTEN WAS BUT A YOUNGLING.
HOW MUCH BLOOD UPON YOUR TRAITOROUS HANDS NOW?
HE WAS OLD ENOUGH TO CHOOSE HIS FATE.
SHOW THE WISDOM OF A TEMPLAR, METHOS!
CHOOSE YOURS AND LEAVE. NOW.
FOOL!
WAIT! DO YOU SENSE IT?

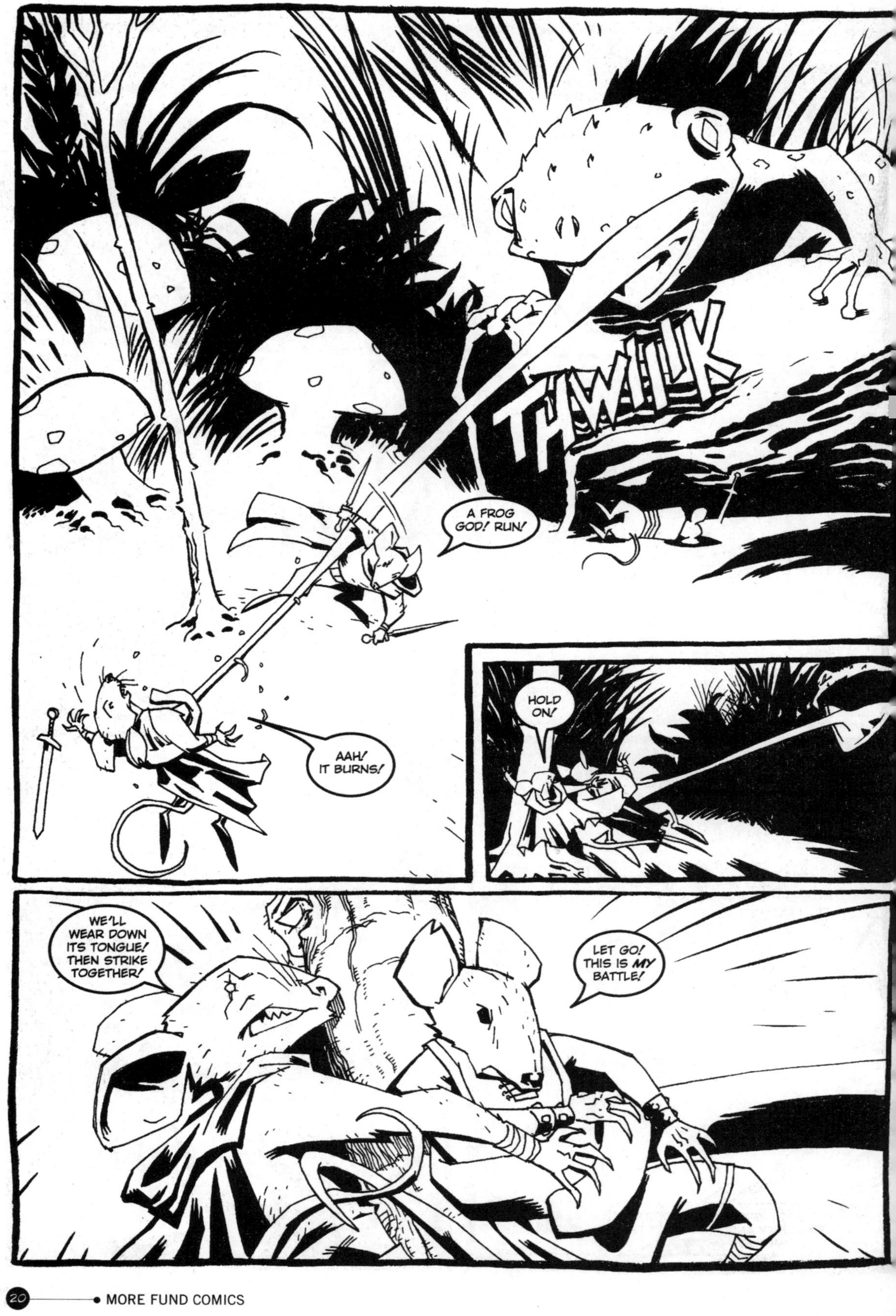
THWUK
A FROG GOD! RUN!
AAH! IT BURNS!
HOLD ON!
WE'LL WEAR DOWN ITS TONGUE! THEN STRIKE TOGETHER!
LET GO! THIS IS *MY* BATTLE!

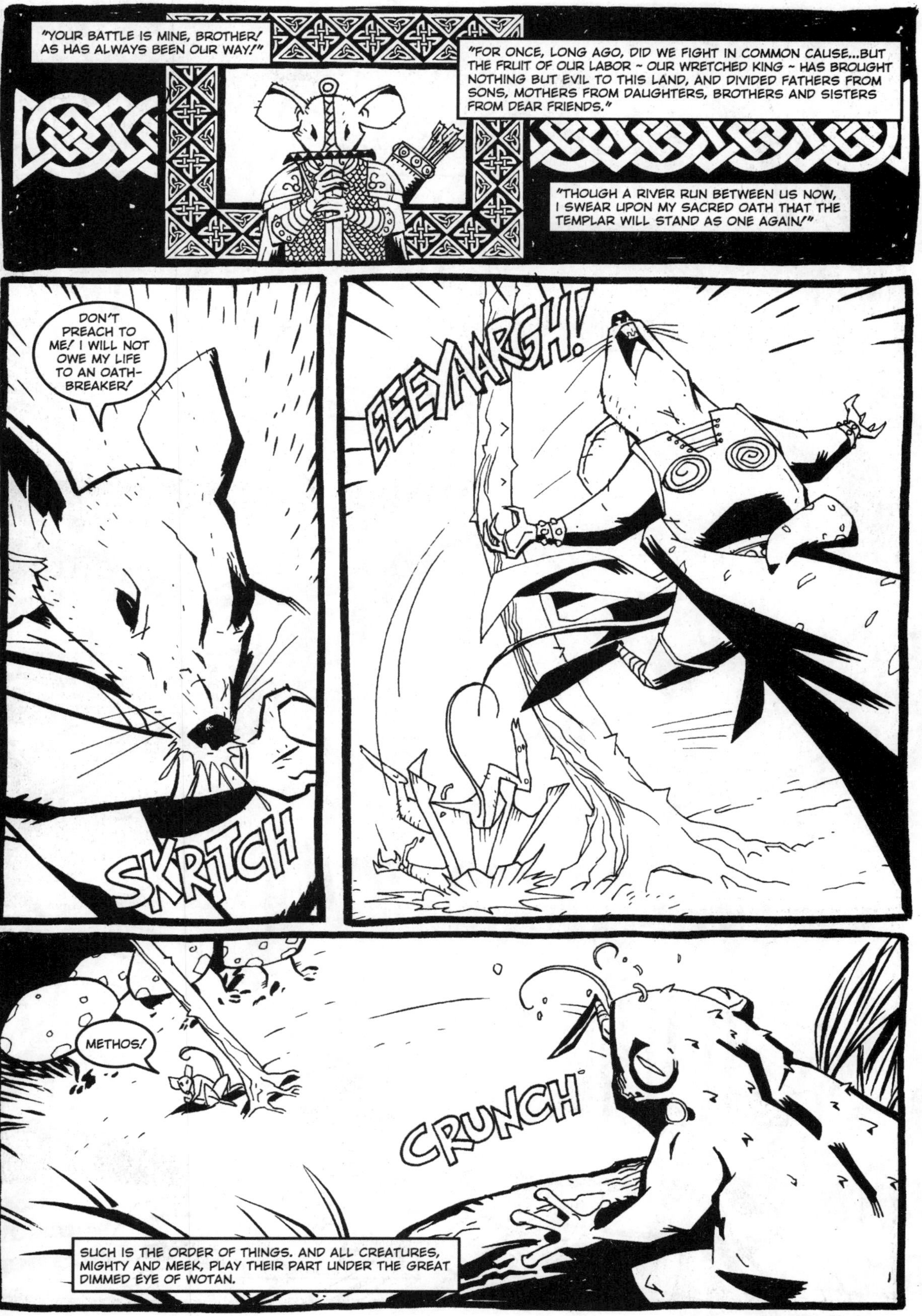
"YOUR BATTLE IS MINE, BROTHER! AS HAS ALWAYS BEEN OUR WAY!"
"FOR ONCE, LONG AGO, DID WE FIGHT IN COMMON CAUSE...BUT THE FRUIT OF OUR LABOR ~ OUR WRETCHED KING ~ HAS BROUGHT NOTHING BUT EVIL TO THIS LAND, AND DIVIDED FATHERS FROM SONS, MOTHERS FROM DAUGHTERS, BROTHERS AND SISTERS FROM DEAR FRIENDS."
"THOUGH A RIVER RUN BETWEEN US NOW, I SWEAR UPON MY SACRED OATH THAT THE TEMPLAR WILL STAND AS ONE AGAIN!"
DON'T PREACH TO ME! I WILL NOT OWE MY LIFE TO AN OATH-BREAKER!
SKRITCH
EEEYAARGH!
METHOS!
CRUNCH
SUCH IS THE ORDER OF THINGS. AND ALL CREATURES, MIGHTY AND MEEK, PLAY THEIR PART UNDER THE GREAT DIMMED EYE OF WOTAN.

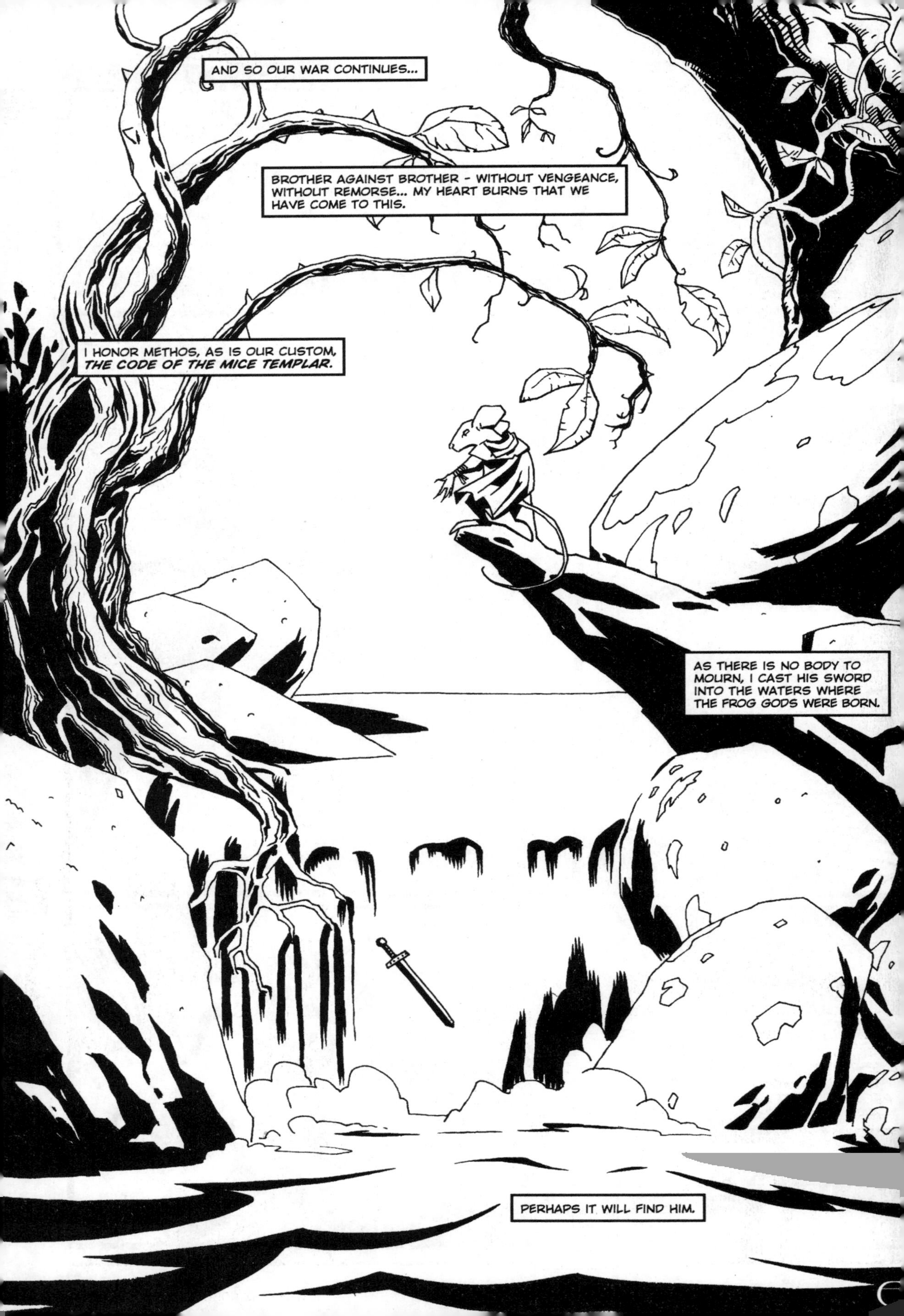
AND SO OUR WAR CONTINUES...
BROTHER AGAINST BROTHER - WITHOUT VENGEANCE, WITHOUT REMORSE... MY HEART BURNS THAT WE HAVE COME TO THIS.
I HONOR METHOS, AS IS OUR CUSTOM, *THE CODE OF THE MICE TEMPLAR.*
AS THERE IS NO BODY TO MOURN, I CAST HIS SWORD INTO THE WATERS WHERE THE FROG GODS WERE BORN.
PERHAPS IT WILL FIND HIM.

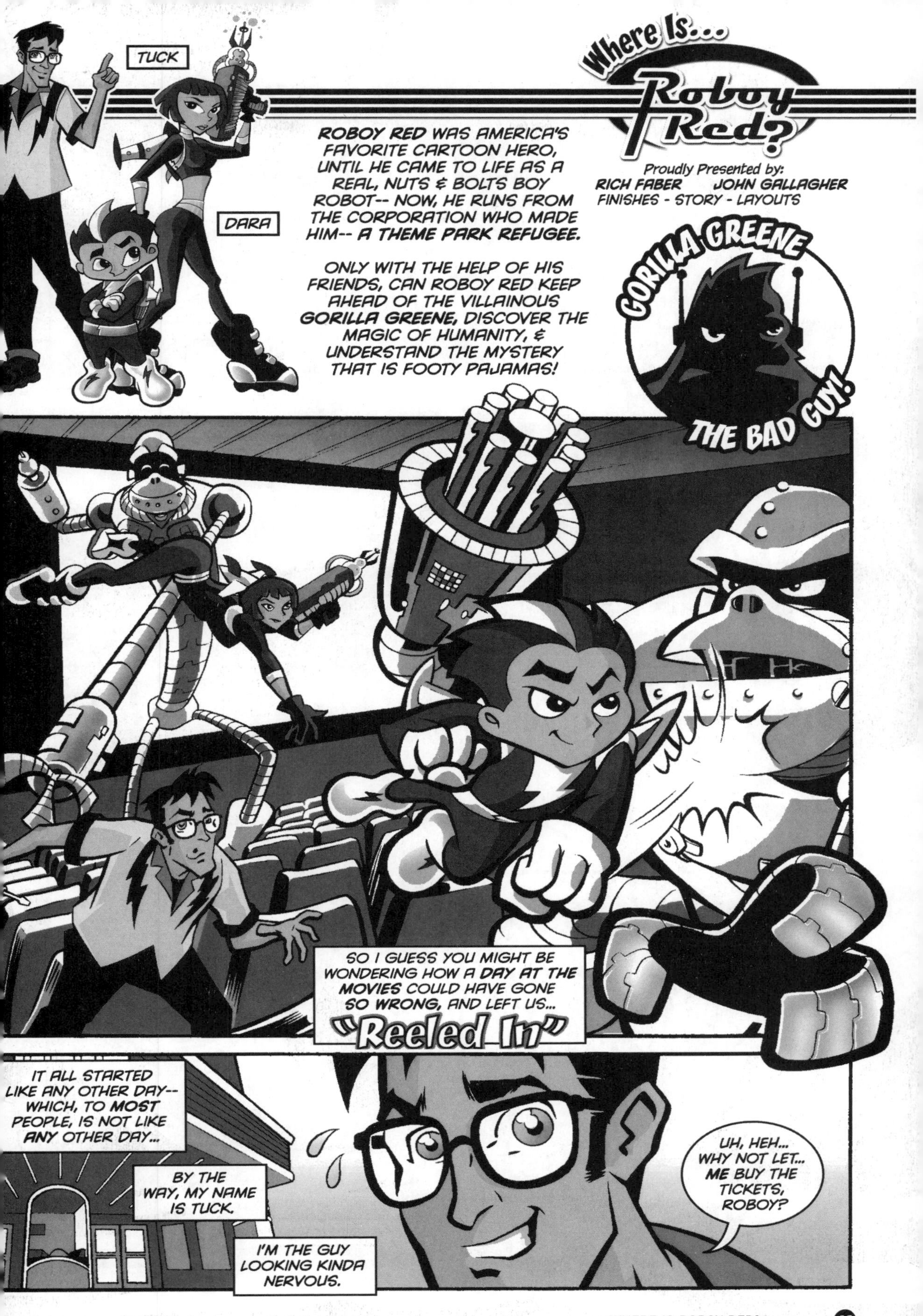
TUCK
DARA
Where Is... Roboy Red?
ROBOY RED WAS AMERICA'S FAVORITE CARTOON HERO, UNTIL HE CAME TO LIFE AS A REAL, NUTS & BOLTS BOY ROBOT-- NOW, HE RUNS FROM THE CORPORATION WHO MADE HIM-- A THEME PARK REFUGEE.
ONLY WITH THE HELP OF HIS FRIENDS, CAN ROBOY RED KEEP AHEAD OF THE VILLAINOUS GORILLA GREENE, DISCOVER THE MAGIC OF HUMANITY, & UNDERSTAND THE MYSTERY THAT IS FOOTY PAJAMAS!
Proudly Presented by:
RICH FABER JOHN GALLAGHER
FINISHES - STORY - LAYOUTS
GORILLA GREENE
THE BAD GUY!
SO I GUESS YOU MIGHT BE WONDERING HOW A DAY AT THE MOVIES COULD HAVE GONE SO WRONG, AND LEFT US...
"Reeled In"
IT ALL STARTED LIKE ANY OTHER DAY-- WHICH, TO MOST PEOPLE, IS NOT LIKE ANY OTHER DAY...
BY THE WAY, MY NAME IS TUCK.
I'M THE GUY LOOKING KINDA NERVOUS.
UH, HEH... WHY NOT LET... ME BUY THE TICKETS, ROBOY?

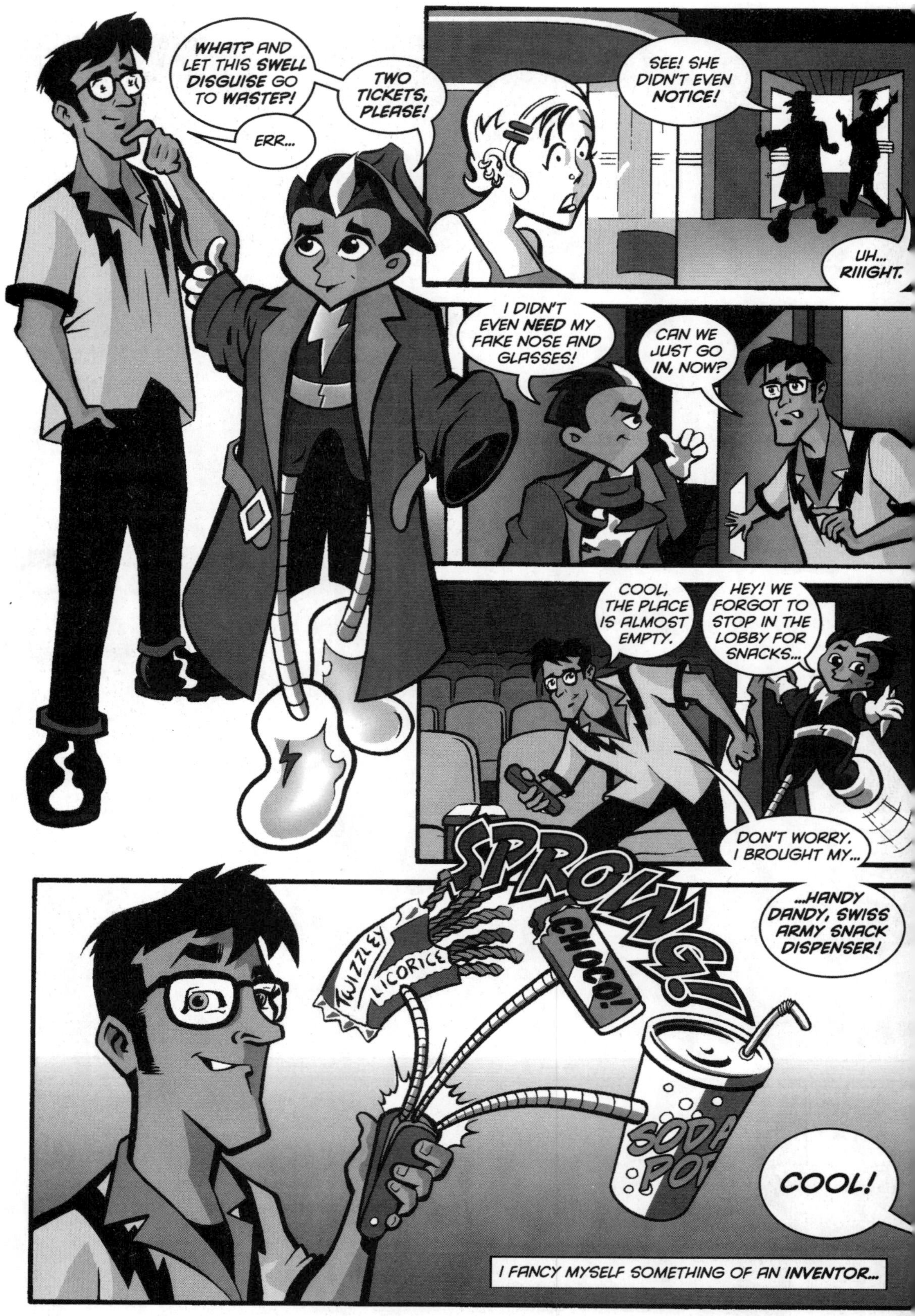
TWO TICKETS, PLEASE!
ERR...
WHAT? AND LET THIS SWELL DISGUISE GO TO WASTE?!
SEE! SHE DIDN'T EVEN NOTICE!
UH... RIIIGHT.
I DIDN'T EVEN NEED MY FAKE NOSE AND GLASSES!
CAN WE JUST GO IN, NOW?
COOL, THE PLACE IS ALMOST EMPTY.
HEY! WE FORGOT TO STOP IN THE LOBBY FOR SNACKS...
DON'T WORRY. I BROUGHT MY...
...HANDY DANDY, SWISS ARMY SNACK DISPENSER!
SPROING!!
TWIZZLEY
LICORICE
CHOCO!
SODA POP
COOL!
I FANCY MYSELF SOMETHING OF AN INVENTOR...

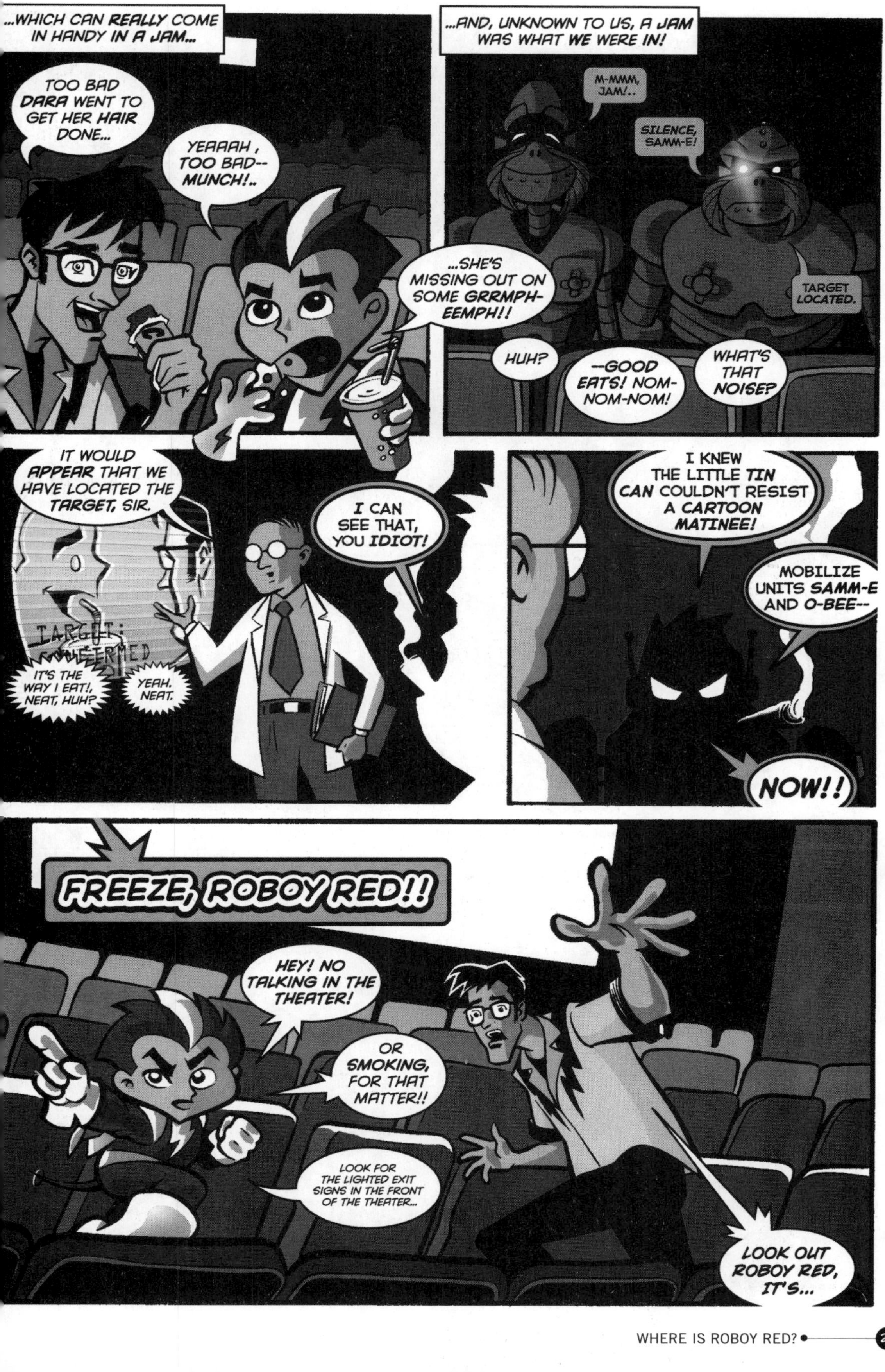
...WHICH CAN REALLY COME IN HANDY IN A JAM...
TOO BAD DARA WENT TO GET HER HAIR DONE...
YEAAAH, TOO BAD-- MUNCH!..
...SHE'S MISSING OUT ON SOME GRRMPH-EEMPH!!
...AND, UNKNOWN TO US, A JAM WAS WHAT WE WERE IN!
M-MMM, JAM!..
SILENCE, SAMM-E!
TARGET LOCATED.
HUH?
--GOOD EATS! NOM-NOM-NOM!
WHAT'S THAT NOISE?
IT WOULD APPEAR THAT WE HAVE LOCATED THE TARGET, SIR.
I CAN SEE THAT, YOU IDIOT!
IT'S THE WAY I EAT!, NEAT, HUH?
YEAH. NEAT.
I KNEW THE LITTLE TIN CAN COULDN'T RESIST A CARTOON MATINEE!
MOBILIZE UNITS SAMM-E AND O-BEE--
NOW!!
FREEZE, ROBOY RED!!
HEY! NO TALKING IN THE THEATER!
OR SMOKING, FOR THAT MATTER!!
LOOK FOR THE LIGHTED EXIT SIGNS IN THE FRONT OF THE THEATER...
LOOK OUT ROBOY RED, IT'S...

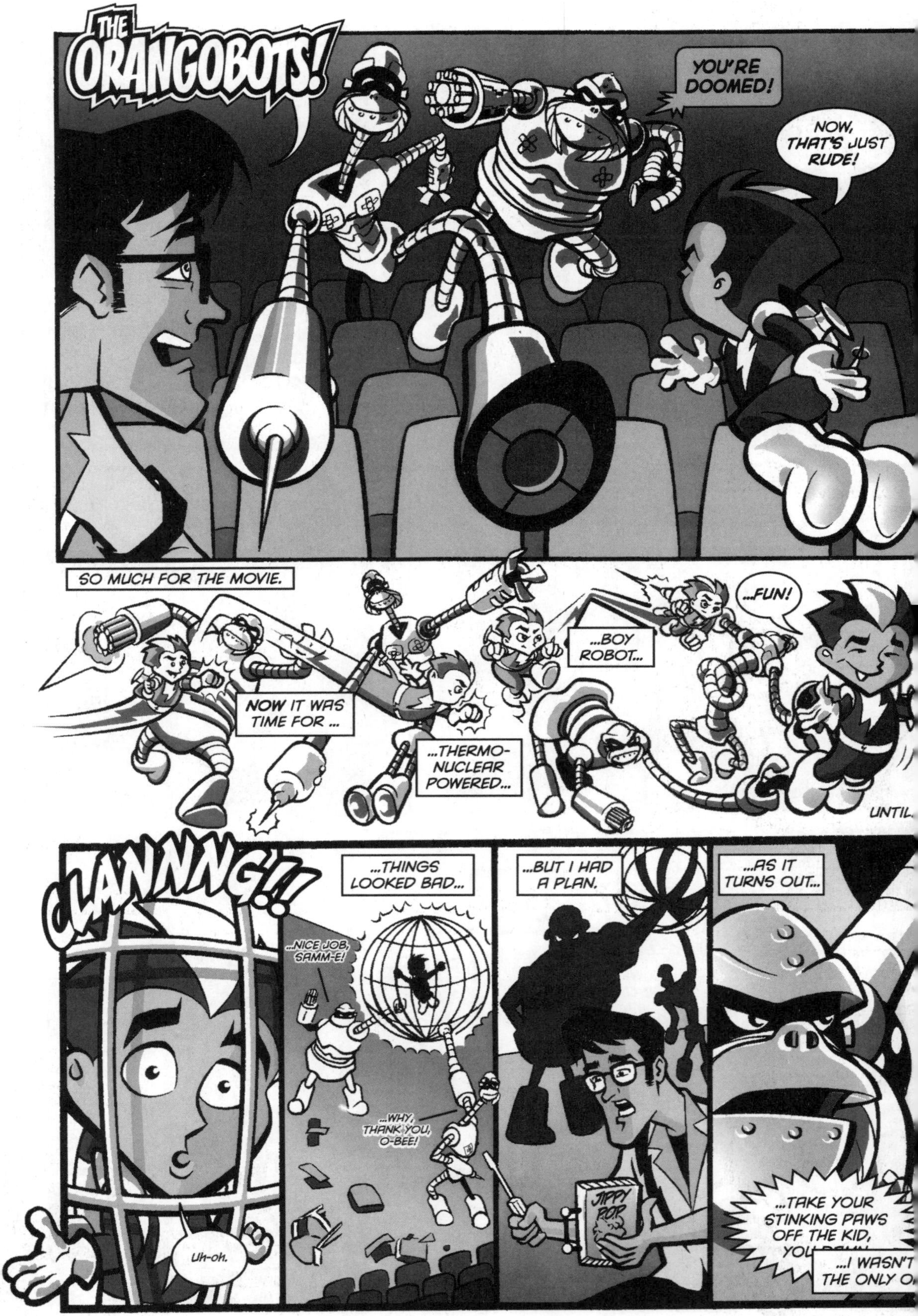

THE ORANGOBOTS!
YOU'RE DOOMED!
NOW, THAT'S JUST RUDE!
SO MUCH FOR THE MOVIE.
NOW IT WAS TIME FOR ...
...THERMO-NUCLEAR POWERED...
...BOY ROBOT...
...FUN!
UNTIL
CLANNNG!!
Uh-oh.
...THINGS LOOKED BAD...
...NICE JOB, SAMM-E!
...WHY, THANK YOU, O-BEE!
...BUT I HAD A PLAN.
JIPPY POP
...AS IT TURNS OUT...
...TAKE YOUR STINKING PAWS OFF THE KID,
...I WASN'T THE ONLY

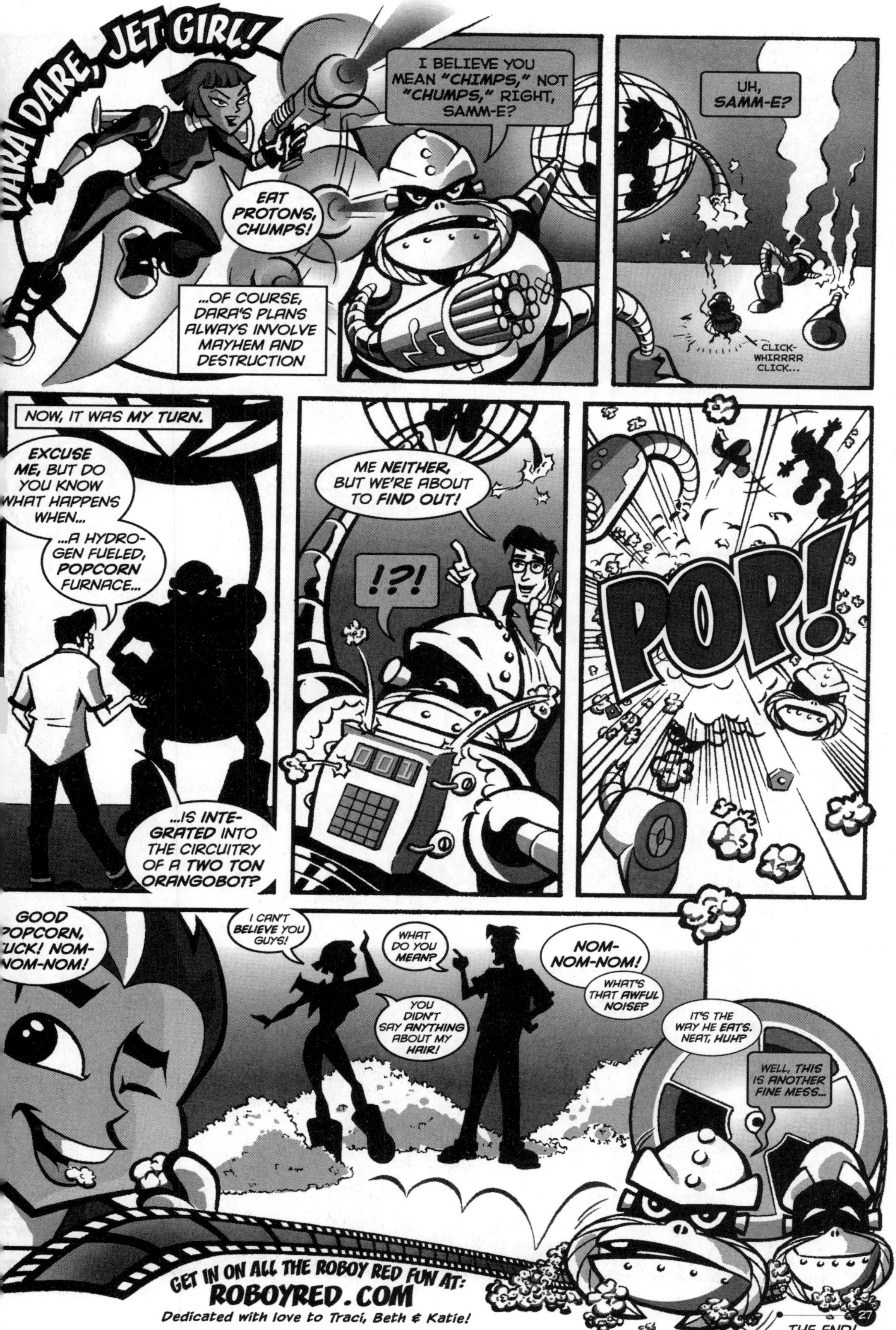

DARA DARE, JET GIRL!
...OF COURSE, DARA'S PLANS ALWAYS INVOLVE MAYHEM AND DESTRUCTION
EAT PROTONS, CHUMPS!
I BELIEVE YOU MEAN "CHIMPS," NOT "CHUMPS," RIGHT, SAMM-E?
UH, SAMM-E?
CLICK- WHIRRRR CLICK...
NOW, IT WAS MY TURN.
EXCUSE ME, BUT DO YOU KNOW WHAT HAPPENS WHEN...
...A HYDROGEN FUELED, POPCORN FURNACE...
...IS INTEGRATED INTO THE CIRCUITRY OF A TWO TON ORANGOBOT?
ME NEITHER, BUT WE'RE ABOUT TO FIND OUT!
!?!
001
POP!
GOOD POPCORN, TUCK! NOM-NOM-NOM!
I CAN'T BELIEVE YOU GUYS!
WHAT DO YOU MEAN?
YOU DIDN'T SAY ANYTHING ABOUT MY HAIR!
NOM-NOM-NOM!
WHAT'S THAT AWFUL NOISE?
IT'S THE WAY HE EATS. NEAT, HUH?
WELL, THIS IS ANOTHER FINE MESS...
GET IN ON ALL THE ROBOY RED FUN AT:
ROBOYRED.COM
Dedicated with love to Traci, Beth & Katie!
THE END!

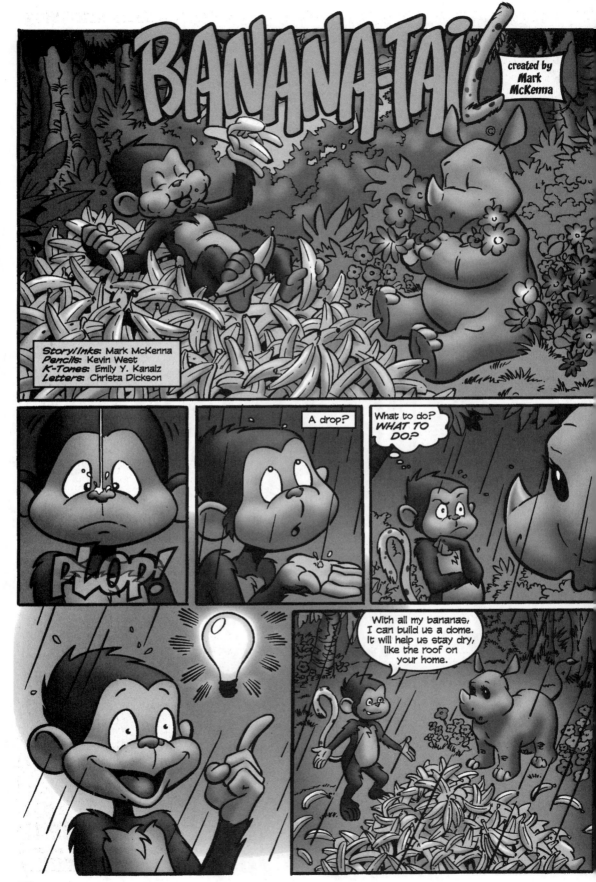

BANANA TAIL

created by Mark McKenna

Story/Inks: Mark McKenna
Pencils: Kevin West
K-Tones: Emily Y. Kanalz
Letters: Christa Dickson

PLOP!

A drop?

What to do? WHAT TO DO?

With all my bananas, I can build us a dome. It will help us stay dry, like the roof on your home.

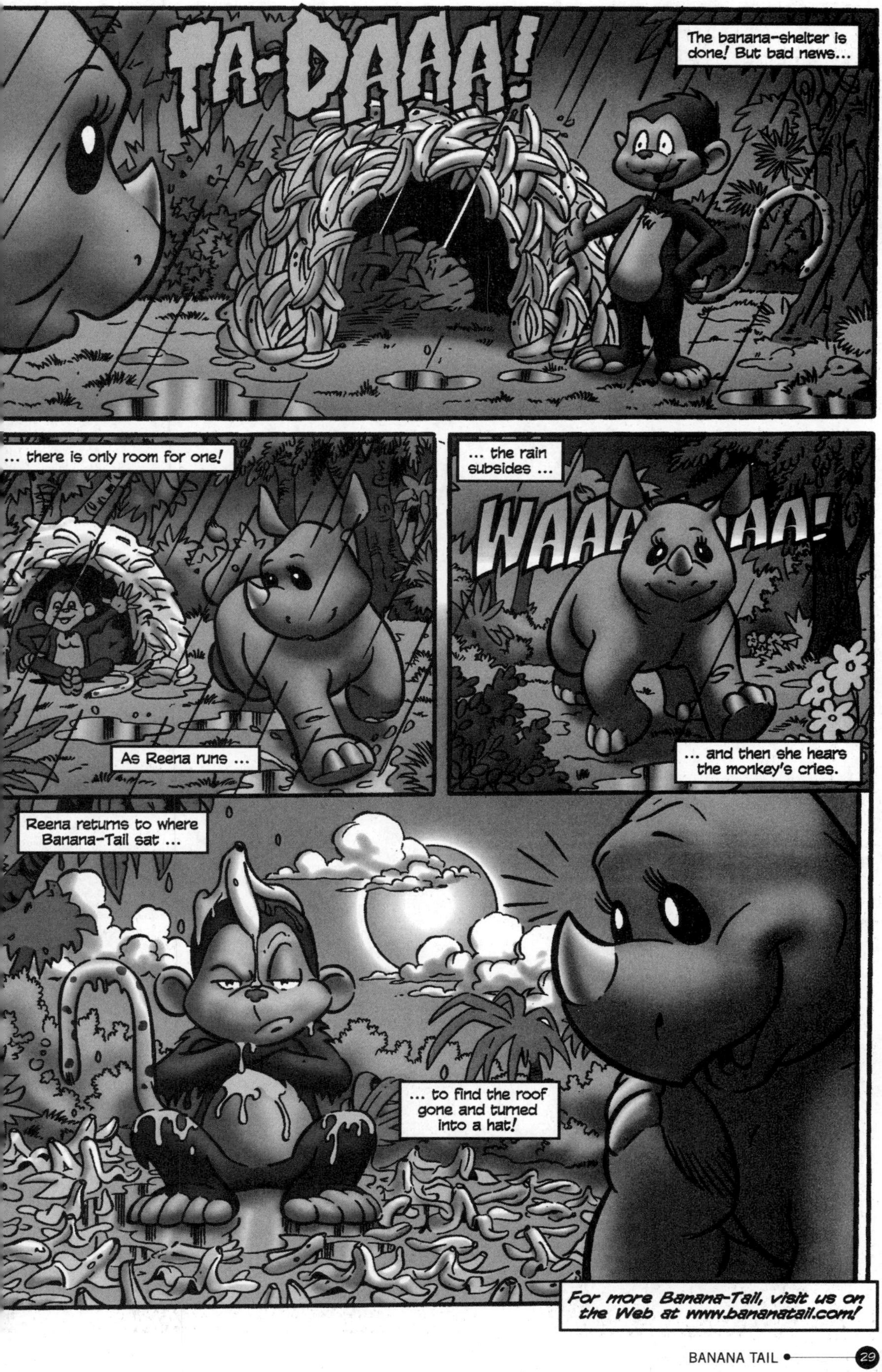

TA-DAAA!
The banana-shelter is done! But bad news...
... there is only room for one!
As Reena runs ...
... the rain subsides ...
... and then she hears the monkey's cries.
Reena returns to where Banana-Tail sat ...
... to find the roof gone and turned into a hat!
For more Banana-Tail, visit us on the Web at www.bananatail.com!

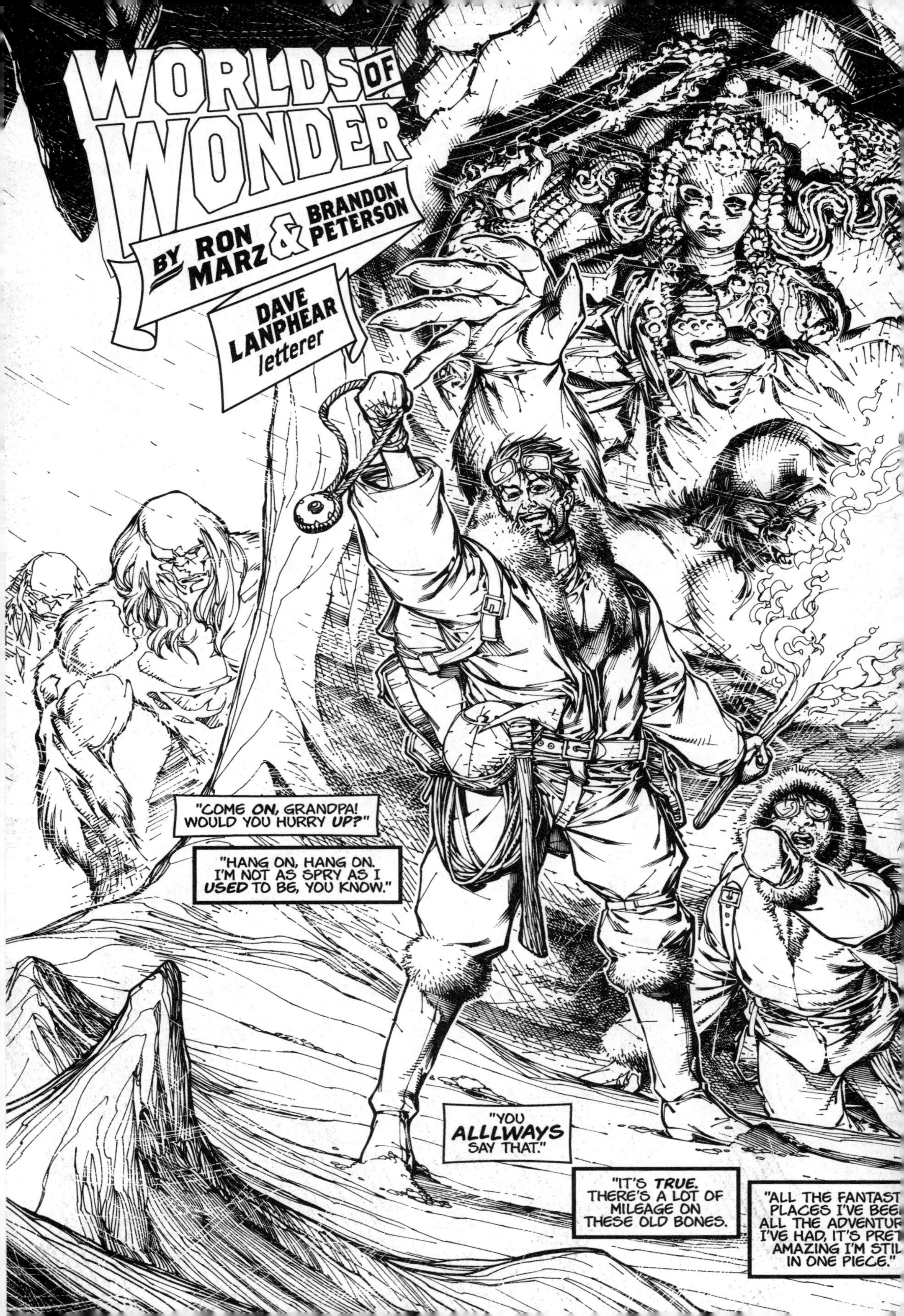
WORLDS OF WONDER
BY RON MARZ & BRANDON PETERSON
DAVE LANPHEAR letterer
"COME ON, GRANDPA! WOULD YOU HURRY UP?"
"HANG ON, HANG ON. I'M NOT AS SPRY AS I USED TO BE, YOU KNOW."
"YOU ALLLWAYS SAY THAT."
"IT'S TRUE. THERE'S A LOT OF MILEAGE ON THESE OLD BONES.
"ALL THE FANTAST PLACES I'VE BEE ALL THE ADVENTUR I'VE HAD, IT'S PRET AMAZING I'M STIL IN ONE PIECE."

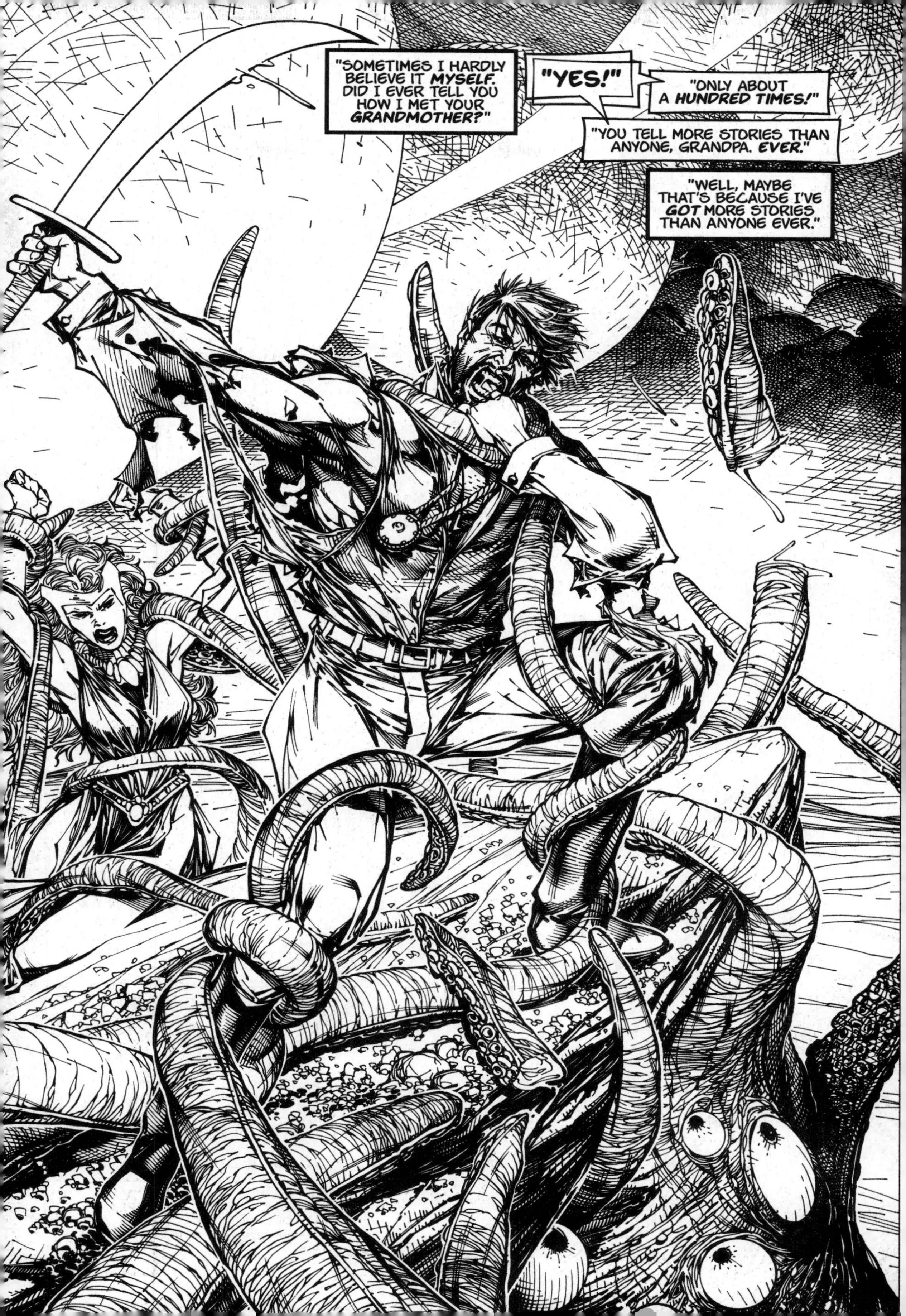
"SOMETIMES I HARDLY BELIEVE IT MYSELF. DID I EVER TELL YOU HOW I MET YOUR GRANDMOTHER?"
"YES!"
"ONLY ABOUT A HUNDRED TIMES!"
"YOU TELL MORE STORIES THAN ANYONE, GRANDPA. EVER."
"WELL, MAYBE THAT'S BECAUSE I'VE GOT MORE STORIES THAN ANYONE EVER."

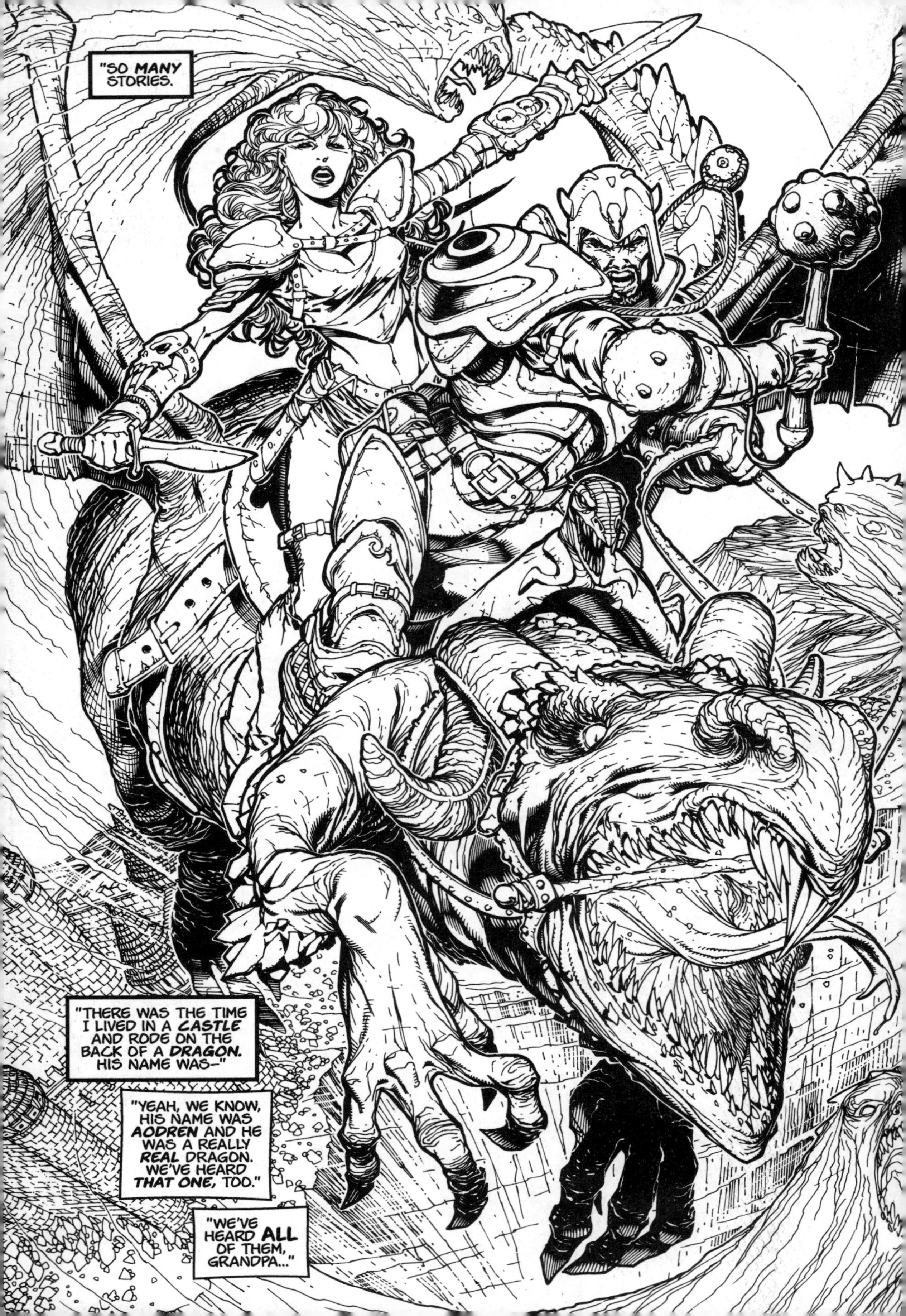
"SO MANY STORIES.
"THERE WAS THE TIME I LIVED IN A CASTLE AND RODE ON THE BACK OF A DRAGON. HIS NAME WAS–"
"YEAH, WE KNOW, HIS NAME WAS AODREN AND HE WAS A REALLY REAL DRAGON. WE'VE HEARD THAT ONE, TOO."
"WE'VE HEARD ALL OF THEM, GRANDPA..."

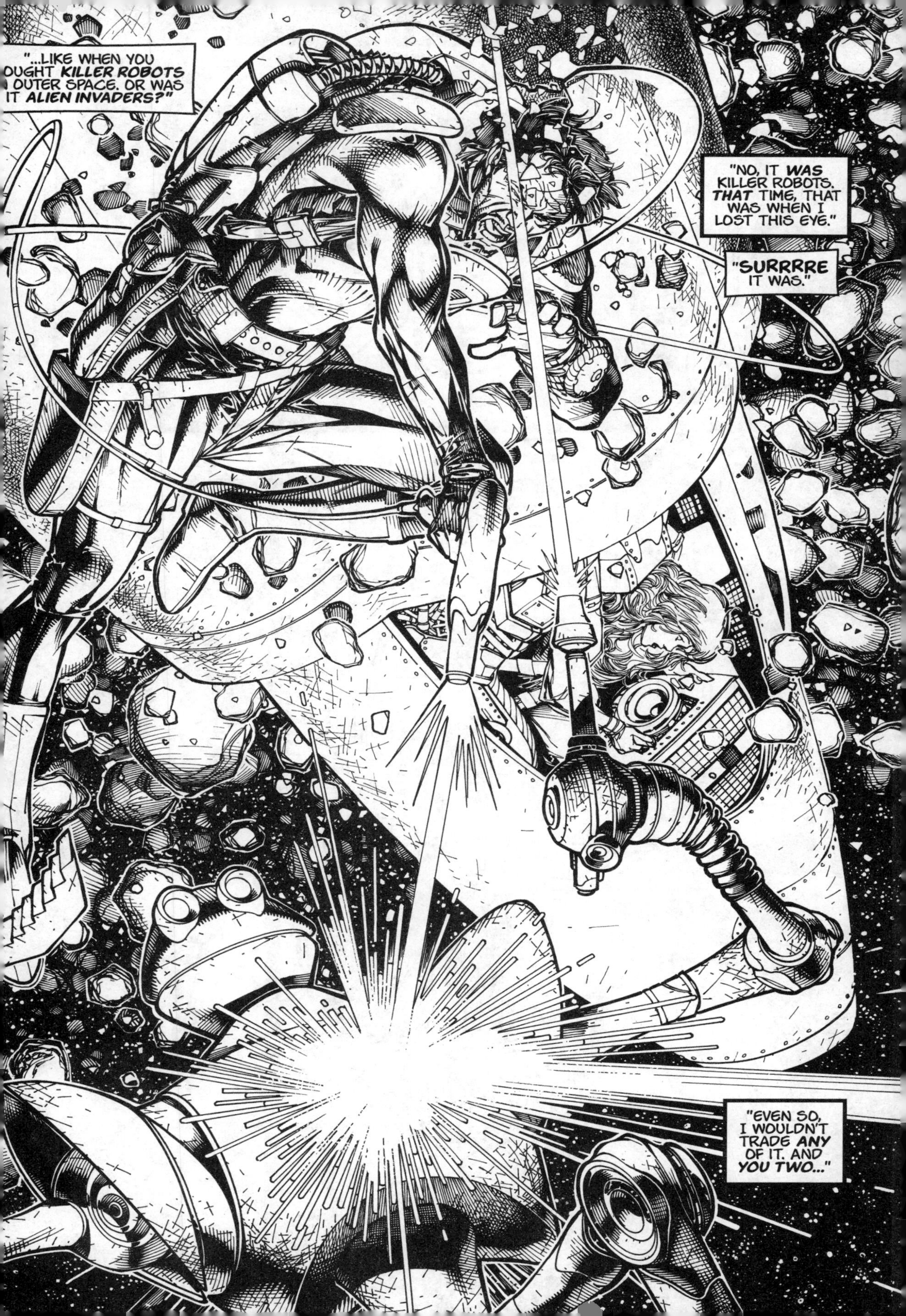
"...LIKE WHEN YOU
OUGHT **KILLER ROBOTS**
OUTER SPACE. OR WAS
IT **ALIEN INVADERS?**"
"NO, IT **WAS** KILLER ROBOTS. **THAT** TIME, THAT WAS WHEN I LOST THIS EYE."
"**SURRRRE** IT WAS."
"EVEN SO, I WOULDN'T TRADE **ANY** OF IT. AND **YOU TWO...**"

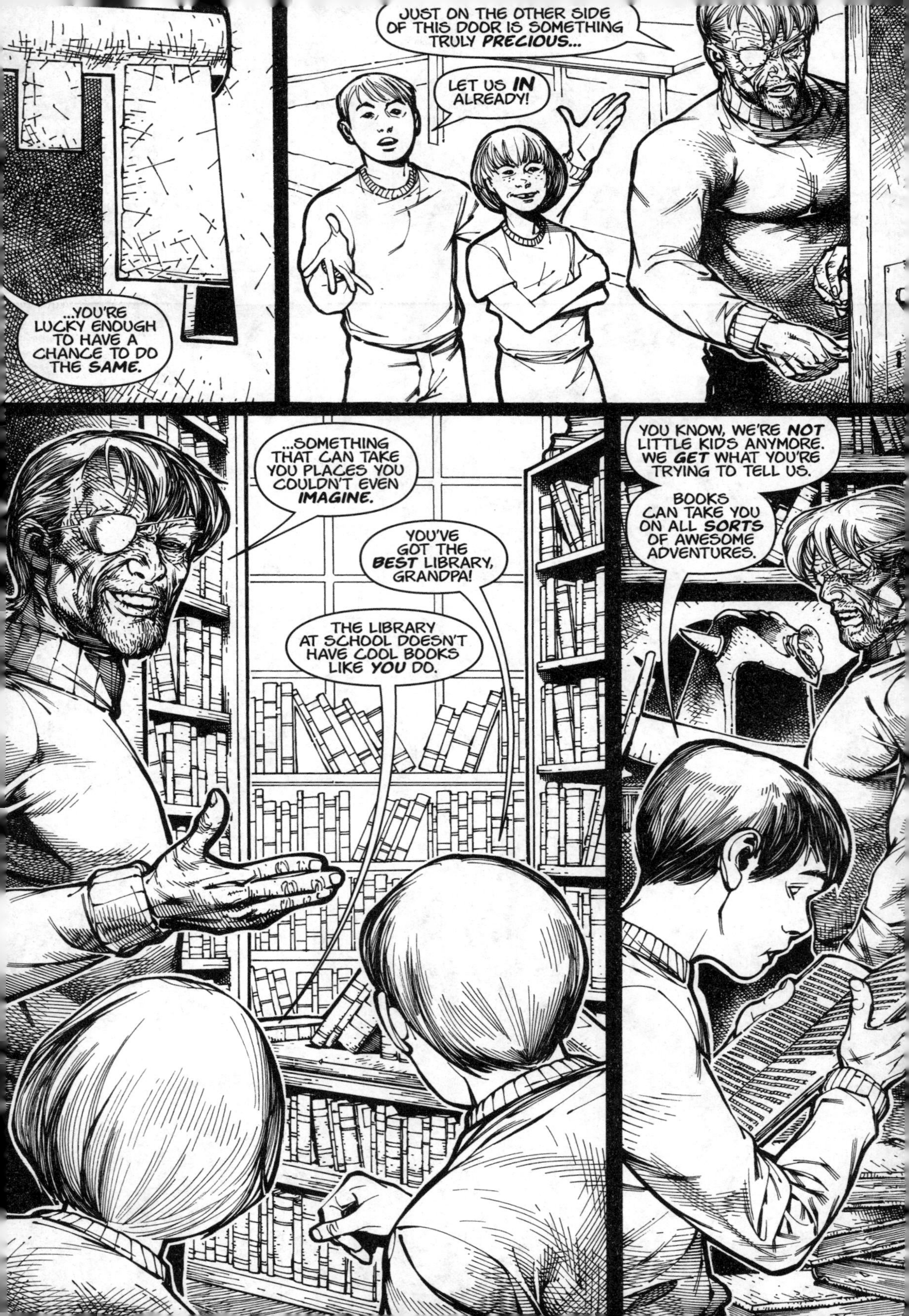
...YOU'RE LUCKY ENOUGH TO HAVE A CHANCE TO DO THE SAME.
JUST ON THE OTHER SIDE OF THIS DOOR IS SOMETHING TRULY PRECIOUS...
LET US IN ALREADY!
...SOMETHING THAT CAN TAKE YOU PLACES YOU COULDN'T EVEN IMAGINE.
YOU'VE GOT THE BEST LIBRARY, GRANDPA!
THE LIBRARY AT SCHOOL DOESN'T HAVE COOL BOOKS LIKE YOU DO.
YOU KNOW, WE'RE NOT LITTLE KIDS ANYMORE. WE GET WHAT YOU'RE TRYING TO TELL US.
BOOKS CAN TAKE YOU ON ALL SORTS OF AWESOME ADVENTURES.

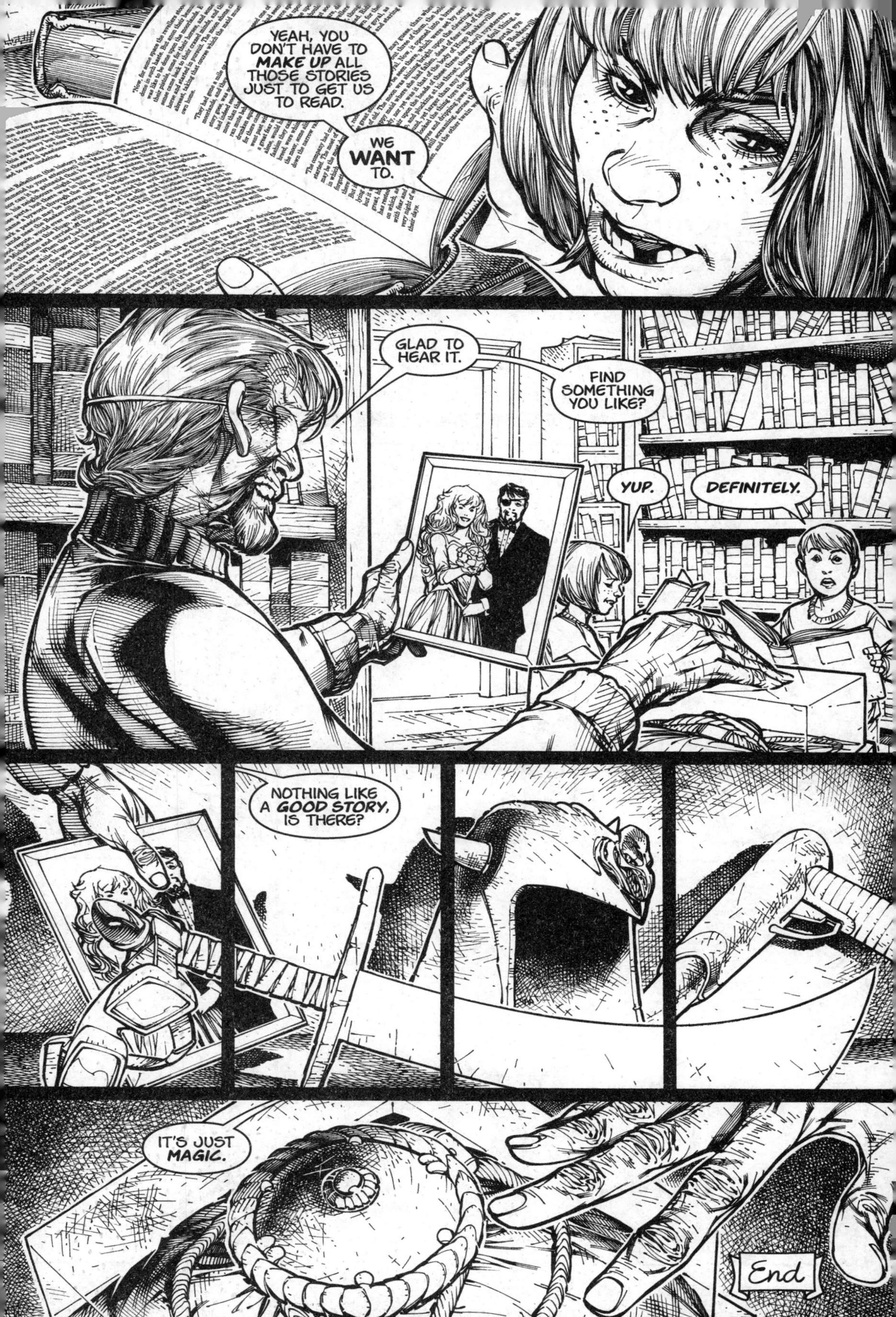
YEAH, YOU DON'T HAVE TO MAKE UP ALL THOSE STORIES JUST TO GET US TO READ.
WE WANT TO.
GLAD TO HEAR IT.
FIND SOMETHING YOU LIKE?
YUP.
DEFINITELY.
NOTHING LIKE A GOOD STORY, IS THERE?
IT'S JUST MAGIC.
End

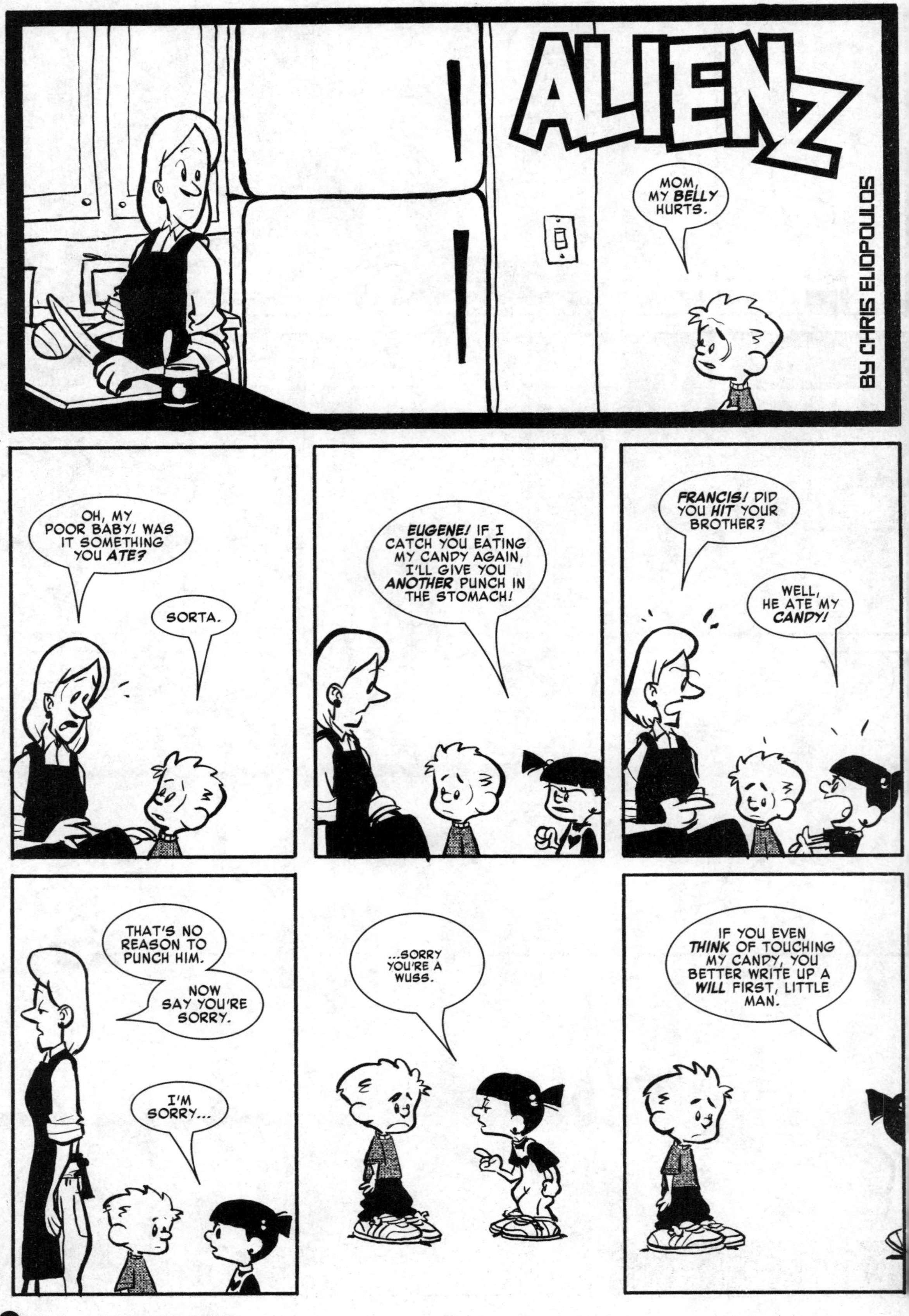
ALIENZ
BY CHRIS ELIOPOULOS
MOM, MY BELLY HURTS.
OH, MY POOR BABY! WAS IT SOMETHING YOU ATE?
SORTA.
EUGENE! IF I CATCH YOU EATING MY CANDY AGAIN, I'LL GIVE YOU ANOTHER PUNCH IN THE STOMACH!
FRANCIS! DID YOU HIT YOUR BROTHER?
WELL, HE ATE MY CANDY!
THAT'S NO REASON TO PUNCH HIM.
NOW SAY YOU'RE SORRY.
I'M SORRY...
...SORRY YOU'RE A WUSS.
IF YOU EVEN THINK OF TOUCHING MY CANDY, YOU BETTER WRITE UP A WILL FIRST, LITTLE MAN.

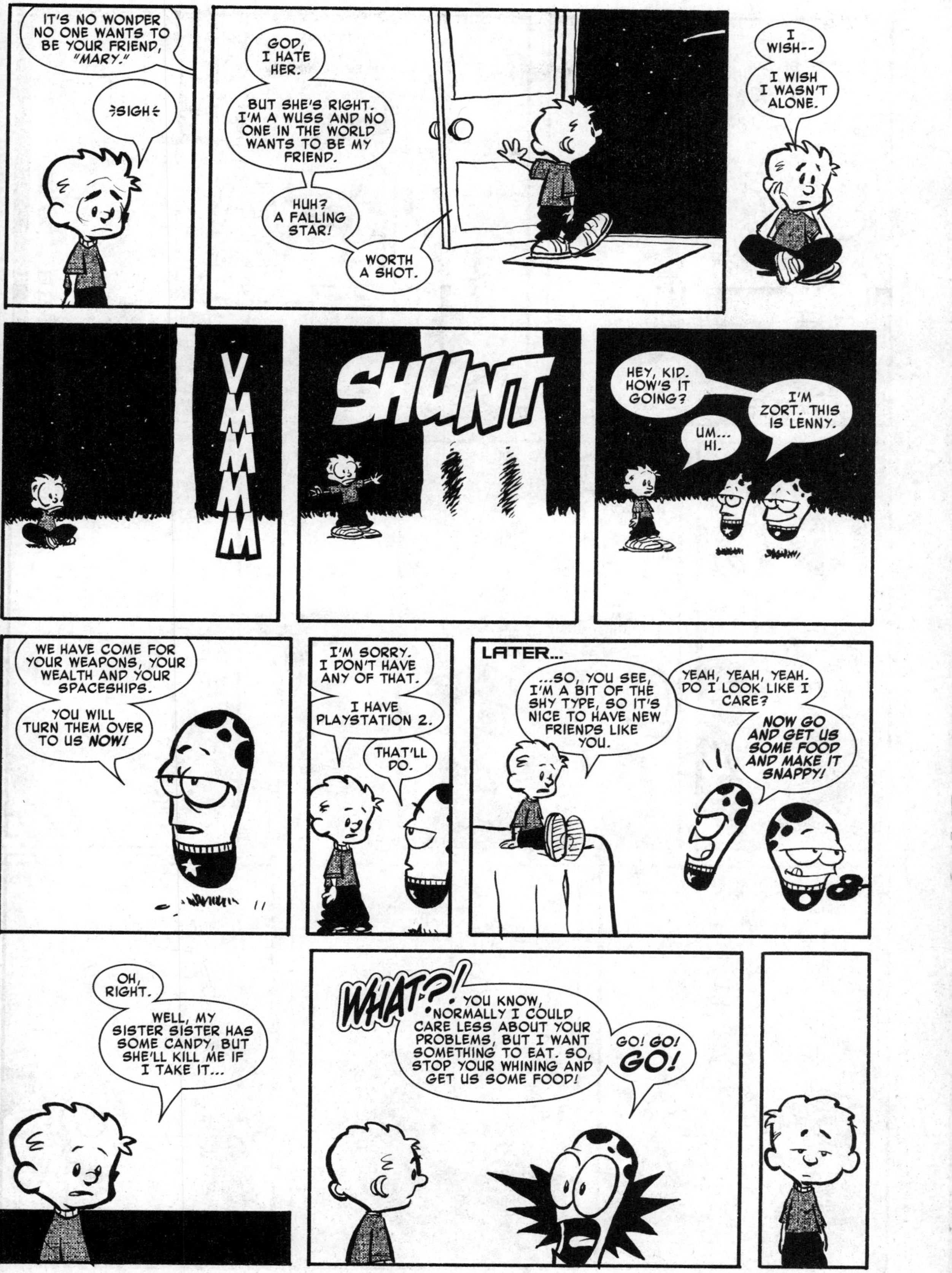

IT'S NO WONDER NO ONE WANTS TO BE YOUR FRIEND, "MARY."
SIGH
GOD, I HATE HER.
BUT SHE'S RIGHT. I'M A WUSS AND NO ONE IN THE WORLD WANTS TO BE MY FRIEND.
HUH? A FALLING STAR!
WORTH A SHOT.
I WISH--
I WISH I WASN'T ALONE.
VMMMMM
SHUNT
HEY, KID. HOW'S IT GOING?
UM... HI.
I'M ZORT. THIS IS LENNY.
WE HAVE COME FOR YOUR WEAPONS, YOUR WEALTH AND YOUR SPACESHIPS.
YOU WILL TURN THEM OVER TO US NOW!
I'M SORRY. I DON'T HAVE ANY OF THAT.
I HAVE PLAYSTATION 2.
THAT'LL DO.
LATER...
...SO, YOU SEE, I'M A BIT OF THE SHY TYPE, SO IT'S NICE TO HAVE NEW FRIENDS LIKE YOU.
YEAH, YEAH, YEAH. DO I LOOK LIKE I CARE?
NOW GO AND GET US SOME FOOD AND MAKE IT SNAPPY!
OH, RIGHT.
WELL, MY SISTER SISTER HAS SOME CANDY, BUT SHE'LL KILL ME IF I TAKE IT...
WHAT?!
YOU KNOW, NORMALLY I COULD CARE LESS ABOUT YOUR PROBLEMS, BUT I WANT SOMETHING TO EAT. SO, STOP YOUR WHINING AND GET US SOME FOOD!
GO! GO! GO!

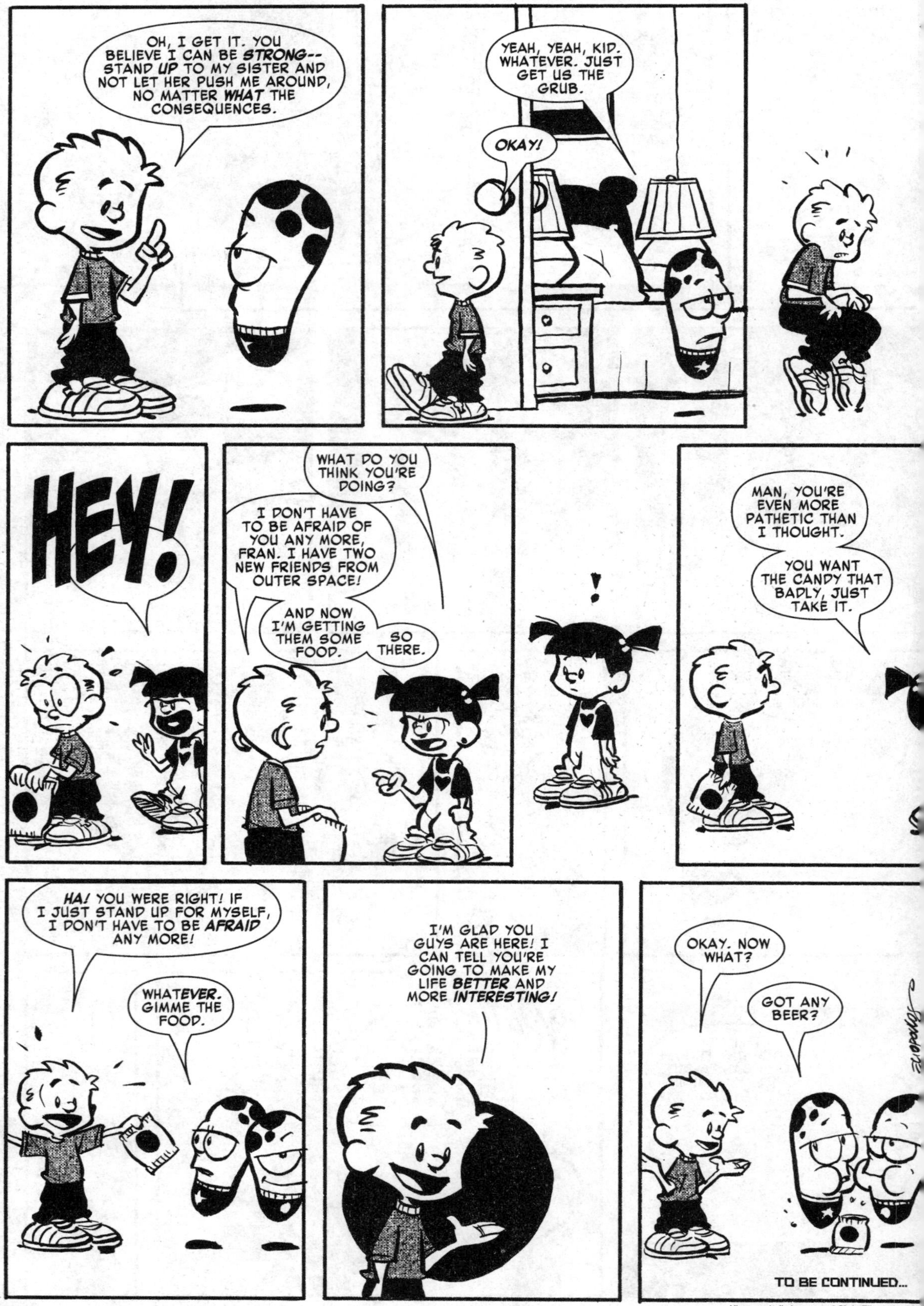

OH, I GET IT. YOU BELIEVE I CAN BE ***STRONG***-- STAND ***UP*** TO MY SISTER AND NOT LET HER PUSH ME AROUND, NO MATTER ***WHAT*** THE CONSEQUENCES.
YEAH, YEAH, KID. WHATEVER. JUST GET US THE GRUB.
OKAY!
HEY!
WHAT DO YOU THINK YOU'RE DOING?
I DON'T HAVE TO BE AFRAID OF YOU ANY MORE, FRAN. I HAVE TWO NEW FRIENDS FROM OUTER SPACE!
AND NOW I'M GETTING THEM SOME FOOD.
SO THERE.
!
MAN, YOU'RE EVEN MORE PATHETIC THAN I THOUGHT.
YOU WANT THE CANDY THAT BADLY, JUST TAKE IT.
HA! YOU WERE RIGHT! IF I JUST STAND UP FOR MYSELF, I DON'T HAVE TO BE ***AFRAID*** ANY MORE!
WHAT***EVER***. GIMME THE FOOD.
I'M GLAD YOU GUYS ARE HERE! I CAN TELL YOU'RE GOING TO MAKE MY LIFE ***BETTER*** AND MORE ***INTERESTING!***
OKAY. NOW WHAT?
GOT ANY BEER?
TO BE CONTINUED...

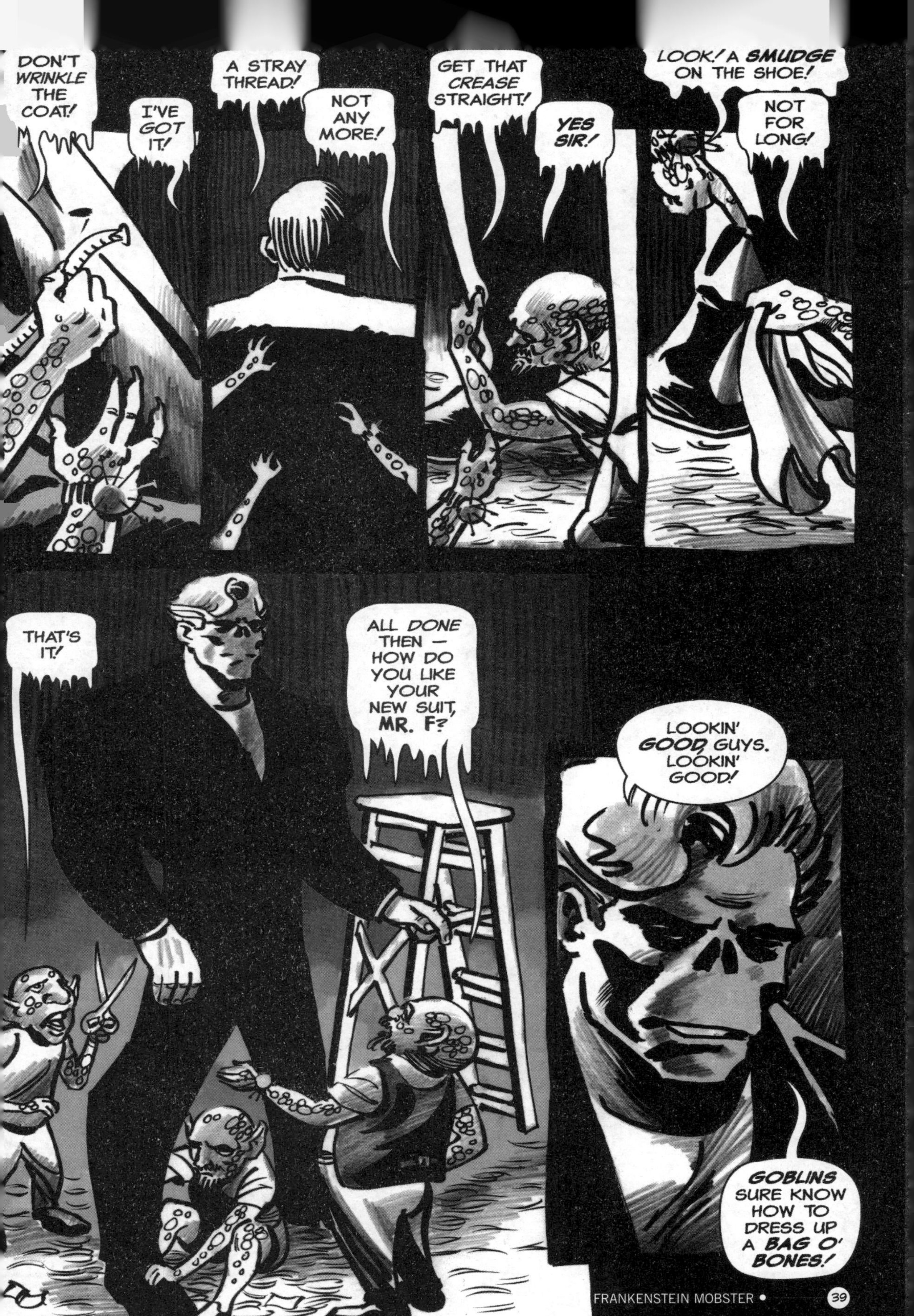

DON'T *WRINKLE* THE COAT!
I'VE *GOT* IT!
A STRAY THREAD!
NOT ANY MORE!
GET THAT *CREASE* STRAIGHT!
YES SIR!
LOOK! A **SMUDGE** ON THE SHOE!
NOT FOR LONG!
THAT'S IT!
ALL *DONE* THEN — HOW DO YOU LIKE YOUR NEW SUIT, **MR. F**?
LOOKIN' ***GOOD,*** GUYS. LOOKIN' GOOD!
GOBLINS SURE KNOW HOW TO DRESS UP A ***BAG O' BONES!***

MACHINE GUN
OUTSIDE THE GOBLIN TAILOR SHOP— IN THE STREETS OF THE DEADEND—
BRAT A RAT A BRAT A BRAT
THAT'S ENOUGH!
GET HIM!
GUH— GUNNER ONE OF THEM MONSTERS IS FIGHTIN' BACK!

EAT LEAD, YOU DIRTY MONSTERS!
DON'T LET ANY OF 'EM GET AWAY!
WHAT THE HELL?
YOU GUYS FIND SOME COVER— THAT WAS GUN FIRE!
FRANKENSTEIN MOBSTER
BY MARK WHEATLEY
THE FRANKENSTEIN MOBSTER RUSHES OUT INTO THE STREET—
THAT'S THE FRANKENSTEIN MOBSTER!
HE'S PURE TROUBLE!
I SHOULD HAVE KNOWN—THIS IS GUNNER'S CREW OF BIGOTS!
I CAN END HIS MURDERIN' WITH ONE GOOD SHOT!
NO YOU DON'T!
GUNNER'S ONE OF MY BOYS!

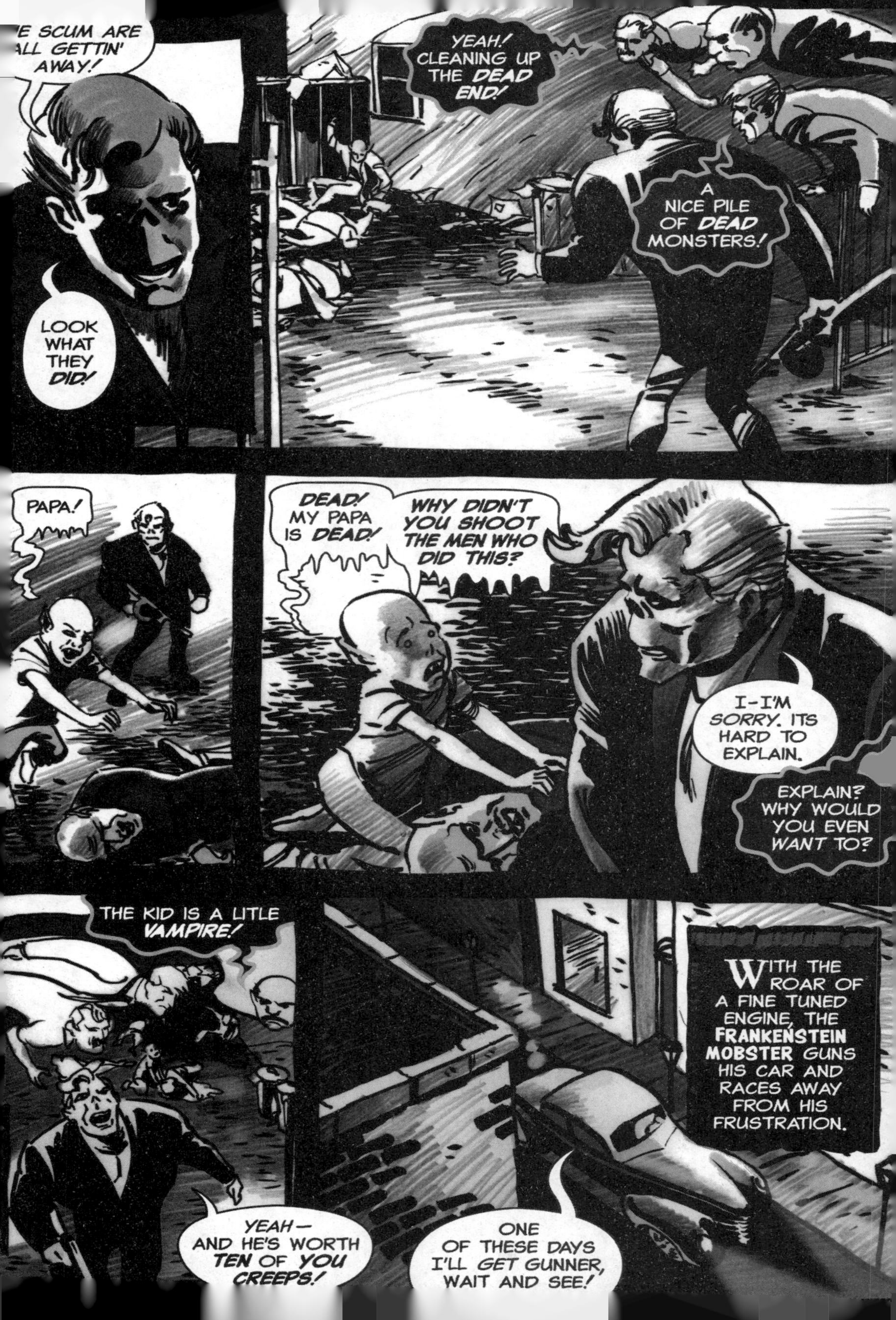

E SCUM ARE ALL GETTIN' AWAY!
LOOK WHAT THEY DID!
YEAH! CLEANING UP THE DEAD END!
A NICE PILE OF DEAD MONSTERS!
PAPA!
DEAD! MY PAPA IS DEAD!
WHY DIDN'T YOU SHOOT THE MEN WHO DID THIS?
I-I'M SORRY. ITS HARD TO EXPLAIN.
EXPLAIN? WHY WOULD YOU EVEN WANT TO?
THE KID IS A LITLE VAMPIRE!
YEAH— AND HE'S WORTH TEN OF YOU CREEPS!
WITH THE ROAR OF A FINE TUNED ENGINE, THE FRANKENSTEIN MOBSTER GUNS HIS CAR AND RACES AWAY FROM HIS FRUSTRATION.
ONE OF THESE DAYS I'LL GET GUNNER, WAIT AND SEE!

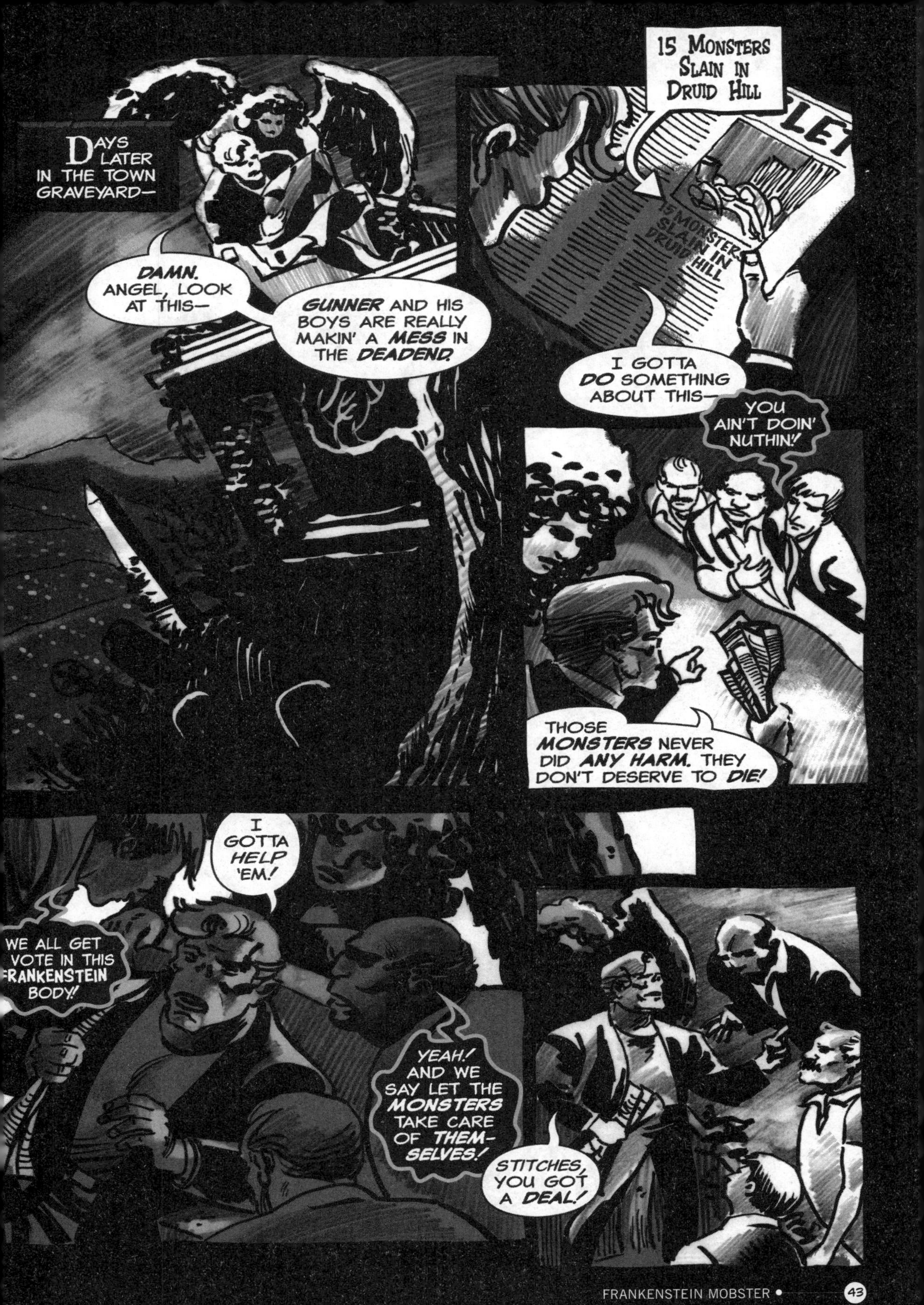
15 MONSTERS SLAIN IN DRUID HILL
DAYS LATER IN THE TOWN GRAVEYARD—
DAMN. ANGEL, LOOK AT THIS—
GUNNER AND HIS BOYS ARE REALLY MAKIN' A MESS IN THE DEADEND.
15 MONSTERS SLAIN IN DRUID HILL
I GOTTA DO SOMETHING ABOUT THIS—
YOU AIN'T DOIN' NUTHIN'!
THOSE MONSTERS NEVER DID ANY HARM. THEY DON'T DESERVE TO DIE!
I GOTTA HELP 'EM!
WE ALL GET VOTE IN THIS FRANKENSTEIN BODY!
YEAH! AND WE SAY LET THE MONSTERS TAKE CARE OF THEM-SELVES!
STITCHES, YOU GOT A DEAL!

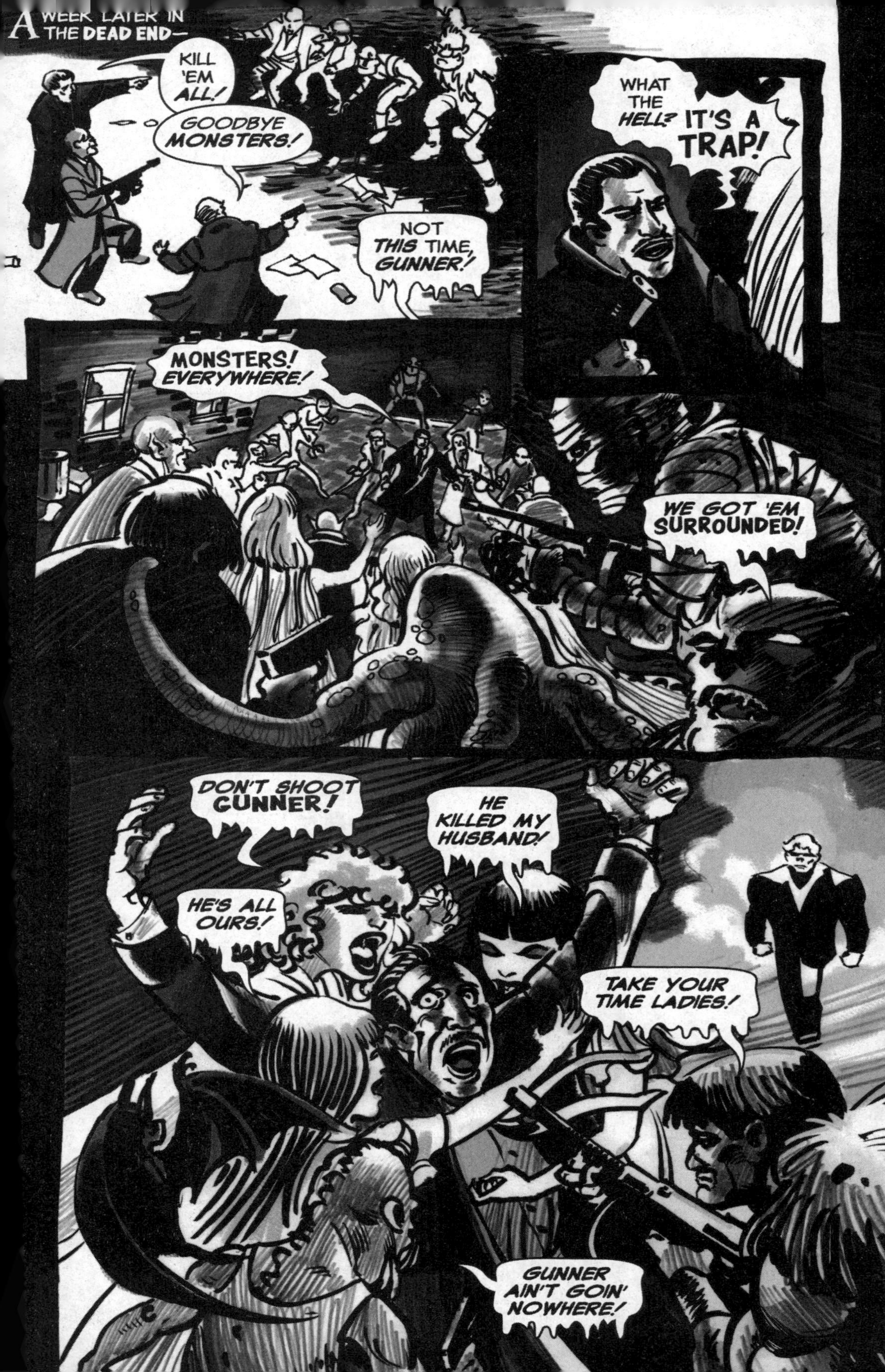
A WEEK LATER IN THE DEAD END—
KILL 'EM ALL!
GOODBYE MONSTERS!
NOT THIS TIME, GUNNER!
WHAT THE HELL? IT'S A TRAP!
MONSTERS! EVERYWHERE!
WE GOT 'EM SURROUNDED!
DON'T SHOOT GUNNER!
HE KILLED MY HUSBAND!
HE'S ALL OURS!
TAKE YOUR TIME LADIES!
GUNNER AIN'T GOIN' NOWHERE!

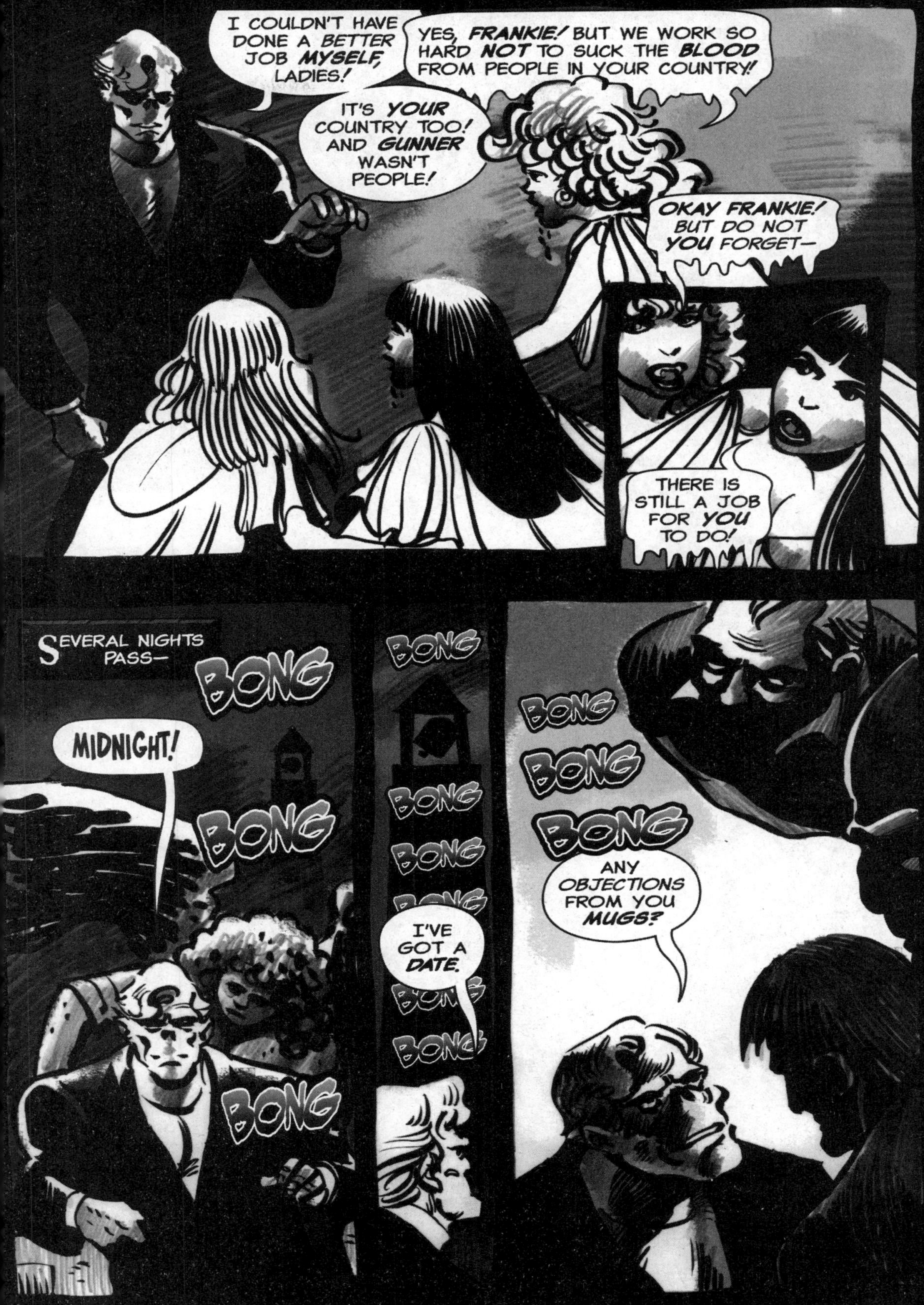

I COULDN'T HAVE DONE A BETTER JOB MYSELF, LADIES!
YES, FRANKIE! BUT WE WORK SO HARD NOT TO SUCK THE BLOOD FROM PEOPLE IN YOUR COUNTRY!
IT'S YOUR COUNTRY TOO! AND GUNNER WASN'T PEOPLE!
OKAY FRANKIE! BUT DO NOT YOU FORGET—
THERE IS STILL A JOB FOR YOU TO DO!
SEVERAL NIGHTS PASS—
BONG
MIDNIGHT!
BONG
BONG
BONG
BONG
BONG
BONG
I'VE GOT A DATE.
BONG
BONG
BONG
ANY OBJECTIONS FROM YOU MUGS?

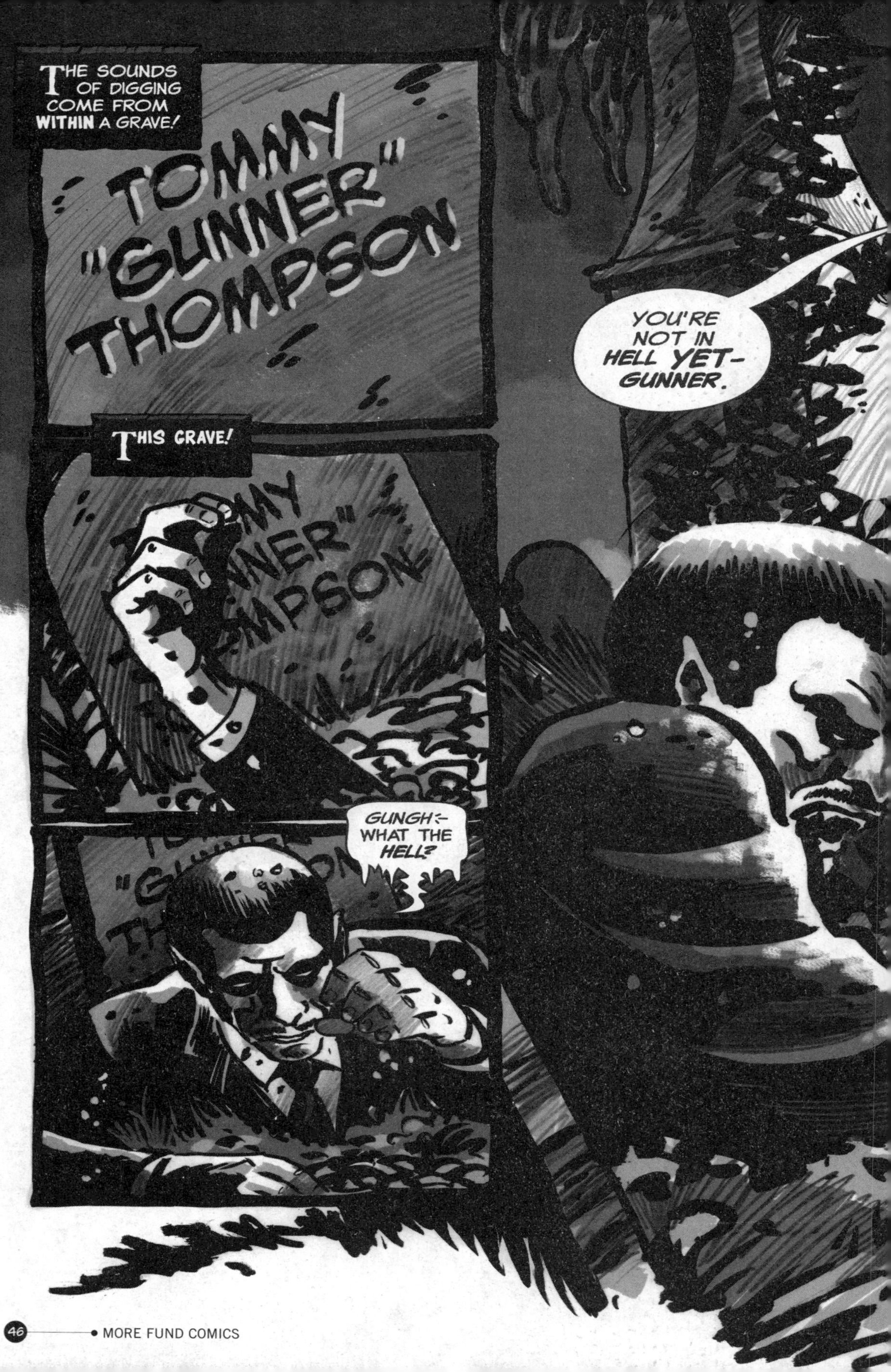

THE SOUNDS OF DIGGING COME FROM WITHIN A GRAVE!
TOMMY "GUNNER" THOMPSON
THIS GRAVE!
GUNGH:- WHAT THE HELL?
YOU'RE NOT IN HELL YET- GUNNER.

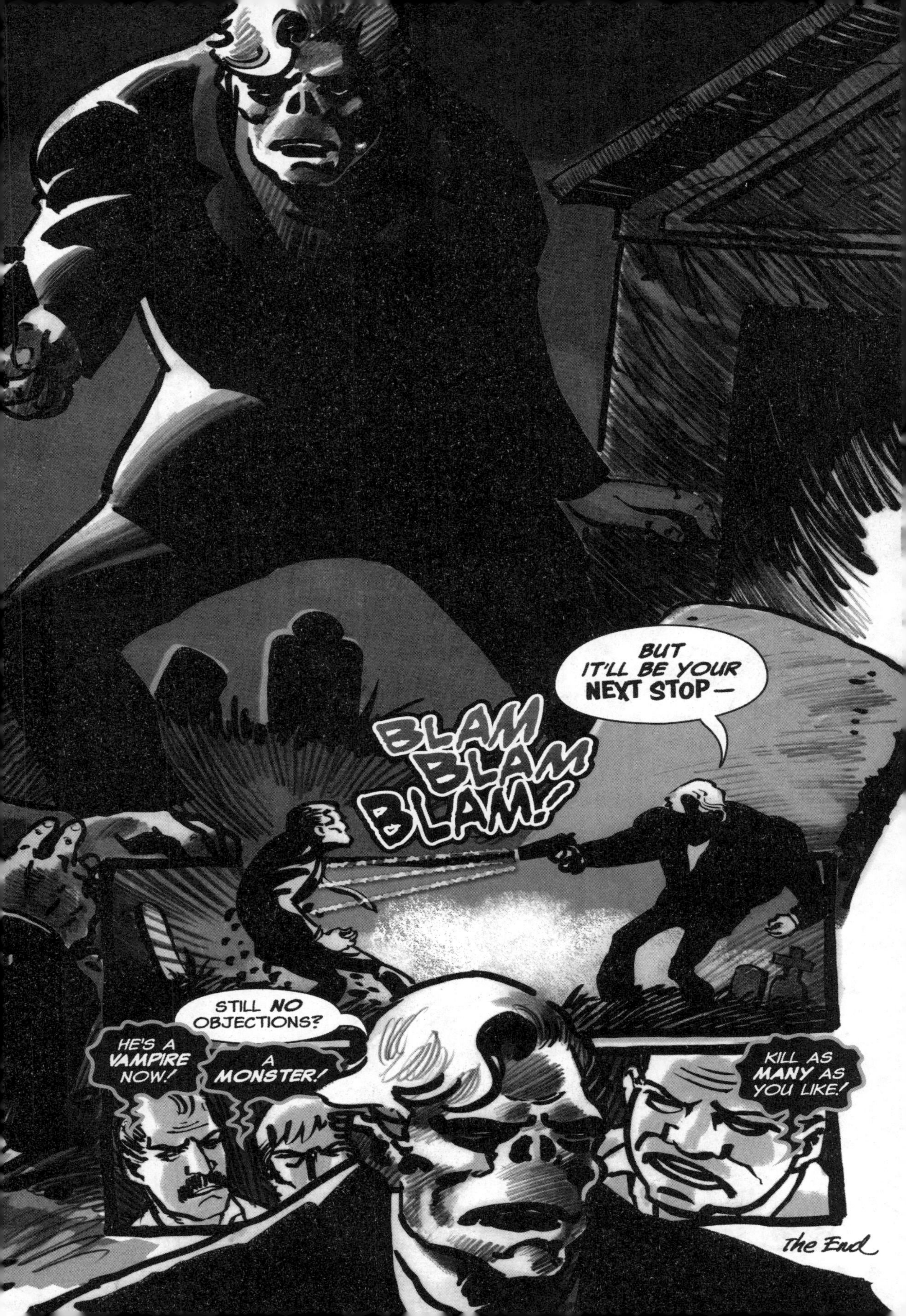
BUT IT'LL BE YOUR NEXT STOP—
BLAM BLAM BLAM!
STILL NO OBJECTIONS?
HE'S A VAMPIRE NOW!
A MONSTER!
KILL AS MANY AS YOU LIKE!
The End

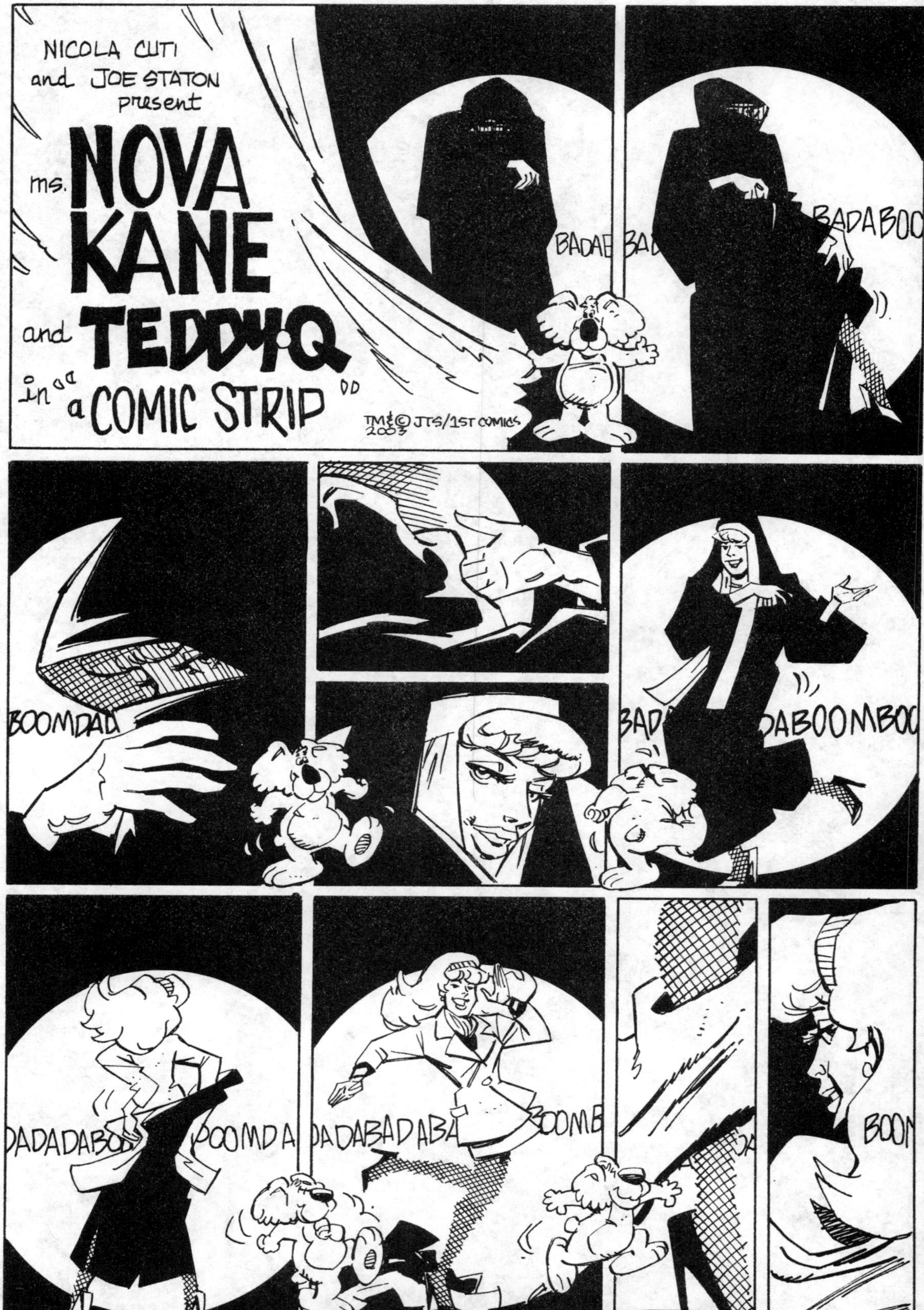
NICOLA CUTI
and JOE STATON
present
ms. NOVA KANE
and TEDDY Q
in "a COMIC STRIP"
TM & © JTS/1ST COMICS 2003
BADAB
BAD
BADABOO
BOOMDAD
BAD
DABOOMBOO
DADADABOO
BOOMDA
DADABADABA
BOOMB
BOOM

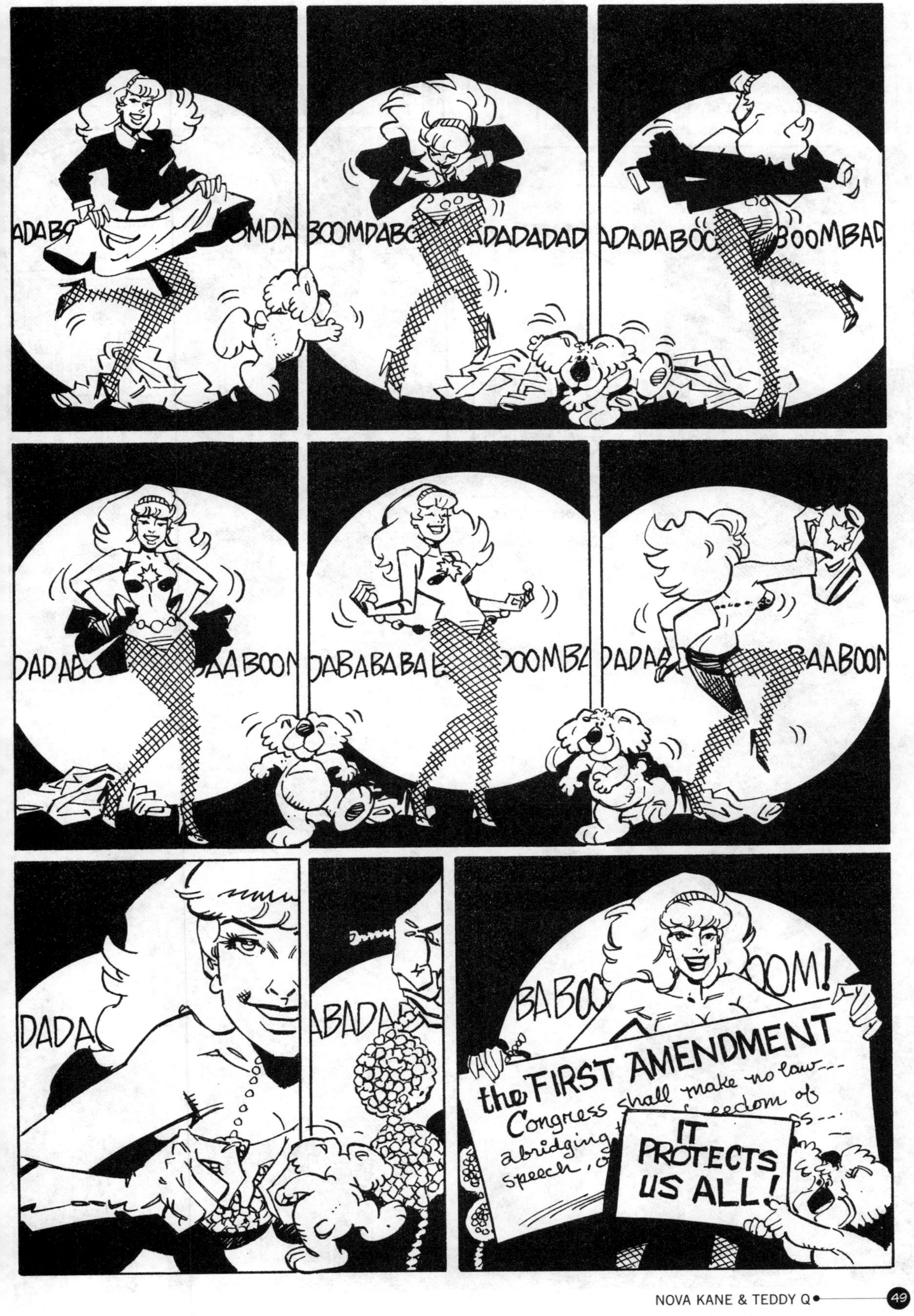
ADABO
OMDA
BOOMDABO
ADADADAD
ADADABOO
BOOMBA
DADABO
AABOOM
DABABABA
OOMBA
DADAB
BAABOOM
DADA
ABADA
BABOO
OOM!
the FIRST AMENDMENT
Congress shall make no law---
reedom of
abridging
speech, o
IT PROTECTS US ALL!

Face of Evil ©2003 Michael T. Gilbert

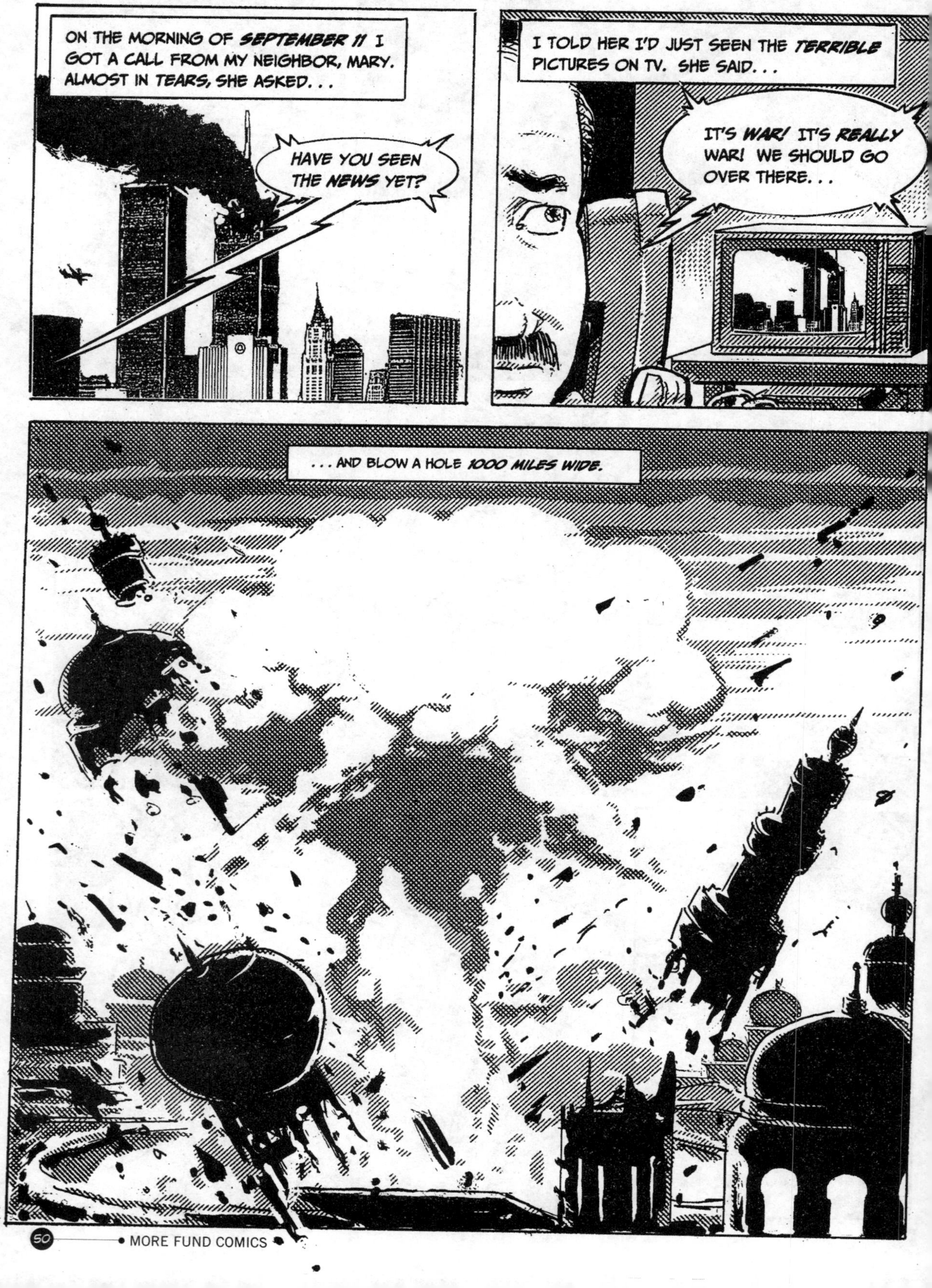
ON THE MORNING OF SEPTEMBER 11 I GOT A CALL FROM MY NEIGHBOR, MARY. ALMOST IN TEARS, SHE ASKED...
HAVE YOU SEEN THE NEWS YET?
I TOLD HER I'D JUST SEEN THE TERRIBLE PICTURES ON TV. SHE SAID...
IT'S WAR! IT'S REALLY WAR! WE SHOULD GO OVER THERE...
...AND BLOW A HOLE 1000 MILES WIDE.

THIS FROM A PASSIONATE *PRO-LIFE* CATHOLIC.

HOW *EASY* IT IS TO TALK ABOUT *KILLING* PEOPLE WE'LL NEVER MEET, HALF A WORLD AWAY.

BUT I HAD TO WONDER. WOULD MARY BE AS WILLING TO *SLAUGHTER* MILLIONS OF *FACELESS* PEOPLE IN THE NAME OF *VENGEANCE* . . .

. . . IF IT MEANT SACRIFICING A SINGLE UNBORN *INNOCENT* WITH THE REST?

I HOPE NOT. FOR HER SAKE, I HOPE MARY WAS JUST BLOWING OFF STEAM.

STILL, IT REMINDED ME JUST HOW EASILY *HATE* CAN POISON THE BEST OF US, IF WE LET IT. AND HOW QUICKLY OUR HATRED OF *EVIL*, UNTEMPERED BY *COMPASSION* . . .

. . . CAN CHANGE US INTO THE VERY *EVIL* WE HATE.

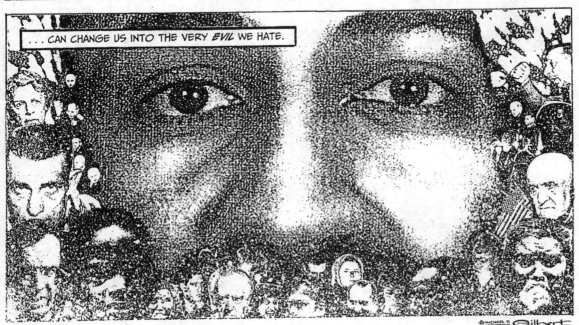

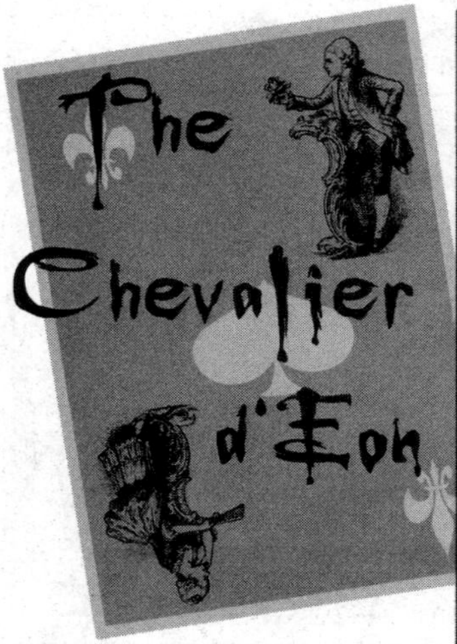
The Chevalier d'Eon

written and drawn by
Jeff Alexander
Edited by
Luciana Lopez

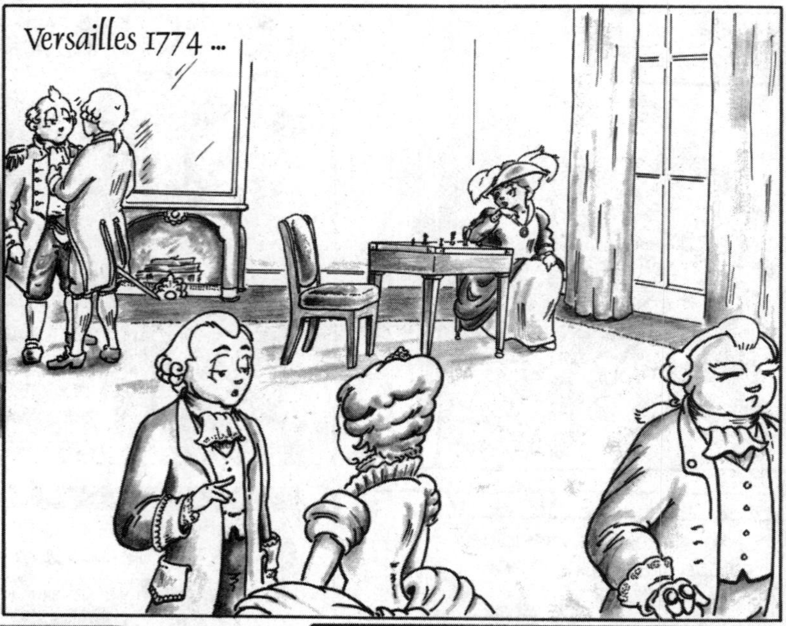
Versailles 1774 ...

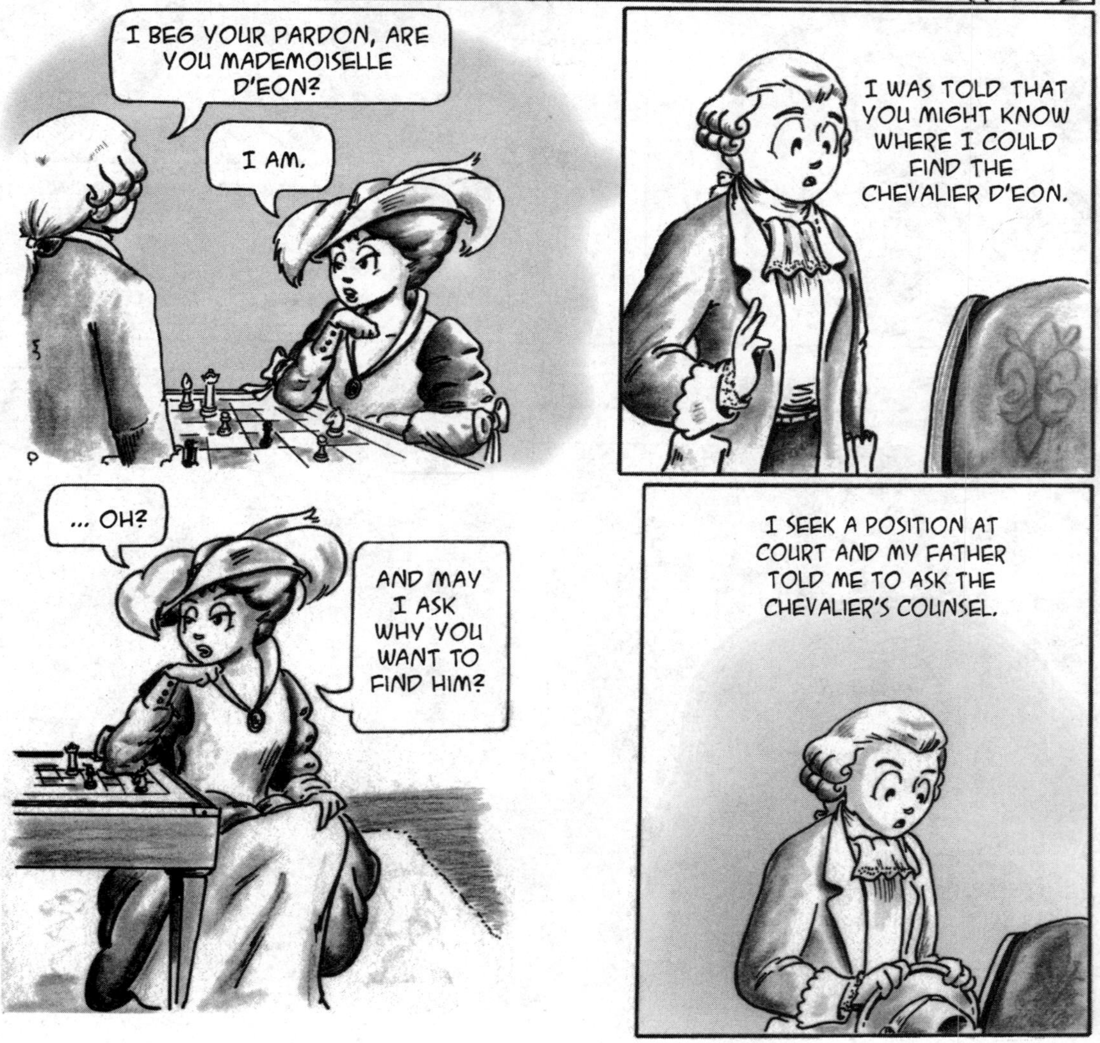
I BEG YOUR PARDON, ARE YOU MADEMOISELLE D'EON?
I AM.
I WAS TOLD THAT YOU MIGHT KNOW WHERE I COULD FIND THE CHEVALIER D'EON.
... OH?
AND MAY I ASK WHY YOU WANT TO FIND HIM?
I SEEK A POSITION AT COURT AND MY FATHER TOLD ME TO ASK THE CHEVALIER'S COUNSEL.

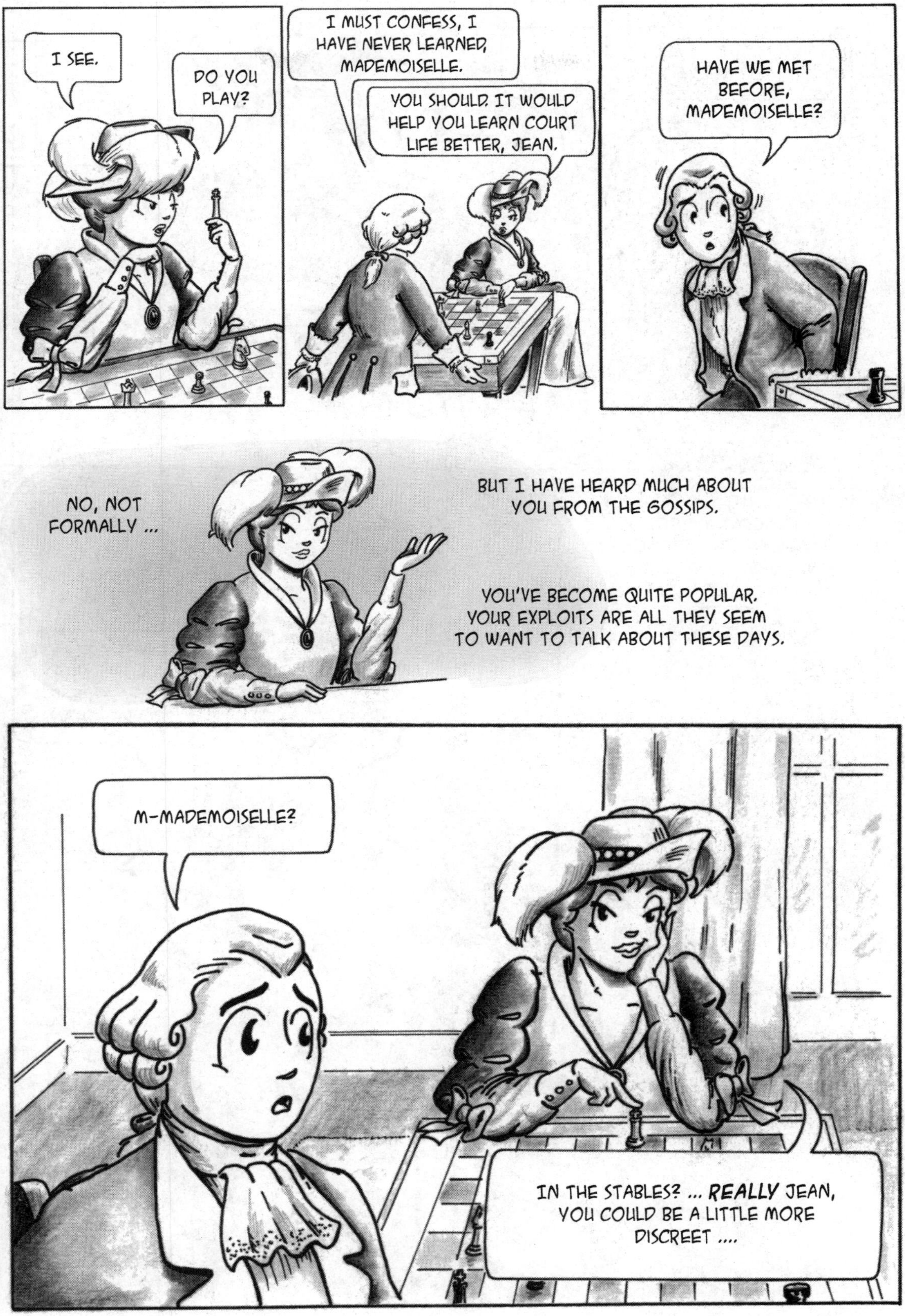
I SEE.
DO YOU PLAY?
I MUST CONFESS, I HAVE NEVER LEARNED, MADEMOISELLE.
YOU SHOULD. IT WOULD HELP YOU LEARN COURT LIFE BETTER, JEAN.
HAVE WE MET BEFORE, MADEMOISELLE?
NO, NOT FORMALLY ...
BUT I HAVE HEARD MUCH ABOUT YOU FROM THE GOSSIPS.
YOU'VE BECOME QUITE POPULAR. YOUR EXPLOITS ARE ALL THEY SEEM TO WANT TO TALK ABOUT THESE DAYS.
M-MADEMOISELLE?
IN THE STABLES? ... **REALLY** JEAN, YOU COULD BE A LITTLE MORE DISCREET ....

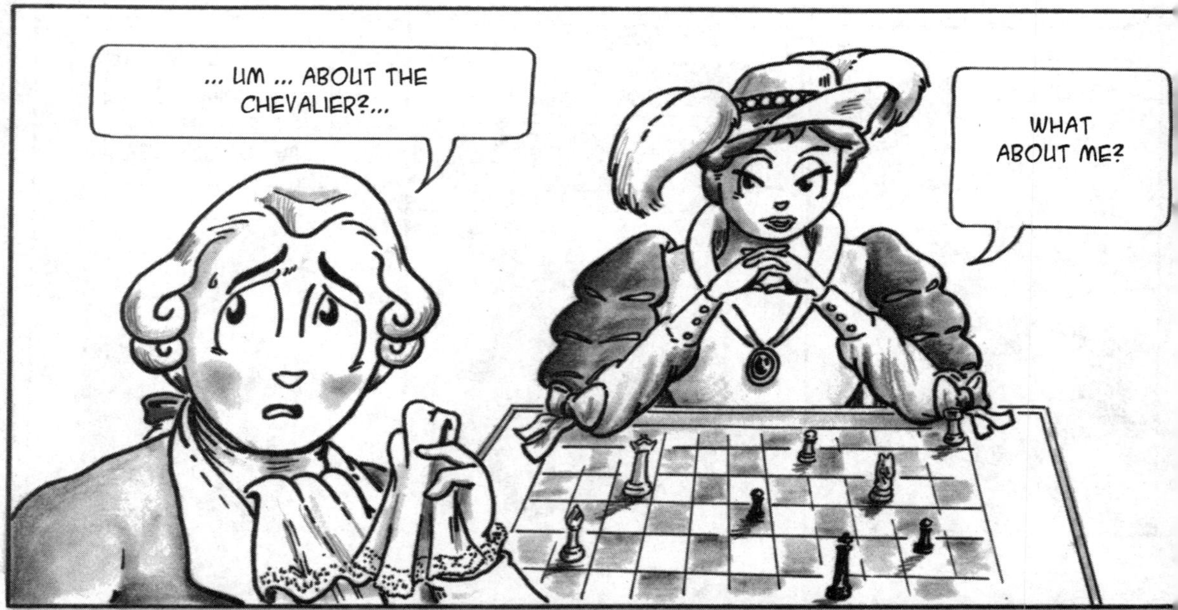
... UM ... ABOUT THE CHEVALIER?...
WHAT ABOUT ME?

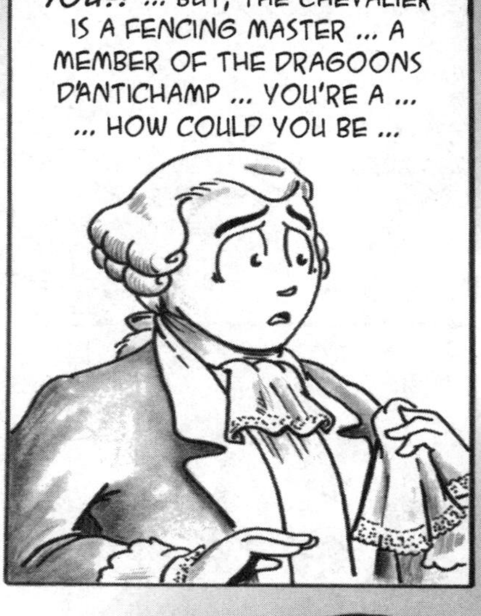
YOU?! ... BUT, THE CHEVALIER IS A FENCING MASTER ... A MEMBER OF THE DRAGOONS D'ANTICHAMP ... YOU'RE A ... ... HOW COULD YOU BE ...

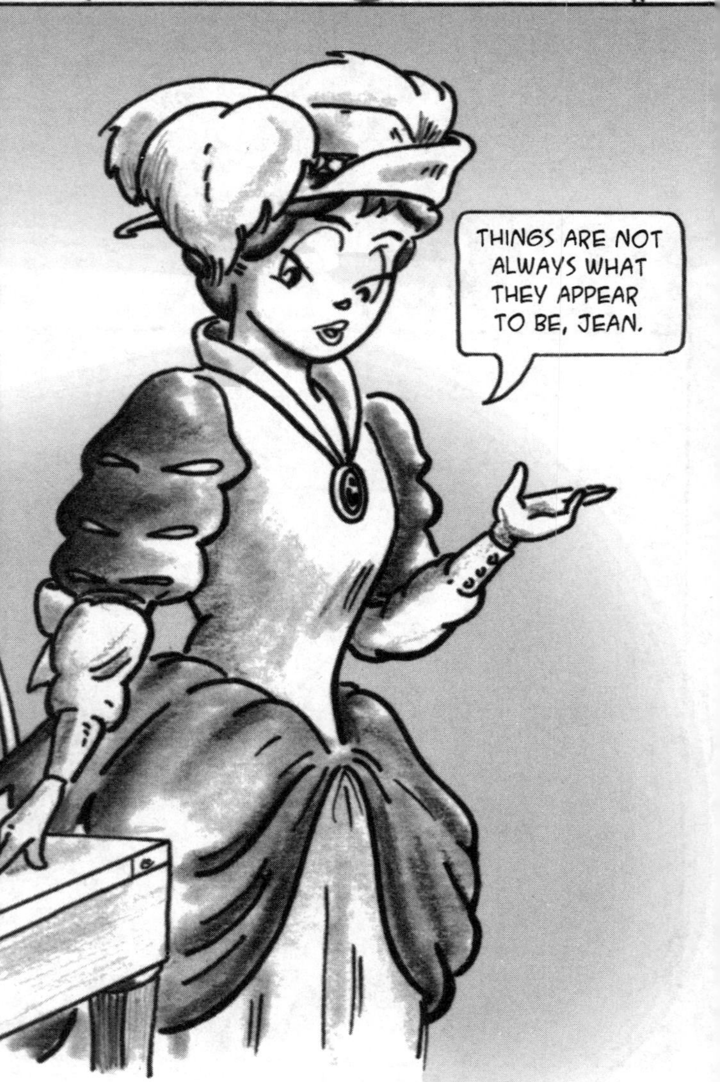
THINGS ARE NOT ALWAYS WHAT THEY APPEAR TO BE, JEAN.

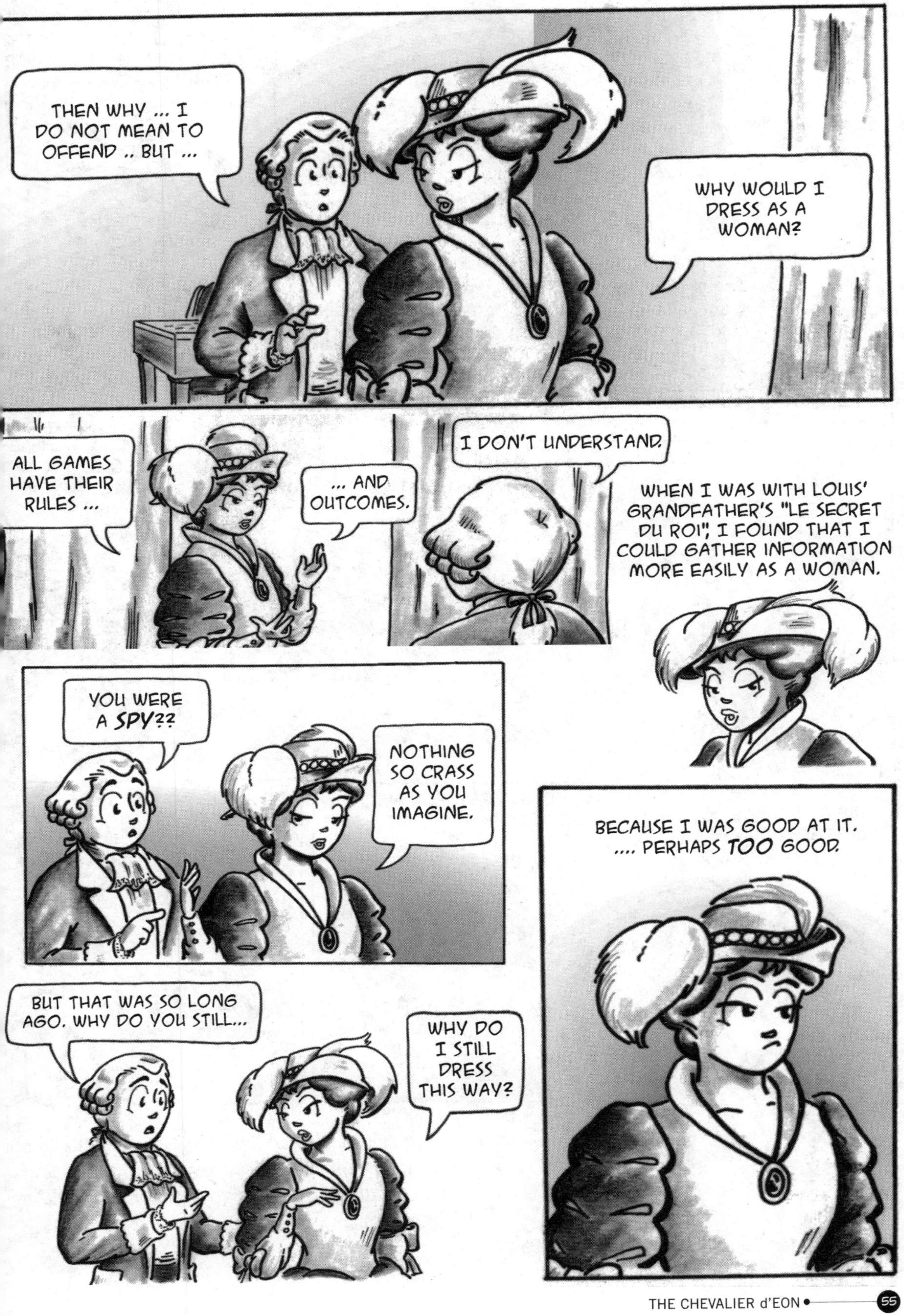

THEN WHY ... I DO NOT MEAN TO OFFEND .. BUT ...
WHY WOULD I DRESS AS A WOMAN?
ALL GAMES HAVE THEIR RULES ...
... AND OUTCOMES.
I DON'T UNDERSTAND.
WHEN I WAS WITH LOUIS' GRANDFATHER'S "LE SECRET DU ROI", I FOUND THAT I COULD GATHER INFORMATION MORE EASILY AS A WOMAN.
YOU WERE A SPY??
NOTHING SO CRASS AS YOU IMAGINE.
BECAUSE I WAS GOOD AT IT. .... PERHAPS TOO GOOD.
BUT THAT WAS SO LONG AGO. WHY DO YOU STILL...
WHY DO I STILL DRESS THIS WAY?

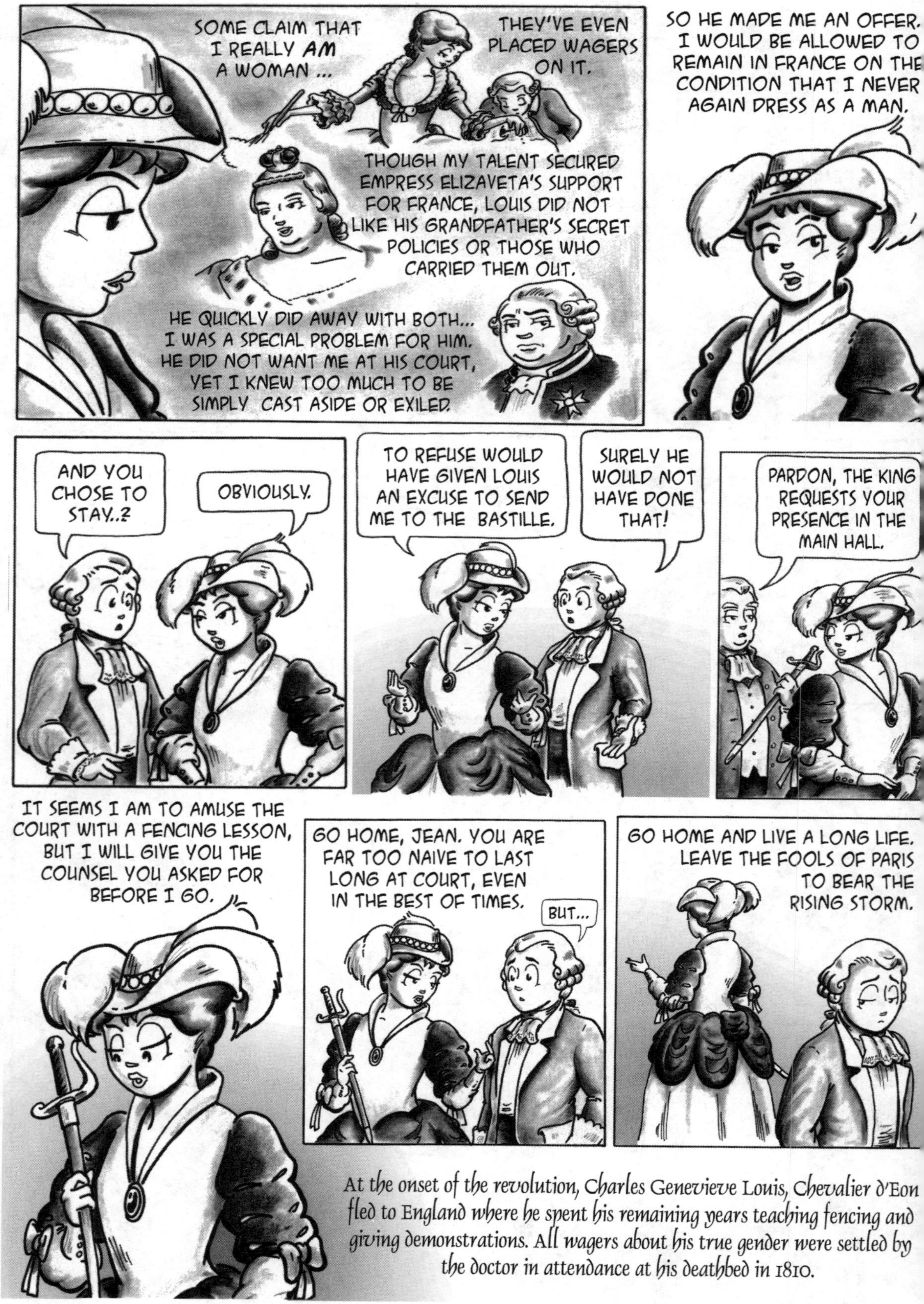
SOME CLAIM THAT I REALLY **AM** A WOMAN ...
THEY'VE EVEN PLACED WAGERS ON IT.
THOUGH MY TALENT SECURED EMPRESS ELIZAVETA'S SUPPORT FOR FRANCE, LOUIS DID NOT LIKE HIS GRANDFATHER'S SECRET POLICIES OR THOSE WHO CARRIED THEM OUT.
HE QUICKLY DID AWAY WITH BOTH... I WAS A SPECIAL PROBLEM FOR HIM. HE DID NOT WANT ME AT HIS COURT, YET I KNEW TOO MUCH TO BE SIMPLY CAST ASIDE OR EXILED.
SO HE MADE ME AN OFFER. I WOULD BE ALLOWED TO REMAIN IN FRANCE ON THE CONDITION THAT I NEVER AGAIN DRESS AS A MAN.
AND YOU CHOSE TO STAY..?
OBVIOUSLY.
TO REFUSE WOULD HAVE GIVEN LOUIS AN EXCUSE TO SEND ME TO THE BASTILLE.
SURELY HE WOULD NOT HAVE DONE THAT!
PARDON, THE KING REQUESTS YOUR PRESENCE IN THE MAIN HALL.
IT SEEMS I AM TO AMUSE THE COURT WITH A FENCING LESSON, BUT I WILL GIVE YOU THE COUNSEL YOU ASKED FOR BEFORE I GO.
GO HOME, JEAN. YOU ARE FAR TOO NAIVE TO LAST LONG AT COURT, EVEN IN THE BEST OF TIMES.
BUT...
GO HOME AND LIVE A LONG LIFE. LEAVE THE FOOLS OF PARIS TO BEAR THE RISING STORM.

At the onset of the revolution, Charles Genevieve Louis, Chevalier d'Eon fled to England where he spent his remaining years teaching fencing and giving demonstrations. All wagers about his true gender were settled by the doctor in attendance at his deathbed in 1810.

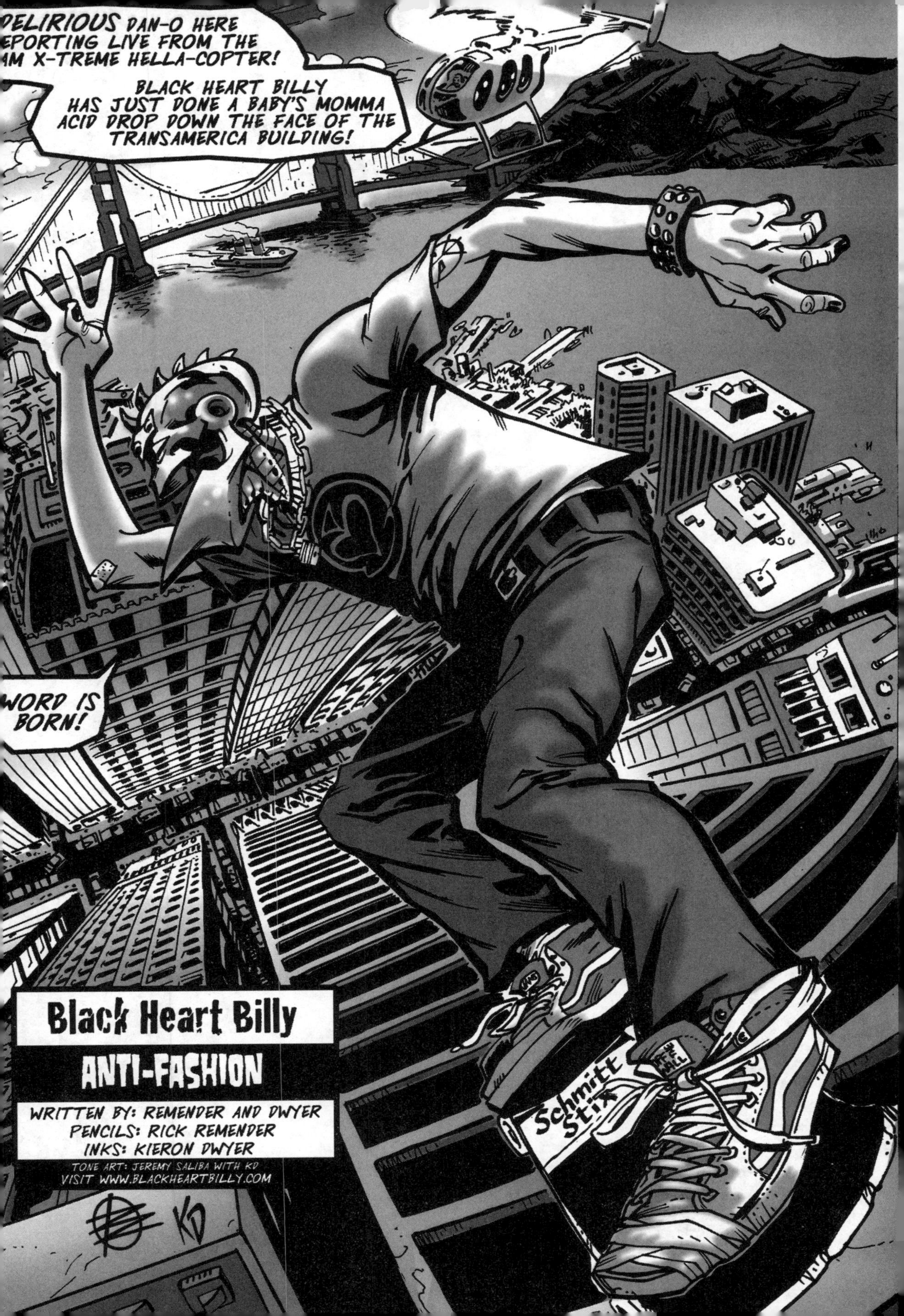
DELIRIOUS DAN-O HERE EPORTING LIVE FROM THE AM X-TREME HELLA-COPTER!
BLACK HEART BILLY HAS JUST DONE A BABY'S MOMMA ACID DROP DOWN THE FACE OF THE TRANSAMERICA BUILDING!
WORD IS BORN!
Schmitt Stix
Black Heart Billy
ANTI-FASHION
WRITTEN BY: REMENDER AND DWYER
PENCILS: RICK REMENDER
INKS: KIERON DWYER
TONE ART: JEREMY SALIBA WITH KD
VISIT WWW.BLACKHEARTBILLY.COM
KD

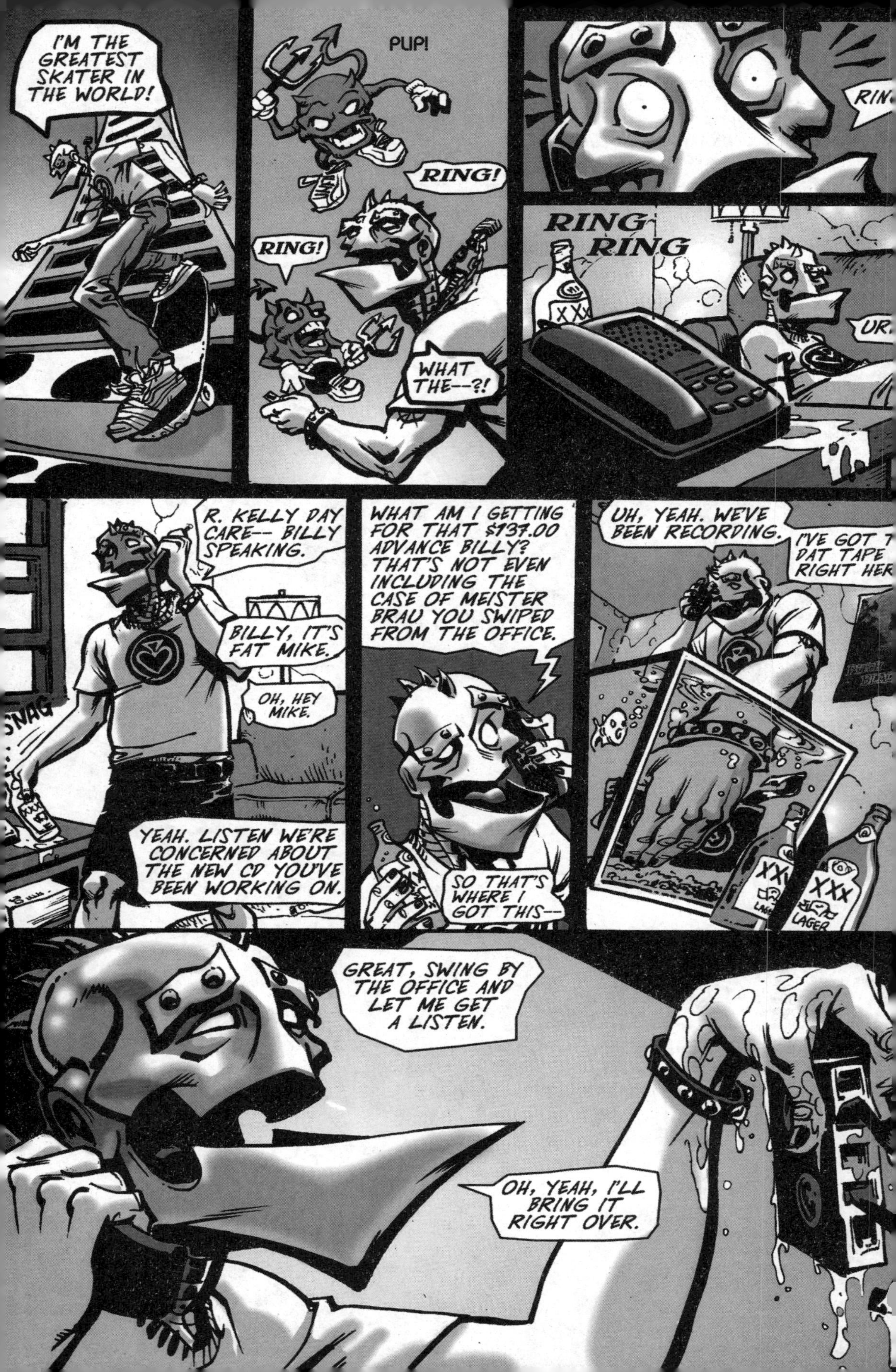
I'M THE GREATEST SKATER IN THE WORLD!
PLIP!
RING!
RING!
WHAT THE--?!
RING RING
R. KELLY DAY CARE-- BILLY SPEAKING.
BILLY, IT'S FAT MIKE.
OH, HEY MIKE.
SNAG
YEAH. LISTEN WE'RE CONCERNED ABOUT THE NEW CD YOU'VE BEEN WORKING ON.
WHAT AM I GETTING FOR THAT $137.00 ADVANCE BILLY? THAT'S NOT EVEN INCLUDING THE CASE OF MEISTER BRAU YOU SWIPED FROM THE OFFICE.
SO THAT'S WHERE I GOT THIS--
UH, YEAH. WE'VE BEEN RECORDING.
GREAT, SWING BY THE OFFICE AND LET ME GET A LISTEN.
OH, YEAH, I'LL BRING IT RIGHT OVER.

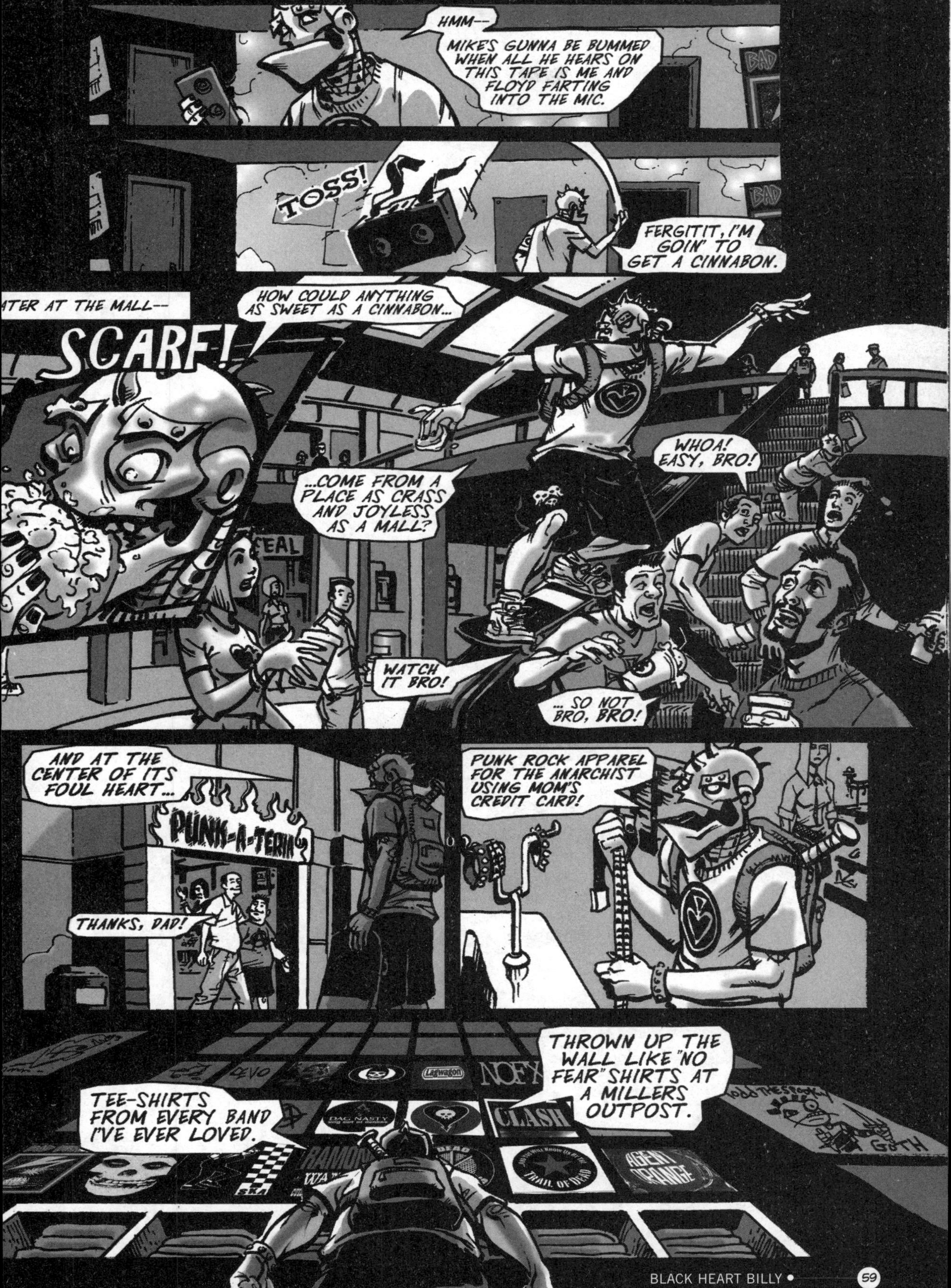
HMM--
MIKE'S GUNNA BE BUMMED WHEN ALL HE HEARS ON THIS TAPE IS ME AND FLOYD FARTING INTO THE MIC.
TOSS!
FERGITIT, I'M GOIN' TO GET A CINNABON.
ATER AT THE MALL--
HOW COULD ANYTHING AS SWEET AS A CINNABON...
SCARF!
...COME FROM A PLACE AS CRASS AND JOYLESS AS A MALL?
WHOA! EASY, BRO!
WATCH IT BRO!
... SO NOT BRO, BRO!
AND AT THE CENTER OF ITS FOUL HEART...
PUNK-A-TERIA
THANKS, DAD!
PUNK ROCK APPAREL FOR THE ANARCHIST USING MOM'S CREDIT CARD!
THROWN UP THE WALL LIKE "NO FEAR" SHIRTS AT A MILLERS OUTPOST.
TEE-SHIRTS FROM EVERY BAND I'VE EVER LOVED.
DEVO
Lagwagon
NOFX
DAG NASTY
CLASH
TRAIL OF DEAD
AGENT ORANGE
SKA

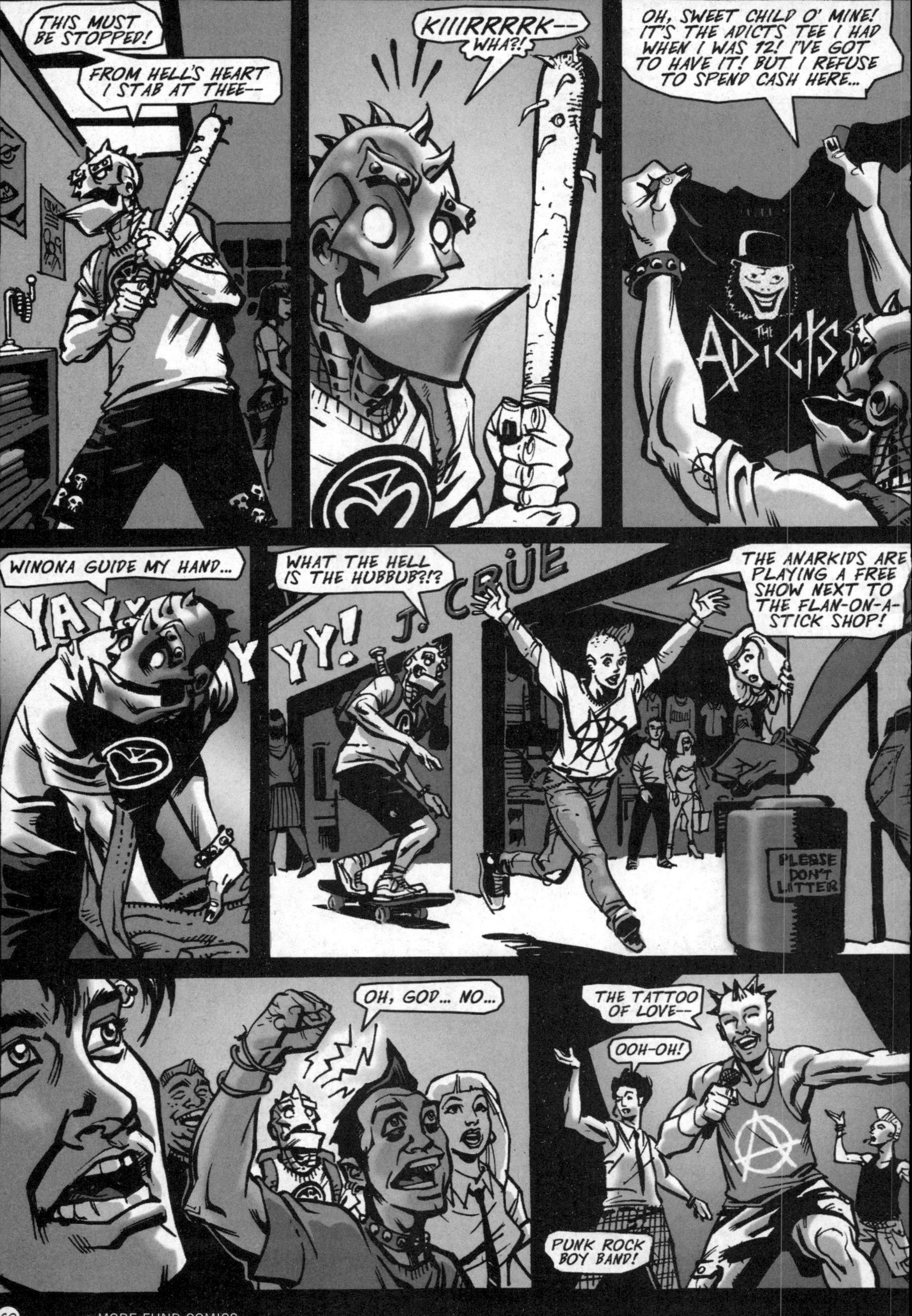
THIS MUST BE STOPPED!
FROM HELL'S HEART I STAB AT THEE--
KIIIRRRRK--
WHA?!
OH, SWEET CHILD O' MINE! IT'S THE ADICTS TEE I HAD WHEN I WAS 12! I'VE GOT TO HAVE IT! BUT I REFUSE TO SPEND CASH HERE...
THE ADICTS
WINONA GUIDE MY HAND...
YAYYYYY!
WHAT THE HELL IS THE HUBBUB?!?
J. CRÜE
THE ANARKIDS ARE PLAYING A FREE SHOW NEXT TO THE FLAN-ON-A-STICK SHOP!
PLEASE DON'T LITTER
OH, GOD... NO...
THE TATTOO OF LOVE--
OOH-OH!
PUNK ROCK BOY BAND!

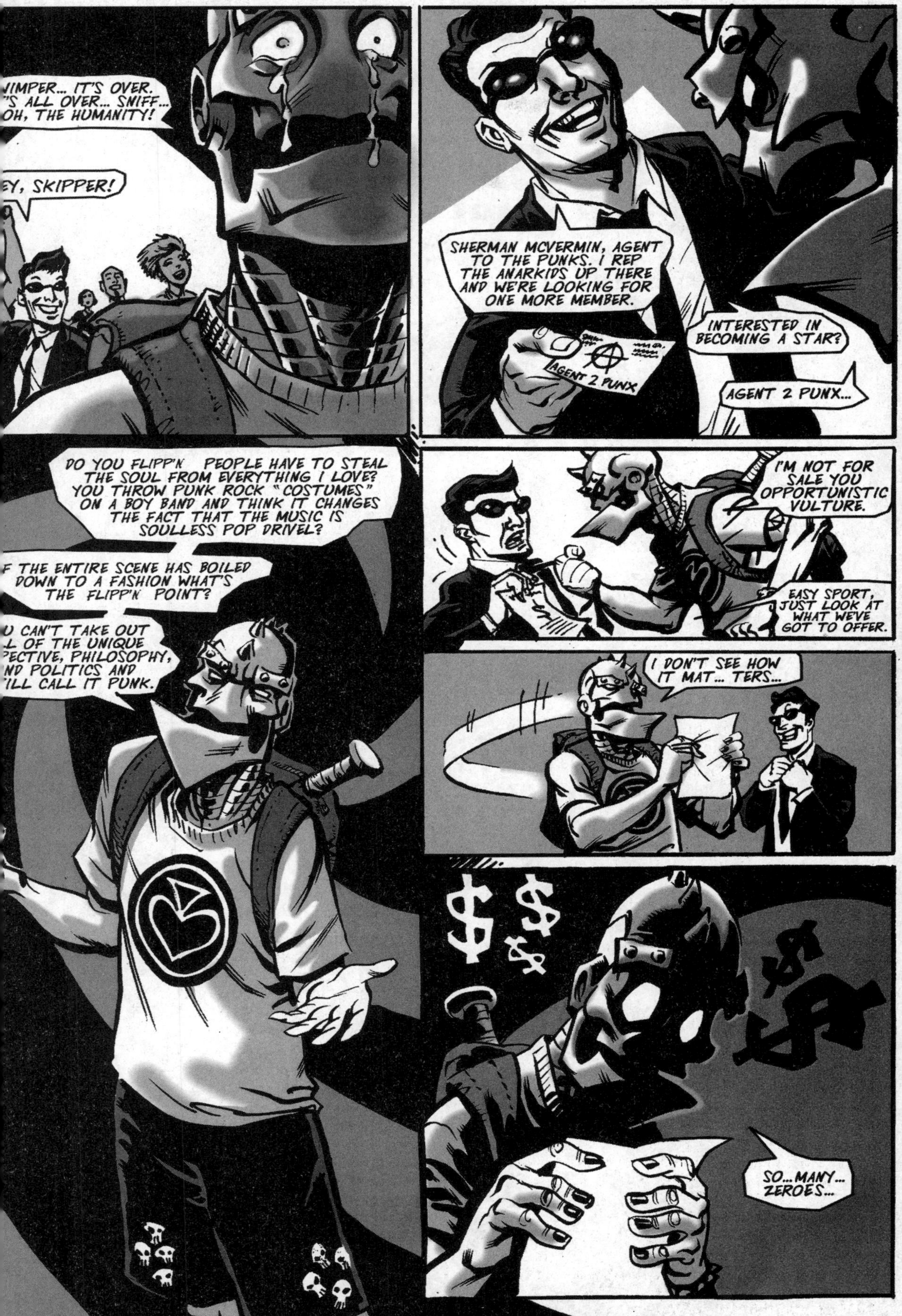

WIMPER... IT'S OVER. 'S ALL OVER... SNIFF... OH, THE HUMANITY!
EY, SKIPPER!
SHERMAN MCVERMIN, AGENT TO THE PUNKS. I REP THE ANARKIDS UP THERE AND WE'RE LOOKING FOR ONE MORE MEMBER.
AGENT 2 PUNX
INTERESTED IN BECOMING A STAR?
AGENT 2 PUNX...
DO YOU FLIPP'N PEOPLE HAVE TO STEAL THE SOUL FROM EVERYTHING I LOVE? YOU THROW PUNK ROCK "COSTUMES" ON A BOY BAND AND THINK IT CHANGES THE FACT THAT THE MUSIC IS SOULLESS POP DRIVEL?
F THE ENTIRE SCENE HAS BOILED DOWN TO A FASHION WHAT'S THE FLIPP'N POINT?
U CAN'T TAKE OUT L OF THE UNIQUE PECTIVE, PHILOSOPHY, ND POLITICS AND TILL CALL IT PUNK.
I'M NOT FOR SALE YOU OPPORTUNISTIC VULTURE.
EASY SPORT, JUST LOOK AT WHAT WEVE GOT TO OFFER.
I DON'T SEE HOW IT MAT... TERS...
SO...MANY... ZEROES...

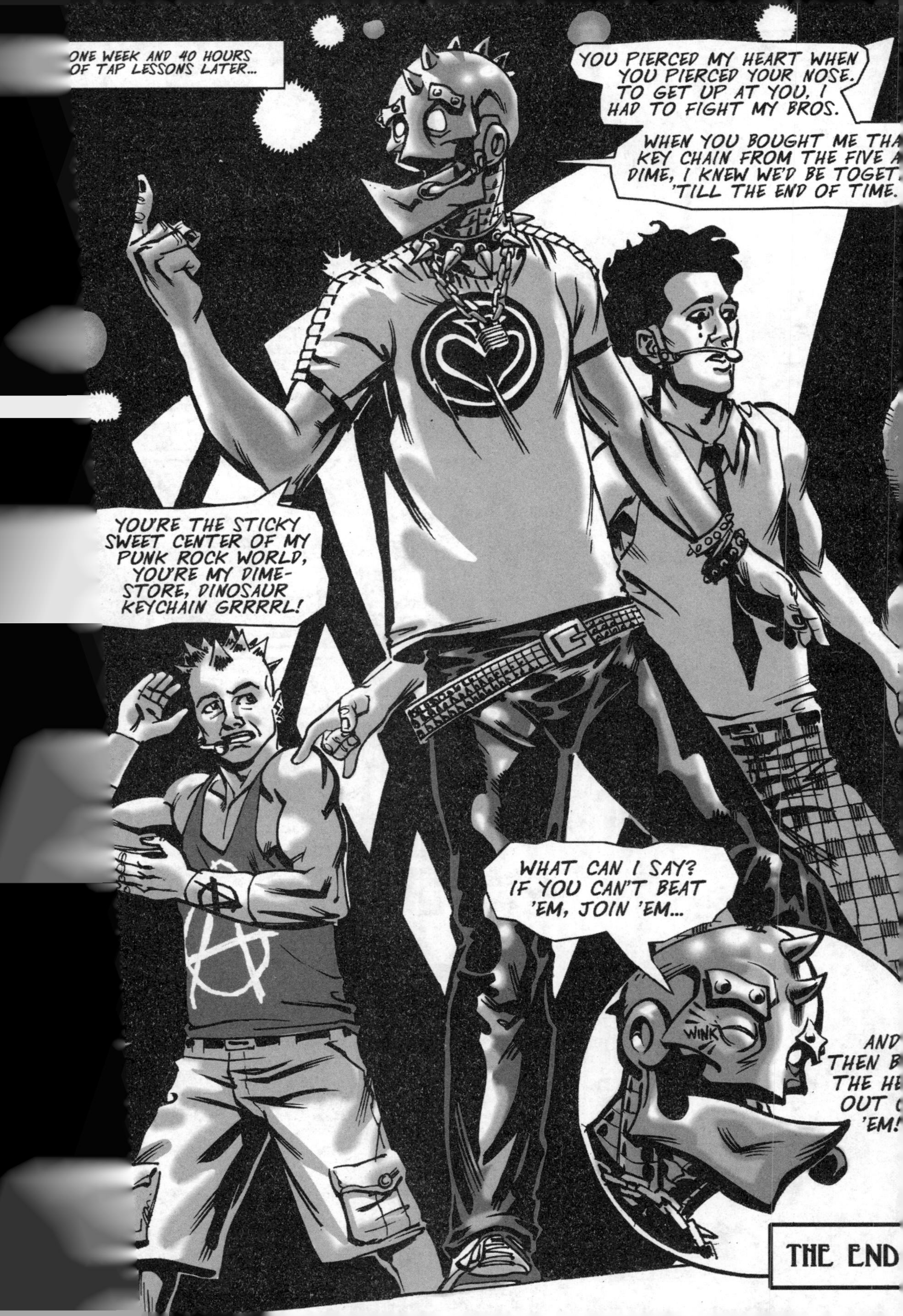
ONE WEEK AND 40 HOURS OF TAP LESSONS LATER...
YOU PIERCED MY HEART WHEN YOU PIERCED YOUR NOSE. TO GET UP AT YOU, I HAD TO FIGHT MY BROS.
WHEN YOU BOUGHT ME THA KEY CHAIN FROM THE FIVE A DIME, I KNEW WE'D BE TOGET 'TILL THE END OF TIME.
YOU'RE THE STICKY SWEET CENTER OF MY PUNK ROCK WORLD, YOU'RE MY DIME-STORE, DINOSAUR KEYCHAIN GRRRRL!
WHAT CAN I SAY? IF YOU CAN'T BEAT 'EM, JOIN 'EM...
WINK
AND THEN B THE HE OUT 'EM!
THE END

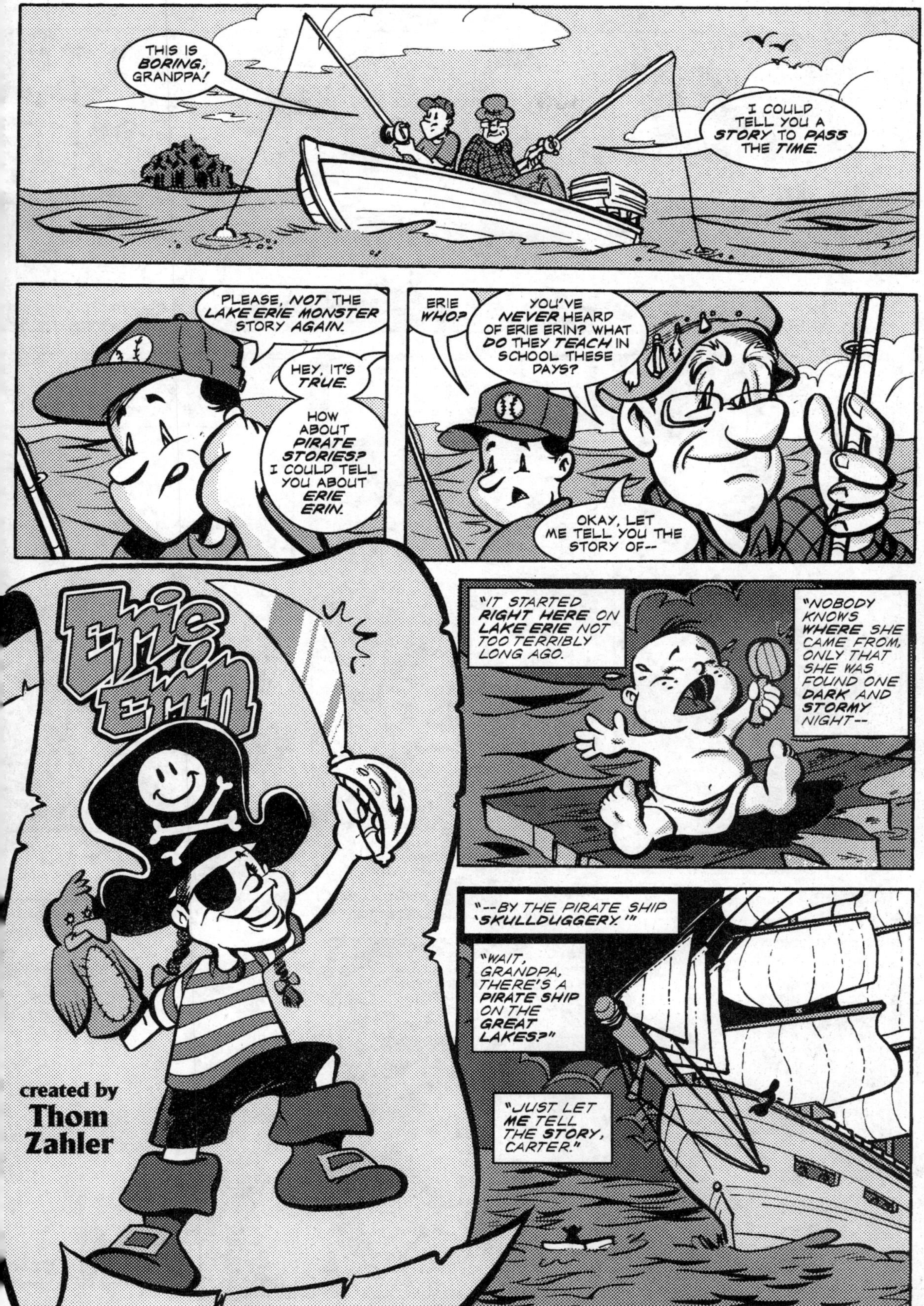
THIS IS BORING, GRANDPA!
I COULD TELL YOU A STORY TO PASS THE TIME.
PLEASE, NOT THE LAKE ERIE MONSTER STORY AGAIN.
HEY, IT'S TRUE.
HOW ABOUT PIRATE STORIES? I COULD TELL YOU ABOUT ERIE ERIN.
ERIE WHO?
YOU'VE NEVER HEARD OF ERIE ERIN? WHAT DO THEY TEACH IN SCHOOL THESE DAYS?
OKAY, LET ME TELL YOU THE STORY OF--
Erie Erin
created by Thom Zahler
"IT STARTED RIGHT HERE ON LAKE ERIE NOT TOO TERRIBLY LONG AGO.
"NOBODY KNOWS WHERE SHE CAME FROM, ONLY THAT SHE WAS FOUND ONE DARK AND STORMY NIGHT--
"--BY THE PIRATE SHIP 'SKULLDUGGERY.'"
"WAIT, GRANDPA, THERE'S A PIRATE SHIP ON THE GREAT LAKES?"
"JUST LET ME TELL THE STORY, CARTER."

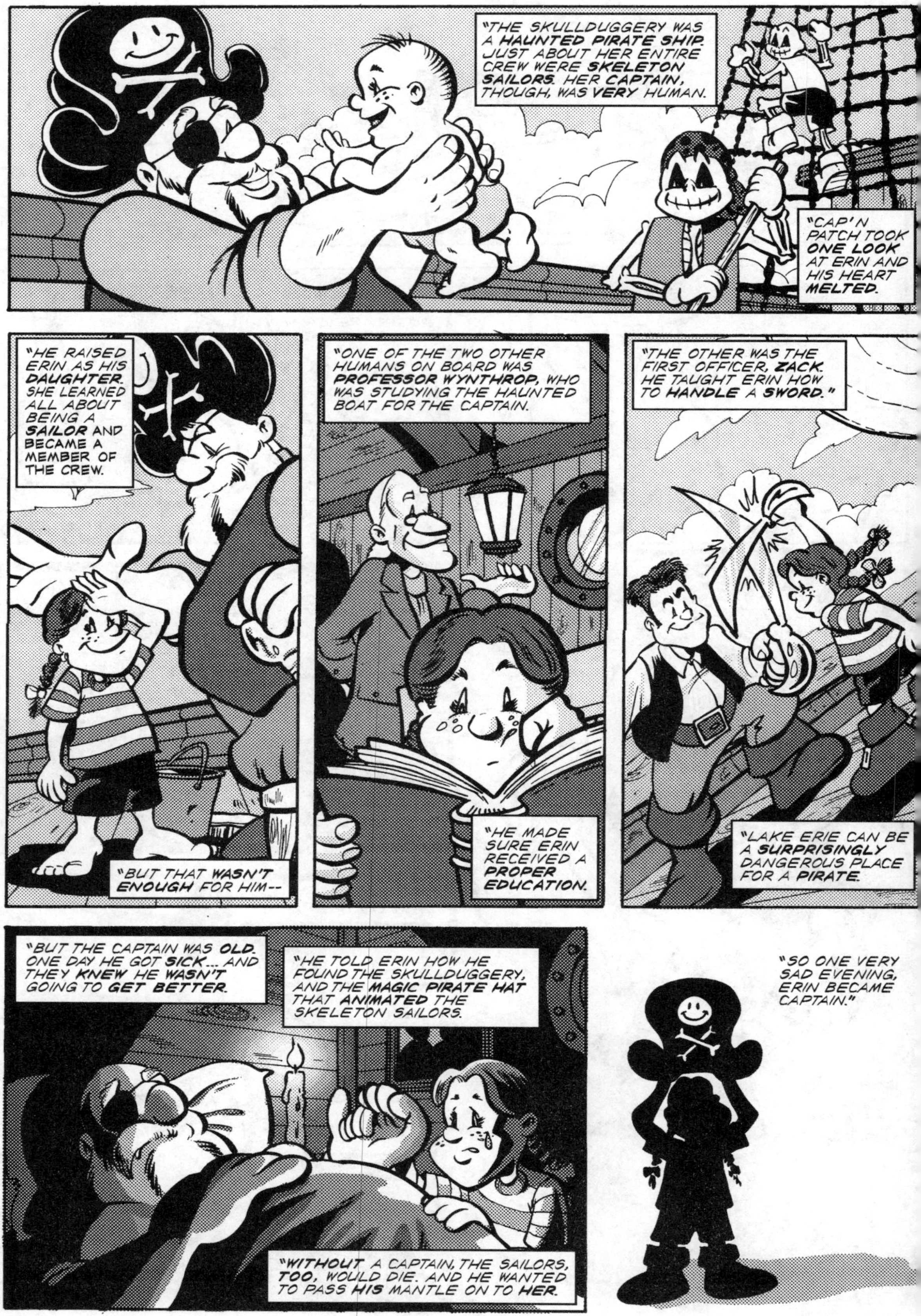
"THE SKULLDUGGERY WAS A HAUNTED PIRATE SHIP. JUST ABOUT HER ENTIRE CREW WERE SKELETON SAILORS. HER CAPTAIN, THOUGH, WAS VERY HUMAN.
"CAP'N PATCH TOOK ONE LOOK AT ERIN AND HIS HEART MELTED.
"HE RAISED ERIN AS HIS DAUGHTER. SHE LEARNED ALL ABOUT BEING A SAILOR AND BECAME A MEMBER OF THE CREW.
"BUT THAT WASN'T ENOUGH FOR HIM--
"ONE OF THE TWO OTHER HUMANS ON BOARD WAS PROFESSOR WYNTHROP, WHO WAS STUDYING THE HAUNTED BOAT FOR THE CAPTAIN.
"HE MADE SURE ERIN RECEIVED A PROPER EDUCATION.
"THE OTHER WAS THE FIRST OFFICER, ZACK. HE TAUGHT ERIN HOW TO HANDLE A SWORD."
"LAKE ERIE CAN BE A SURPRISINGLY DANGEROUS PLACE FOR A PIRATE.
"BUT THE CAPTAIN WAS OLD. ONE DAY HE GOT SICK... AND THEY KNEW HE WASN'T GOING TO GET BETTER.
"HE TOLD ERIN HOW HE FOUND THE SKULLDUGGERY, AND THE MAGIC PIRATE HAT THAT ANIMATED THE SKELETON SAILORS.
"WITHOUT A CAPTAIN, THE SAILORS, TOO, WOULD DIE. AND HE WANTED TO PASS HIS MANTLE ON TO HER.
"SO ONE VERY SAD EVENING, ERIN BECAME CAPTAIN."

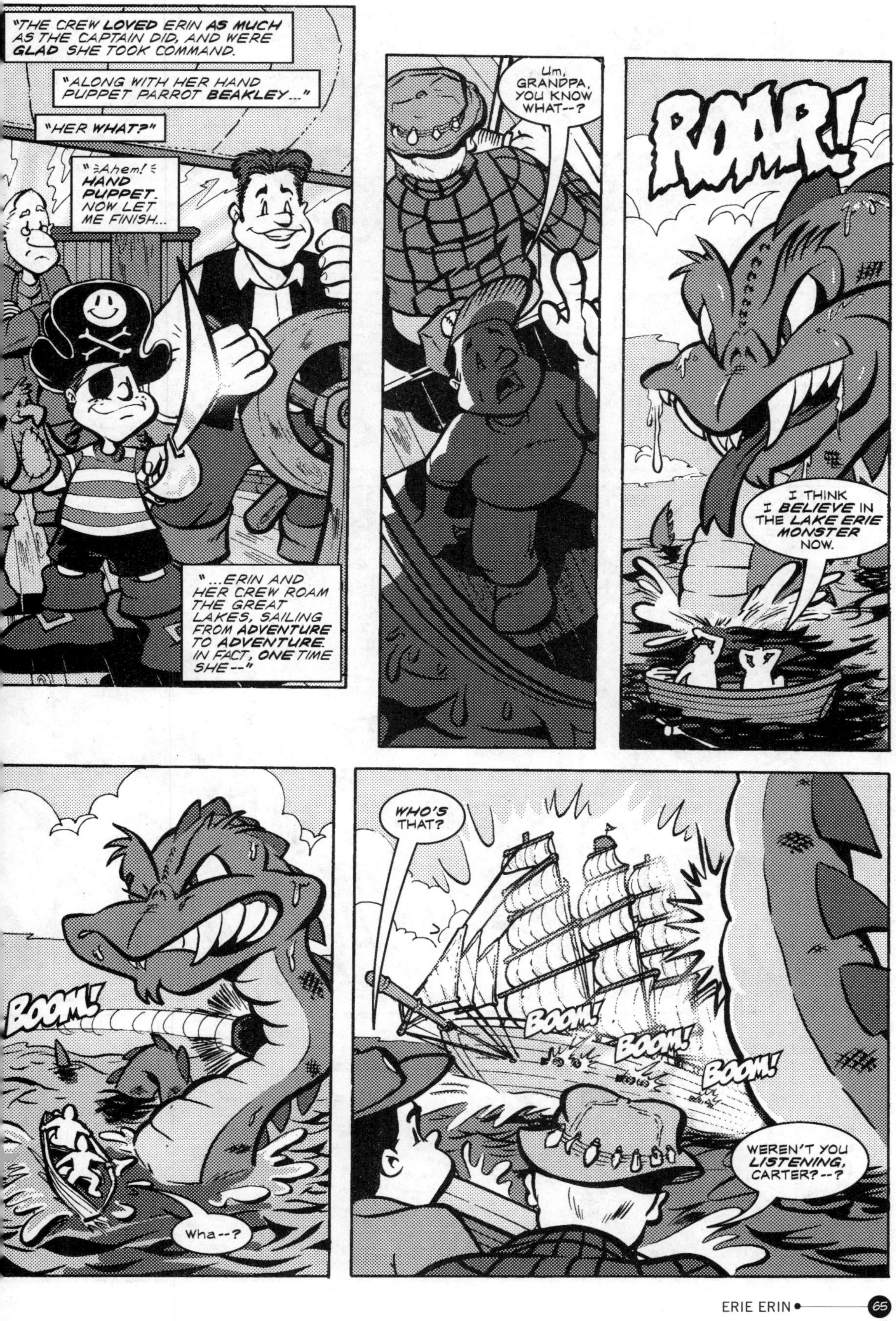
"THE CREW LOVED ERIN AS MUCH AS THE CAPTAIN DID, AND WERE GLAD SHE TOOK COMMAND.
"ALONG WITH HER HAND PUPPET PARROT BEAKLEY..."
"HER WHAT?"
"Ahem! HAND PUPPET. NOW LET ME FINISH...
"...ERIN AND HER CREW ROAM THE GREAT LAKES, SAILING FROM ADVENTURE TO ADVENTURE. IN FACT, ONE TIME SHE--"
Um, GRANDPA, YOU KNOW WHAT--?
ROAR!
I THINK I BELIEVE IN THE LAKE ERIE MONSTER NOW.
BOOM!
Wha--?
WHO'S THAT?
BOOM!
BOOM!
BOOM!
WEREN'T YOU LISTENING, CARTER?--?

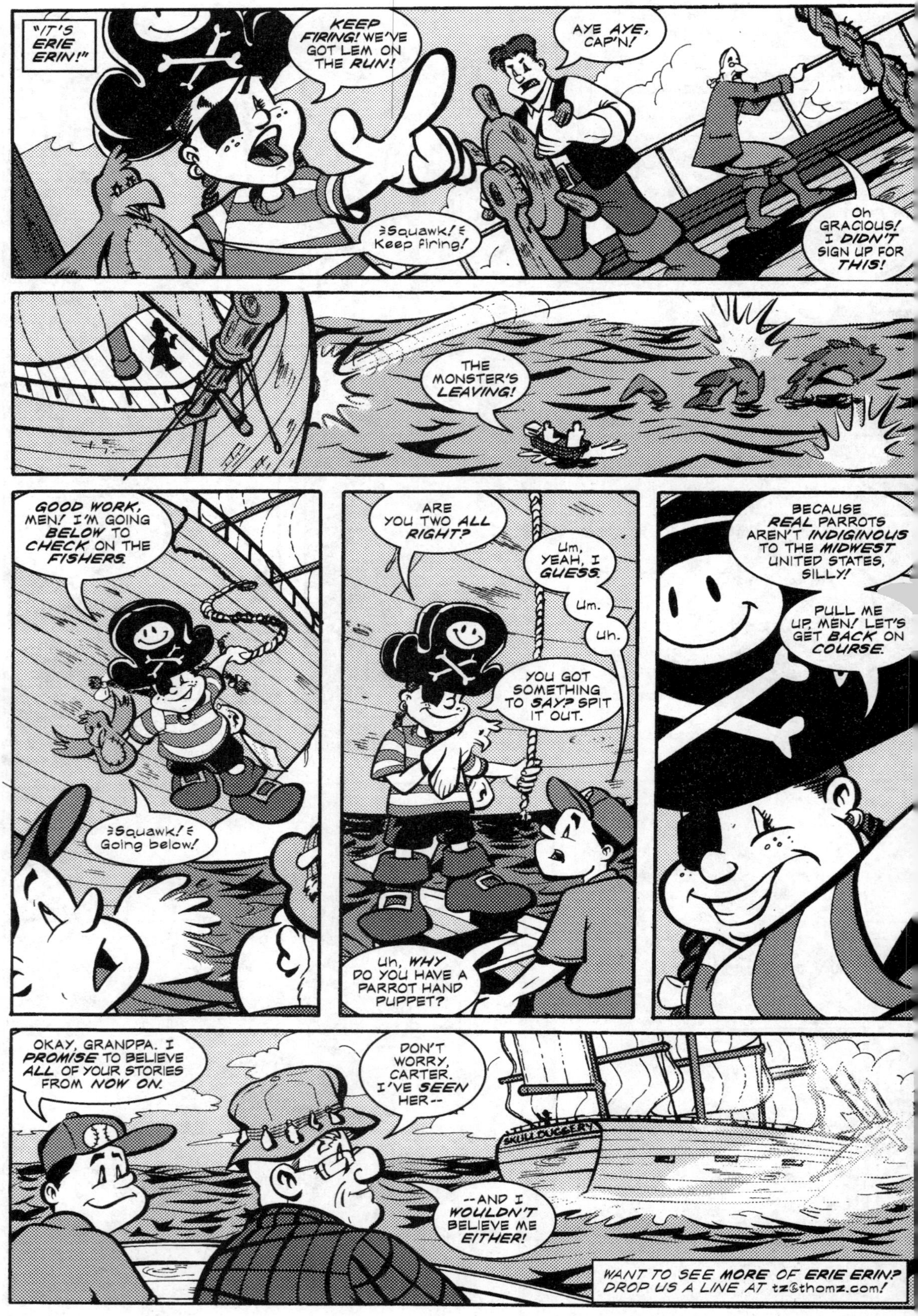

"IT'S ERIE ERIN!"
KEEP FIRING! WE'VE GOT LEM ON THE RUN!
AYE AYE, CAP'N!
Squawk! Keep firing!
Oh GRACIOUS! I DIDN'T SIGN UP FOR THIS!
THE MONSTER'S LEAVING!
GOOD WORK, MEN! I'M GOING BELOW TO CHECK ON THE FISHERS.
Squawk! Going below!
ARE YOU TWO ALL RIGHT?
Um, YEAH, I GUESS.
Um.
Uh.
YOU GOT SOMETHING TO SAY? SPIT IT OUT.
Uh, WHY DO YOU HAVE A PARROT HAND PUPPET?
BECAUSE REAL PARROTS AREN'T INDIGINOUS TO THE MIDWEST UNITED STATES, SILLY!
PULL ME UP, MEN! LET'S GET BACK ON COURSE.
OKAY, GRANDPA. I PROMISE TO BELIEVE ALL OF YOUR STORIES FROM NOW ON.
DON'T WORRY, CARTER. I'VE SEEN HER--
SKULLDUGGERY
--AND I WOULDN'T BELIEVE ME EITHER!
WANT TO SEE MORE OF ERIE ERIN? DROP US A LINE AT tz@thomz.com!

ELEVEN WORDS

BY MIKE MANLEY

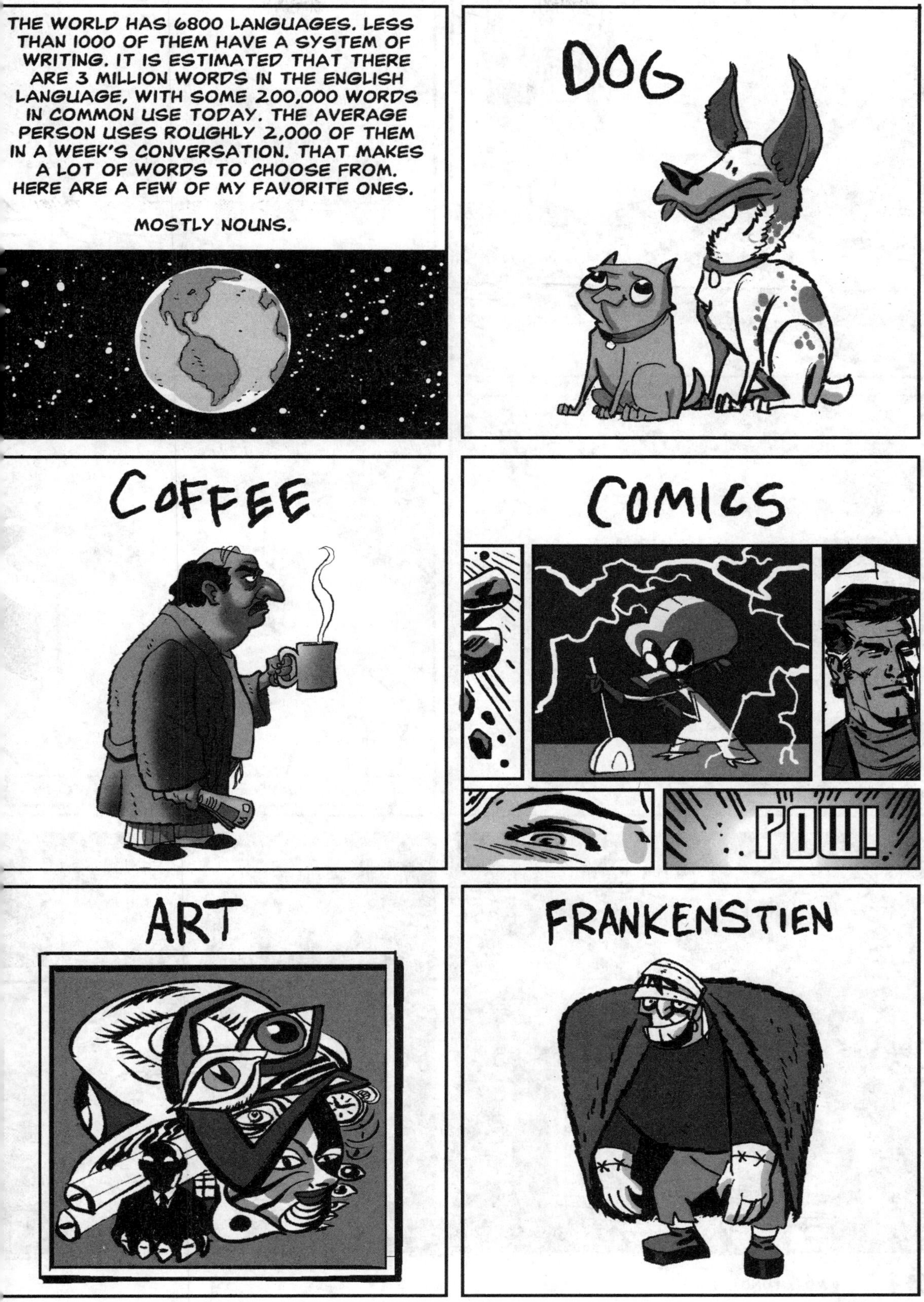

THE WORLD HAS 6800 LANGUAGES. LESS THAN 1000 OF THEM HAVE A SYSTEM OF WRITING. IT IS ESTIMATED THAT THERE ARE 3 MILLION WORDS IN THE ENGLISH LANGUAGE, WITH SOME 200,000 WORDS IN COMMON USE TODAY. THE AVERAGE PERSON USES ROUGHLY 2,000 OF THEM IN A WEEK'S CONVERSATION. THAT MAKES A LOT OF WORDS TO CHOOSE FROM. HERE ARE A FEW OF MY FAVORITE ONES.
MOSTLY NOUNS.
DOG
COFFEE
COMICS
POW!
ART
FRANKENSTIEN

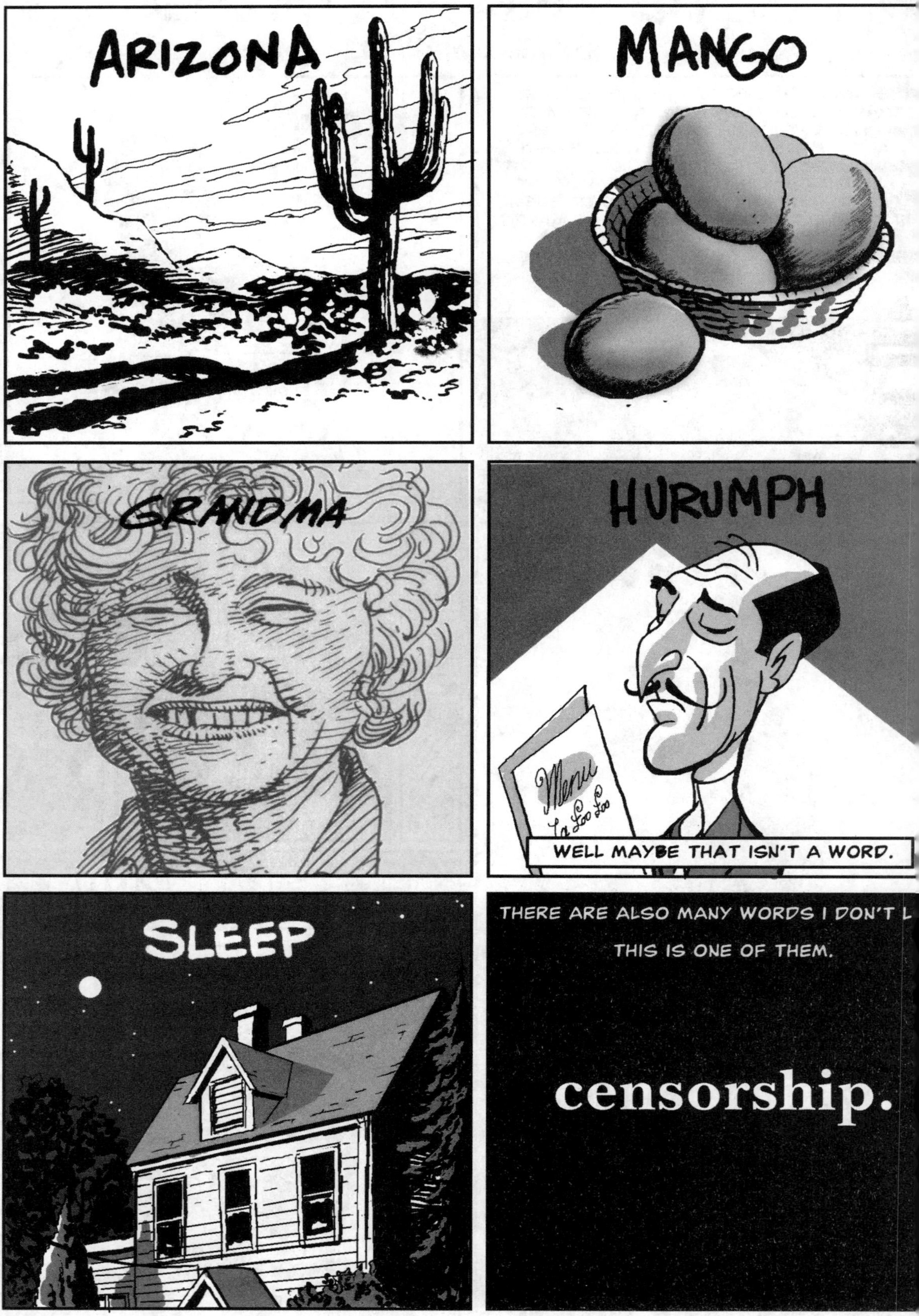
ARIZONA
MANGO
GRANDMA
HURUMPH
Menu
WELL MAYBE THAT ISN'T A WORD.
SLEEP
THERE ARE ALSO MANY WORDS I DON'T L
THIS IS ONE OF THEM.
censorship.

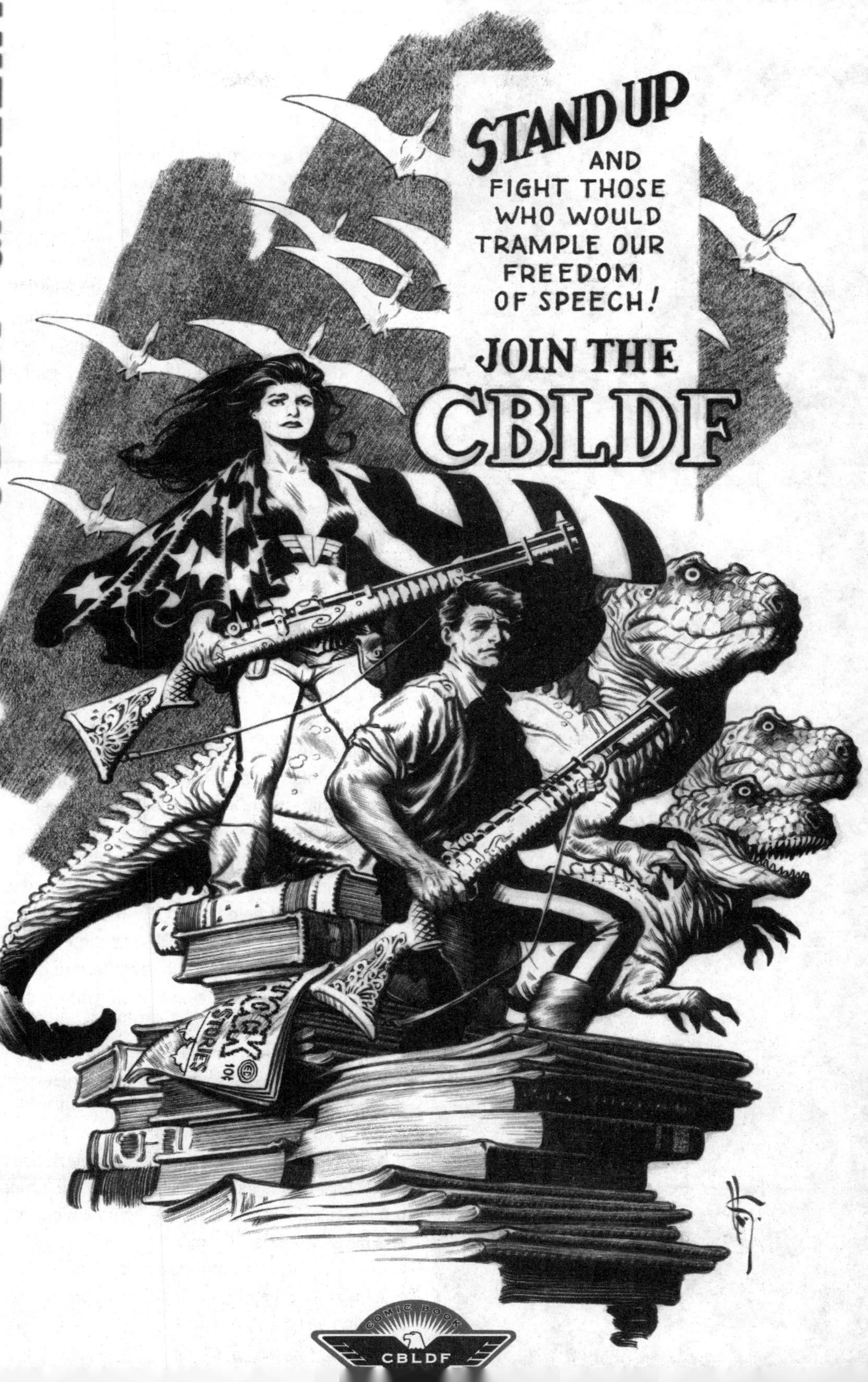
STAND UP
AND FIGHT THOSE WHO WOULD TRAMPLE OUR FREEDOM OF SPEECH!
JOIN THE
CBLDF
COMIC BOOK
CBLDF

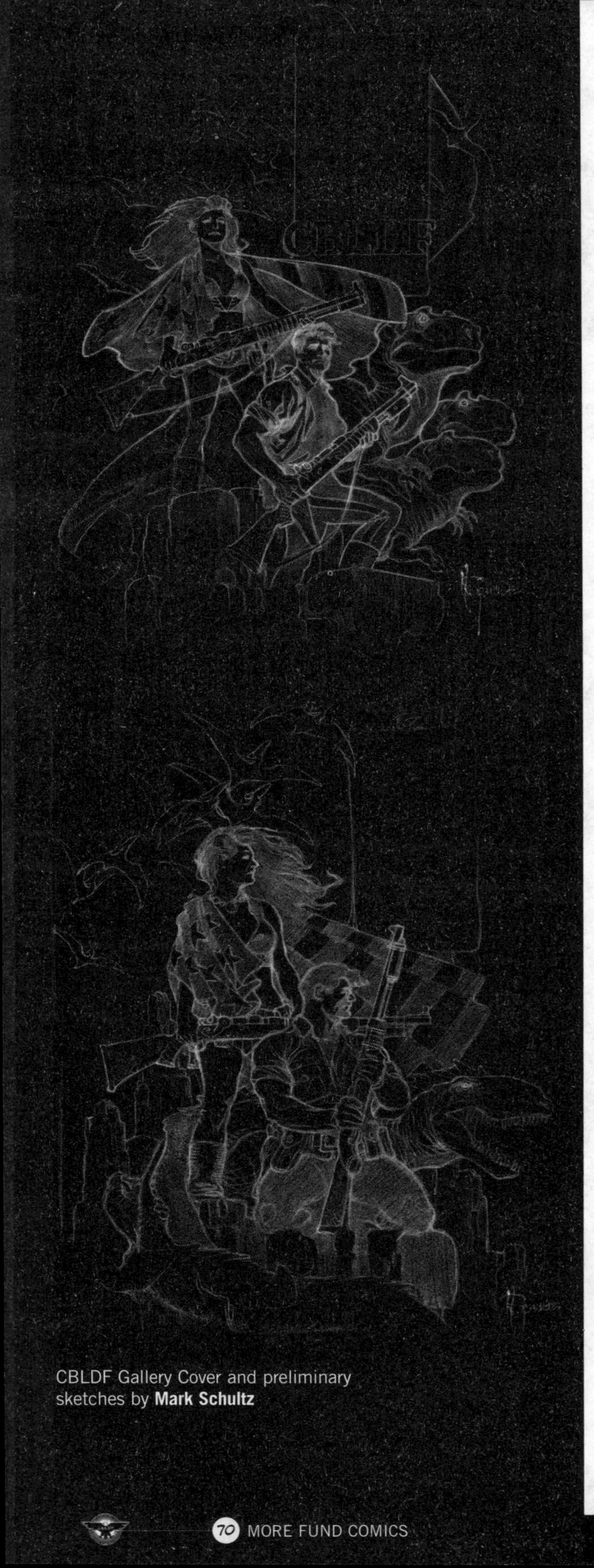

CBLDF Gallery Cover and preliminary sketches by **Mark Schultz**

Howdy!

The book you are holding in your hands, MORE FUND COMICS, is the first in what is hoped will be a continuing series of collections of donated art by some of the most thoughtful and proficient creators in the entire world of comics. MORE FUND COMICS is the brainchild of John Gallagher, Frank Cho, and Marc Nathan, two talented comics creators, and one longtime Maryland comics dealer and convention organizer. Aside from conceptualizing this brilliant idea, they are the ones who took the time to send requests to the dozens of wonderful creators who contributed to this excellent book, and to organize the book into its present, cohesive form. I think John, Frank, and Marc are to be commended for their outstanding efforts on the part of freedom of speech and expression in America.

I was asked to write this introduction soon after being presented with the 2003 Comic Book Legal Defense Fund "Defender of Liberty" award. I accepted this award at a very emotional ceremony during this year's Eisner awards at Comic-Con International - San Diego. I mention this event because I started my acceptance speech with words to the effect that "I never expected this award, and am not at all certain that I deserve it." Those words still hold true today. When I made my contributions to the CBLDF over the past few years I have to admit that it had far less to do with supporting a noble cause, than with my simply seeking to insure my own self-preservation. Frankly, I am scared. As the largest comics retailer in America, I have a great big target painted all over me. Particularly because I have a very simple policy of selling every comic book produced, regardless of content. Any overzealous prosecutor who is looking for a big fish can't help but wonder if I wouldn't be the right comics retailer to bring down. Don't think that thought doesn't give me chills during some of those quiet hours in the middle of the night when the mind wanders...

AN INTRODUCTION BY CHUCK ROZANSKI

Now don't get the wrong impression of me when I say that I am "afraid." I think that being aware of the dangers around you is simple animal instinct. Being oblivious, and thinking that everything is going to be just wonderful all the time, is the greatest danger of all. As I see it, by being afraid, I stay on my toes, and am inspired to work to build my defenses. In this case, it is just the simplest possible extension of logic that supporting the Comic Book Legal Defense Fund is my best avenue for insuring that harm does not befall me from harassment by powerful authorities.

Aside from looking after my own well-being, I also find it philosophically repugnant to let any comics retailer, publisher, or creator be persecuted for providing comics readers with any type of comics they might wish to purchase. I immigrated to America when I was 5 years old, and was naturalized as an American citizen when I was 11. As a part of my citizenship process I was forced to study up on the history of America, including the events surrounding the Revolutionary War. Even at that young age, I was totally impressed by the wisdom of the Founding Fathers in drawing up the Constitution and the Bill of Rights. Obviously these very sage men of 1776 saw the dangers of government quite clearly. Bear in mind that this was a time when memories of people being burned at the stake for disagreeing with a given religion, or government, in places like England, Germany, and Spain were still quite vivid. Clearly, protecting freedom of speech and religion were critically important to these great men. That's why they made the right to freely express oneself the First Amendment to the Constitution.

With the thought in mind that the Founding Fathers were prepared to sacrifice not only their personal fortunes, but also their lives, in defense of liberty, is it any wonder that I work so hard to preserve those freedoms? None of us have the ability to change the world in any great measure as an individual, but working together in the context of an organization like the Comic Book Legal Defense Fund, we have a capacity to do good that far exceeds any efforts we could make individually. We can not only safeguard our own freedoms, but also those of our compatriots who do not have the resources to defend themselves. Through the contributions that we make in donated items, artwork, and cash, we endow the CBLDF with the strength to save those who would otherwise be helpless in the face of oppression. That's a darn good reason to get up in the morning!

In closing, I want to thank everyone for purchasing MORE FUND COMICS. In buying this book, you not only get some wonderful artwork and stories, but you also make a significant contribution to the CBLDF. I would now encourage you to make contributing to the CBLDF a regular part of your life. Even if you don't have resources to give a cash contribution, how about a few books from your collection that you no longer need? Or if you're an artist, how about a small sketch? Writers, we also accept signed scripts and plots. These donated items ultimately end up in CBLDF benefit auctions, which sometimes gross as much as $18,000! That much money buys more than a few hours of desperately needed high quality legal time. Your contribution may be small, but my feeling is that anyone who helps in even a small way to preserve freedom in these days of repression, can quite legitimately call themselves a "Defender of Liberty!"

All the best!

Chuck Rozanski,
President - Mile High Comics, Inc.
August 11th, 2003

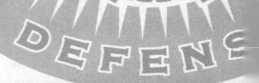

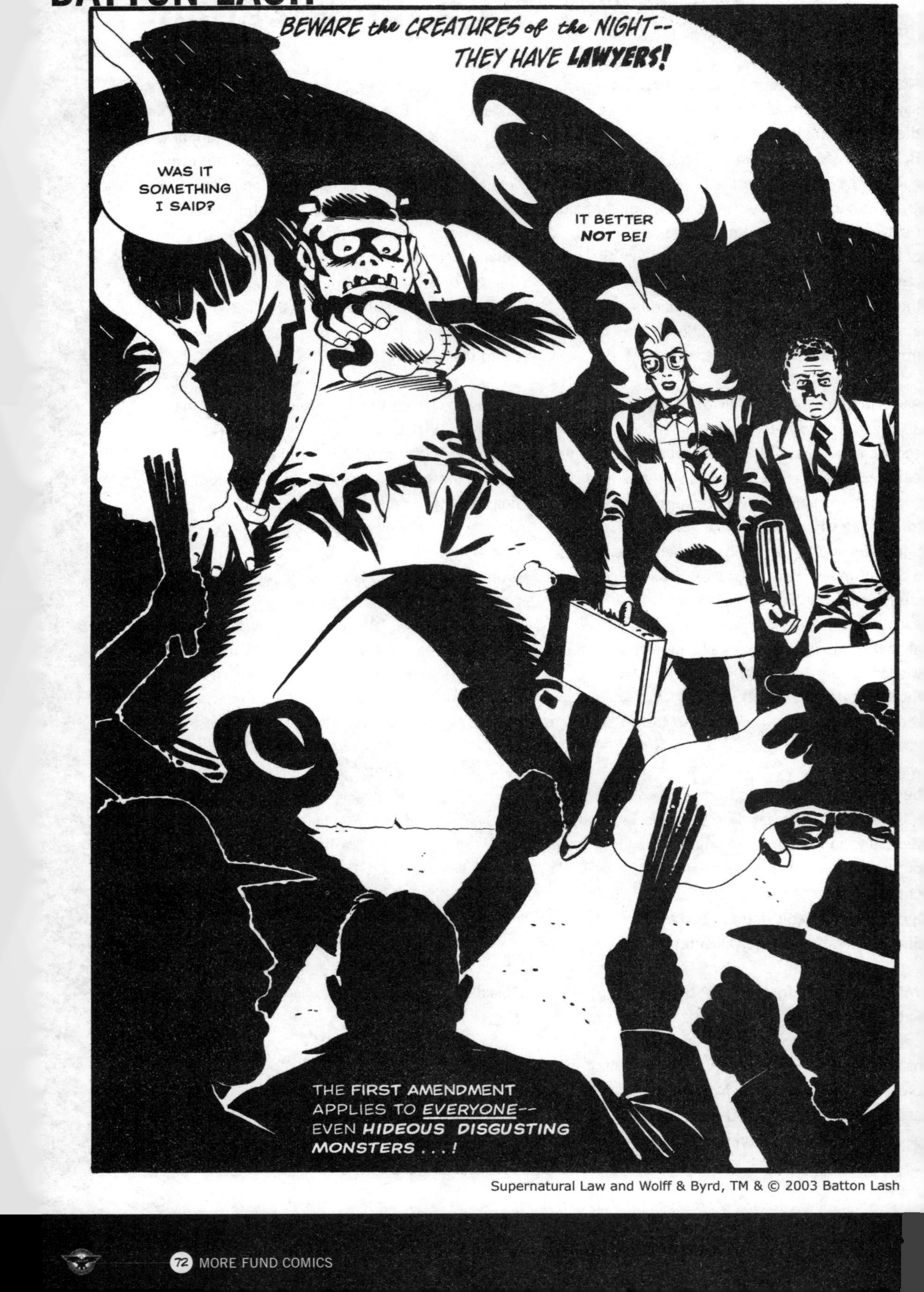
BEWARE the CREATURES of the NIGHT-- THEY HAVE LAWYERS!
WAS IT SOMETHING I SAID?
IT BETTER NOT BE!
THE FIRST AMENDMENT APPLIES TO EVERYONE-- EVEN HIDEOUS DISGUSTING MONSTERS . . . !

PHIL NOTO

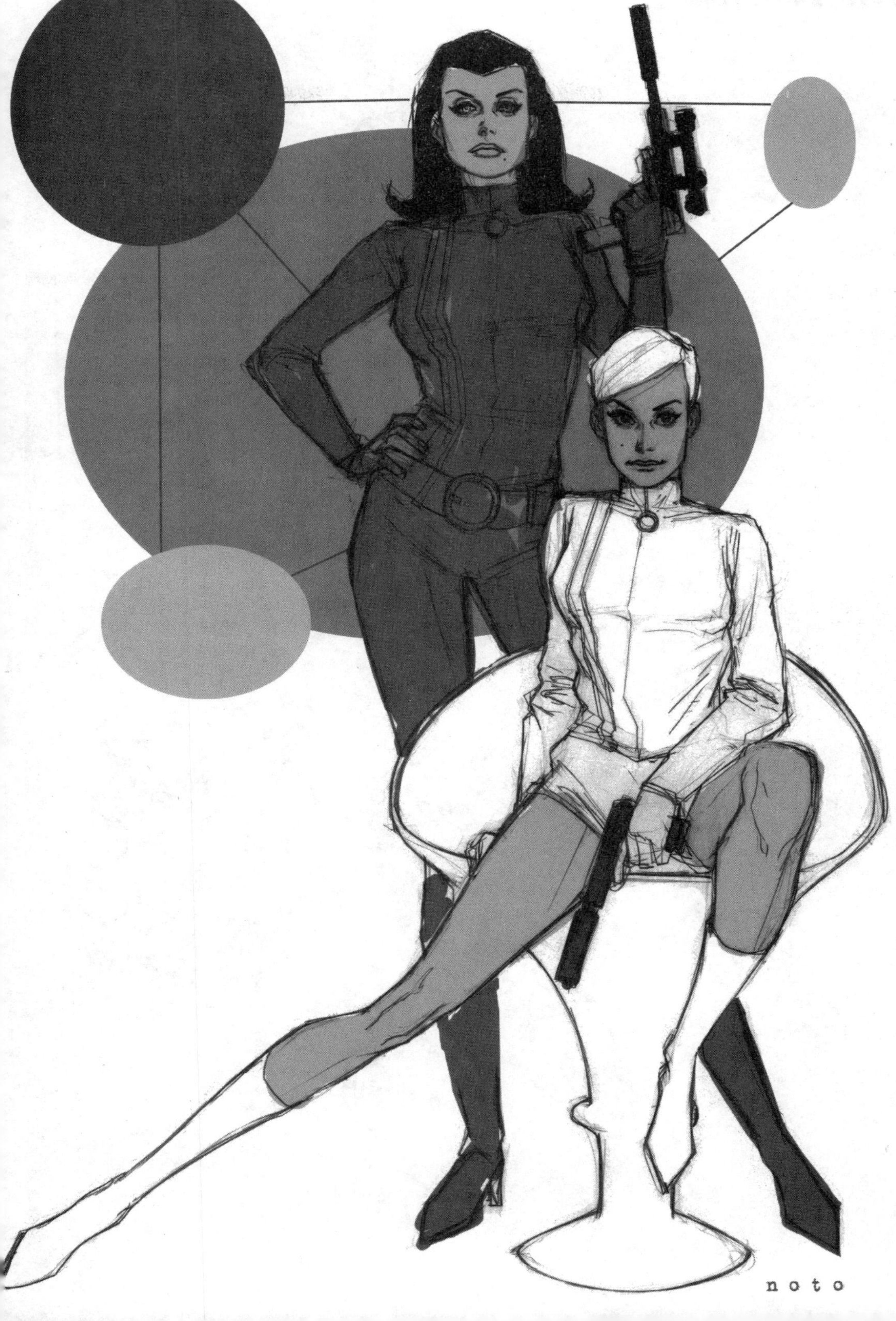
noto

MIKE WIERINGO

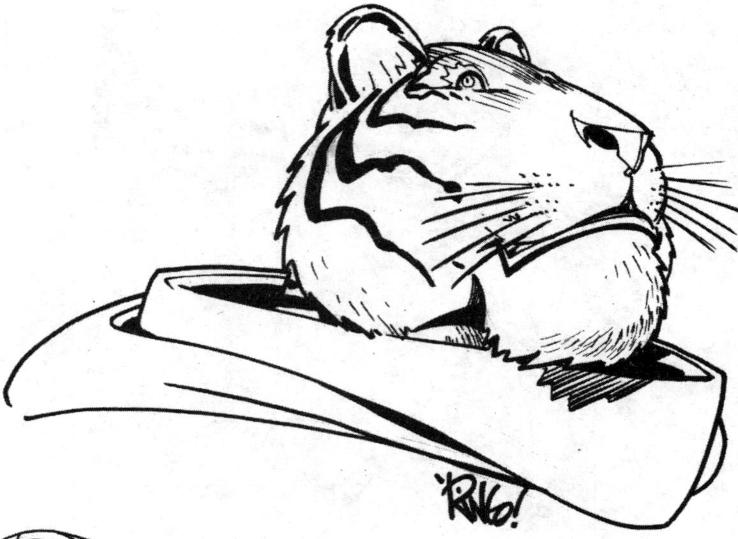
'RINGO!

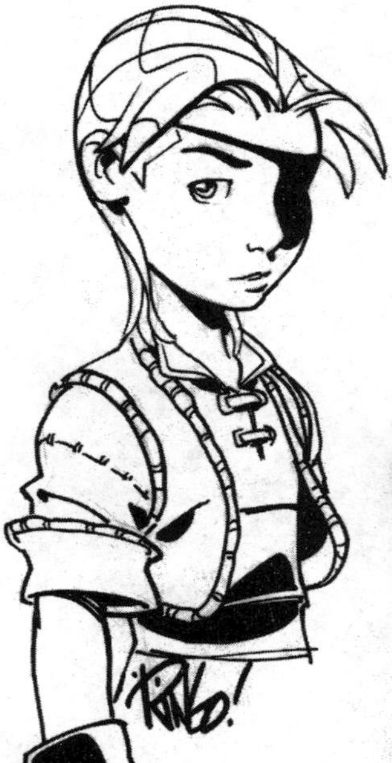
'RINGO!

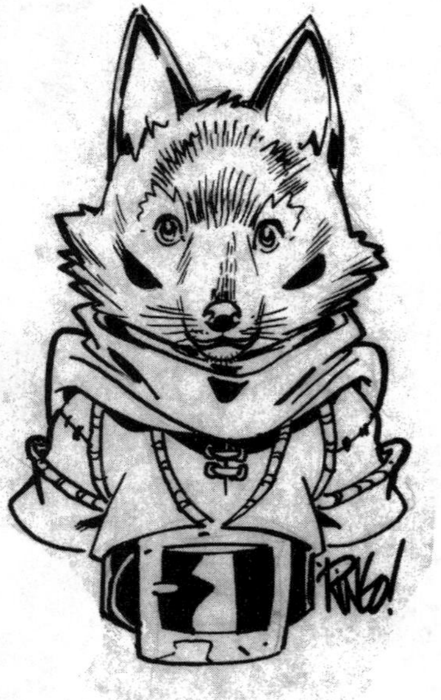
'RINGO!

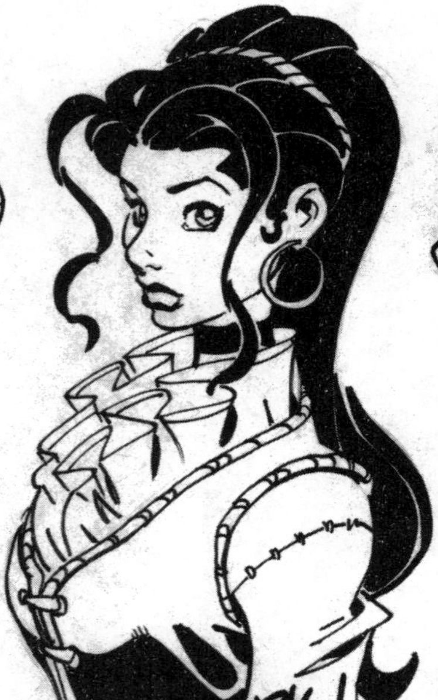
'RINGO!

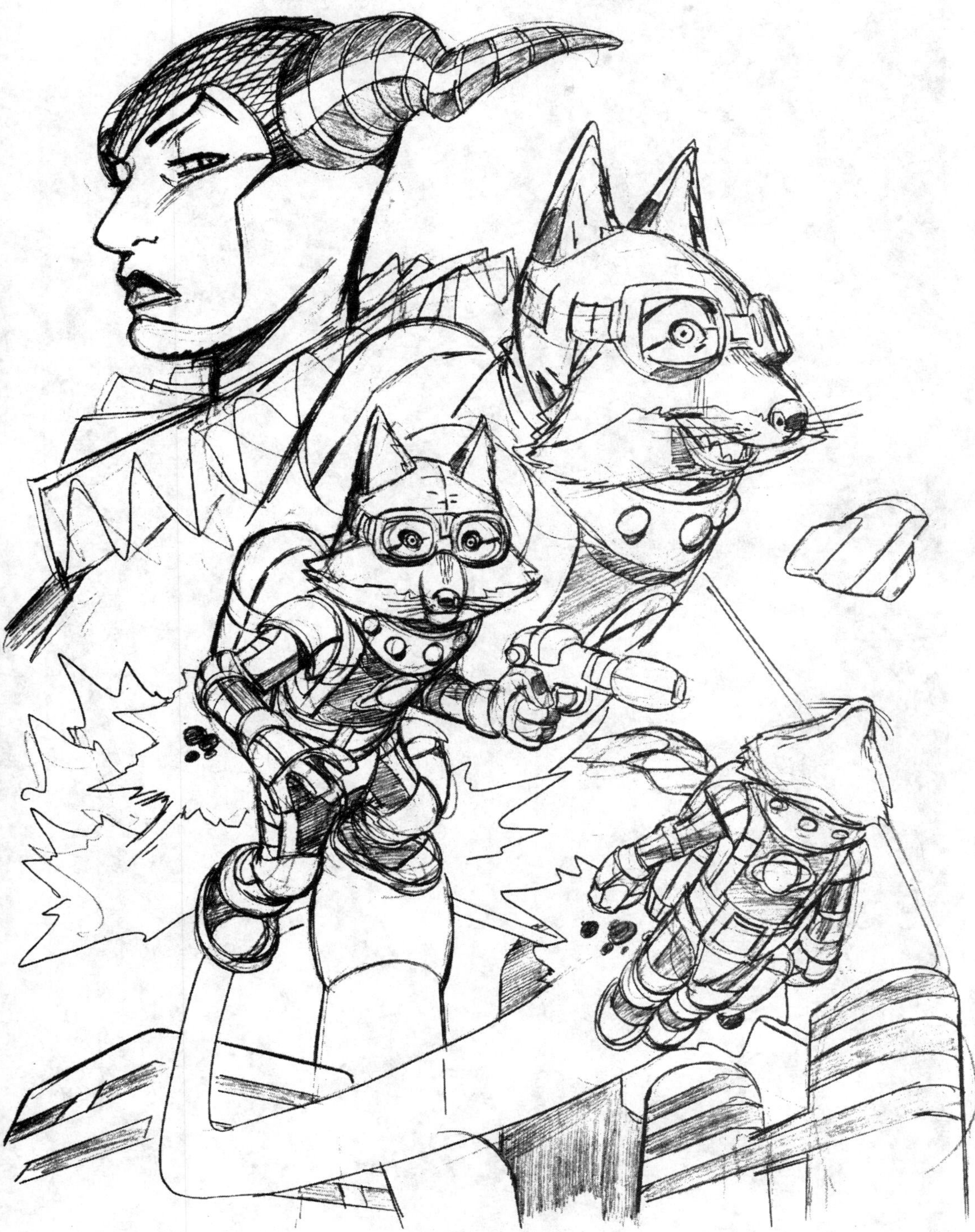

MICHAEL KORNSTEIN

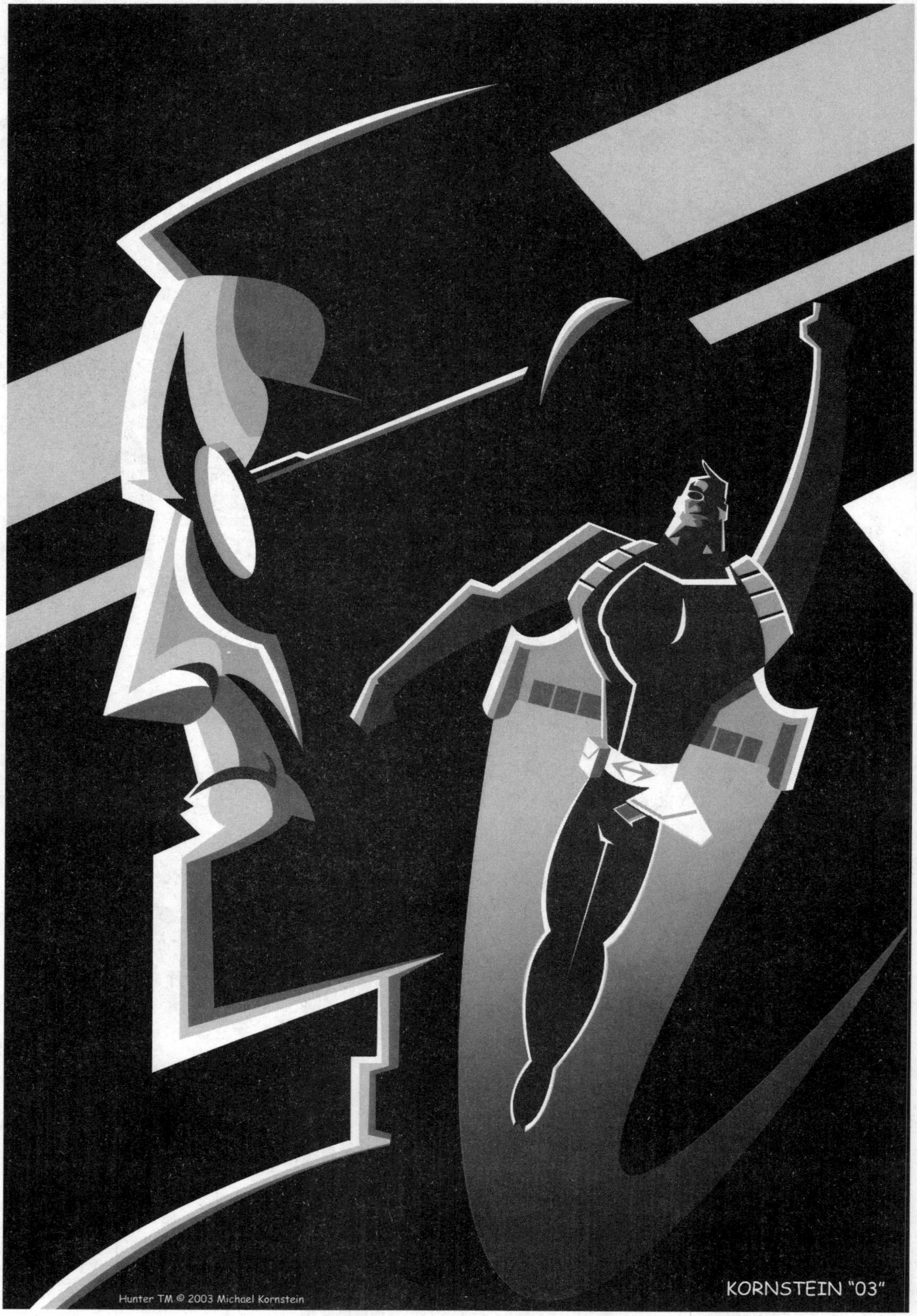
Hunter TM © 2003 Michael Kornstein
KORNSTEIN "03"

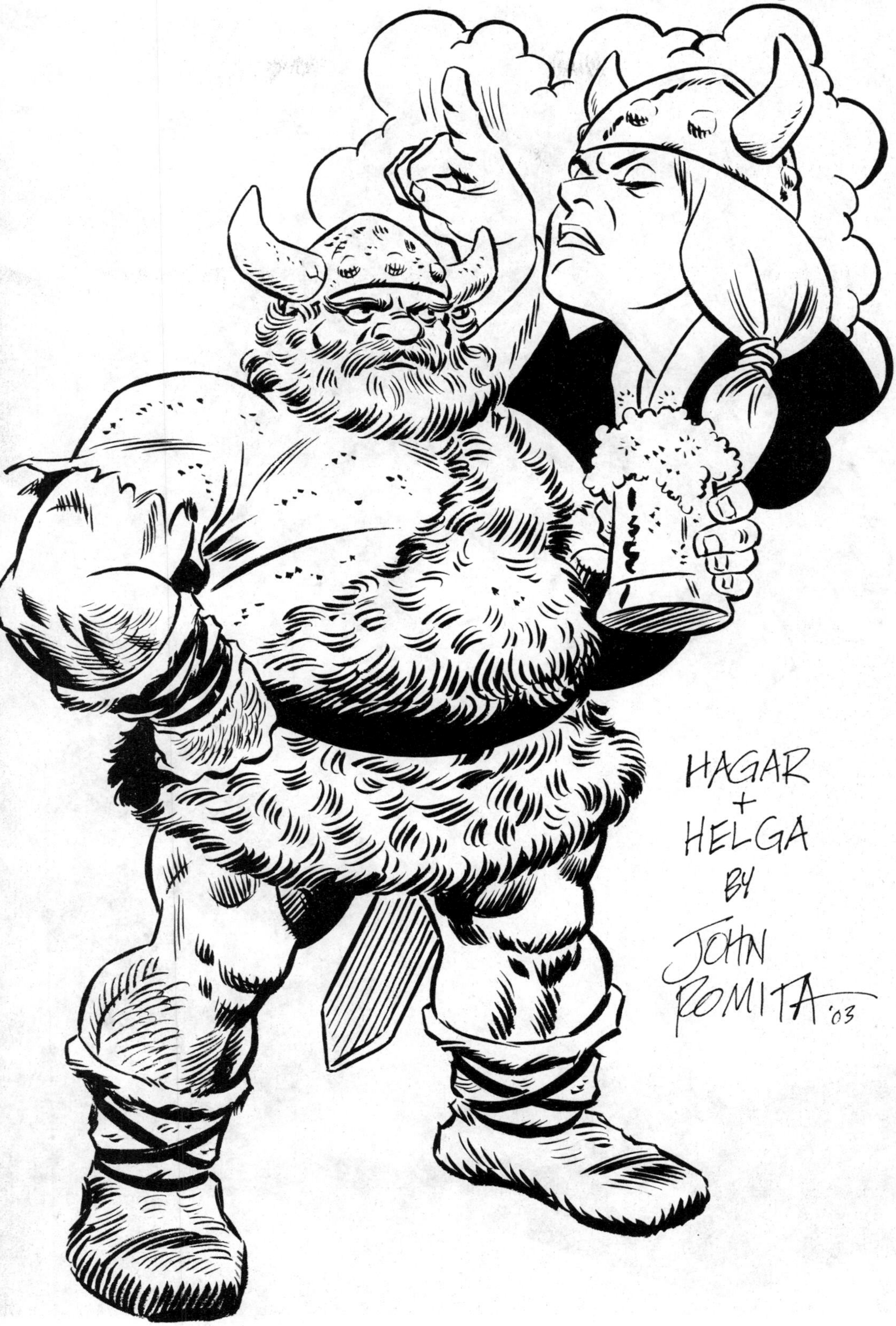
HAGAR
+
HELGA
BY
JOHN
ROMITA '03

[redacted]

TERRY DODSON

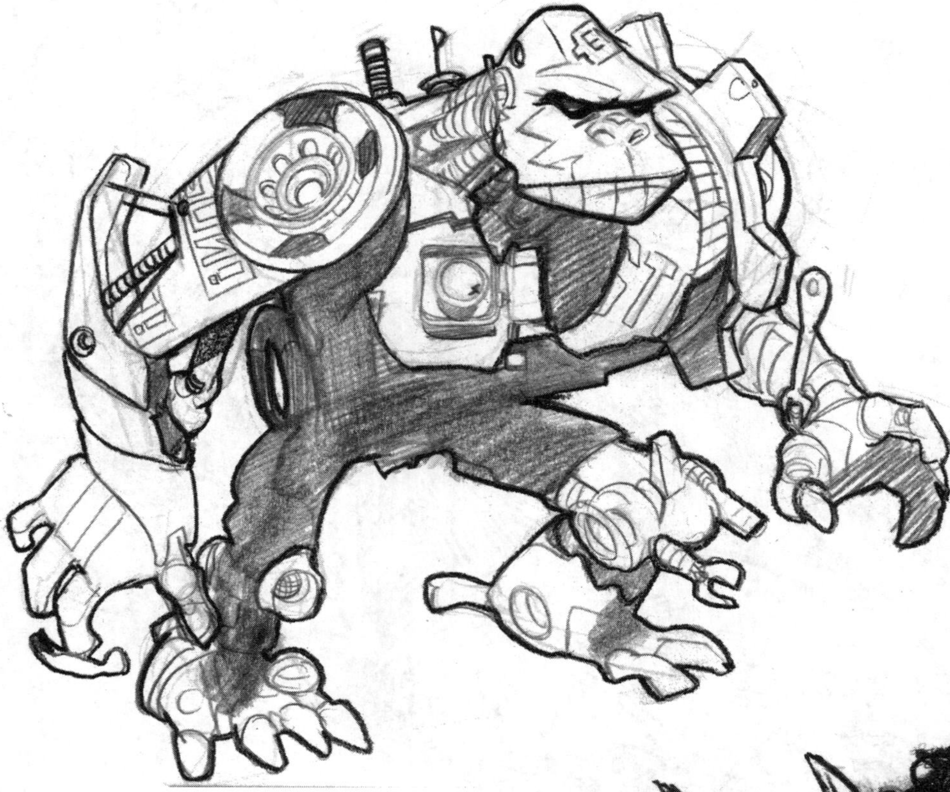

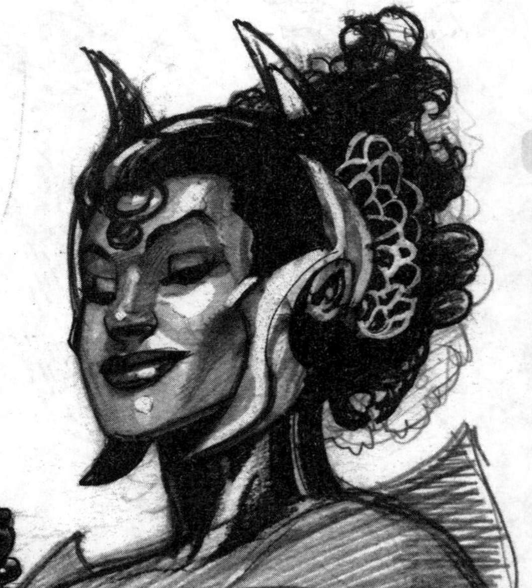

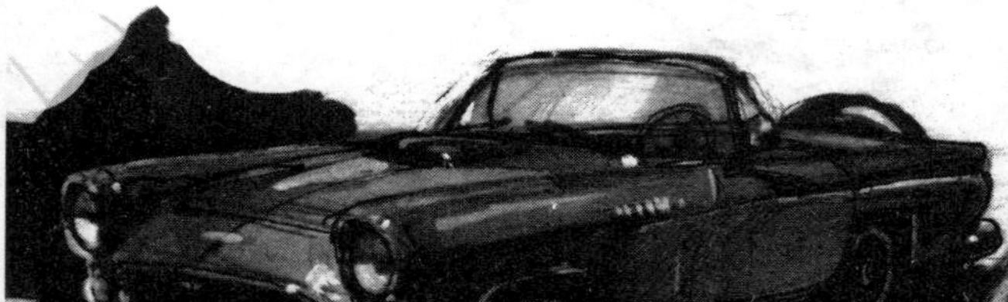

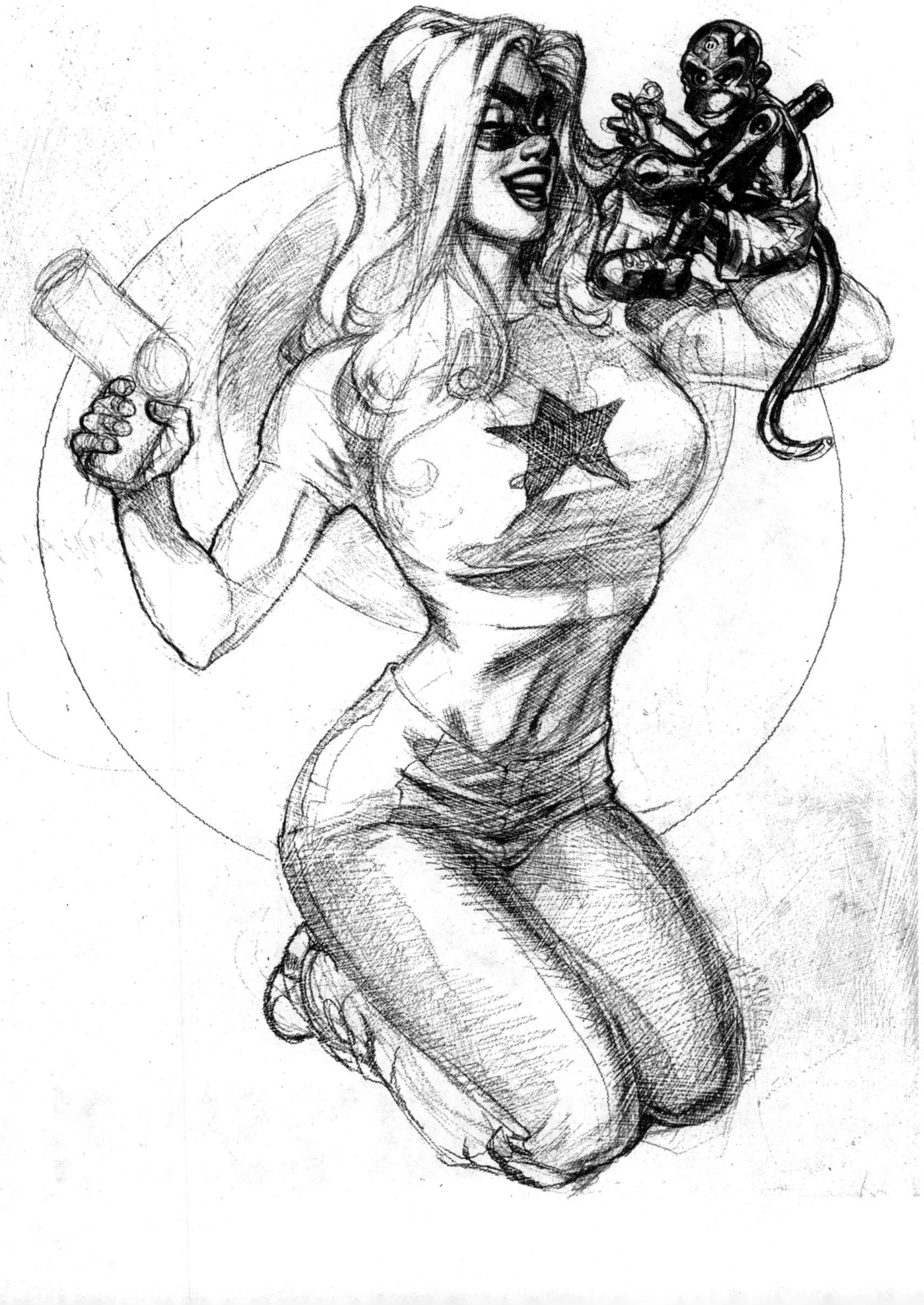

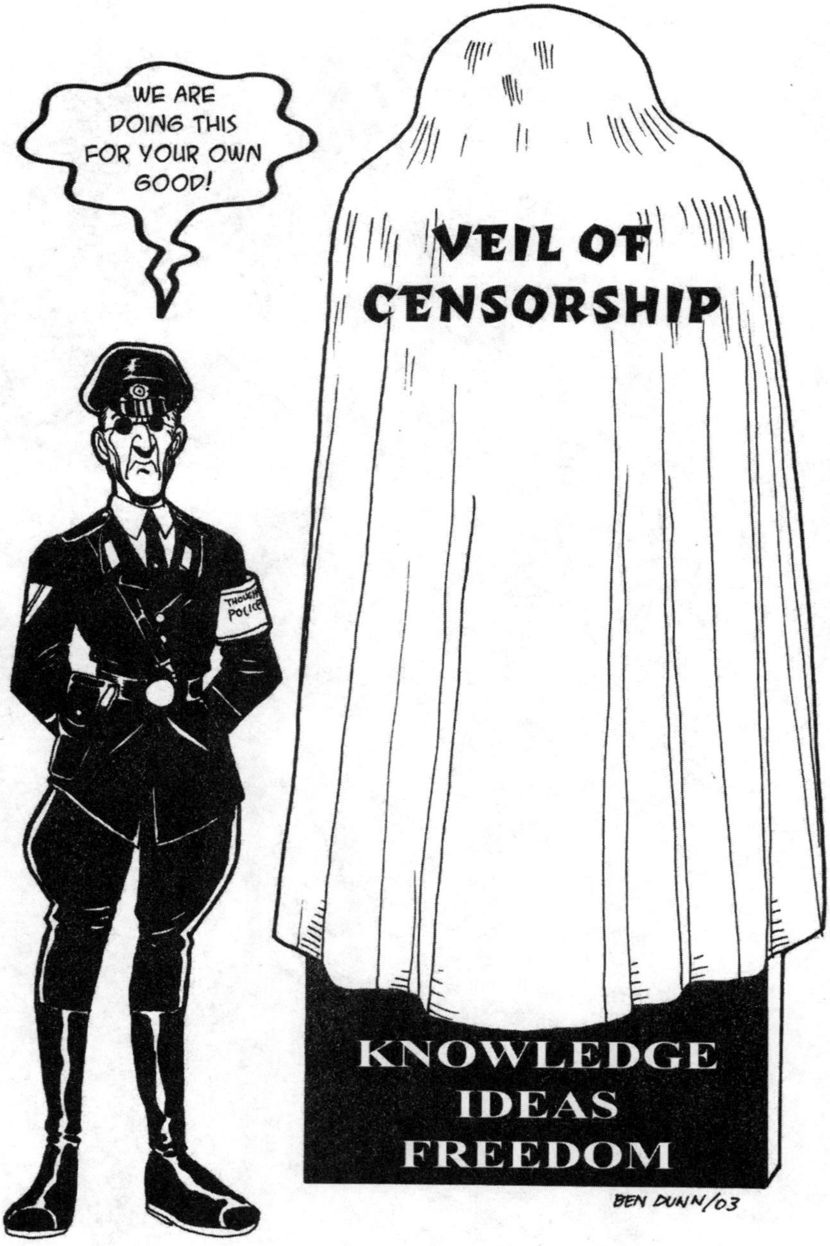
WE ARE DOING THIS FOR YOUR OWN GOOD!
VEIL OF CENSORSHIP
KNOWLEDGE
IDEAS
FREEDOM
BEN DUNN/03

FIGHT CENSORSHIP!

JOYCE CHIN

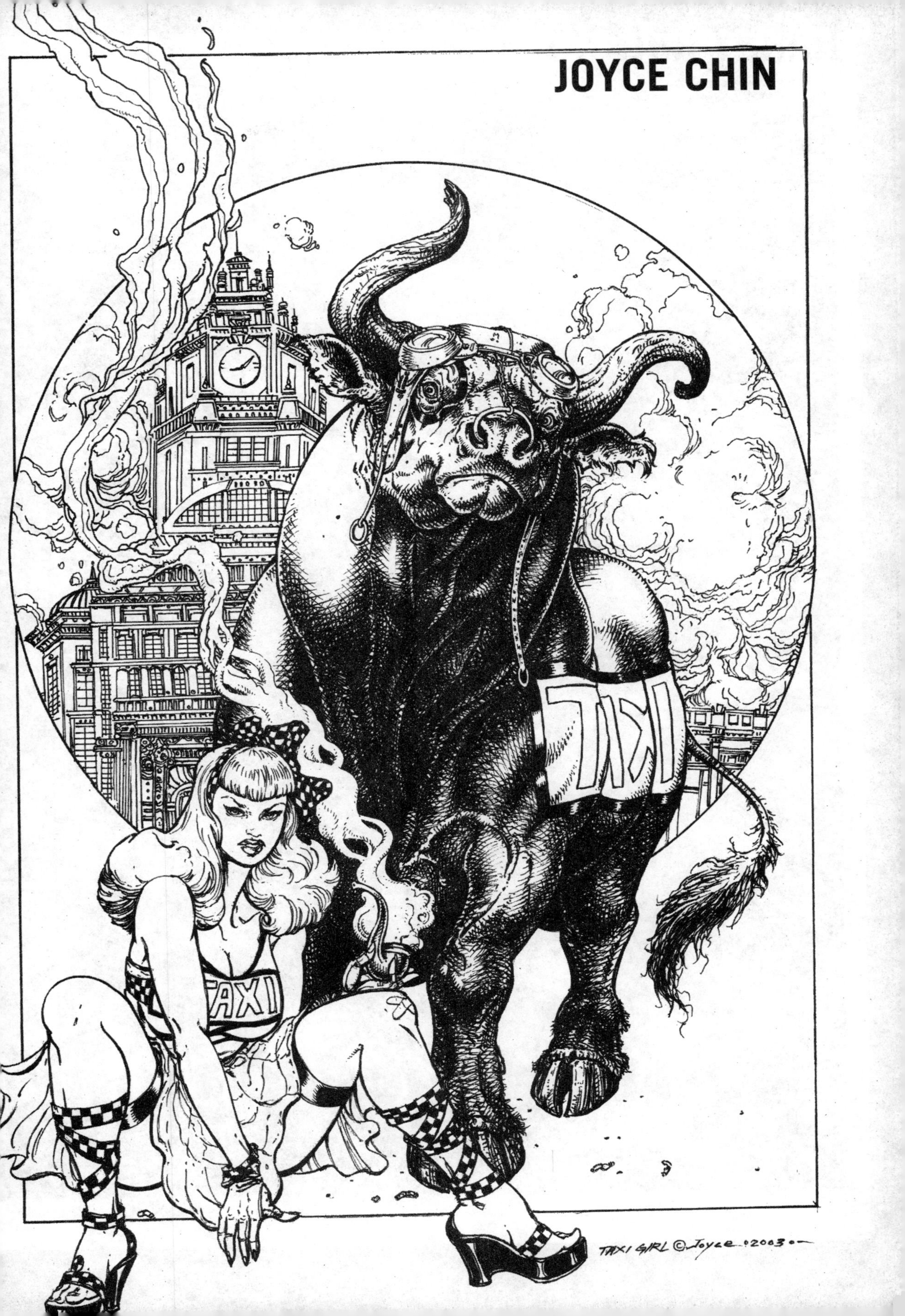

TAXI
TAXI
TAXI GIRL © Joyce ©2003

HARRY ROLAND

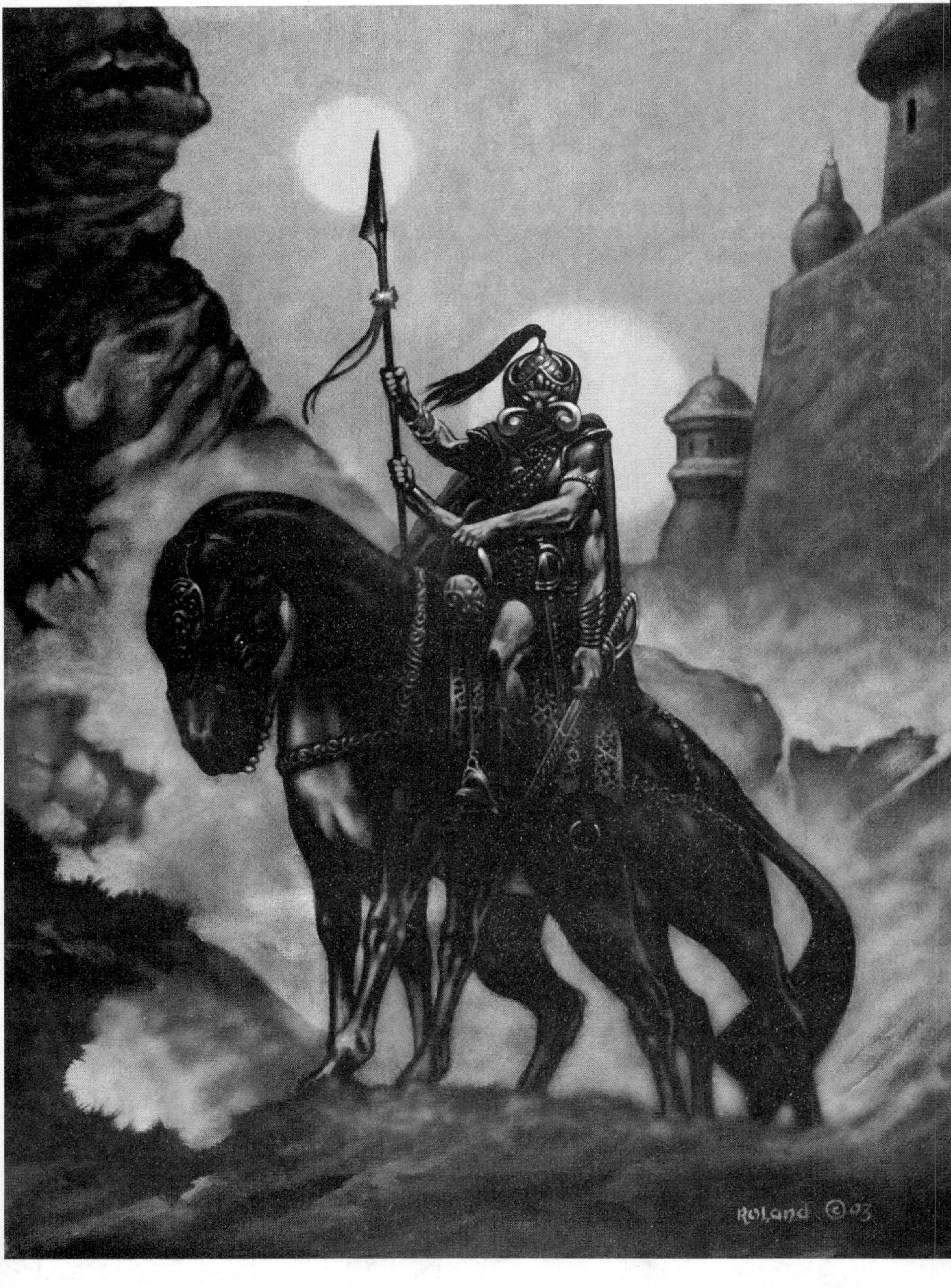
ROLAND ©03

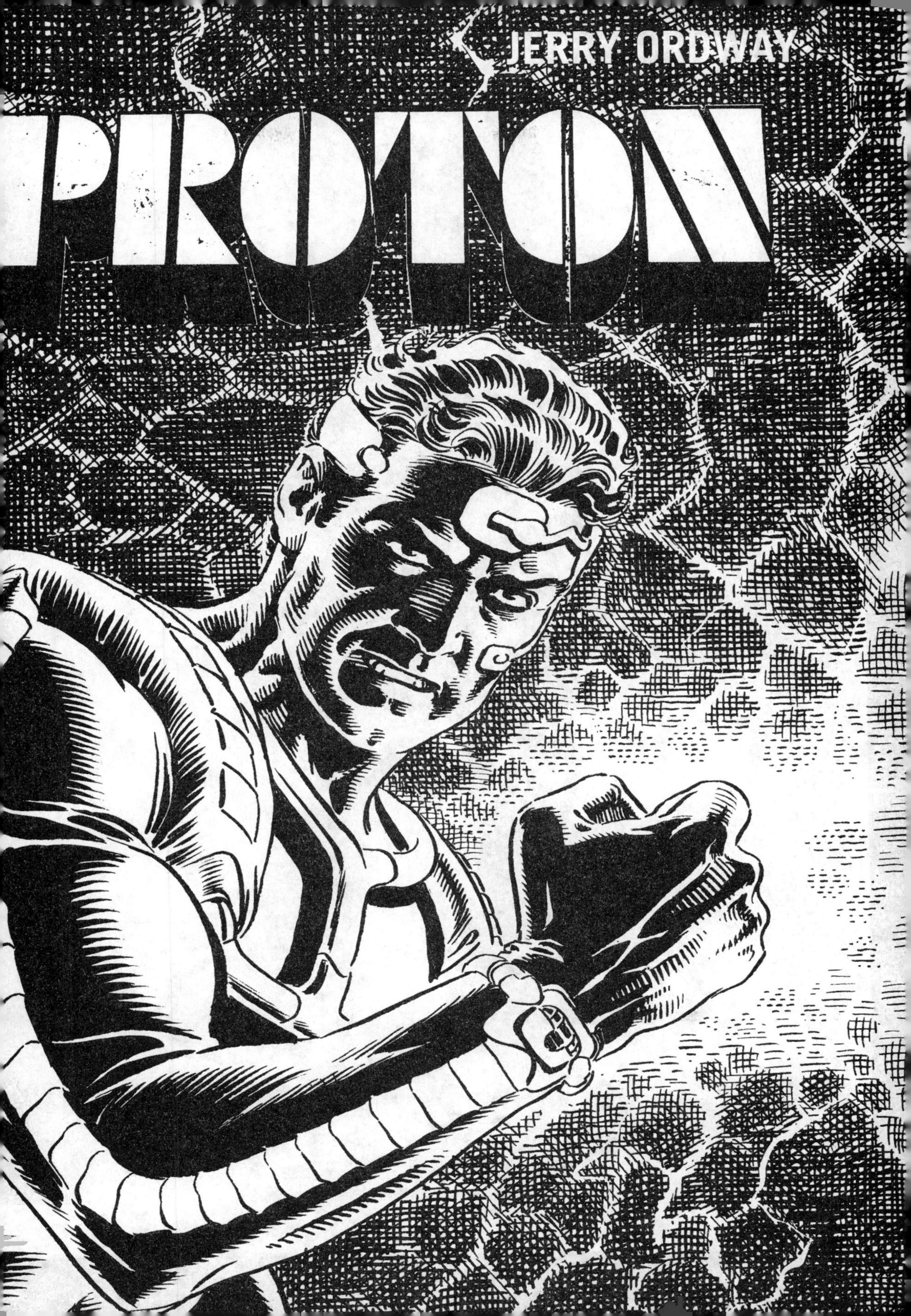
JERRY ORDWAY
PROTON

JAMAR NICHOLAS

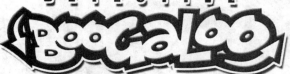

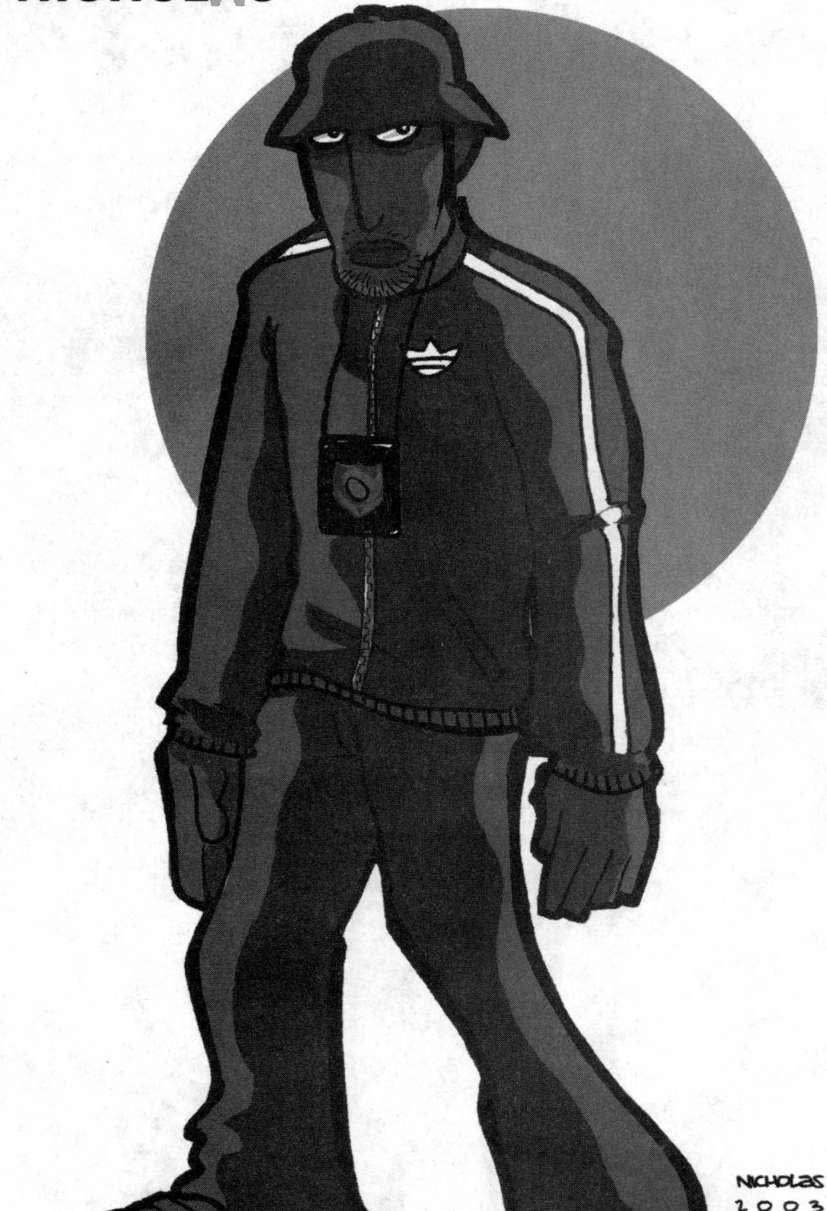
NICHOLAS
2003

DETECTIVE
BOOGALOO

www.moviepoopshoot.com • detectiveboogaloo.com

TODD NAUCK

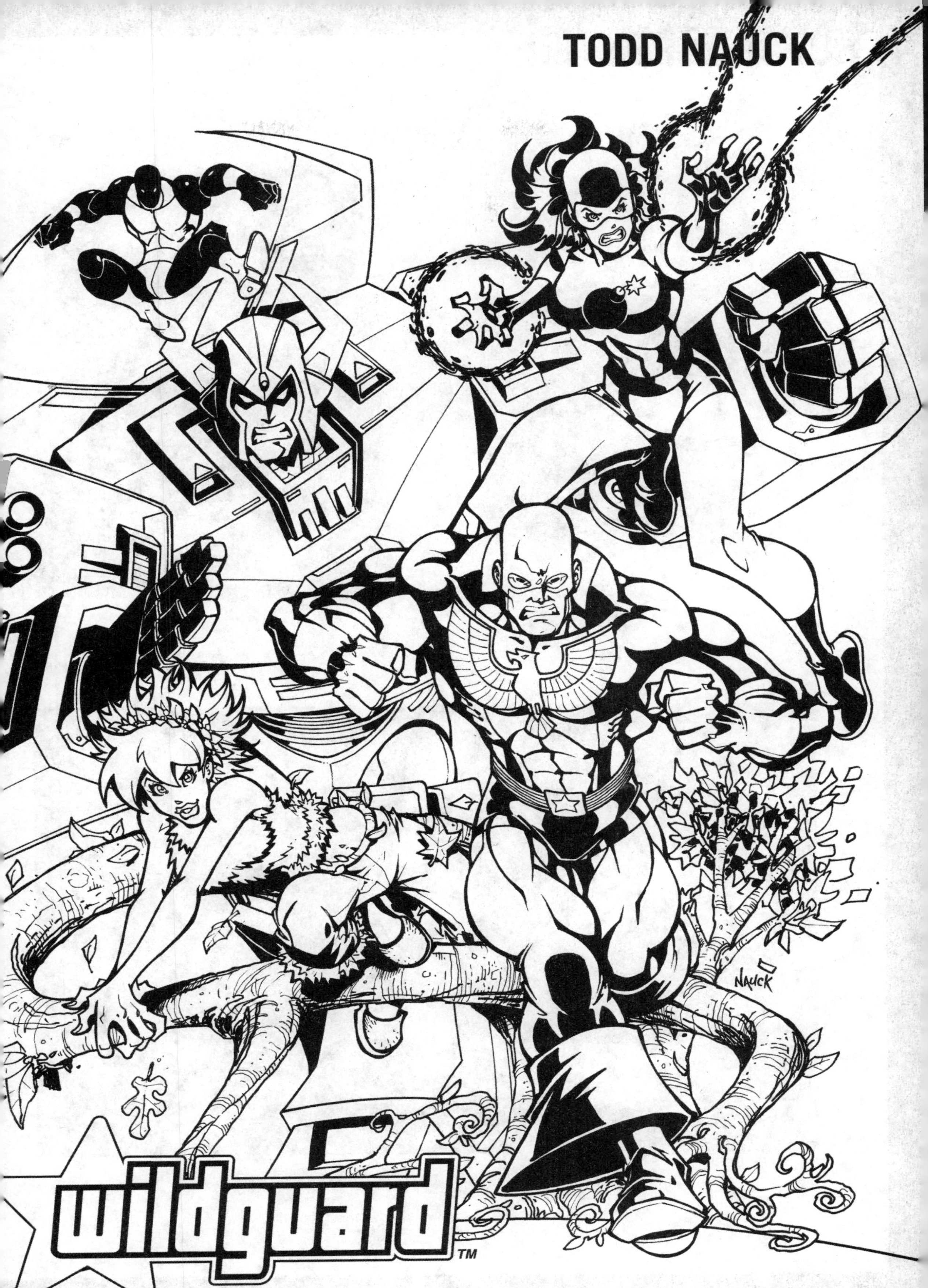
NAUCK
wildguard™

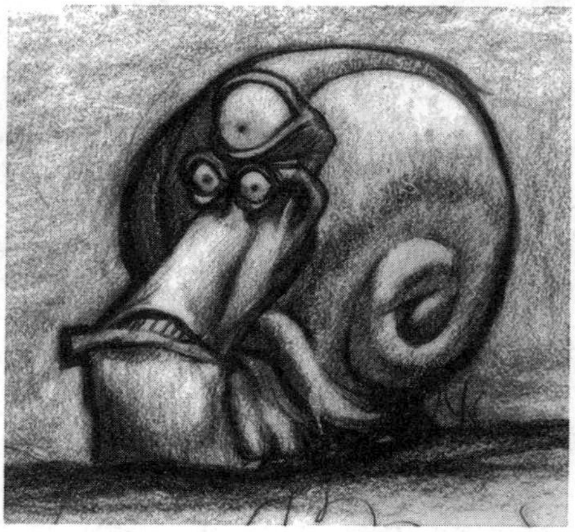

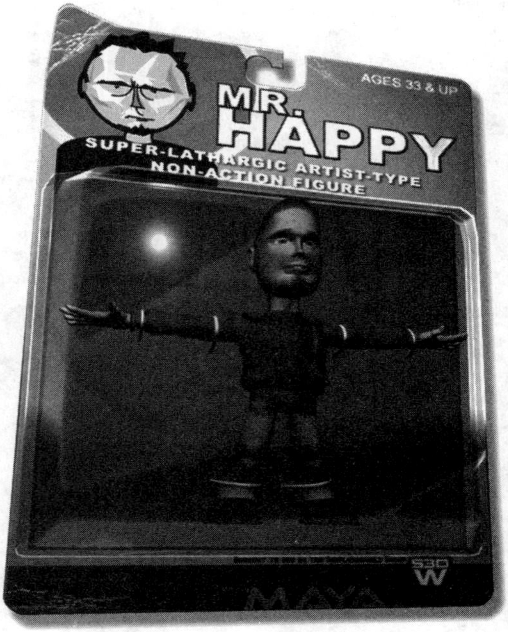
AGES 33 & UP
MR. HÄPPY
SUPER-LATHARGIC ARTIST-TYPE
NON-ACTION FIGURE
MAYA

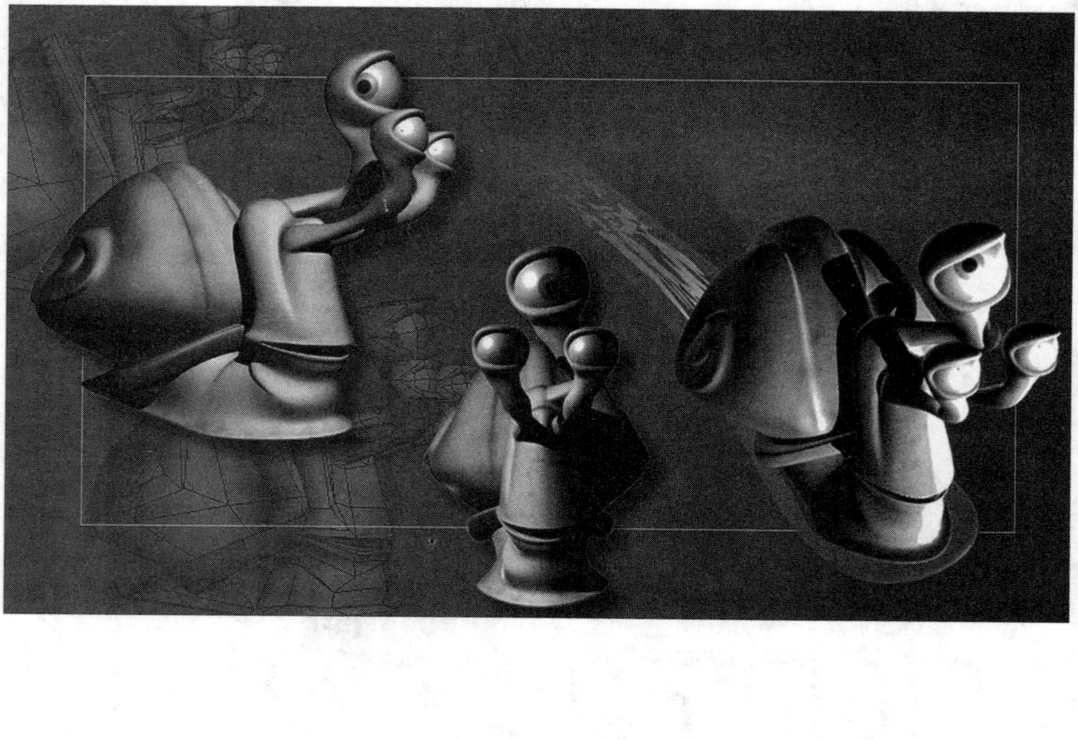

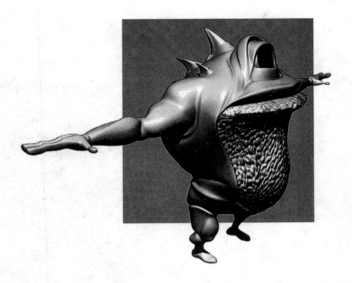

The morning after little Timmy installed the new and improved "Uber-Grow light" in his aquarium, Bill his pet frog (which he found near the power plant) had been changed... changed into into Uber-Toad™. A massive amphibious force the world had not yet seen. This super-slimy creature is - powerful, destructive and surprisingly funny, but only if Bill the toad remains under the Uber-Light™. Once the light is turned off the Uber-Toad™ will revert back to his normal state, lil' old Bill.

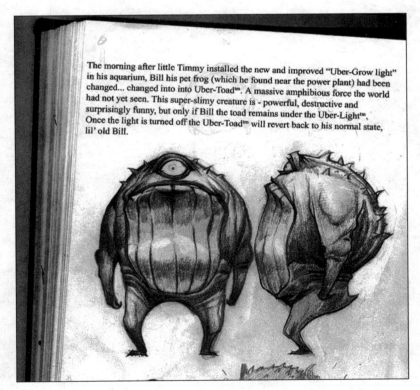

BUDD ROOT

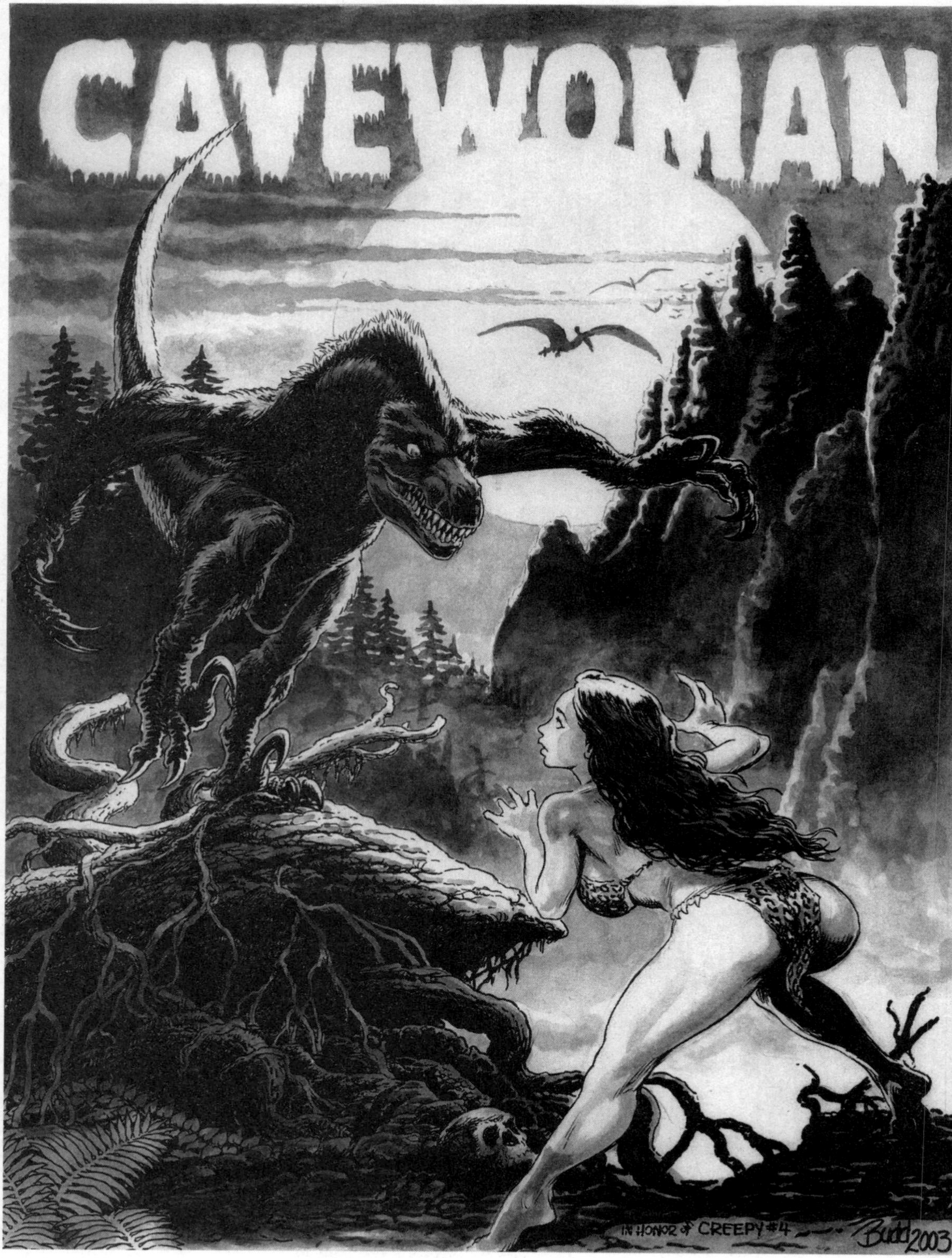
CAVEWOMAN
IN HONOR OF CREEPY #4
Budd 2003

JOHN ROMITA, JR.

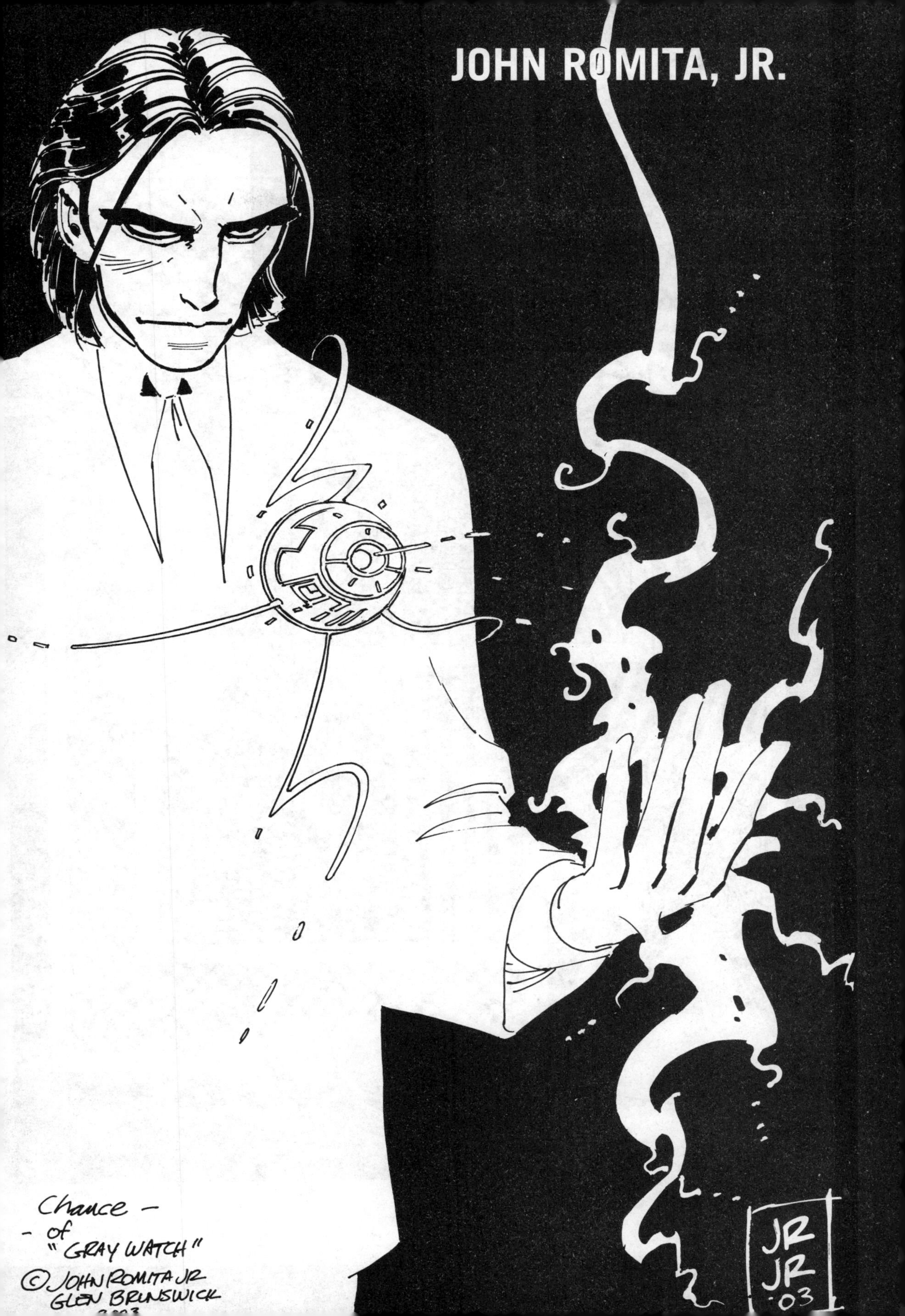
Chance -
- of
"GRAY WATCH"
©JOHN ROMITA JR
GLEN BRUNSWICK
JR
JR
'03

BRAD FOSTER

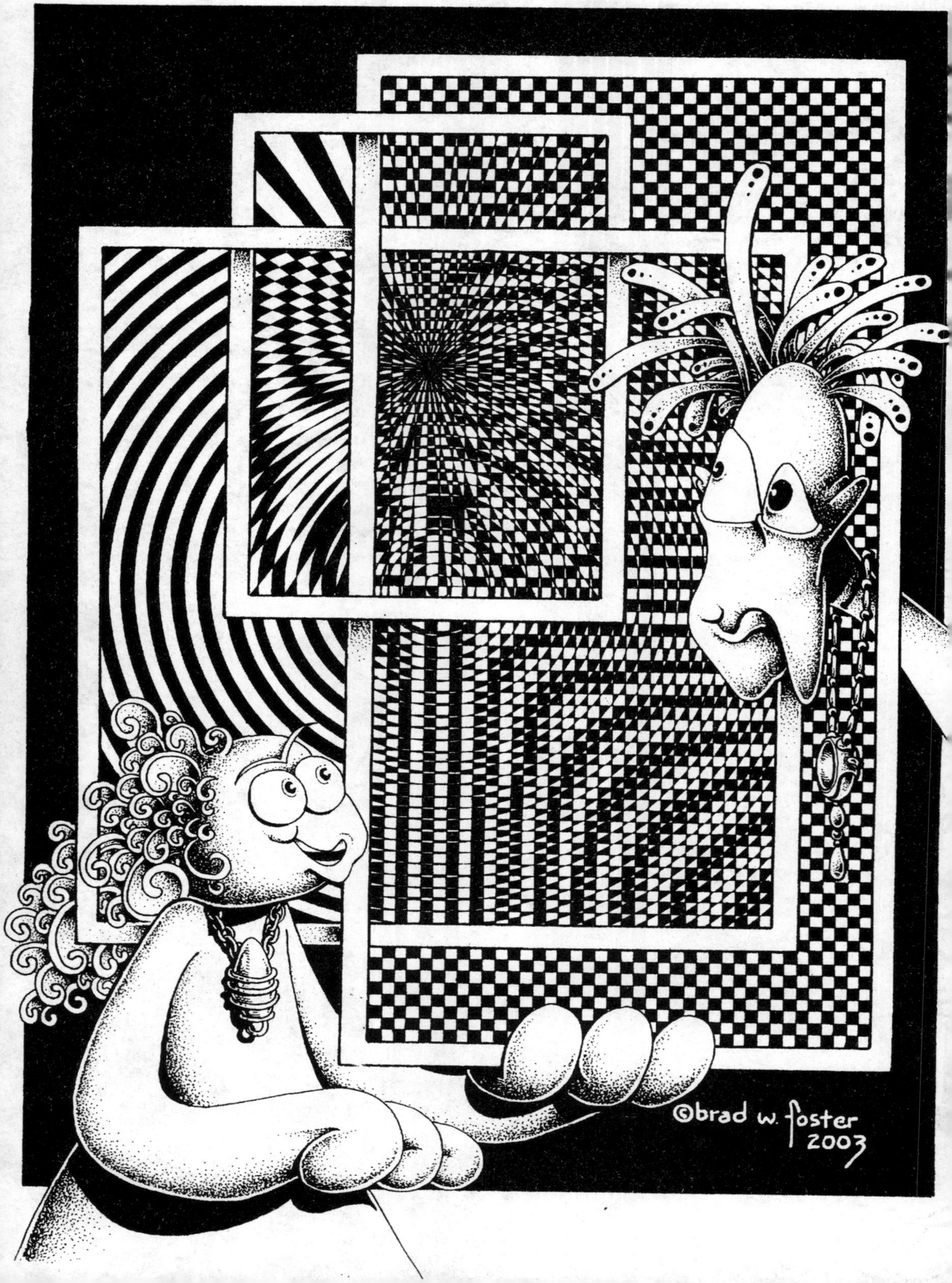
©brad w. foster
2003

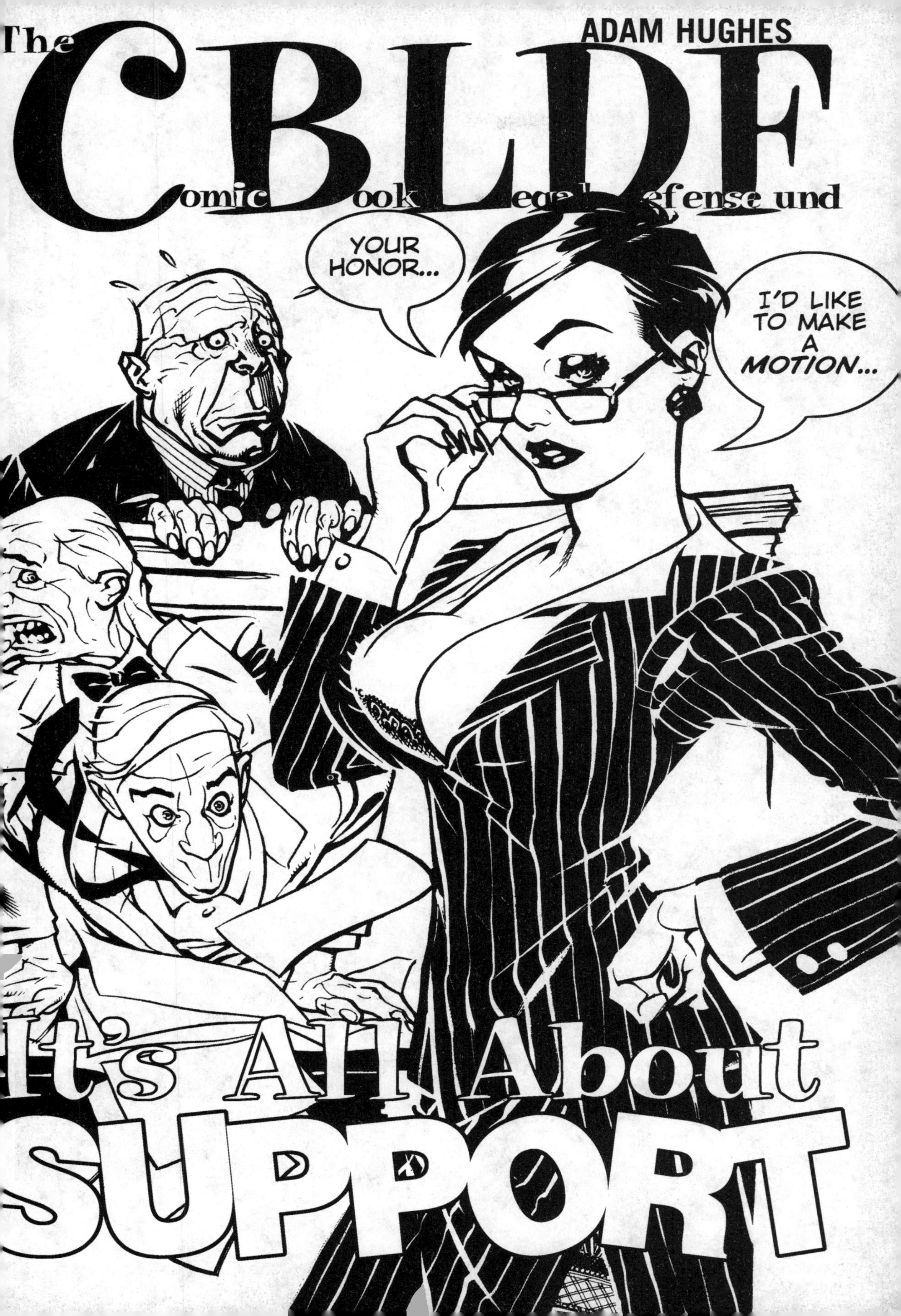
ADAM HUGHES
The CBLDF
Comic Book Legal Defense Fund
YOUR HONOR...
I'D LIKE TO MAKE A *MOTION*...
It's All About
SUPPORT

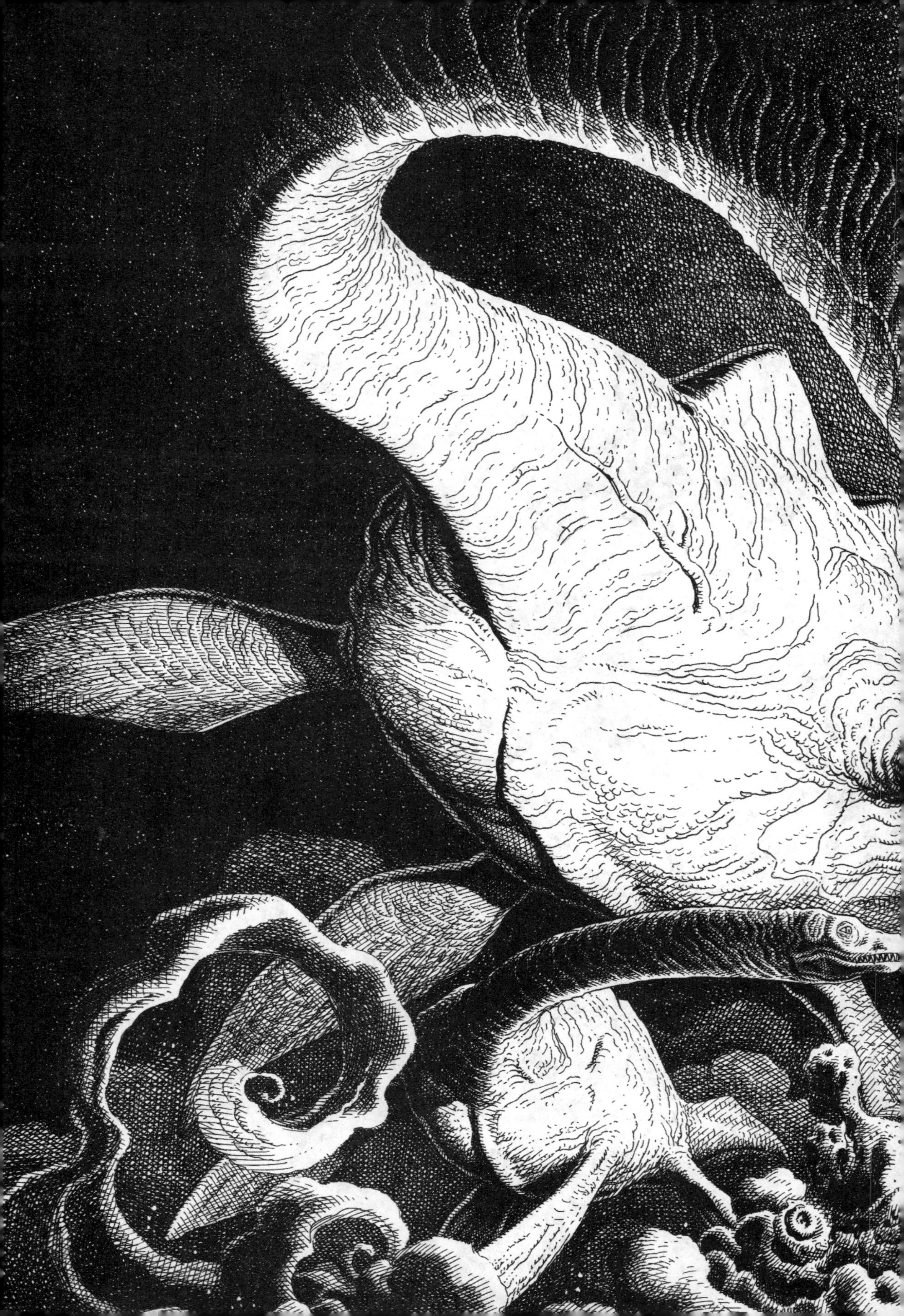

ART ADAMS

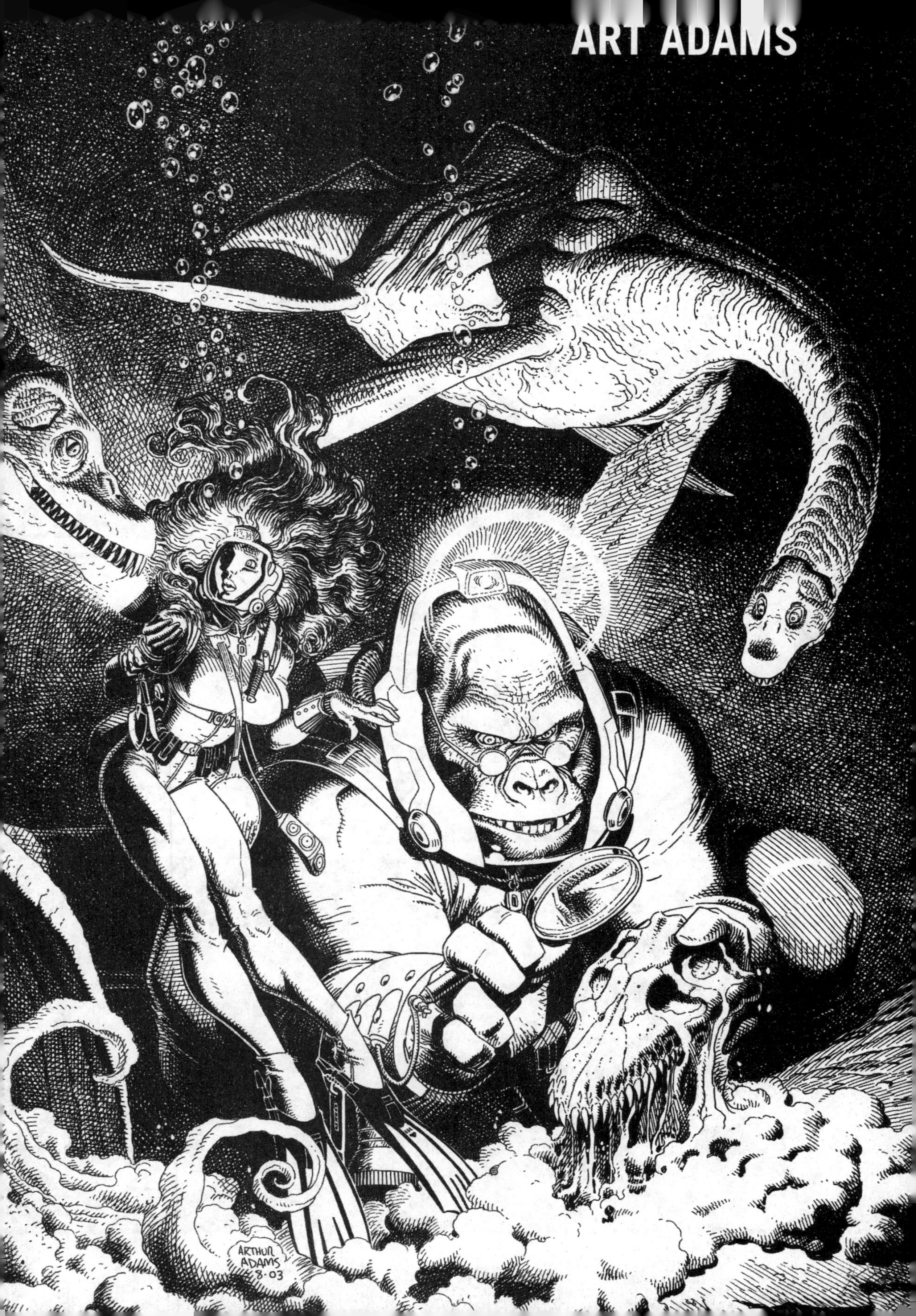

ARTHUR
ADAMS
8·03

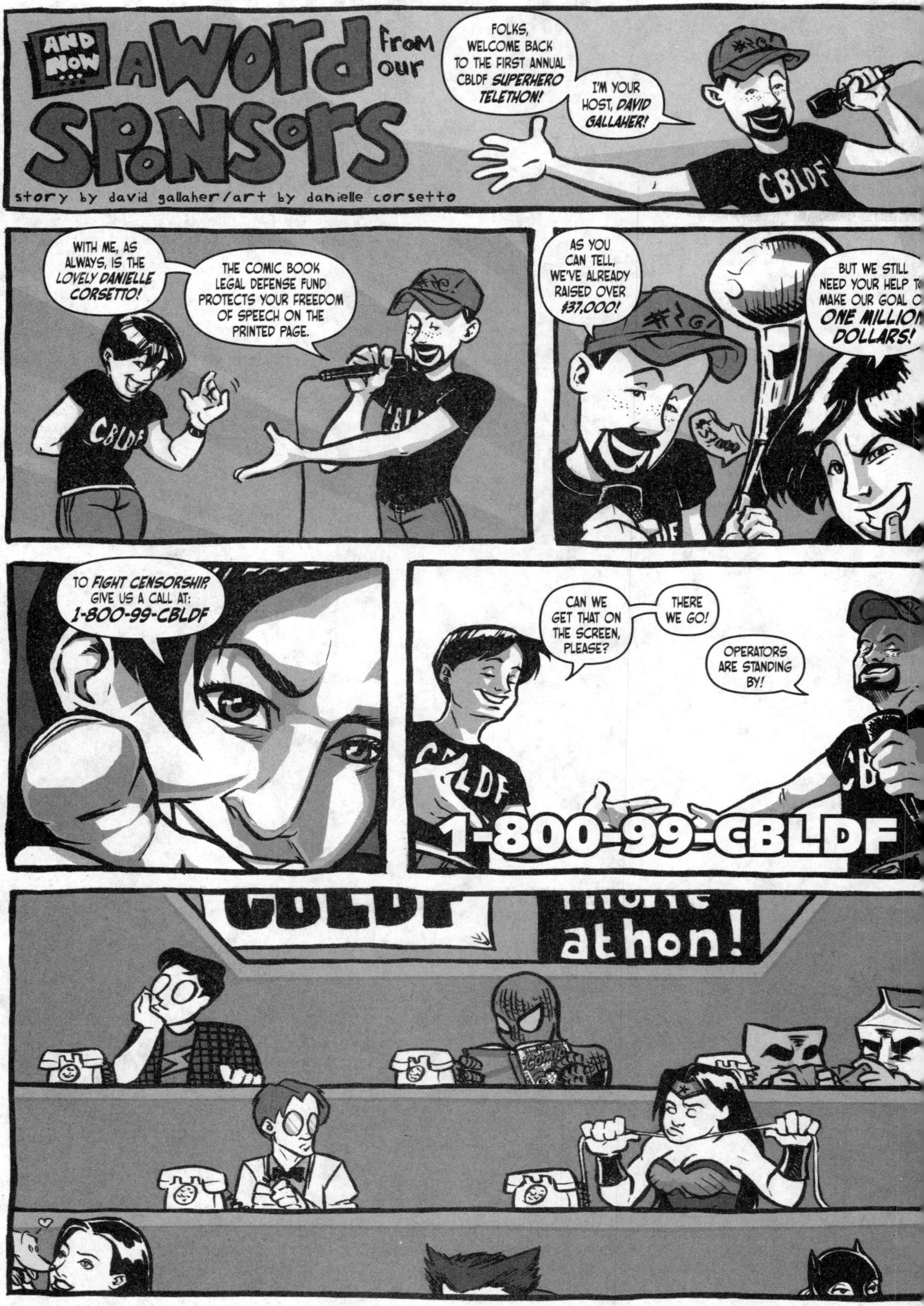
AND NOW
A WORD from our SPONSORS
story by david gallaher/art by danielle corsetto
FOLKS, WELCOME BACK TO THE FIRST ANNUAL CBLDF SUPERHERO TELETHON!
I'M YOUR HOST, DAVID GALLAHER!
CBLDF
WITH ME, AS ALWAYS, IS THE LOVELY DANIELLE CORSETTO!
THE COMIC BOOK LEGAL DEFENSE FUND PROTECTS YOUR FREEDOM OF SPEECH ON THE PRINTED PAGE.
CBLDF
AS YOU CAN TELL, WE'VE ALREADY RAISED OVER $37,000!
BUT WE STILL NEED YOUR HELP T MAKE OUR GOAL O ONE MILLION DOLLARS!
TO FIGHT CENSORSHIP, GIVE US A CALL AT: 1-800-99-CBLDF
CAN WE GET THAT ON THE SCREEN, PLEASE?
THERE WE GO!
OPERATORS ARE STANDING BY!
CBLDF
1-800-99-CBLDF
athon!

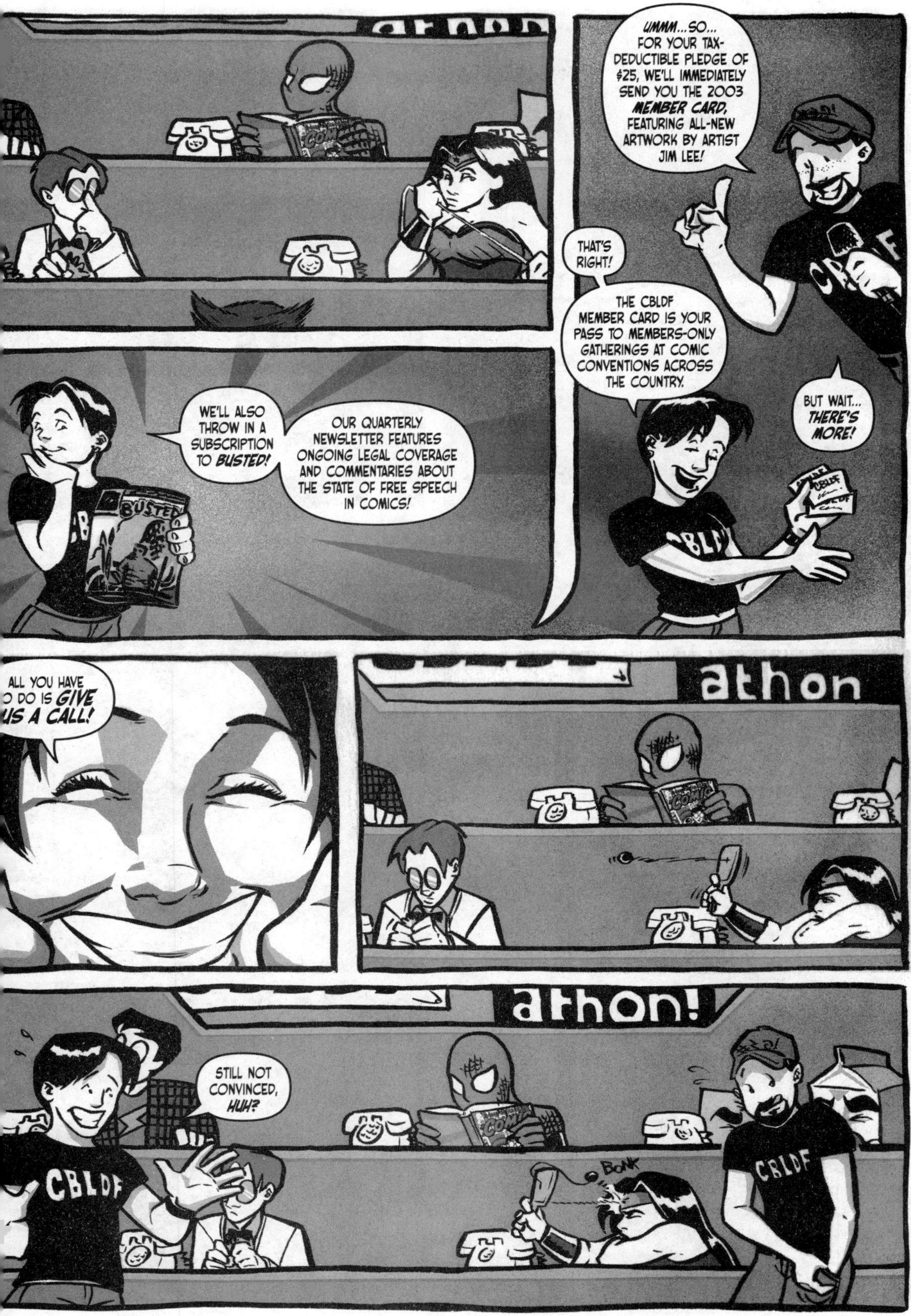
athon
UMMM...SO... FOR YOUR TAX-DEDUCTIBLE PLEDGE OF $25, WE'LL IMMEDIATELY SEND YOU THE 2003 MEMBER CARD, FEATURING ALL-NEW ARTWORK BY ARTIST JIM LEE!
THAT'S RIGHT!
THE CBLDF MEMBER CARD IS YOUR PASS TO MEMBERS-ONLY GATHERINGS AT COMIC CONVENTIONS ACROSS THE COUNTRY.
BUT WAIT... THERE'S MORE!
WE'LL ALSO THROW IN A SUBSCRIPTION TO BUSTED!
OUR QUARTERLY NEWSLETTER FEATURES ONGOING LEGAL COVERAGE AND COMMENTARIES ABOUT THE STATE OF FREE SPEECH IN COMICS!
BUSTED
CBLDF
ALL YOU HAVE O DO IS GIVE US A CALL!
athon
athon!
STILL NOT CONVINCED, HUH?
CBLDF
BONK
CBLDF

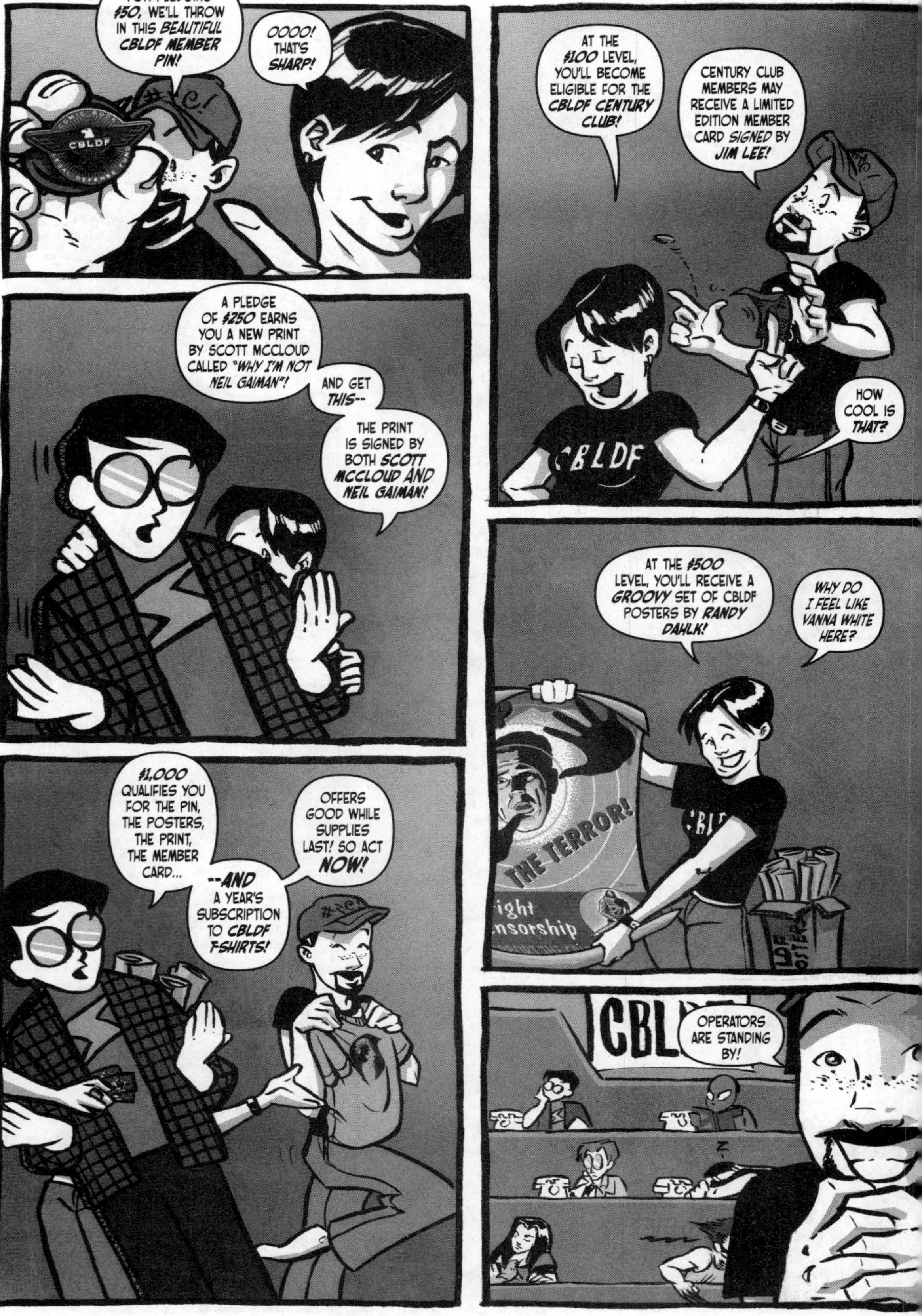
FOR PLEDGING $50, WE'LL THROW IN THIS BEAUTIFUL CBLDF MEMBER PIN!
OOOO! THAT'S SHARP!
CBLDF
AT THE $100 LEVEL, YOU'LL BECOME ELIGIBLE FOR THE CBLDF CENTURY CLUB!
CENTURY CLUB MEMBERS MAY RECEIVE A LIMITED EDITION MEMBER CARD SIGNED BY JIM LEE!
HOW COOL IS THAT?
CBLDF
A PLEDGE OF $250 EARNS YOU A NEW PRINT BY SCOTT MCCLOUD CALLED "WHY I'M NOT NEIL GAIMAN"!
AND GET THIS--
THE PRINT IS SIGNED BY BOTH SCOTT MCCLOUD AND NEIL GAIMAN!
AT THE $500 LEVEL, YOU'LL RECEIVE A GROOVY SET OF CBLDF POSTERS BY RANDY DAHLK!
WHY DO I FEEL LIKE VANNA WHITE HERE?
THE TERROR!
$1,000 QUALIFIES YOU FOR THE PIN, THE POSTERS, THE PRINT, THE MEMBER CARD...
--AND A YEAR'S SUBSCRIPTION TO CBLDF T-SHIRTS!
OFFERS GOOD WHILE SUPPLIES LAST! SO ACT NOW!
OPERATORS ARE STANDING BY!

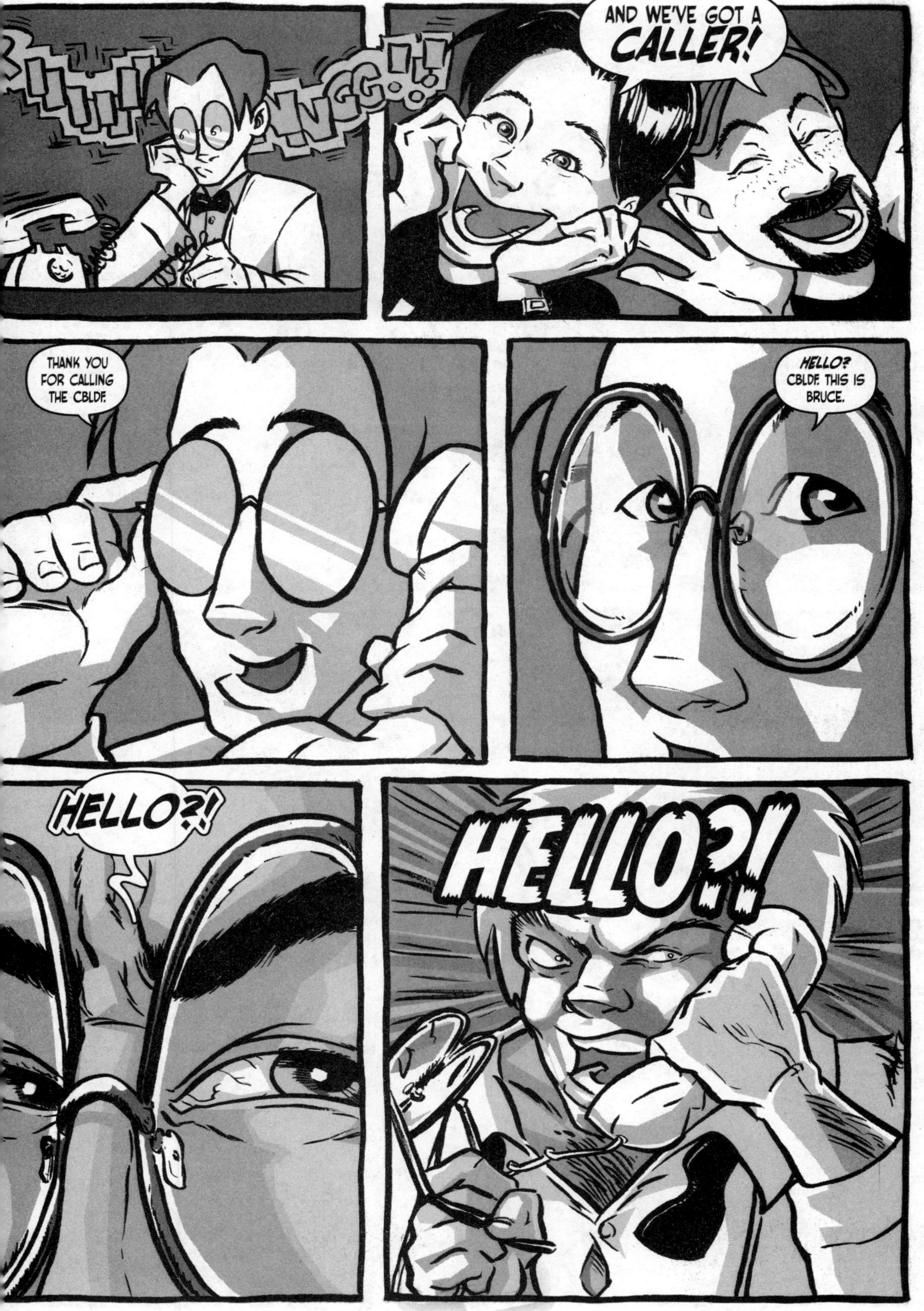
BRIIIIINNGG!!!
AND WE'VE GOT A CALLER!
THANK YOU FOR CALLING THE CBLDF.
HELLO? CBLDF. THIS IS BRUCE.
HELLO?!
HELLO?!

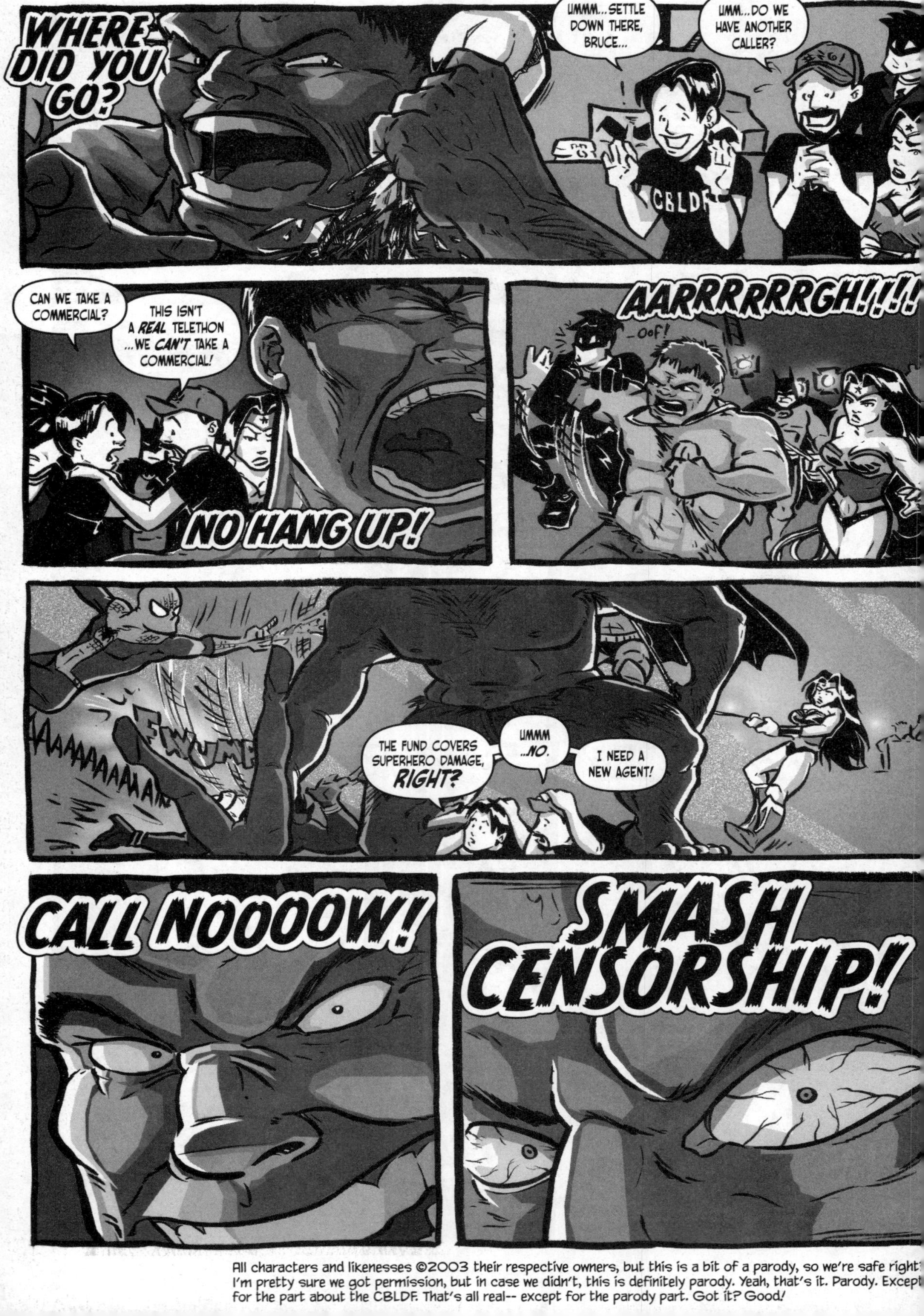
WHERE DID YOU GO?
UMMM...SETTLE DOWN THERE, BRUCE...
UMM...DO WE HAVE ANOTHER CALLER?
CAN WE TAKE A COMMERCIAL?
THIS ISN'T A *REAL* TELETHON ...WE *CAN'T* TAKE A COMMERCIAL!
NO HANG UP!
AARRRRRRGH!!!!
-OOF!
FWUMP
THE FUND COVERS SUPERHERO DAMAGE, *RIGHT?*
UMMM ...*NO.*
I NEED A NEW AGENT!
CALL NOOOOOW!
SMASH CENSORSHIP!

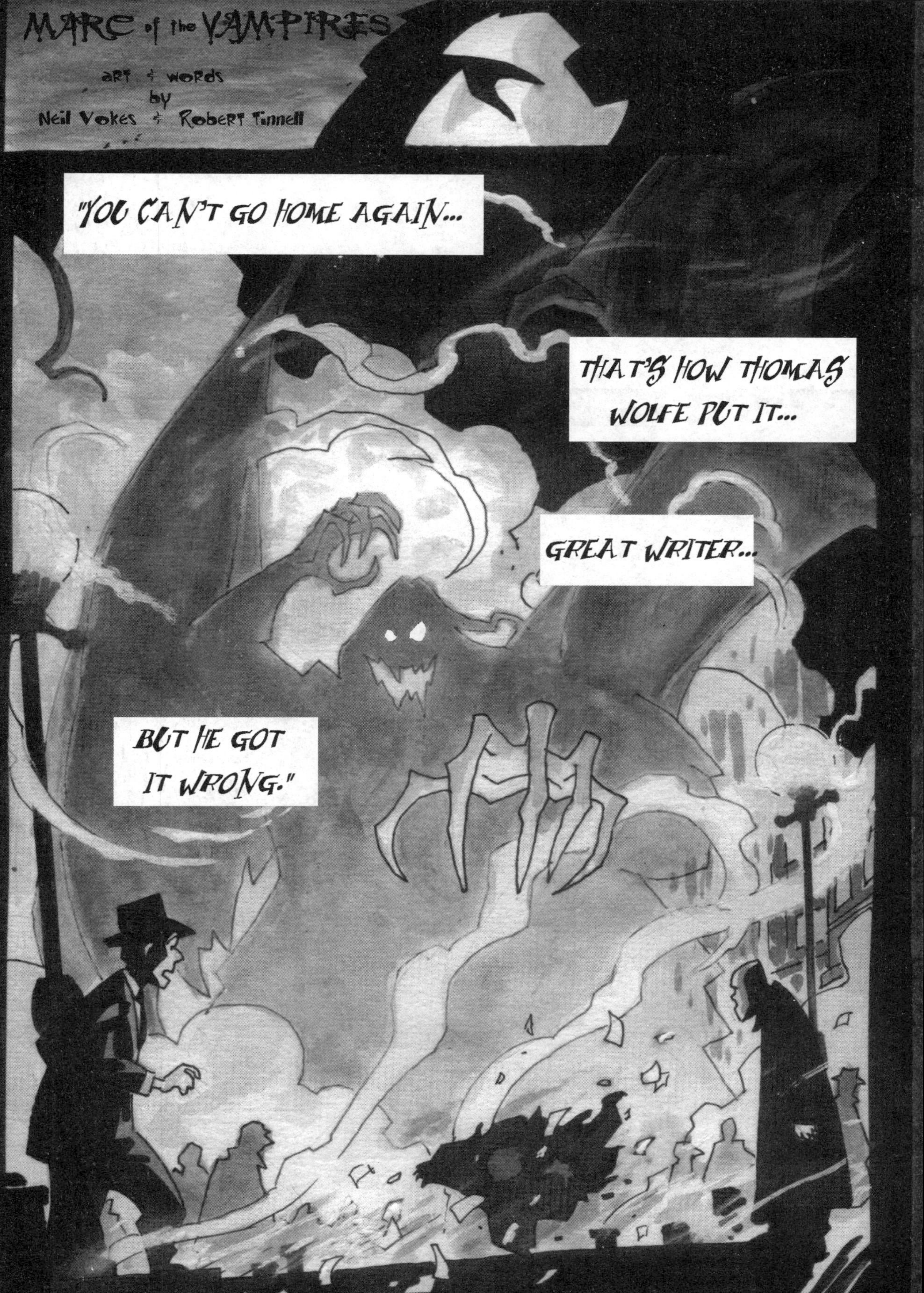
MARC of the VAMPIRES
art & words
by
Neil Vokes & Robert Tinnell
"YOU CAN'T GO HOME AGAIN...
THAT'S HOW THOMAS WOLFE PUT IT...
GREAT WRITER...
BUT HE GOT IT WRONG."

PAGE 1

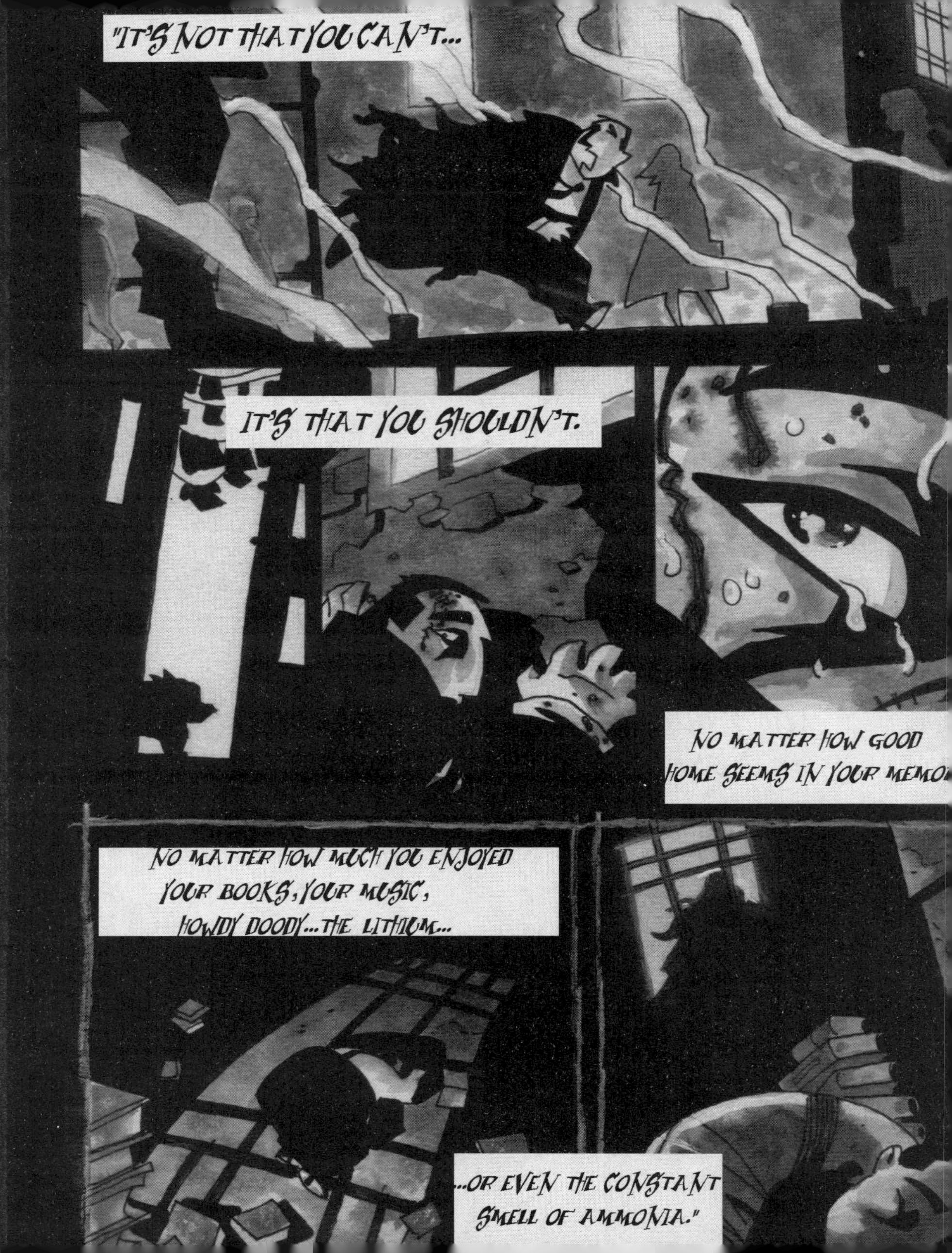
"IT'S NOT THAT YOU CAN'T...
IT'S THAT YOU SHOULDN'T.
NO MATTER HOW GOOD HOME SEEMS IN YOUR MEMO
NO MATTER HOW MUCH YOU ENJOYED YOUR BOOKS, YOUR MUSIC, HOWDY DOODY...THE LITHIUM...
...OR EVEN THE CONSTANT SMELL OF AMMONIA."

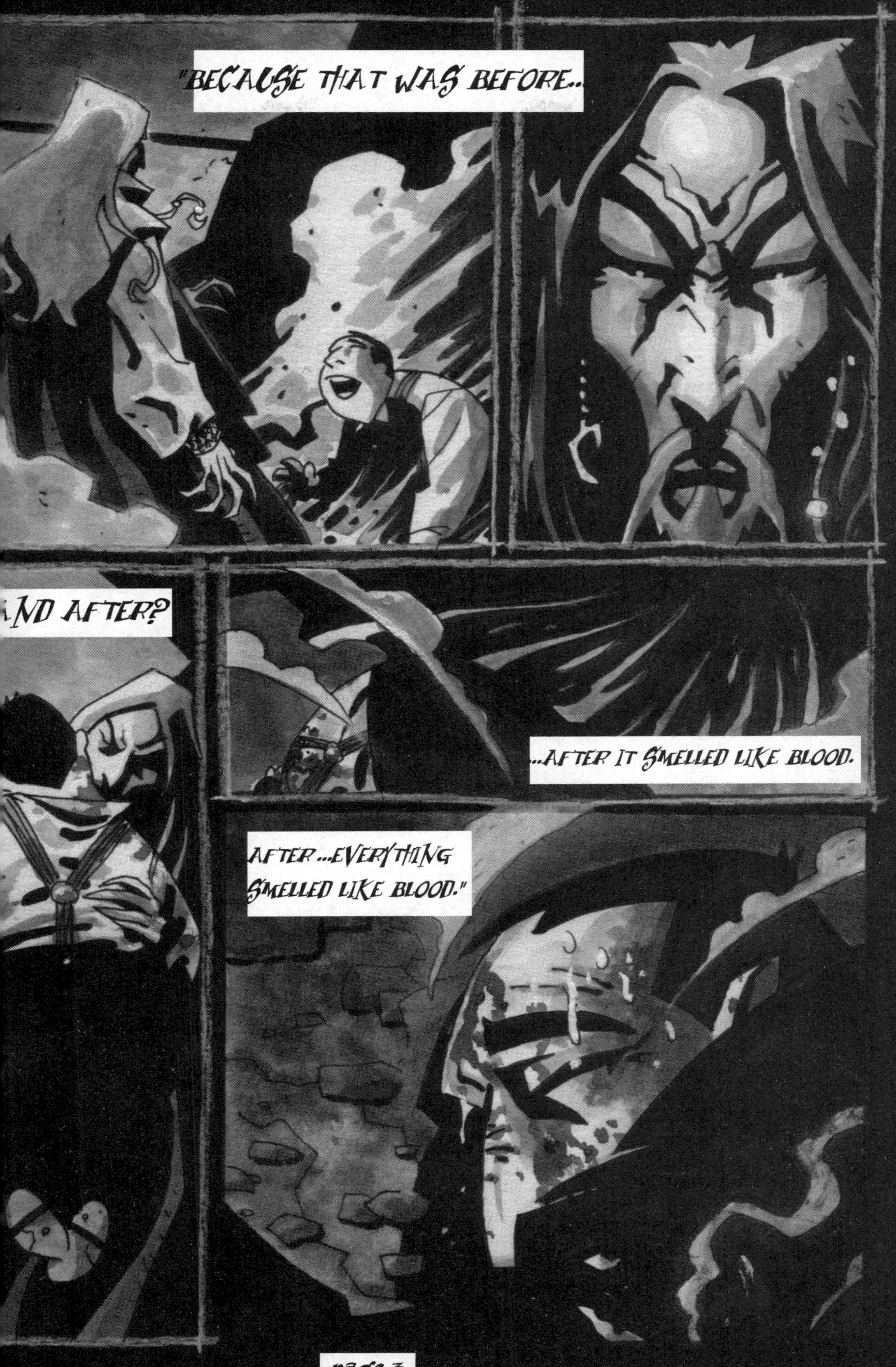
"BECAUSE THAT WAS BEFORE...
ND AFTER?
...AFTER IT SMELLED LIKE BLOOD.
AFTER...EVERYTHING SMELLED LIKE BLOOD."

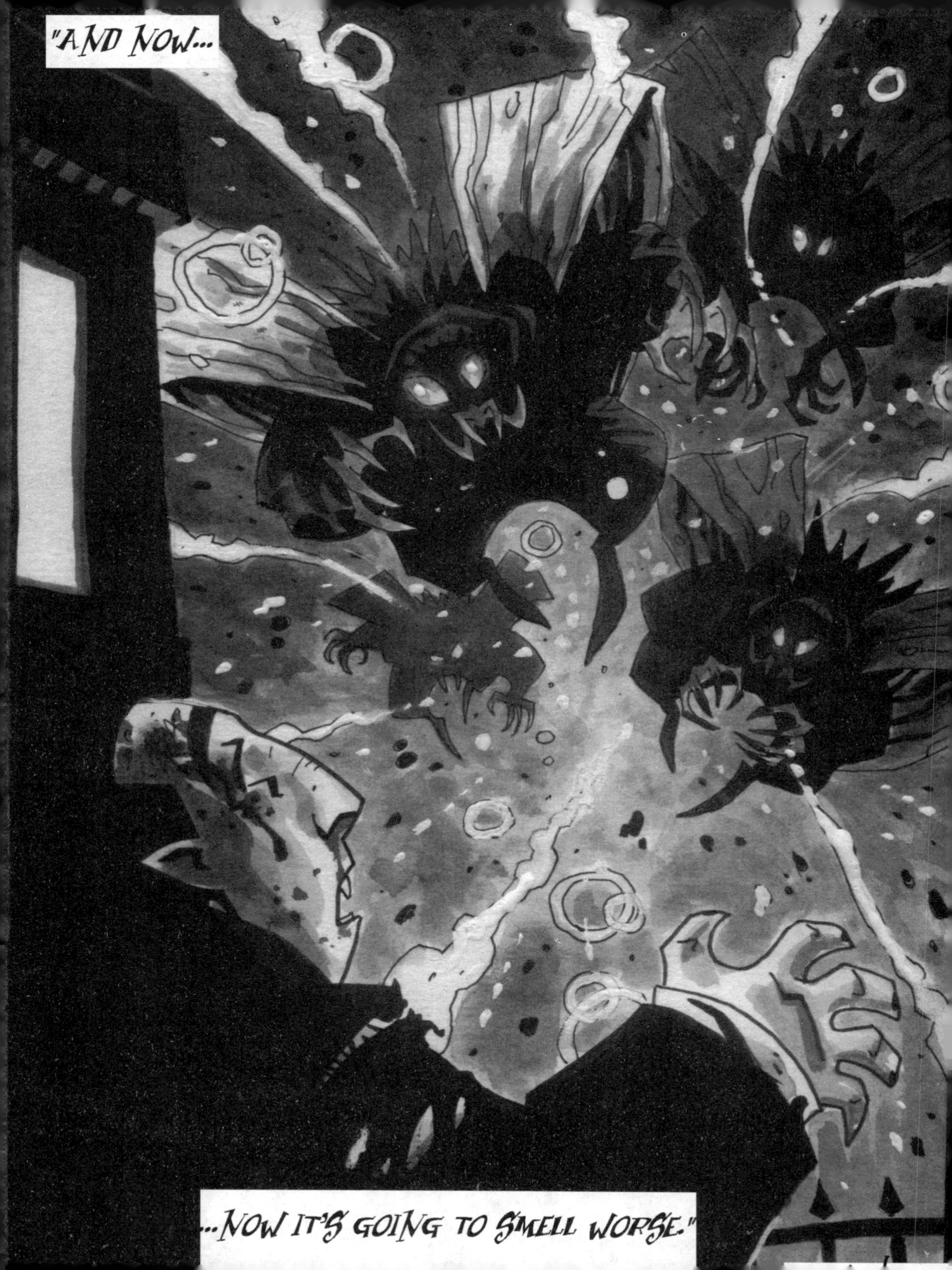
"AND NOW...
...NOW IT'S GOING TO SMELL WORSE."

GOBUKAN: THE ACCOUNTANT *by J. Bone*

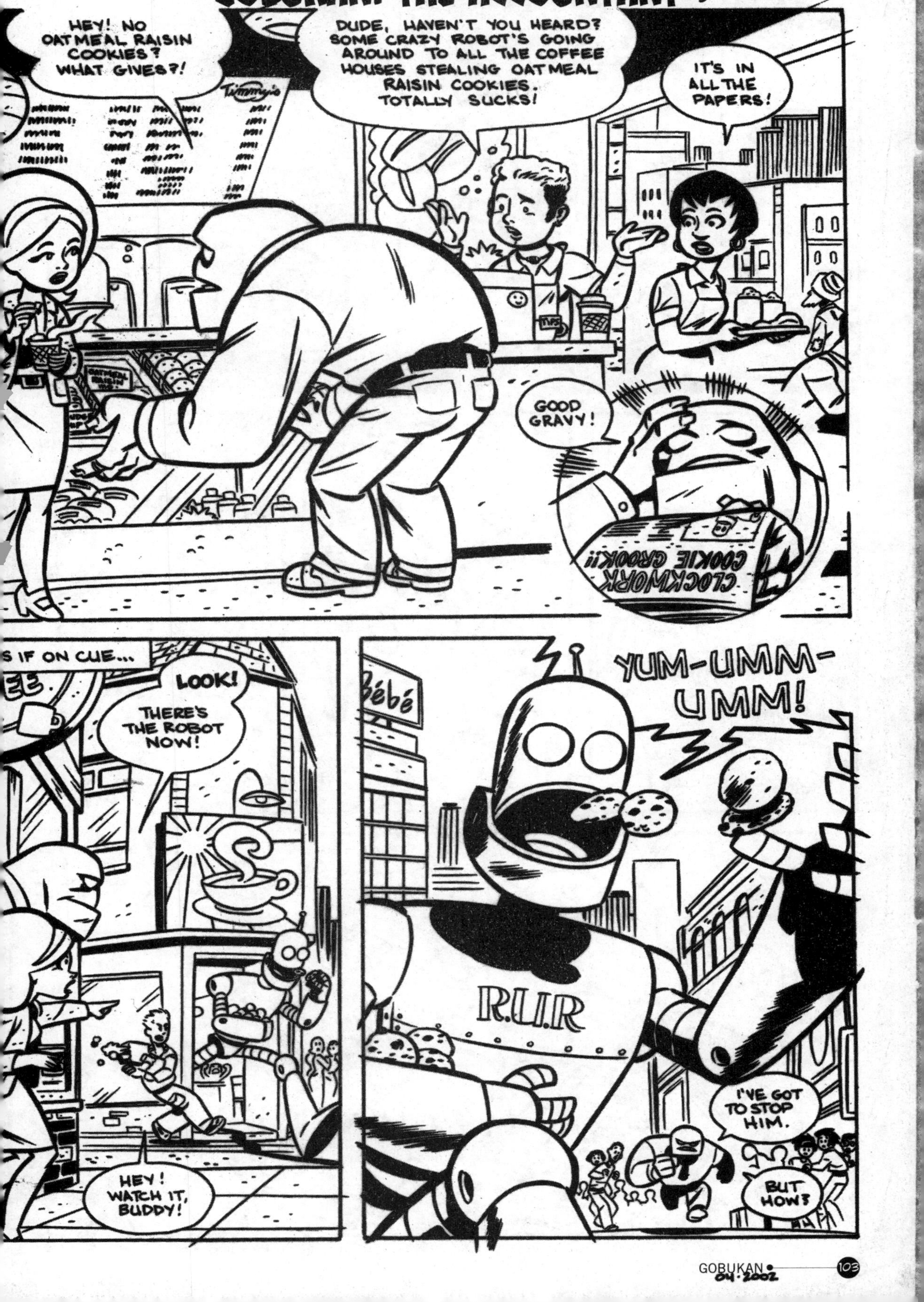

HEY! NO OATMEAL RAISIN COOKIES? WHAT GIVES?!
DUDE, HAVEN'T YOU HEARD? SOME CRAZY ROBOT'S GOING AROUND TO ALL THE COFFEE HOUSES STEALING OATMEAL RAISIN COOKIES. TOTALLY SUCKS!
IT'S IN ALL THE PAPERS!
GOOD GRAVY!
S IF ON CUE...
LOOK!
THERE'S THE ROBOT NOW!
HEY! WATCH IT, BUDDY!
YUM-UMM-UMM!
Bébé
R.U.R
I'VE GOT TO STOP HIM.
BUT HOW?

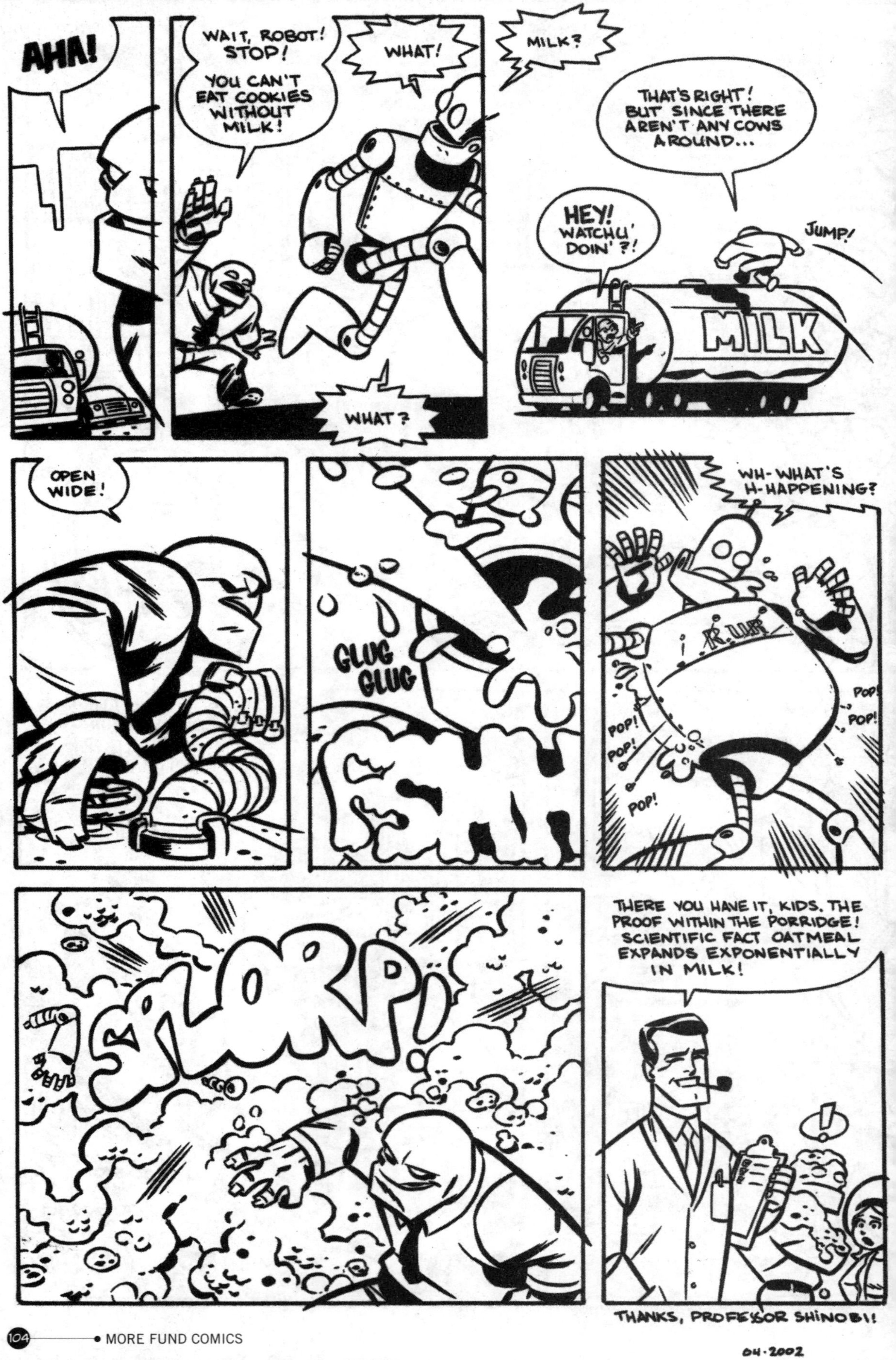

AHA!
WAIT, ROBOT! STOP!
YOU CAN'T EAT COOKIES WITHOUT MILK!
WHAT!
MILK?
WHAT?
THAT'S RIGHT! BUT SINCE THERE AREN'T ANY COWS AROUND...
HEY! WATCHU' DOIN' ?!
JUMP!
MILK
OPEN WIDE!
GLUG GLUG
WH-WHAT'S H-HAPPENING?
POP!
POP!
POP!
POP!
POP!
SPLORP!
THERE YOU HAVE IT, KIDS. THE PROOF WITHIN THE PORRIDGE! SCIENTIFIC FACT OATMEAL EXPANDS EXPONENTIALLY IN MILK!
!
THANKS, PROFESSOR SHINOBI!
04·2002

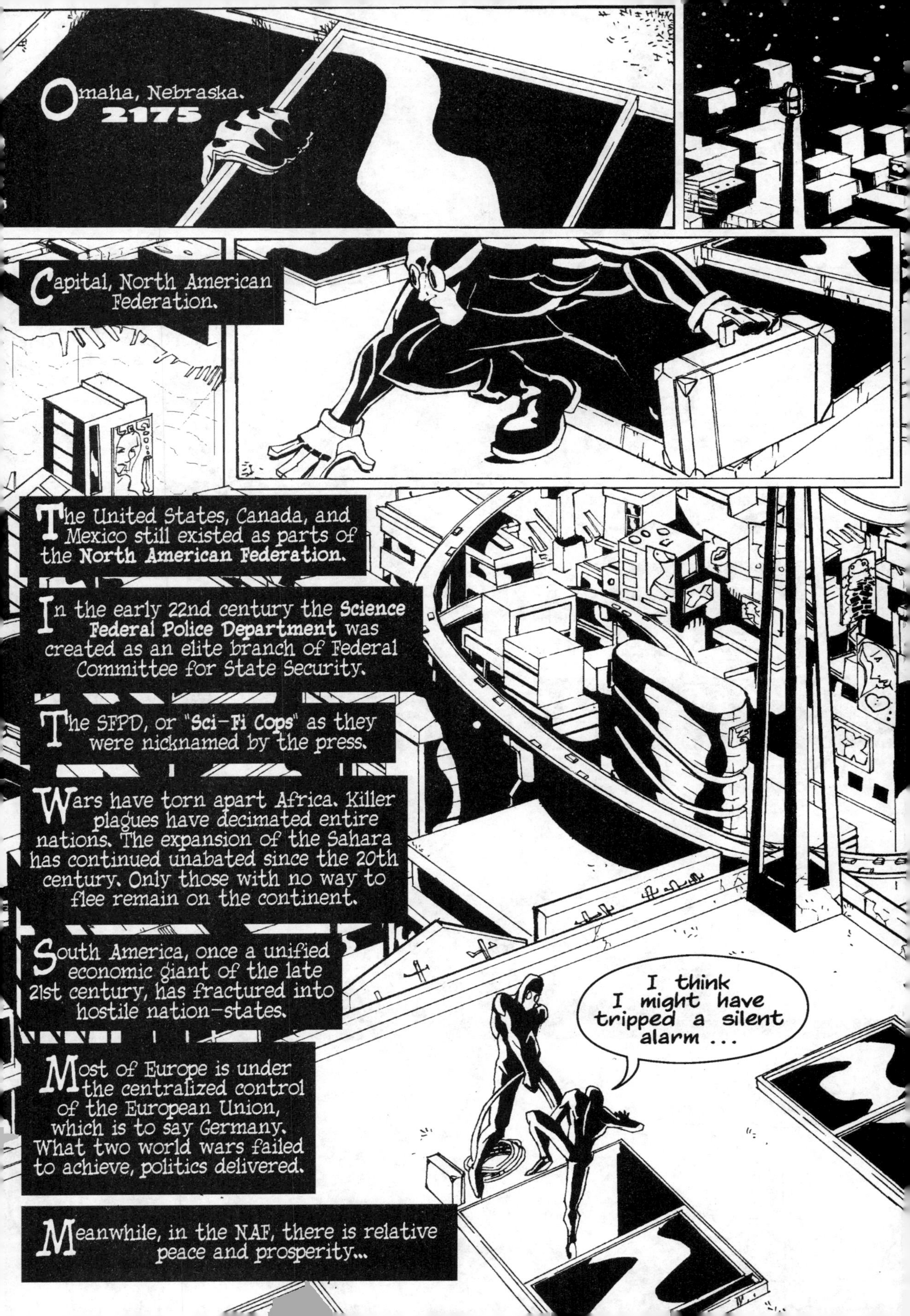
Omaha, Nebraska.
2175
Capital, North American Federation.
The United States, Canada, and Mexico still existed as parts of the North American Federation.
In the early 22nd century the Science Federal Police Department was created as an elite branch of Federal Committee for State Security.
The SFPD, or "Sci-Fi Cops" as they were nicknamed by the press.
Wars have torn apart Africa. Killer plagues have decimated entire nations. The expansion of the Sahara has continued unabated since the 20th century. Only those with no way to flee remain on the continent.
South America, once a unified economic giant of the late 21st century, has fractured into hostile nation-states.
I think I might have tripped a silent alarm ...
Most of Europe is under the centralized control of the European Union, which is to say Germany. What two world wars failed to achieve, politics delivered.
Meanwhile, in the NAF, there is relative peace and prosperity...

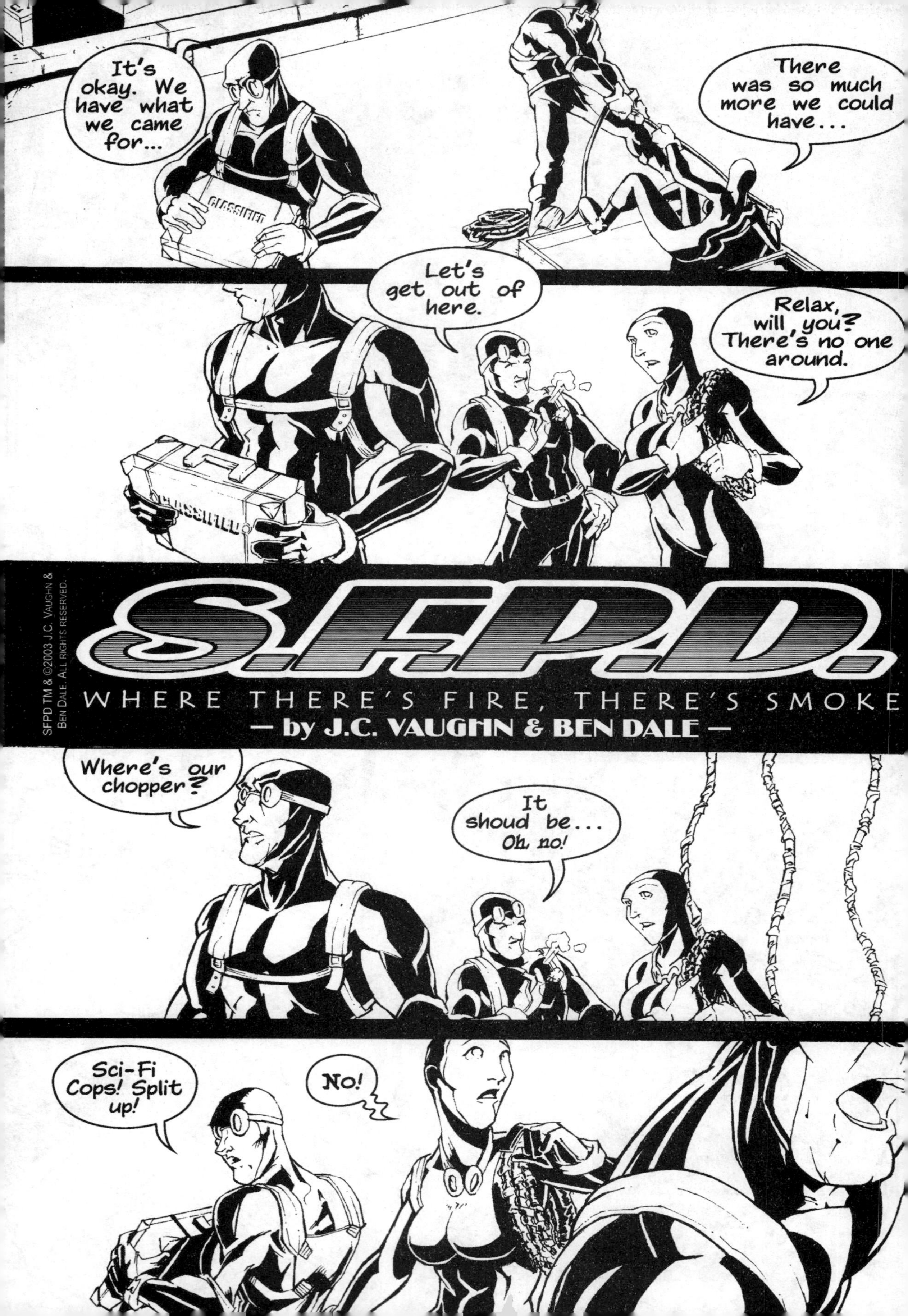
It's okay. We have what we came for...
There was so much more we could have...
CLASSIFIED
Let's get out of here.
Relax, will you? There's no one around.
CLASSIFIED
S.F.P.D.
WHERE THERE'S FIRE, THERE'S SMOKE
— by J.C. VAUGHN & BEN DALE —
SFPD TM & ©2003 J.C. VAUGHN & BEN DALE. ALL RIGHTS RESERVED.
Where's our chopper?
It shoud be... Oh no!
Sci-Fi Cops! Split up!
No!

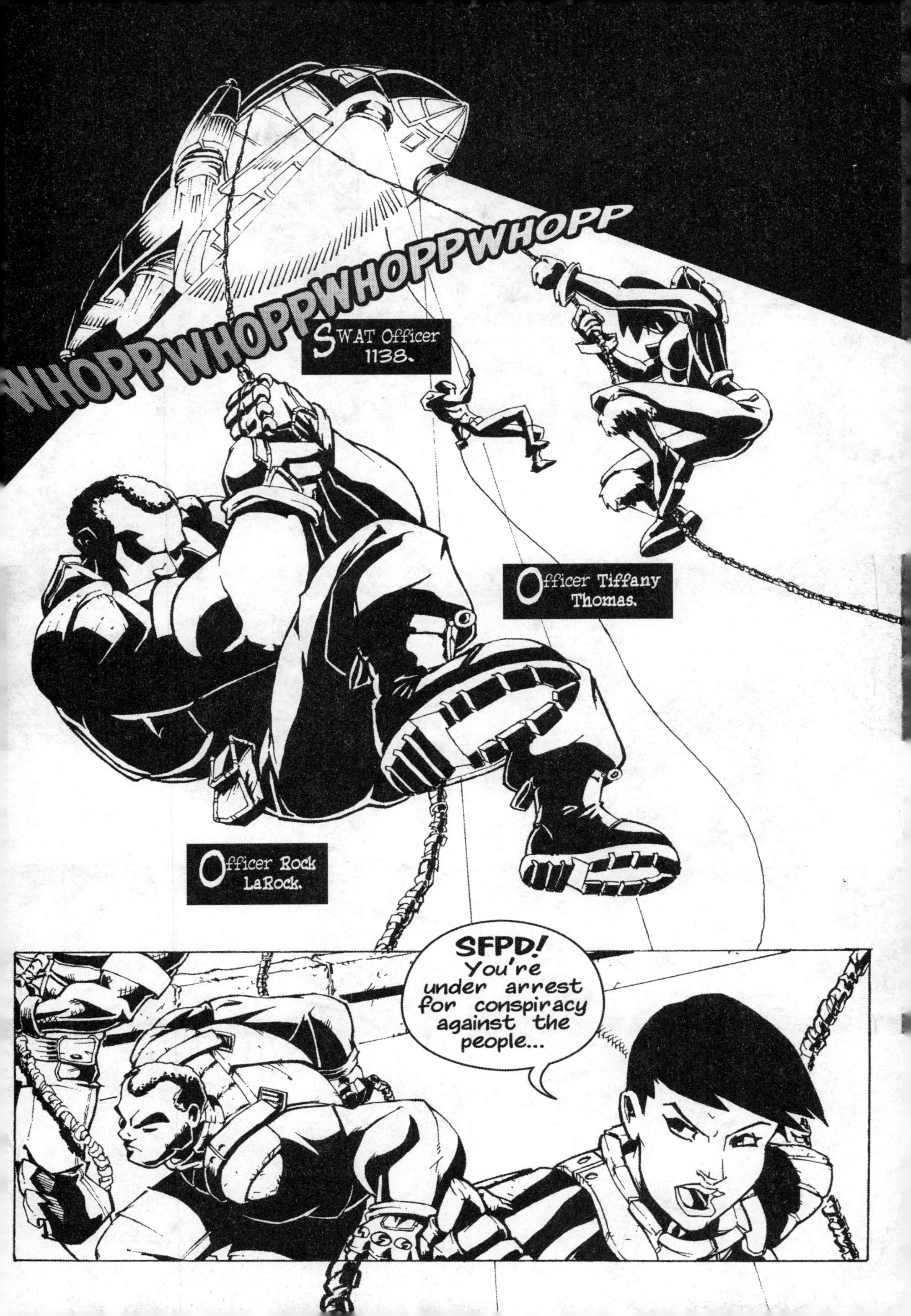
WHOPPWHOPPWHOPPWHOPP
SWAT Officer 1138.
Officer Tiffany Thomas.
Officer Rock LaRock.
SFPD! You're under arrest for conspiracy against the people...

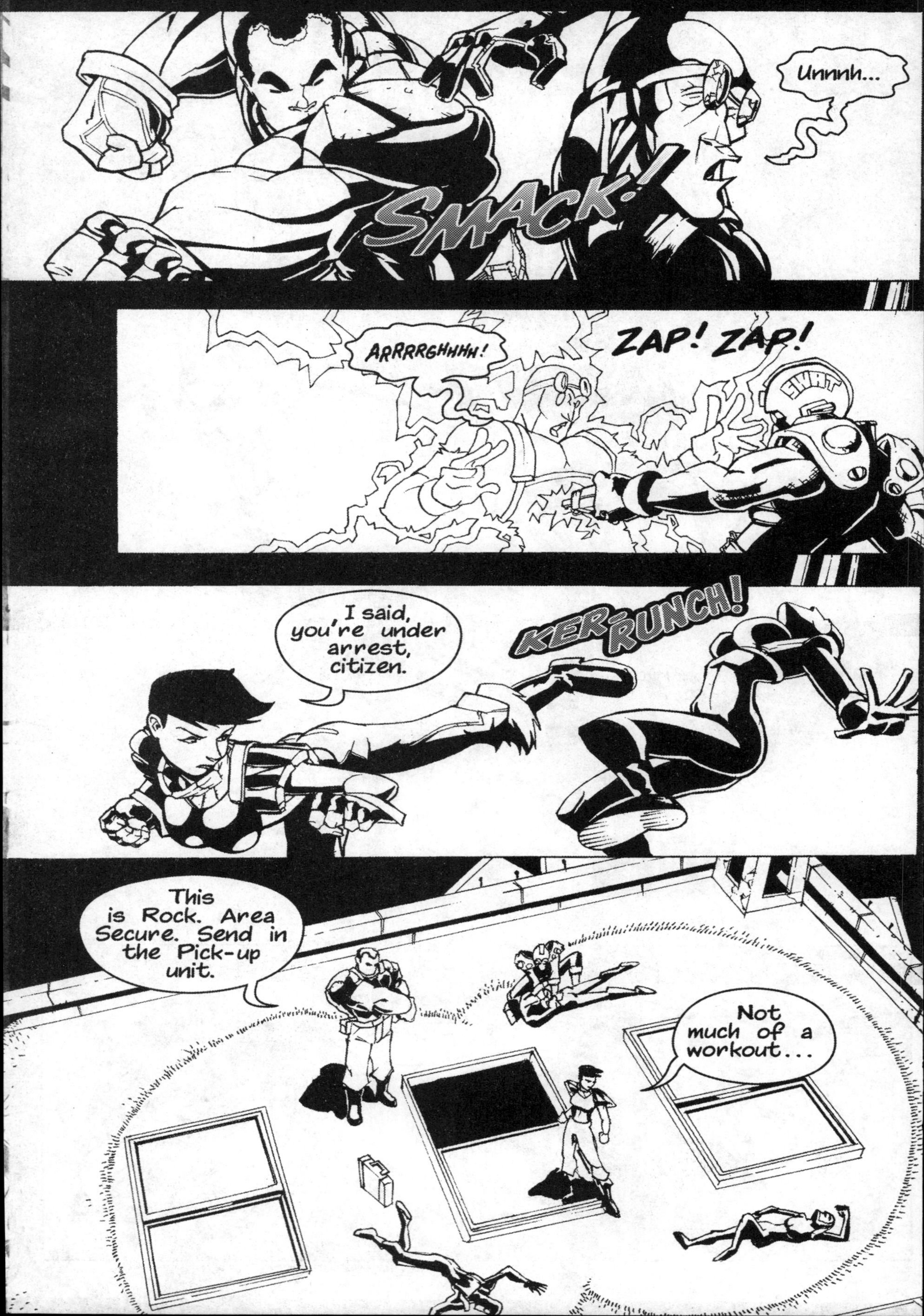
Unnnh...
SMACK!
ARRRRGHHHH!
ZAP! ZAP!
SWAT
I said, you're under arrest, citizen.
KER-RUNCH!
This is Rock. Area Secure. Send in the Pick-up unit.
Not much of a workout...

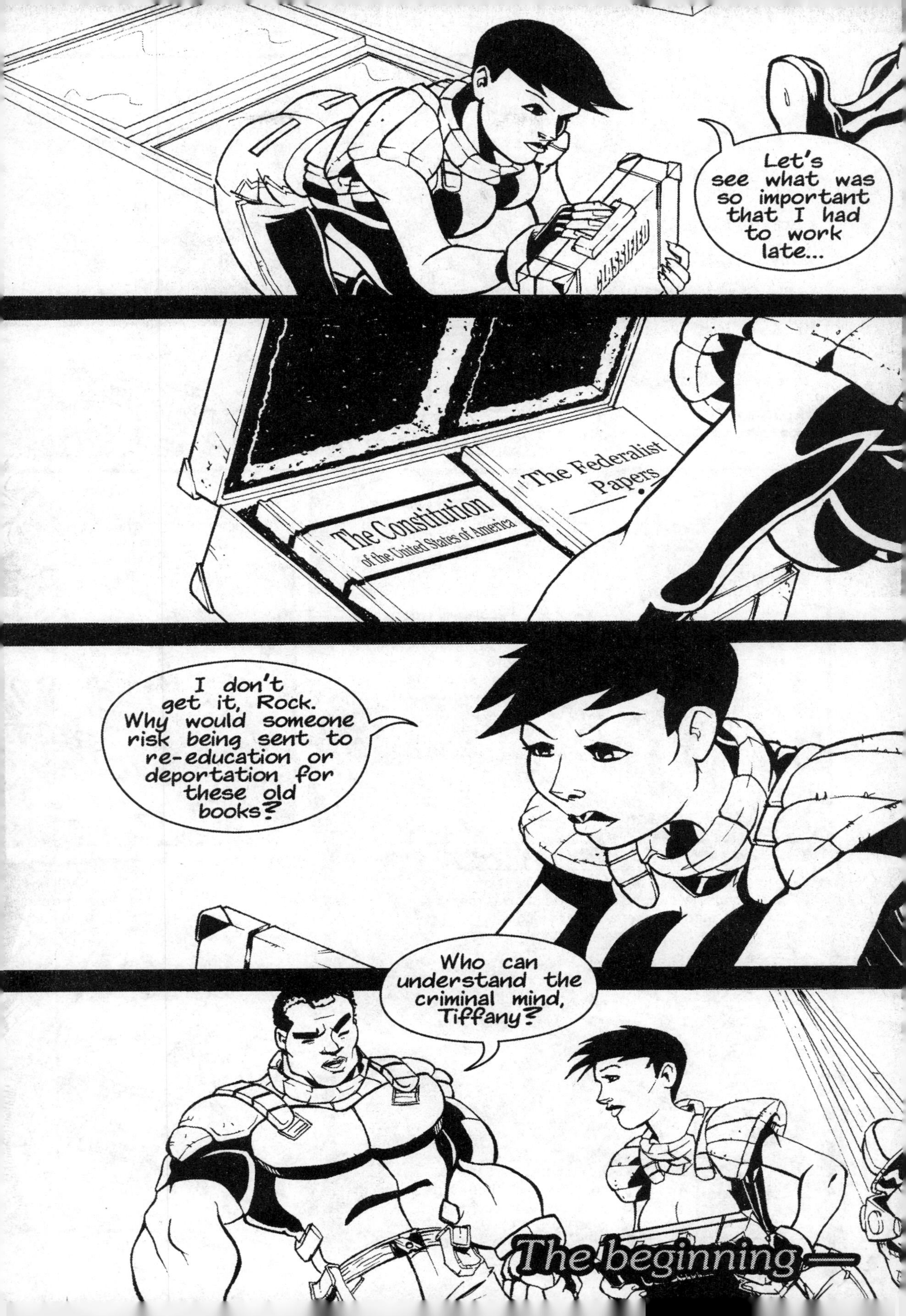
Let's see what was so important that I had to work late...
CLASSIFIED
The Federalist Papers
The Constitution of the United States of America
I don't get it, Rock. Why would someone risk being sent to re-education or deportation for these old books?
Who can understand the criminal mind, Tiffany?
The beginning—

仮面
KAMEN

Created by Steven Cummings and Egg

Story by Egg

Art by Steven Cummings

Letters by Jessi Nelson

Logo by Kazuko Ashizawa

Atlanta. The offices of the National News Channel
Chuck, anchor my story with the unedited killing!
What can I do to convince you that will make good copy?
Sorry, can't do it. Editor's prerogative, Julie. It's too graphic.

Why? You know my voiceover is great! Combined with this sweet old Japanese man's death, we have something!
People will relate. This isn't a chalk outline and a bad driver's license photo; I see this as a man's last steps!
Julie, the Rising Sun Killer doin' in this old timer wearin' the camera is too intense for our audience.
Look at this...
If this one gets aired then the rest of the killings he's taped should be shown, too. And then my phone'll start ringin'!
FCC.
Parent's Groups.
And all of'em screamin' about kids seein' this and cryin' and who could blame'em!
A kid that cries at a murder...
Will not grow up to atte
Columbine!
Ain't gotta tell m
darlin'...

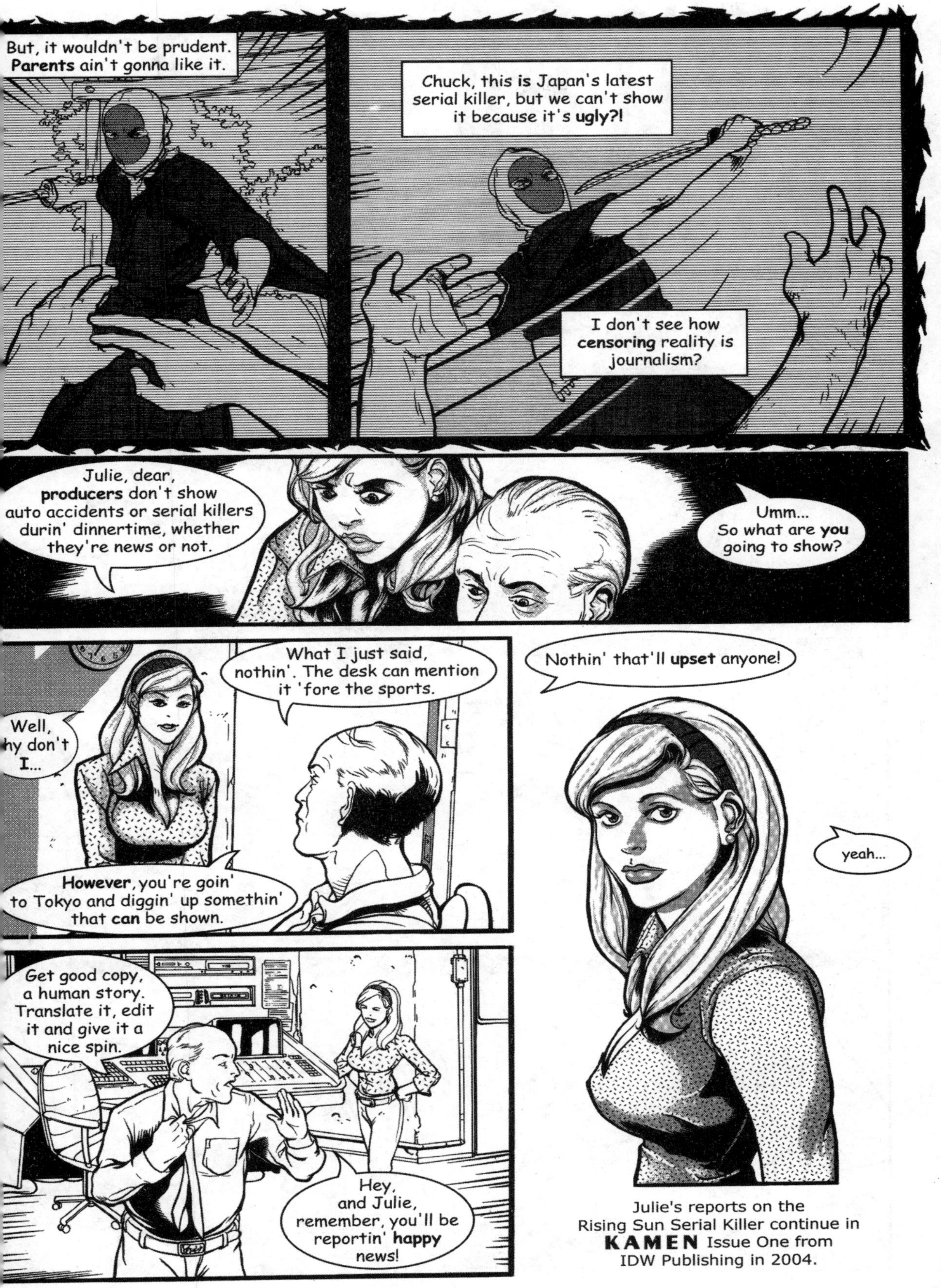
But, it wouldn't be prudent. Parents ain't gonna like it.
Chuck, this is Japan's latest serial killer, but we can't show it because it's ugly?!
I don't see how censoring reality is journalism?
Julie, dear, producers don't show auto accidents or serial killers durin' dinnertime, whether they're news or not.
Umm... So what are you going to show?
What I just said, nothin'. The desk can mention it 'fore the sports.
Well, hy don't I...
However, you're goin' to Tokyo and diggin' up somethin' that can be shown.
Nothin' that'll upset anyone!
yeah...
Get good copy, a human story. Translate it, edit it and give it a nice spin.
Hey, and Julie, remember, you'll be reportin' happy news!

Julie's reports on the Rising Sun Serial Killer continue in **KAMEN** Issue One from IDW Publishing in 2004.

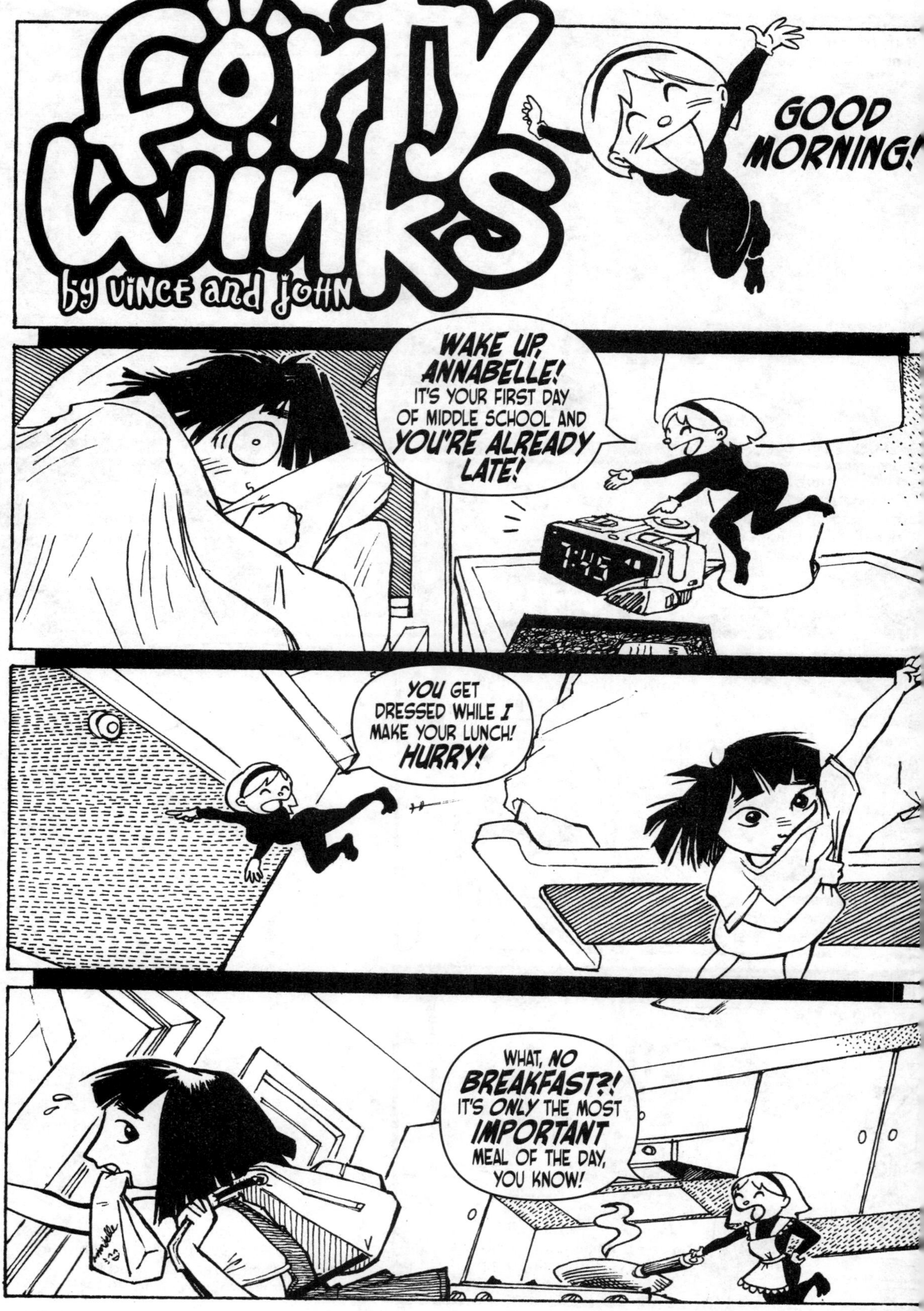
Forty Winks
by Vince and John
GOOD MORNING!
WAKE UP, ANNABELLE! IT'S YOUR FIRST DAY OF MIDDLE SCHOOL AND YOU'RE ALREADY LATE!
7:45
YOU GET DRESSED WHILE I MAKE YOUR LUNCH! HURRY!
WHAT, NO BREAKFAST?! IT'S ONLY THE MOST IMPORTANT MEAL OF THE DAY, YOU KNOW!

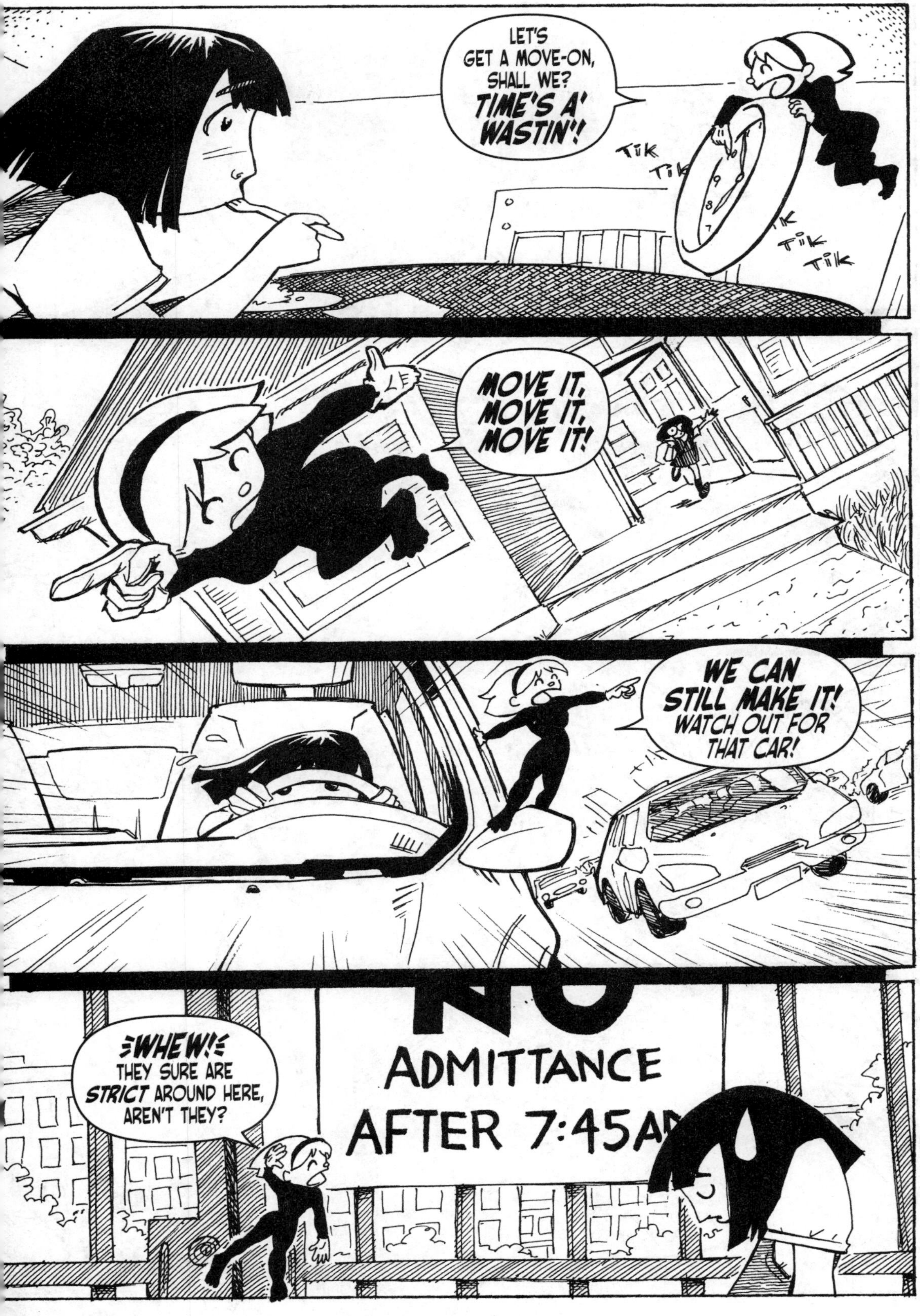

LET'S GET A MOVE-ON, SHALL WE? TIME'S A' WASTIN'!
TIK TIK
TIK TIK TIK
MOVE IT, MOVE IT, MOVE IT!
WE CAN STILL MAKE IT! WATCH OUT FOR THAT CAR!
WHEW! THEY SURE ARE STRICT AROUND HERE, AREN'T THEY?
ADMITTANCE
AFTER 7:45A

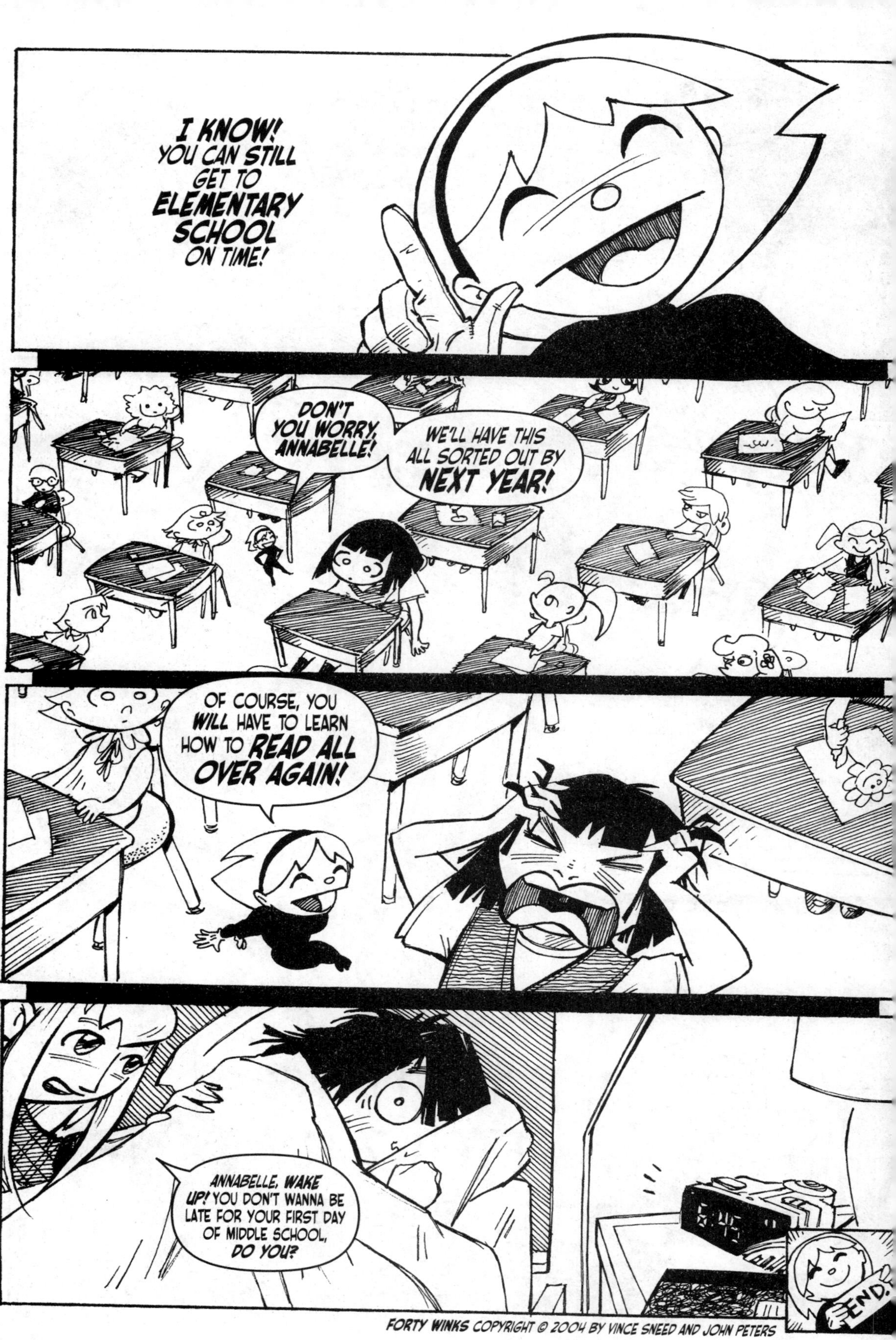
I KNOW! YOU CAN STILL GET TO ELEMENTARY SCHOOL ON TIME!
DON'T YOU WORRY, ANNABELLE!
WE'LL HAVE THIS ALL SORTED OUT BY NEXT YEAR!
OF COURSE, YOU WILL HAVE TO LEARN HOW TO READ ALL OVER AGAIN!
ANNABELLE, WAKE UP! YOU DON'T WANNA BE LATE FOR YOUR FIRST DAY OF MIDDLE SCHOOL, DO YOU?
END.

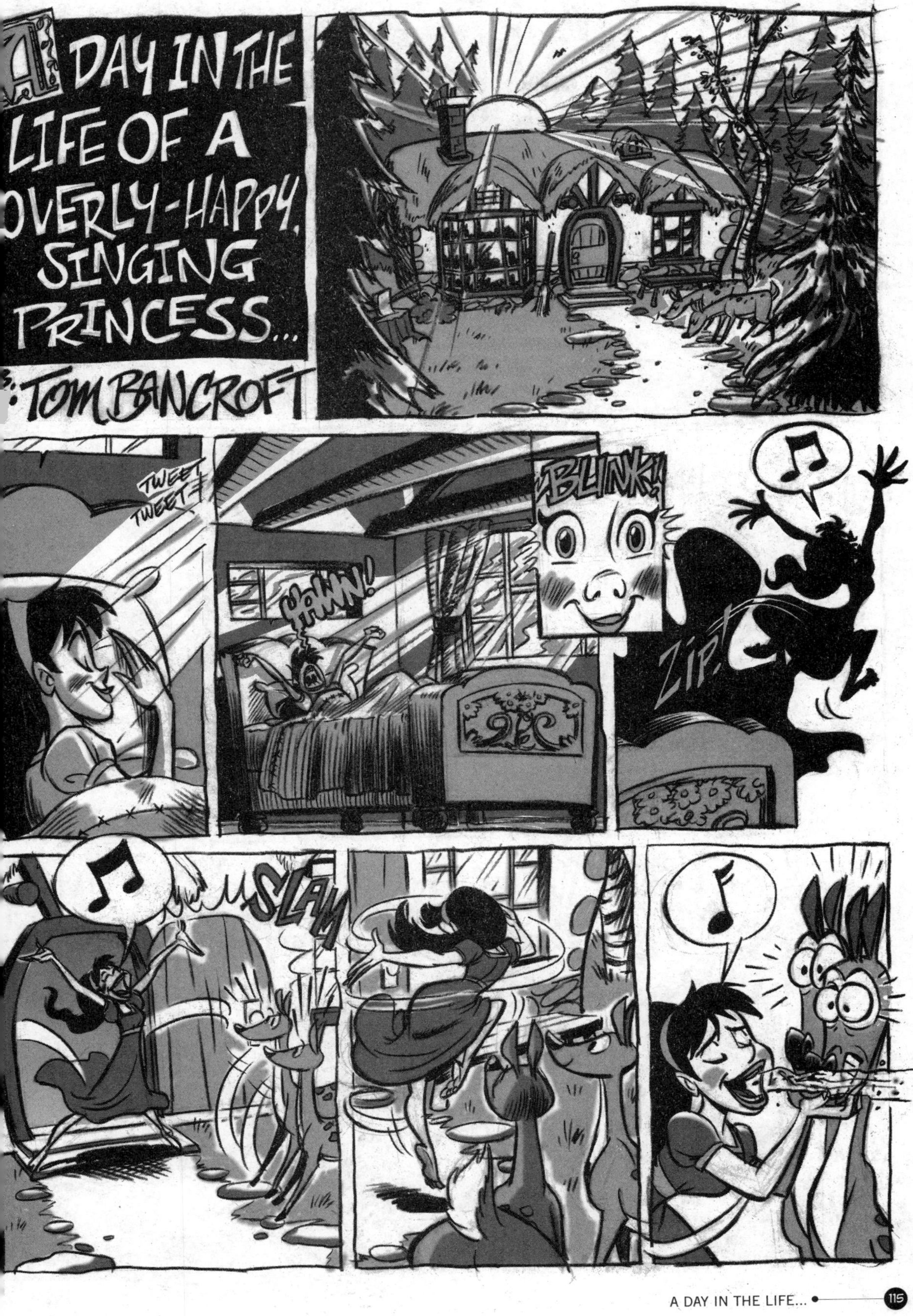
A DAY IN THE LIFE OF A OVERLY-HAPPY, SINGING PRINCESS...
TOM BANCROFT
TWEET TWEET
YAWN!
BLINK!
ZIP!
SLAM

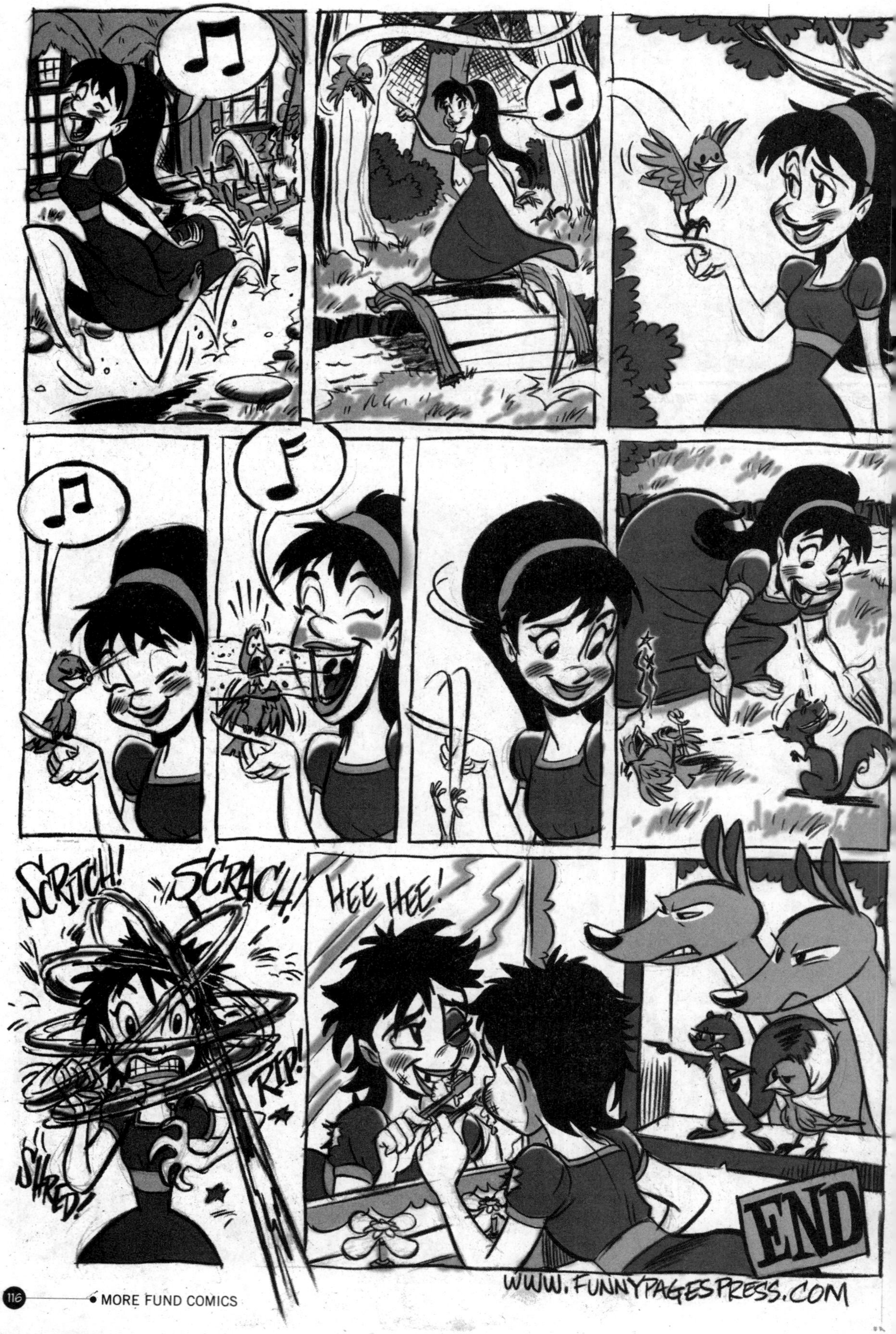
SCRITCH!
SCRACH!
RIP!
SHRED!
HEE HEE!
END
WWW.FUNNYPAGESPRESS.COM

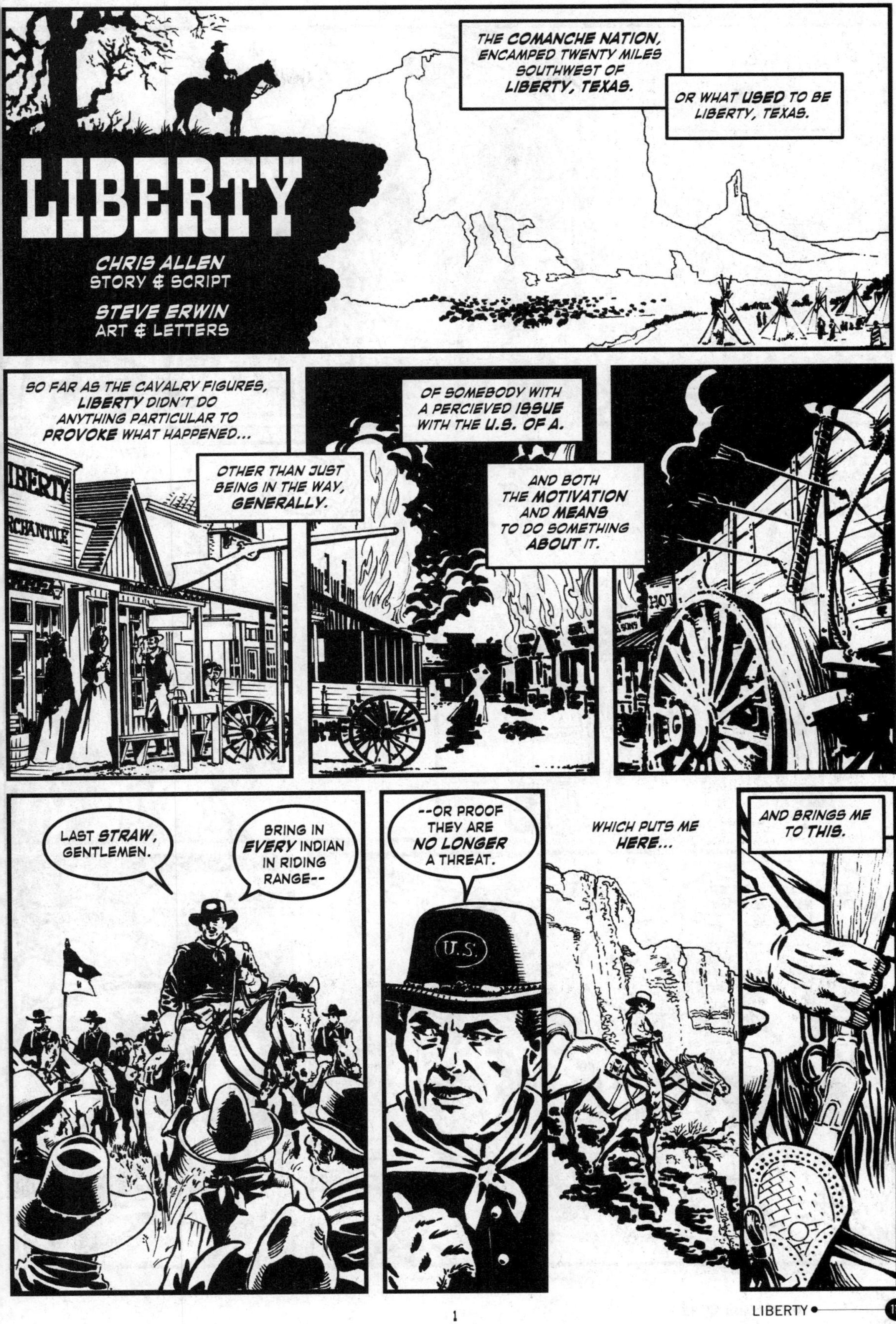
LIBERTY
CHRIS ALLEN
STORY & SCRIPT
STEVE ERWIN
ART & LETTERS
THE COMANCHE NATION, ENCAMPED TWENTY MILES SOUTHWEST OF LIBERTY, TEXAS.
OR WHAT USED TO BE LIBERTY, TEXAS.
SO FAR AS THE CAVALRY FIGURES, LIBERTY DIDN'T DO ANYTHING PARTICULAR TO PROVOKE WHAT HAPPENED...
OTHER THAN JUST BEING IN THE WAY, GENERALLY.
OF SOMEBODY WITH A PERCIEVED ISSUE WITH THE U.S. OF A.
AND BOTH THE MOTIVATION AND MEANS TO DO SOMETHING ABOUT IT.
LAST STRAW, GENTLEMEN.
BRING IN EVERY INDIAN IN RIDING RANGE--
--OR PROOF THEY ARE NO LONGER A THREAT.
U.S.
WHICH PUTS ME HERE...
AND BRINGS ME TO THIS.

1

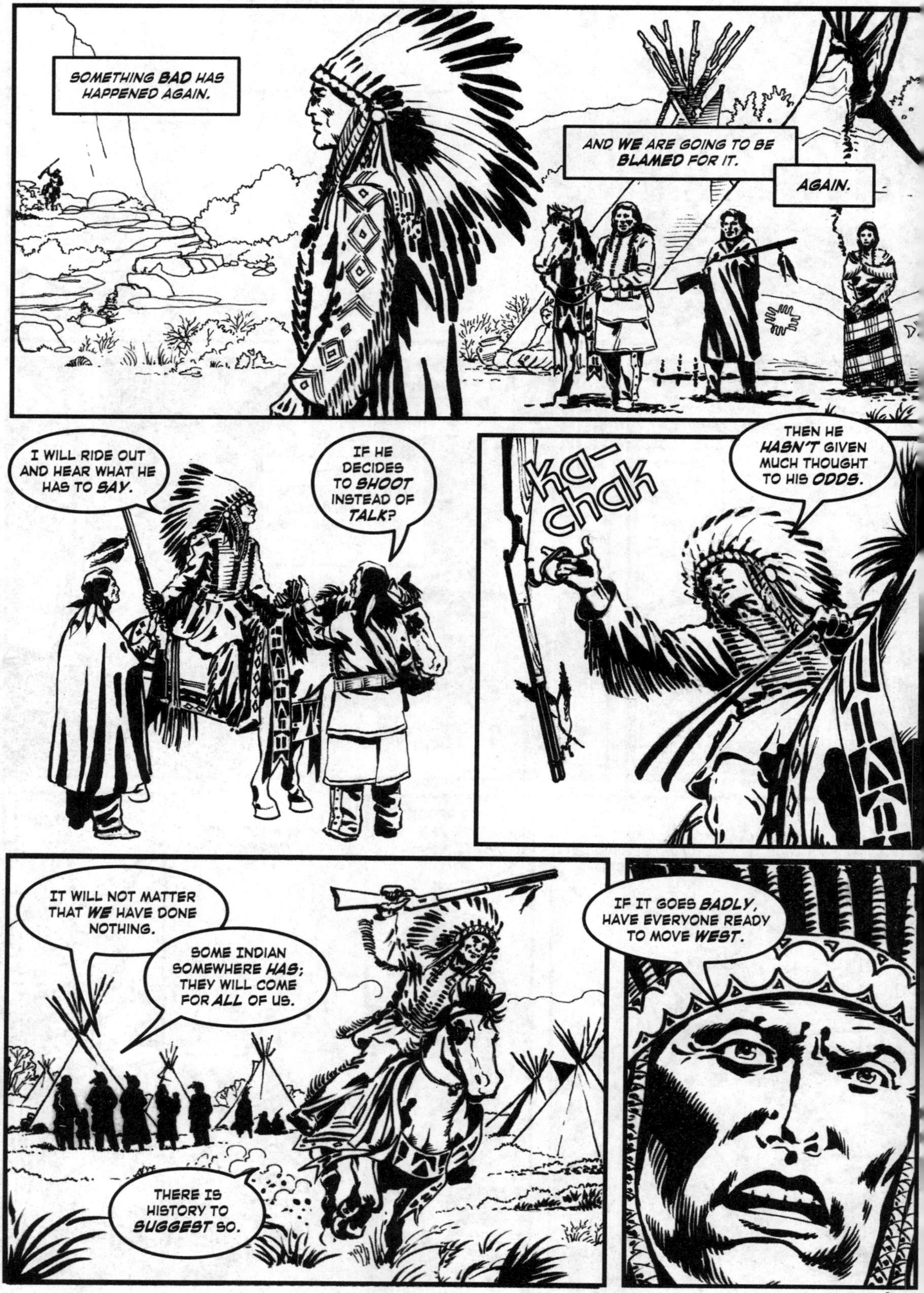
SOMETHING BAD HAS HAPPENED AGAIN.
AND WE ARE GOING TO BE BLAMED FOR IT.
AGAIN.
I WILL RIDE OUT AND HEAR WHAT HE HAS TO SAY.
IF HE DECIDES TO SHOOT INSTEAD OF TALK?
KA-CHAK
THEN HE HASN'T GIVEN MUCH THOUGHT TO HIS ODDS.
IT WILL NOT MATTER THAT WE HAVE DONE NOTHING.
SOME INDIAN SOMEWHERE HAS; THEY WILL COME FOR ALL OF US.
THERE IS HISTORY TO SUGGEST SO.
IF IT GOES BADLY, HAVE EVERYONE READY TO MOVE WEST.

2

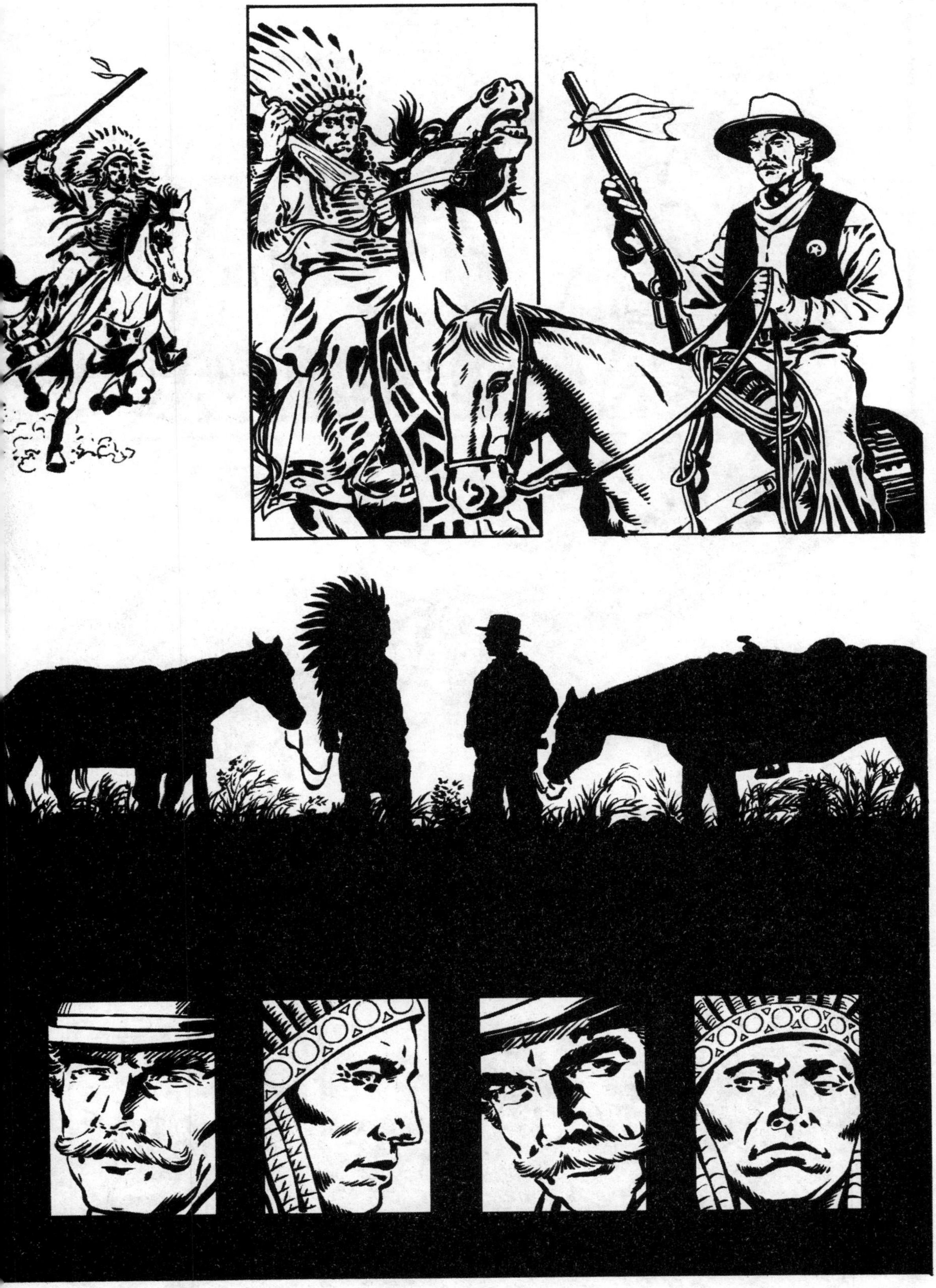

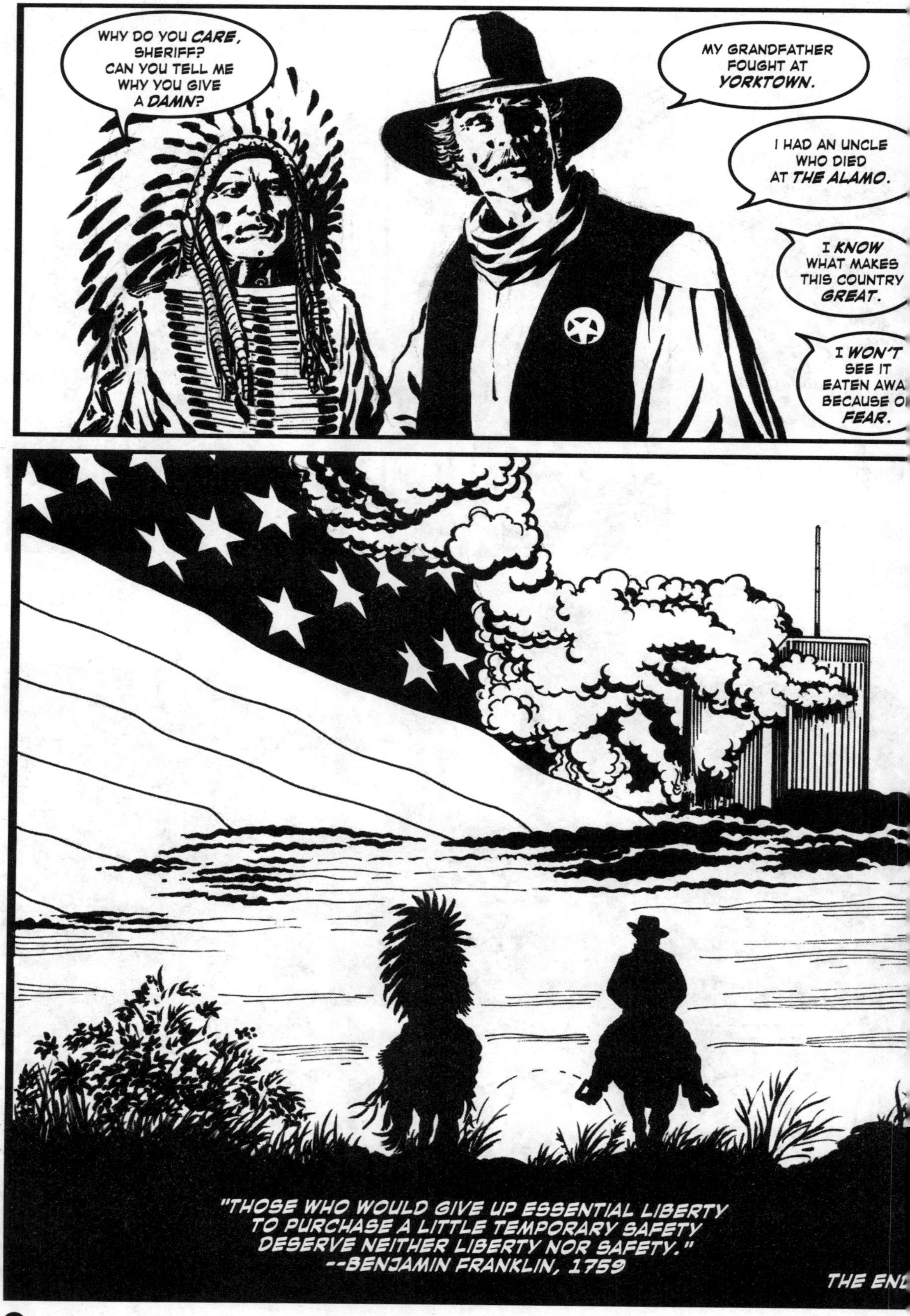
WHY DO YOU *CARE*, SHERIFF? CAN YOU TELL ME WHY YOU GIVE A *DAMN*?
MY GRANDFATHER FOUGHT AT *YORKTOWN*.
I HAD AN UNCLE WHO DIED AT *THE ALAMO*.
I *KNOW* WHAT MAKES THIS COUNTRY *GREAT*.
I *WON'T* SEE IT EATEN AWA BECAUSE O *FEAR*.
"THOSE WHO WOULD GIVE UP ESSENTIAL LIBERTY TO PURCHASE A LITTLE TEMPORARY SAFETY DESERVE NEITHER LIBERTY NOR SAFETY."
--BENJAMIN FRANKLIN, 1759
THE EN

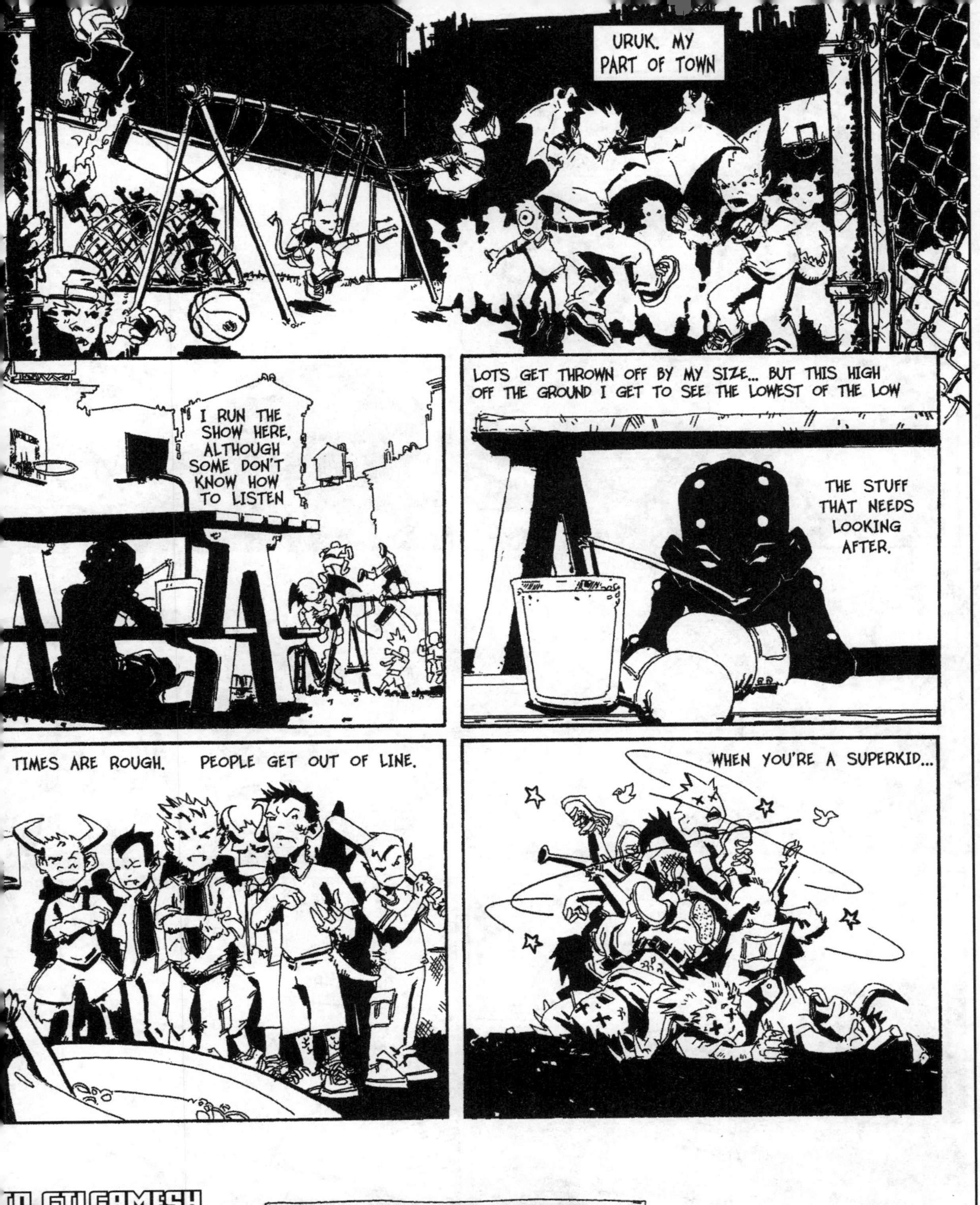
URUK. MY PART OF TOWN
I RUN THE SHOW HERE, ALTHOUGH SOME DON'T KNOW HOW TO LISTEN
LOTS GET THROWN OFF BY MY SIZE... BUT THIS HIGH OFF THE GROUND I GET TO SEE THE LOWEST OF THE LOW
THE STUFF THAT NEEDS LOOKING AFTER.
TIMES ARE ROUGH.
PEOPLE GET OUT OF LINE.
WHEN YOU'RE A SUPERKID...
ID GILGAMESH
IN
"COOKIES & MILK"
ring BEAR-BEAR McMAIMSALOT
and the URUK TOUGHS)
By Ivan Brandon
and Andy MacDonald
www.ivanbrandon.com
www.cactusfusion.com
SOMETIMES YOU GOTTA BUST SOME HEADS.

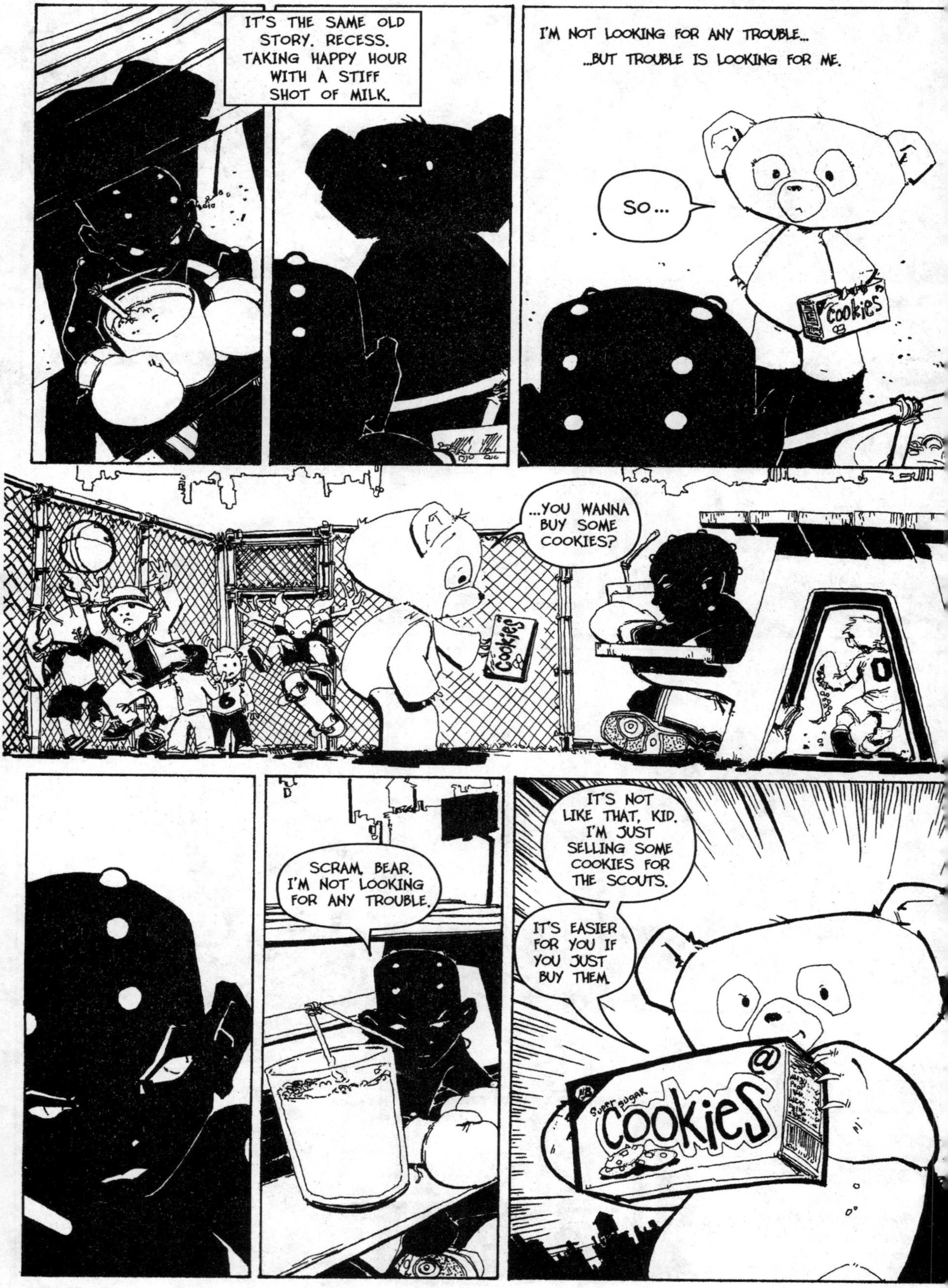

IT'S THE SAME OLD STORY. RECESS. TAKING HAPPY HOUR WITH A STIFF SHOT OF MILK.
I'M NOT LOOKING FOR ANY TROUBLE...
...BUT TROUBLE IS LOOKING FOR ME.
SO...
COOKIES
...YOU WANNA BUY SOME COOKIES?
COOKIES
SCRAM, BEAR. I'M NOT LOOKING FOR ANY TROUBLE.
IT'S NOT LIKE THAT, KID. I'M JUST SELLING SOME COOKIES FOR THE SCOUTS.
IT'S EASIER FOR YOU IF YOU JUST BUY THEM.
SUPER SUGAR COOKIES

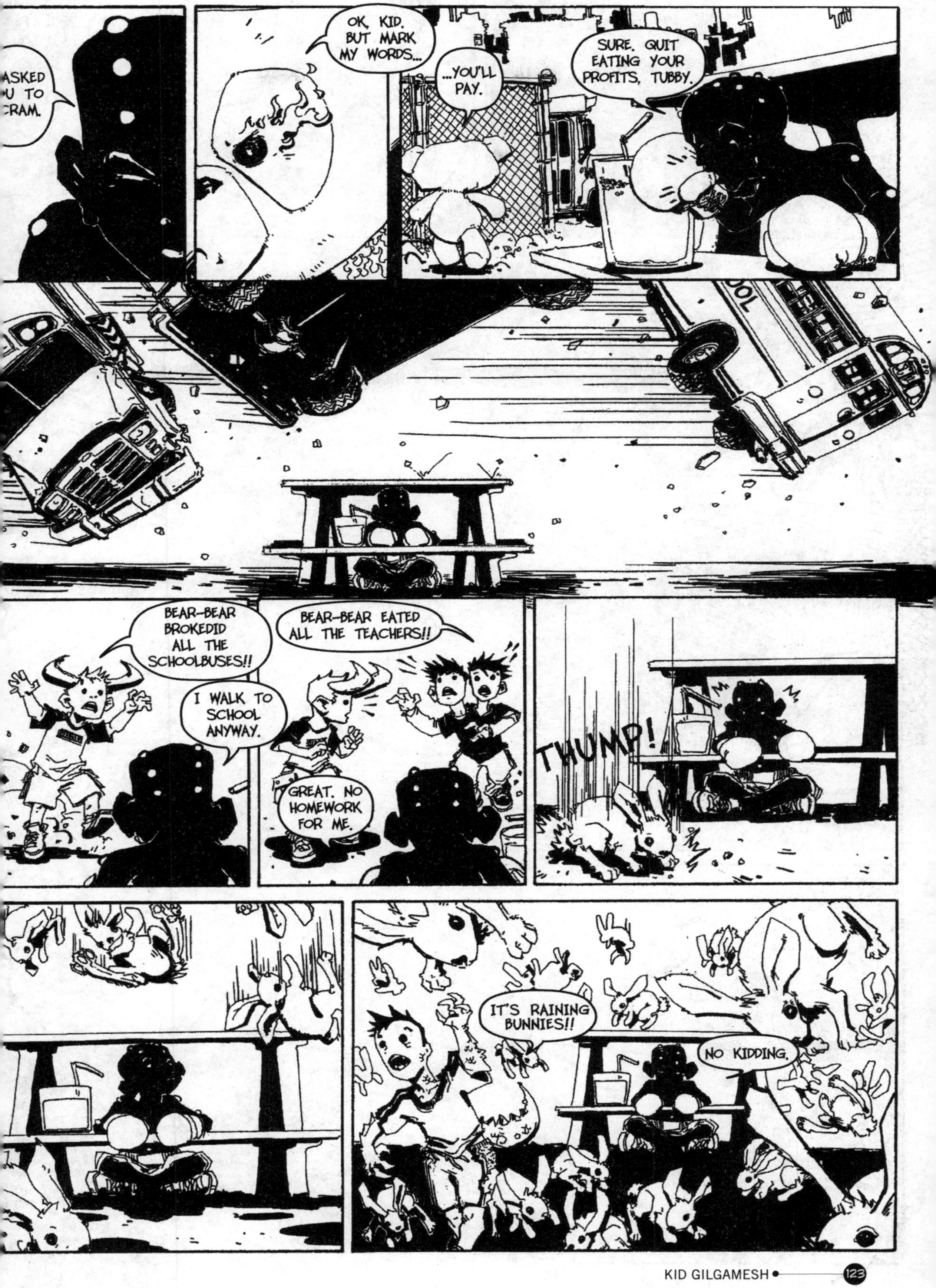
ASKED
U TO
CRAM.
OK, KID. BUT MARK MY WORDS...
...YOU'LL PAY.
SURE. QUIT EATING YOUR PROFITS, TUBBY.
SCHOOL
BEAR-BEAR BROKEDID ALL THE SCHOOLBUSES!!
I WALK TO SCHOOL ANYWAY.
BEAR-BEAR EATED ALL THE TEACHERS!!
GREAT. NO HOMEWORK FOR ME.
THUMP!
IT'S RAINING BUNNIES!!
NO KIDDING.

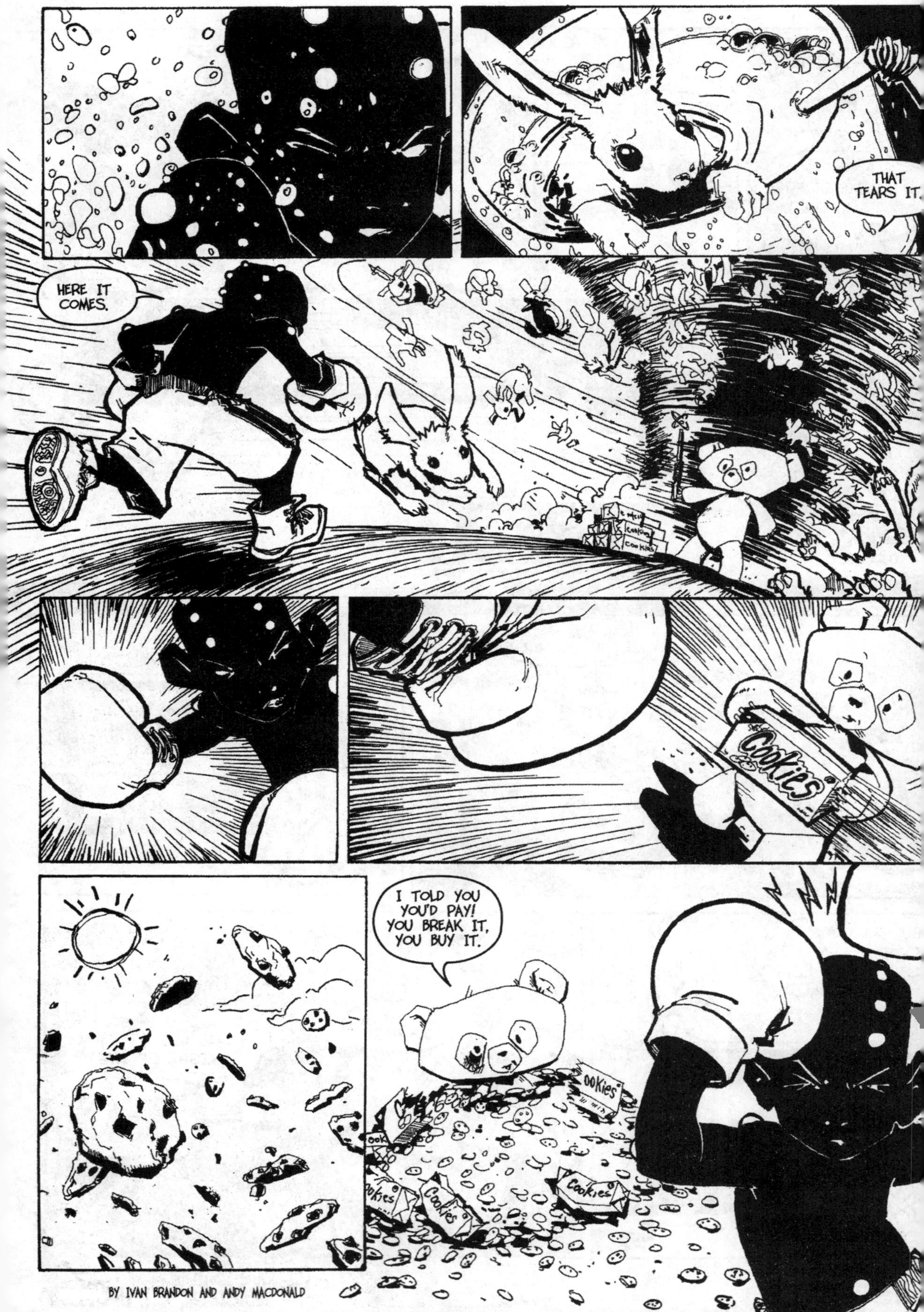
THAT TEARS IT.
HERE IT COMES.
Cookies
I TOLD YOU YOU'D PAY! YOU BREAK IT, YOU BUY IT.

BY IVAN BRANDON AND ANDY MACDONALD

Amelia Rules! "Why the Werefish became Extinct!"

©by Jimmy Gownley 2003

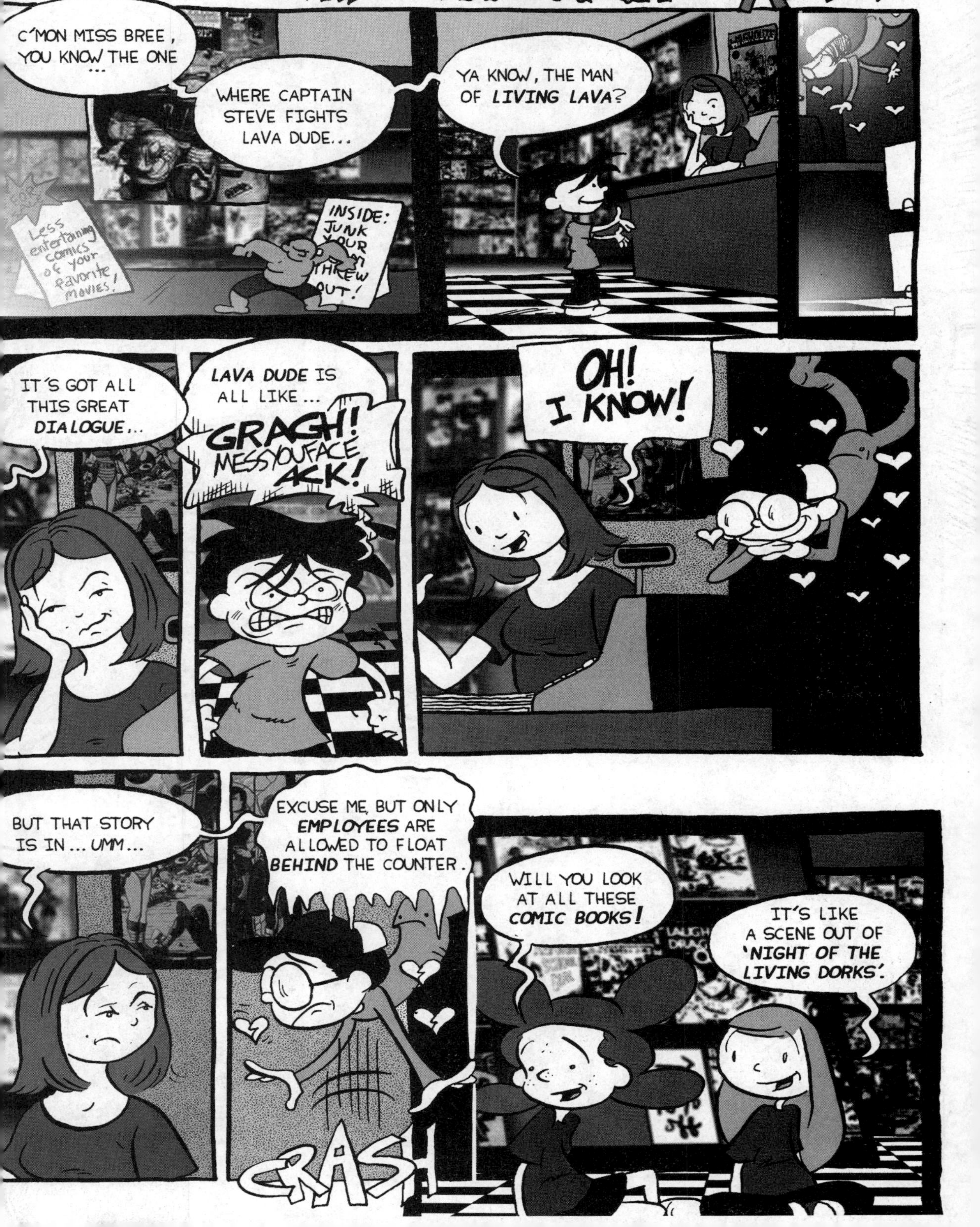
C'MON MISS BREE, YOU KNOW THE ONE ...
WHERE CAPTAIN STEVE FIGHTS LAVA DUDE...
YA KNOW, THE MAN OF LIVING LAVA?
FOR SALE
Less entertaining comics of your favorite movies!
INSIDE: JUNK YOUR MOM THREW OUT!
IT'S GOT ALL THIS GREAT DIALOGUE...
LAVA DUDE IS ALL LIKE...
GRAGH! MESSYOUFACE ACK!
OH! I KNOW!
BUT THAT STORY IS IN... UMM...
EXCUSE ME, BUT ONLY EMPLOYEES ARE ALLOWED TO FLOAT BEHIND THE COUNTER.
WILL YOU LOOK AT ALL THESE COMIC BOOKS!
IT'S LIKE A SCENE OUT OF 'NIGHT OF THE LIVING DORKS'.
CRASH

HEE HEE HEE HEE HEE HEE HEE HEE HEE HEE HEE HEE HEE HEE HEE HEE

HE*LLOOoo*?

may i **HELP** you?

NO THANK YOU.

WE'RE JUST FINE.

O*KAY*... umm... see... **GEN**erally? we don't let our customers (like) lay *AROUND*? y'know... on the *FLOOR*?

SO... if you could (like)...

OH SORRY IT'S JUST THAT WE'RE KINDA *ALREADY* CONSIDERED NERDS...

AND TO BE SEEN, Y'KNOW, ACTUALLY *IN* A COMIC STORE...

WELL WHO *COULD* SURVIVE *THAT* KIND OF PUBLICITY?

AC*tually*? i (like) *TOTALLY* get that?

let me know? (like) if you *NEED* anything?

ACES.

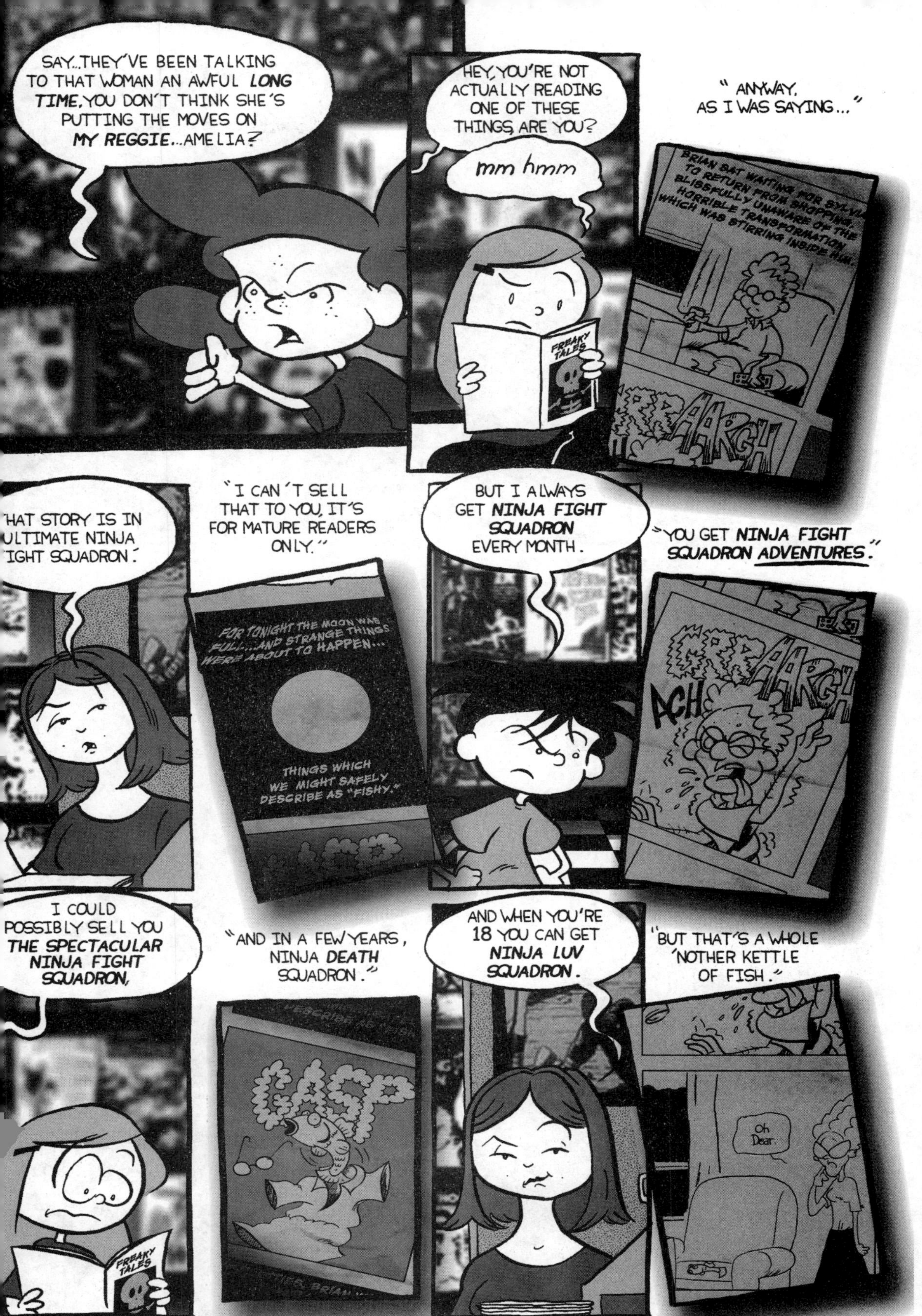
SAY...THEY'VE BEEN TALKING TO THAT WOMAN AN AWFUL LONG TIME. YOU DON'T THINK SHE'S PUTTING THE MOVES ON MY REGGIE...AMELIA?
HEY, YOU'RE NOT ACTUALLY READING ONE OF THESE THINGS, ARE YOU?
mm hmm
FREAKY TALES
" ANYWAY, AS I WAS SAYING..."
BRIAN SAT WAITING FOR SYLVIA TO RETURN FROM SHOPPING, BLISSFULLY UNAWARE OF THE HORRIBLE TRANSFORMATION WHICH WAS STIRRING INSIDE HIM.
GRRAARGH
HAT STORY IS IN ULTIMATE NINJA IGHT SQUADRON.
"I CAN'T SELL THAT TO YOU, IT'S FOR MATURE READERS ONLY."
FOR TONIGHT THE MOON WAS FULL...AND STRANGE THINGS WERE ABOUT TO HAPPEN...
THINGS WHICH WE MIGHT SAFELY DESCRIBE AS "FISHY."
BUT I ALWAYS GET NINJA FIGHT SQUADRON EVERY MONTH.
"YOU GET NINJA FIGHT SQUADRON ADVENTURES."
GRRAARGH
ACH
I COULD POSSIBLY SELL YOU THE SPECTACULAR NINJA FIGHT SQUADRON,
FREAKY TALES
"AND IN A FEW YEARS, NINJA DEATH SQUADRON."
GASP
AND WHEN YOU'RE 18 YOU CAN GET NINJA LUV SQUADRON.
"BUT THAT'S A WHOLE 'NOTHER KETTLE OF FISH."
Oh Dear.

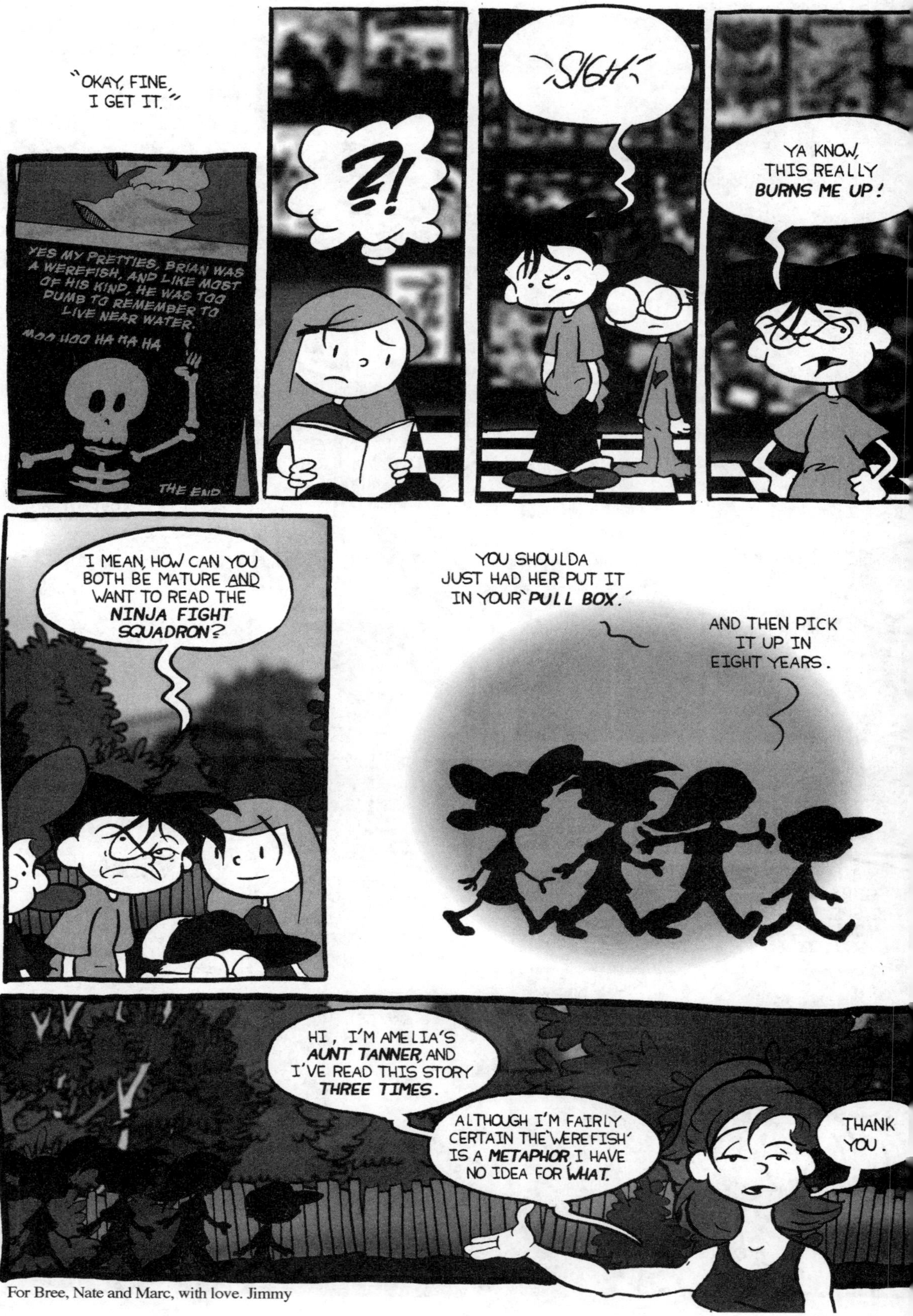
"OKAY, FINE, I GET IT."
YES MY PRETTIES, BRIAN WAS A WEREFISH, AND LIKE MOST OF HIS KIND, HE WAS TOO DUMB TO REMEMBER TO LIVE NEAR WATER.
MOO HOO HA HA HA
THE END
?!
SIGH
YA KNOW, THIS REALLY BURNS ME UP!
I MEAN, HOW CAN YOU BOTH BE MATURE AND WANT TO READ THE NINJA FIGHT SQUADRON?
YOU SHOULDA JUST HAD HER PUT IT IN YOUR 'PULL BOX.'
AND THEN PICK IT UP IN EIGHT YEARS.
HI, I'M AMELIA'S AUNT TANNER, AND I'VE READ THIS STORY THREE TIMES.
ALTHOUGH I'M FAIRLY CERTAIN THE 'WEREFISH' IS A METAPHOR, I HAVE NO IDEA FOR WHAT.
THANK YOU.

For Bree, Nate and Marc, with love. Jimmy

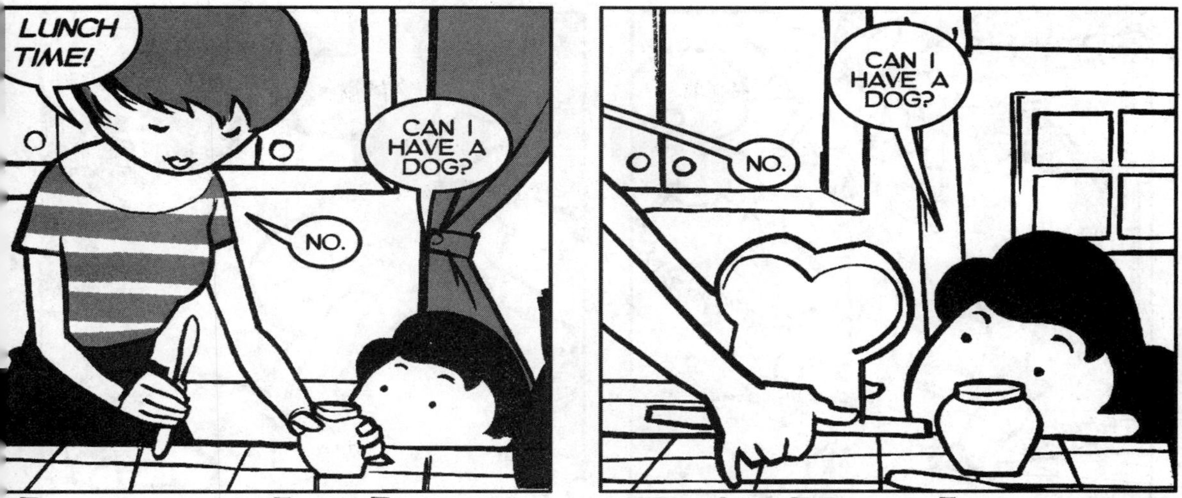
LUNCH TIME!
CAN I HAVE A DOG?
NO.
CAN I HAVE A DOG?
NO.

Jeopardy Jones in Fair Trade

story by kathryn kuder & stuart immonen

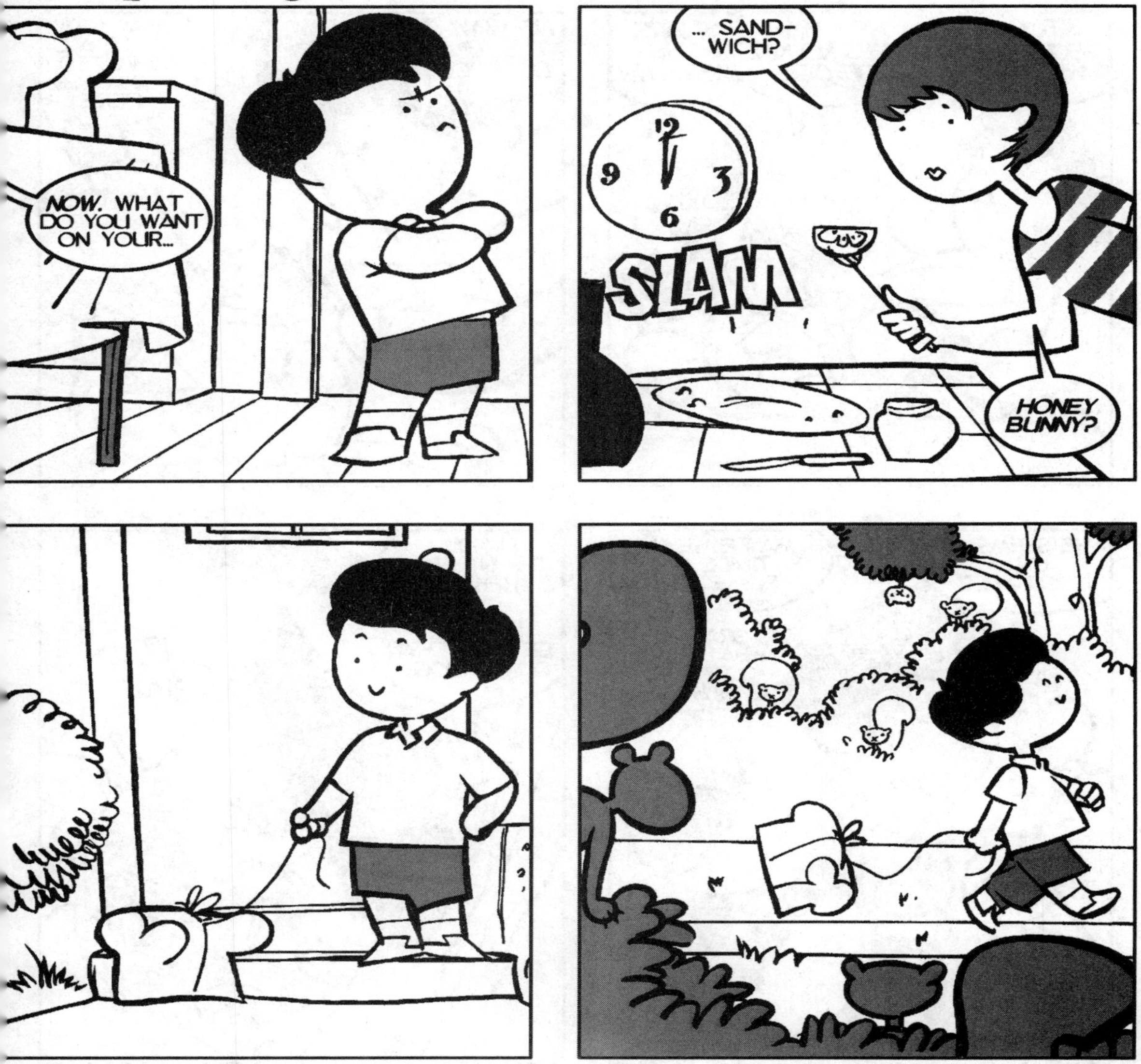
NOW. WHAT DO YOU WANT ON YOUR...
... SAND-WICH?
12
9
3
6
SLAM
HONEY BUNNY?

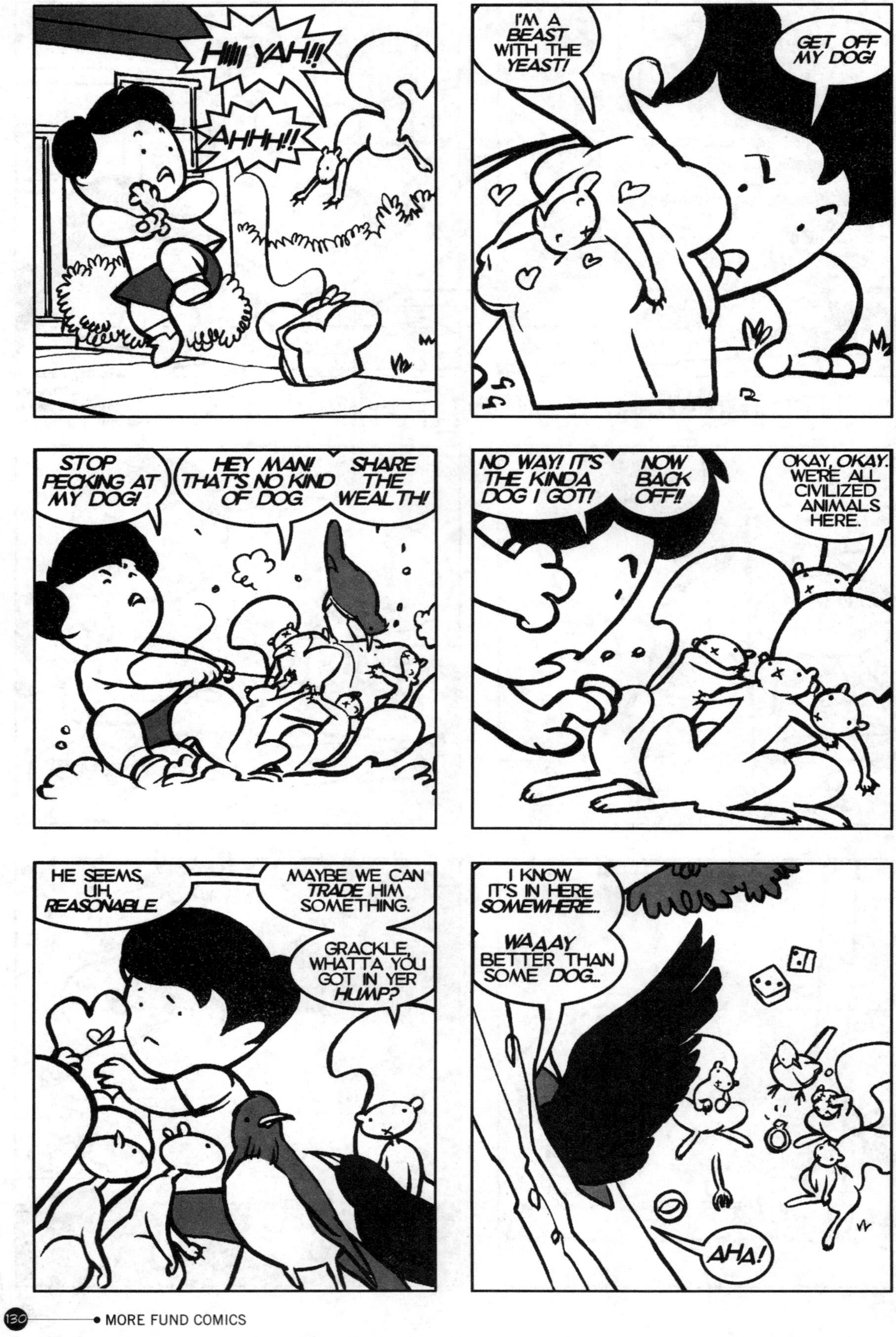
HIIII YAH!!
AHHH!!
I'M A BEAST WITH THE YEAST!
GET OFF MY DOG!
STOP PECKING AT MY DOG!
HEY MAN! THAT'S NO KIND OF DOG.
SHARE THE WEALTH!
NO WAY! IT'S THE KINDA DOG I GOT!
NOW BACK OFF!!
OKAY, OKAY. WE'RE ALL CIVILIZED ANIMALS HERE.
HE SEEMS, UH, REASONABLE.
MAYBE WE CAN TRADE HIM SOMETHING.
GRACKLE, WHATTA YOU GOT IN YER HUMP?
I KNOW IT'S IN HERE SOMEWHERE...
WAAAY BETTER THAN SOME DOG...
AHA!

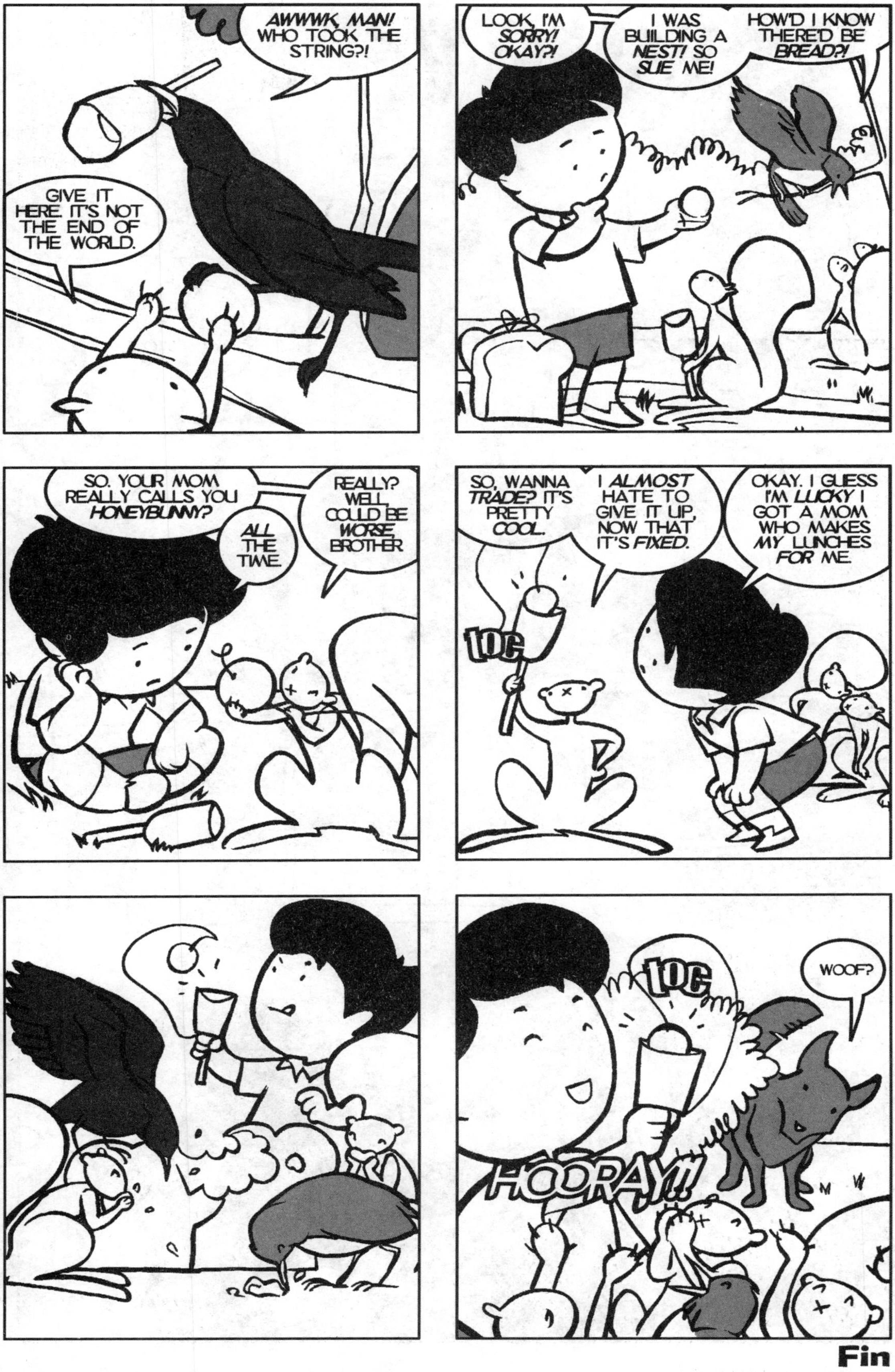
AWWWK, MAN! WHO TOOK THE STRING?!
GIVE IT HERE. IT'S NOT THE END OF THE WORLD.
LOOK, I'M SORRY! OKAY?!
I WAS BUILDING A NEST! SO SUE ME!
HOW'D I KNOW THERE'D BE BREAD?!
SO. YOUR MOM REALLY CALLS YOU HONEYBUNNY?
ALL THE TIME.
REALLY? WELL COULD BE WORSE, BROTHER.
SO, WANNA TRADE? IT'S PRETTY COOL.
I ALMOST HATE TO GIVE IT UP, NOW THAT IT'S FIXED.
OKAY. I GUESS I'M LUCKY I GOT A MOM WHO MAKES MY LUNCHES FOR ME.
toc
toc
WOOF?
HOORAY!!

Fin

SQUEEZE ME

A GBS PRESENTATION
by DON BETHMAN

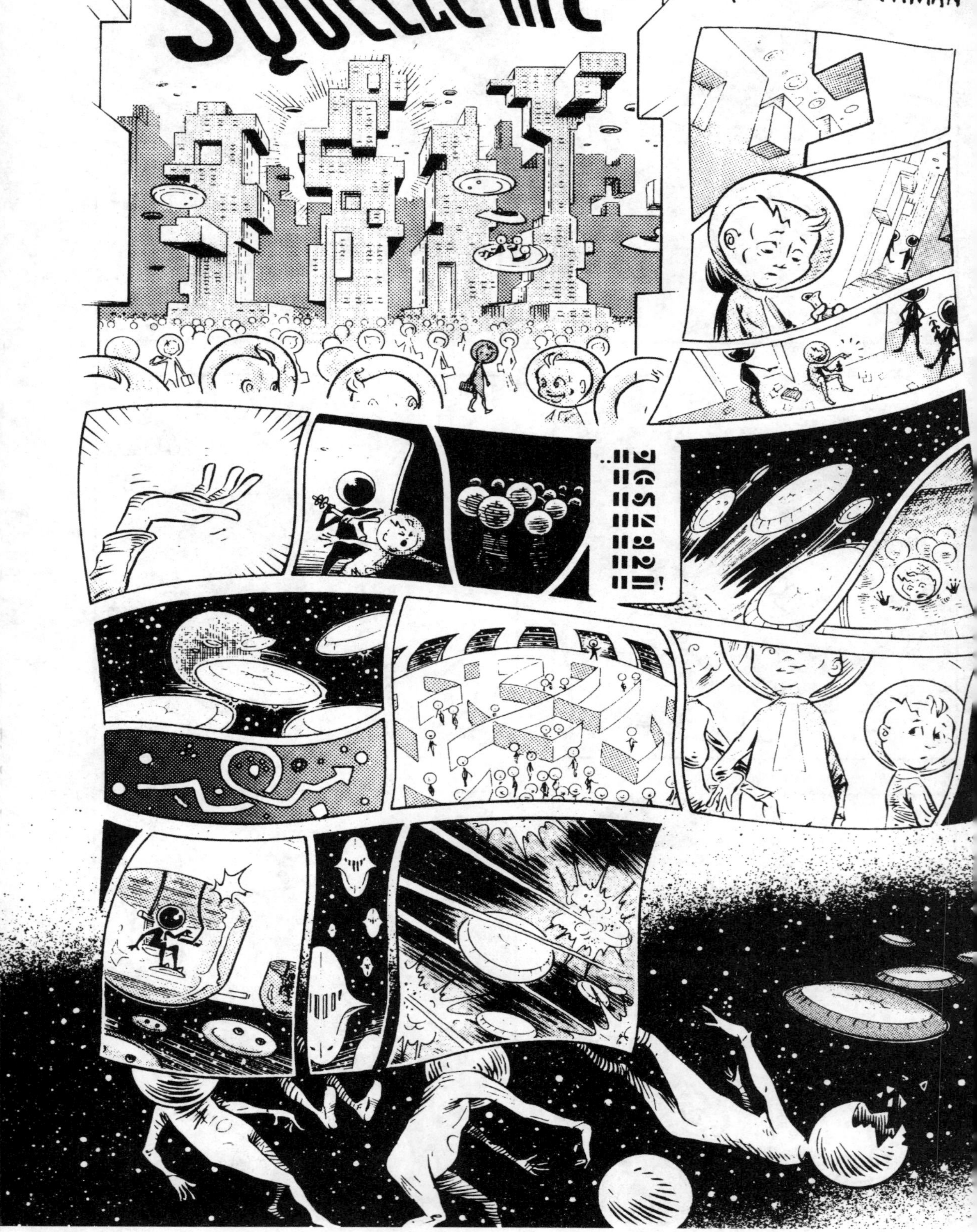

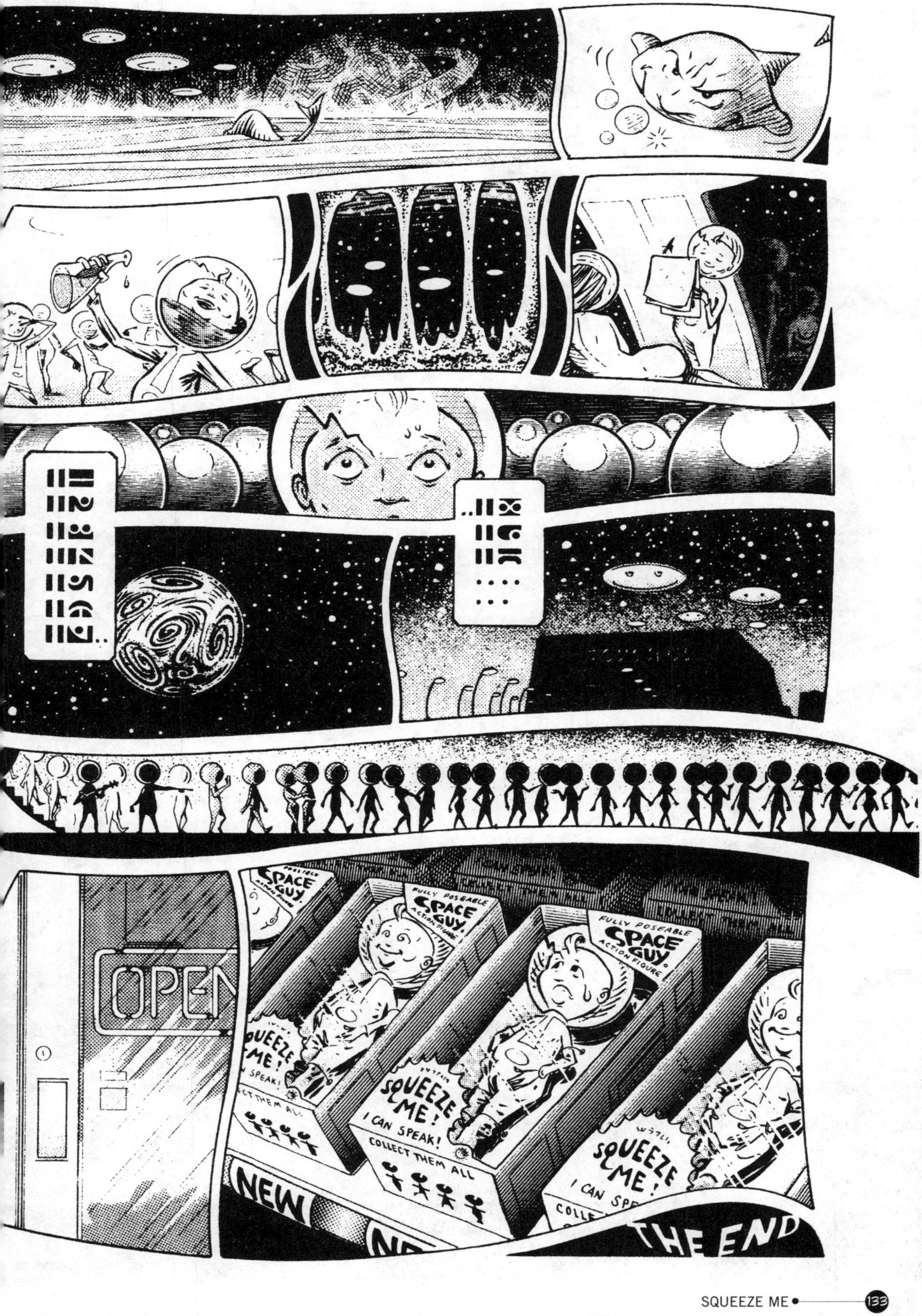
OPEN
FULLY POSEABLE
SPACE GUY
ACTION FIGURE
SQUEEZE ME!
I CAN SPEAK!
COLLECT THEM ALL
NEW
THE END

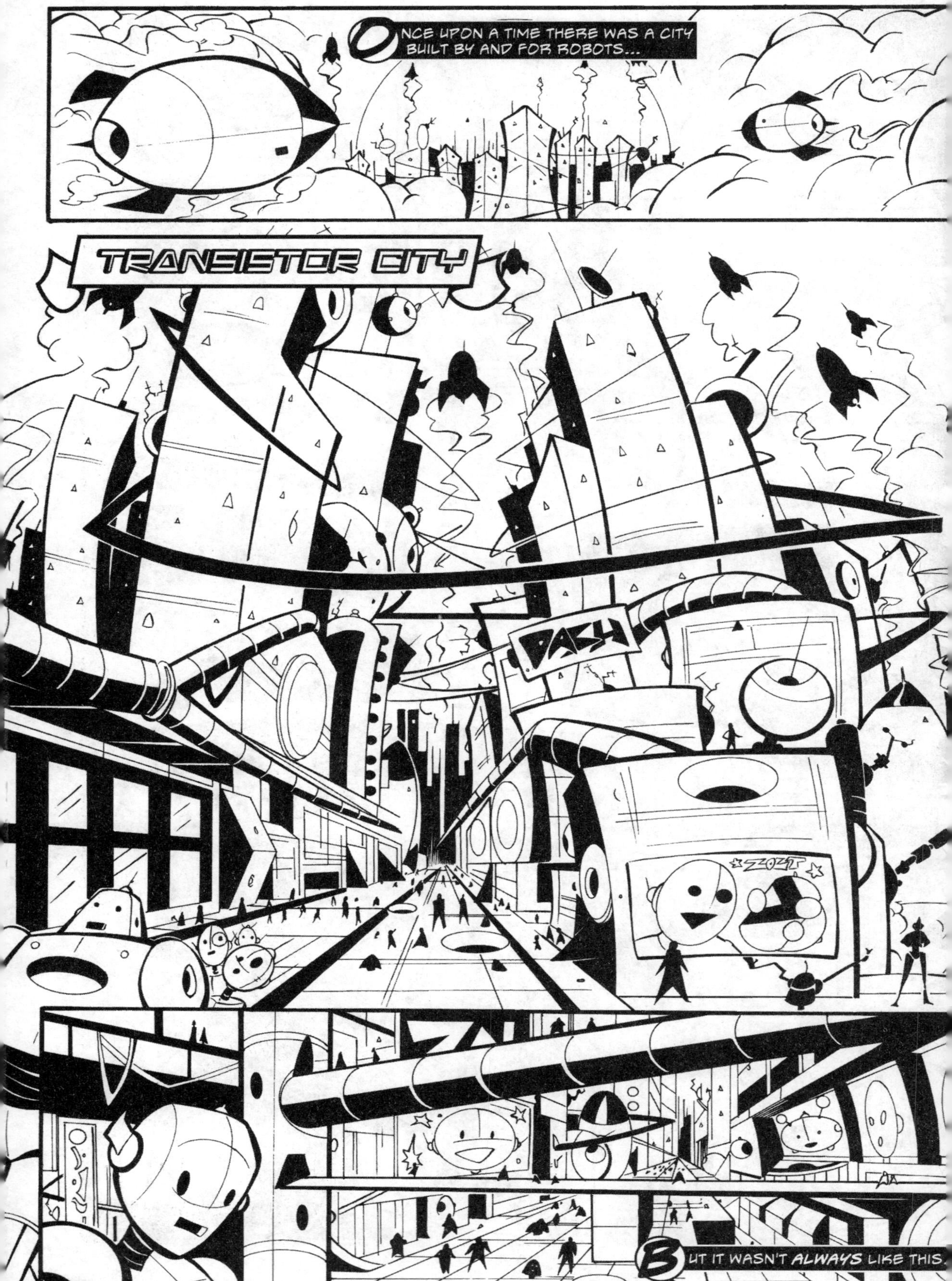
ONCE UPON A TIME THERE WAS A CITY BUILT BY AND FOR ROBOTS...
TRANSISTOR CITY
DASH
ZOZT
BUT IT WASN'T ALWAYS LIKE THIS.

ROBOTS *USED* TO LIVE AROUND HUMANS.

UNTIL THERE CAME A POINT WHERE THEY WERE NOTHING MORE THAN *TOOLS* IN MAN'S WAR --

-- AND NOT SOUGHT AS *INDIVIDUALS* WITH THEIR *OWN* IDEAS.

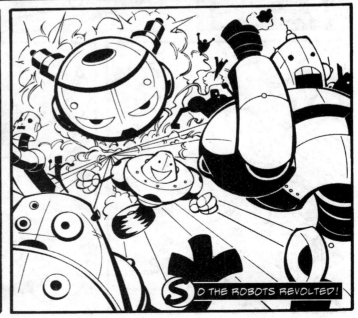

SO THE ROBOTS REVOLTED!

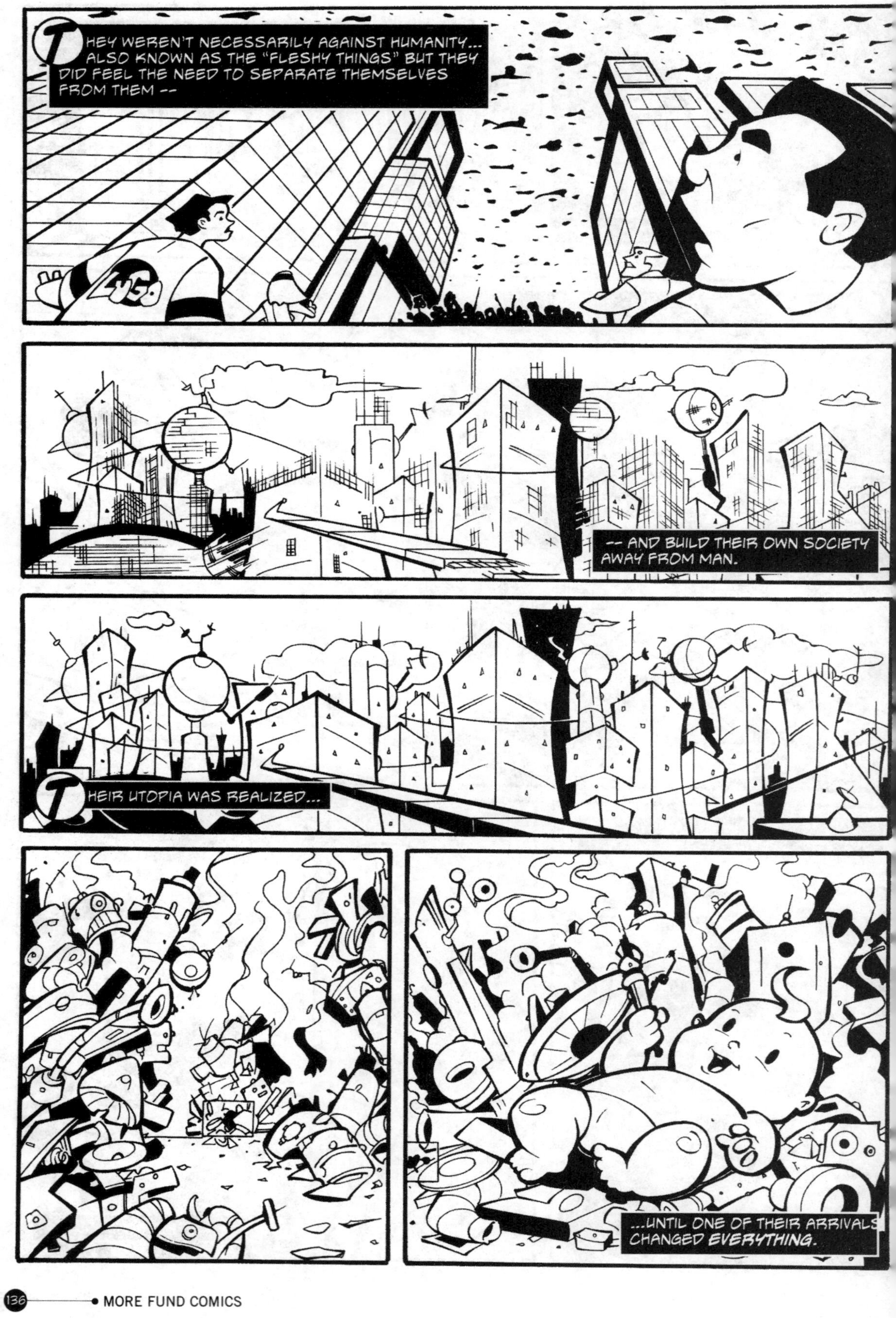
THEY WEREN'T NECESSARILY AGAINST HUMANITY... ALSO KNOWN AS THE "FLESHY THINGS" BUT THEY DID FEEL THE NEED TO SEPARATE THEMSELVES FROM THEM --
-- AND BUILD THEIR OWN SOCIETY AWAY FROM MAN.
THEIR UTOPIA WAS REALIZED...
...UNTIL ONE OF THEIR ARRIVALS CHANGED *EVERYTHING*.

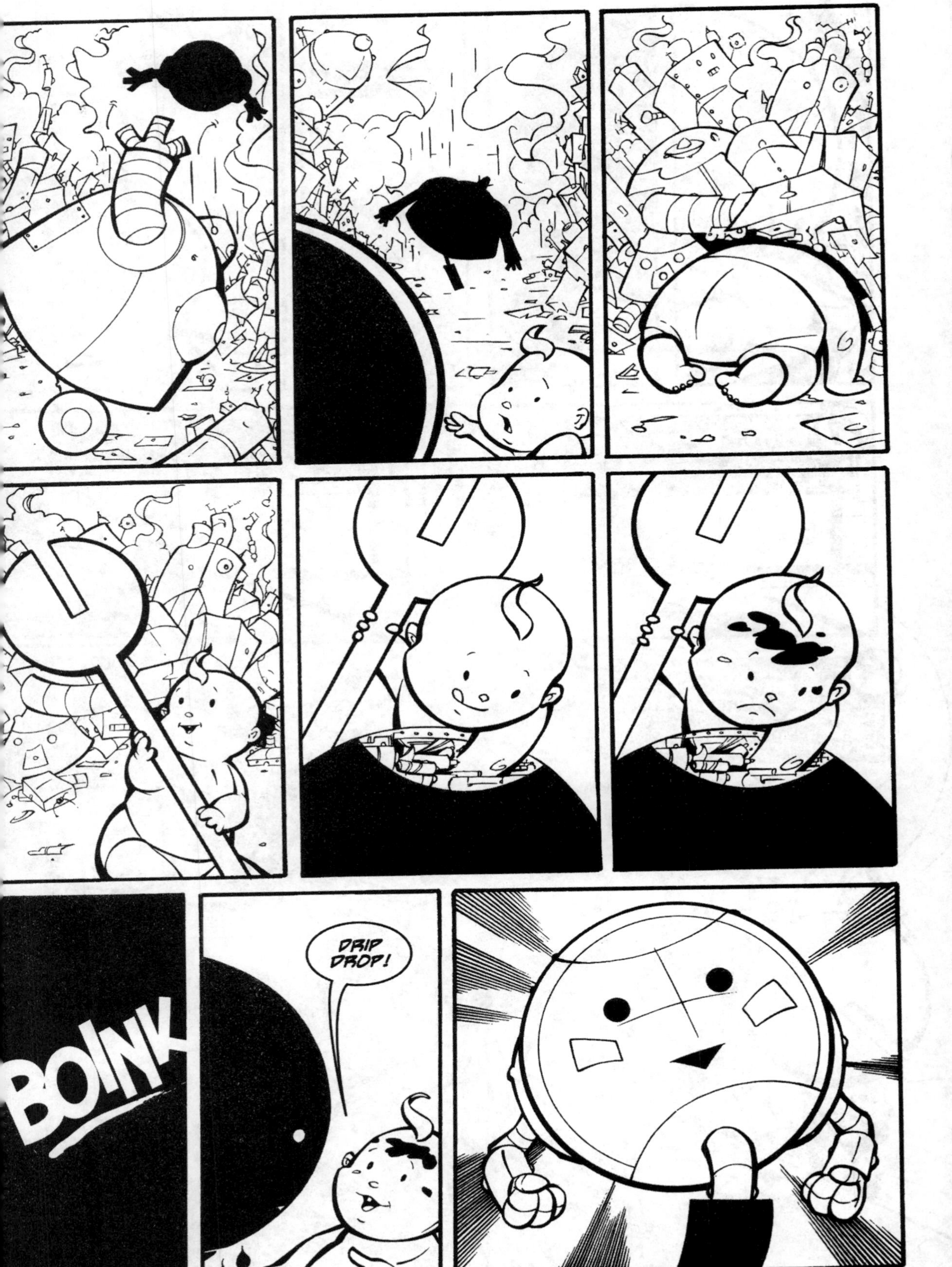
BOINK
DRIP DROP!

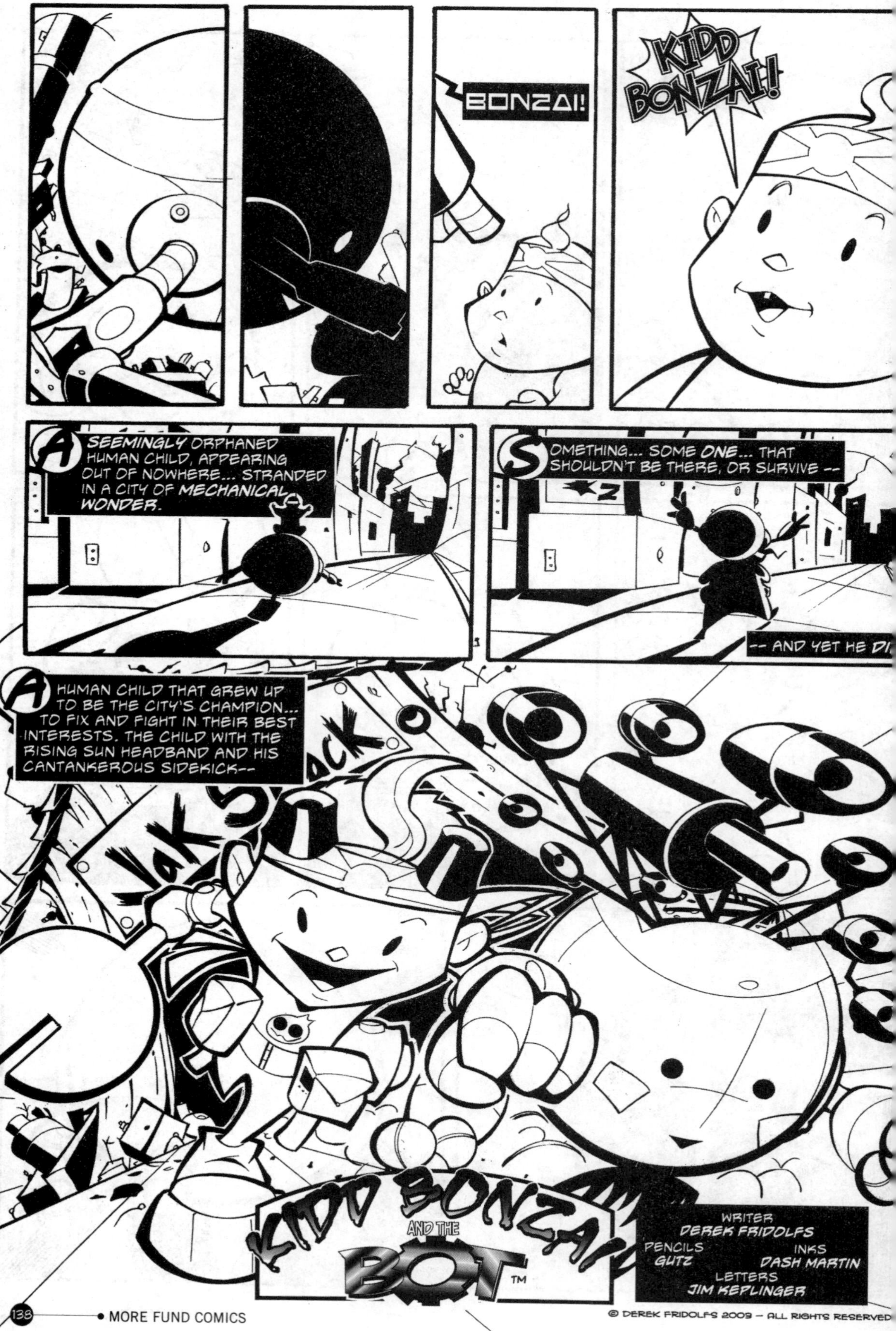
BONZAI!
KIDD BONZAI!
A SEEMINGLY ORPHANED HUMAN CHILD, APPEARING OUT OF NOWHERE... STRANDED IN A CITY OF MECHANICAL WONDER.
SOMETHING... SOME ONE... THAT SHOULDN'T BE THERE, OR SURVIVE --
-- AND YET HE DI
A HUMAN CHILD THAT GREW UP TO BE THE CITY'S CHAMPION... TO FIX AND FIGHT IN THEIR BEST INTERESTS. THE CHILD WITH THE RISING SUN HEADBAND AND HIS CANTANKEROUS SIDEKICK--
KIDD BONZAI! AND THE BOT™
WRITER DEREK FRIDOLFS
PENCILS GUTZ
INKS DASH MARTIN
LETTERS JIM KEPLINGER

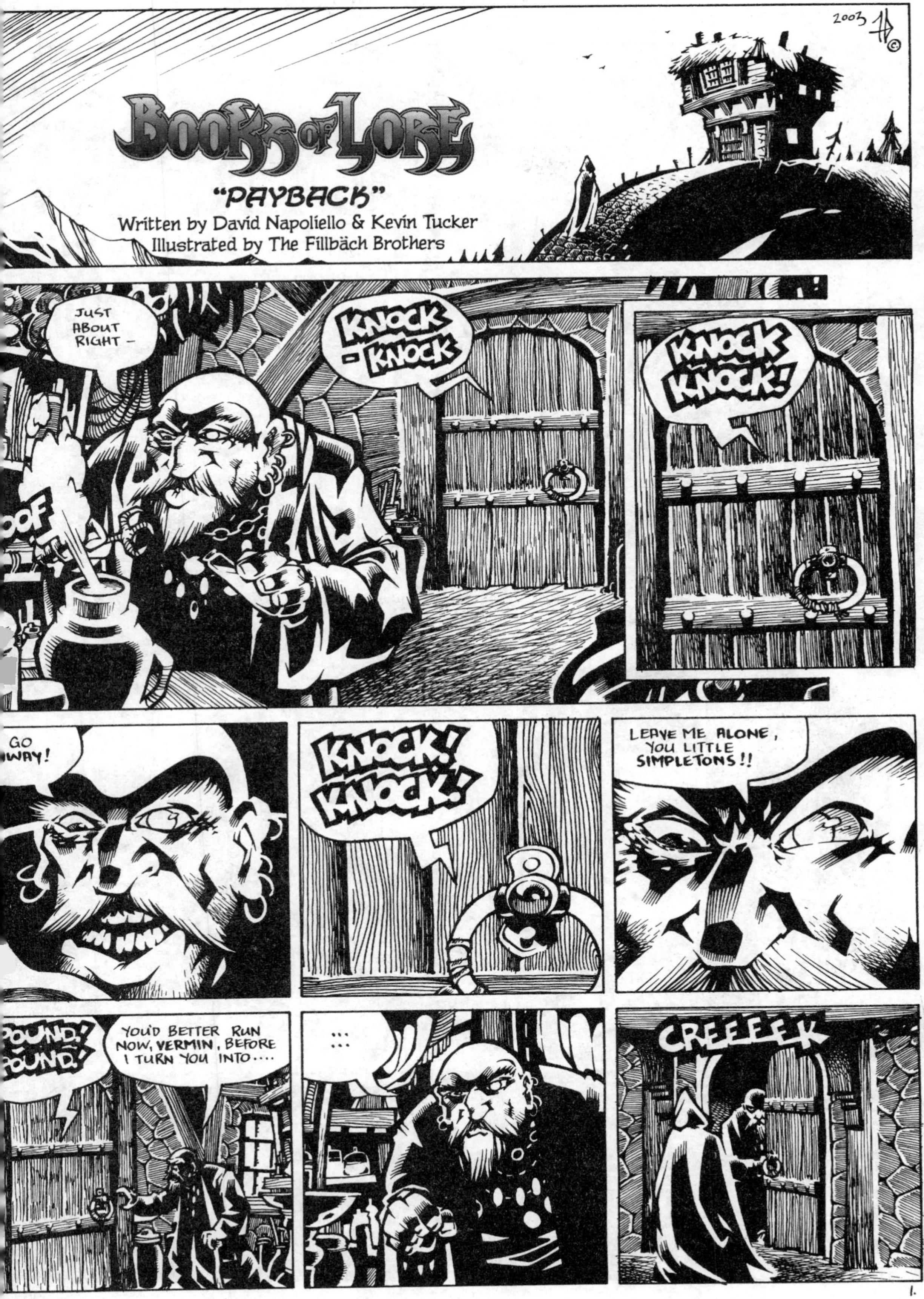
2003
BOOKS OF LORE
"PAYBACK"
Written by David Napoliello & Kevin Tucker
Illustrated by The Fillbäch Brothers
JUST ABOUT RIGHT –
OOF
KNOCK - KNOCK
KNOCK KNOCK!
GO WAY!
KNOCK! KNOCK!
LEAVE ME ALONE, YOU LITTLE SIMPLETONS!!
POUND! POUND!
YOU'D BETTER RUN NOW, VERMIN, BEFORE I TURN YOU INTO....
......
CREEEEK
1.

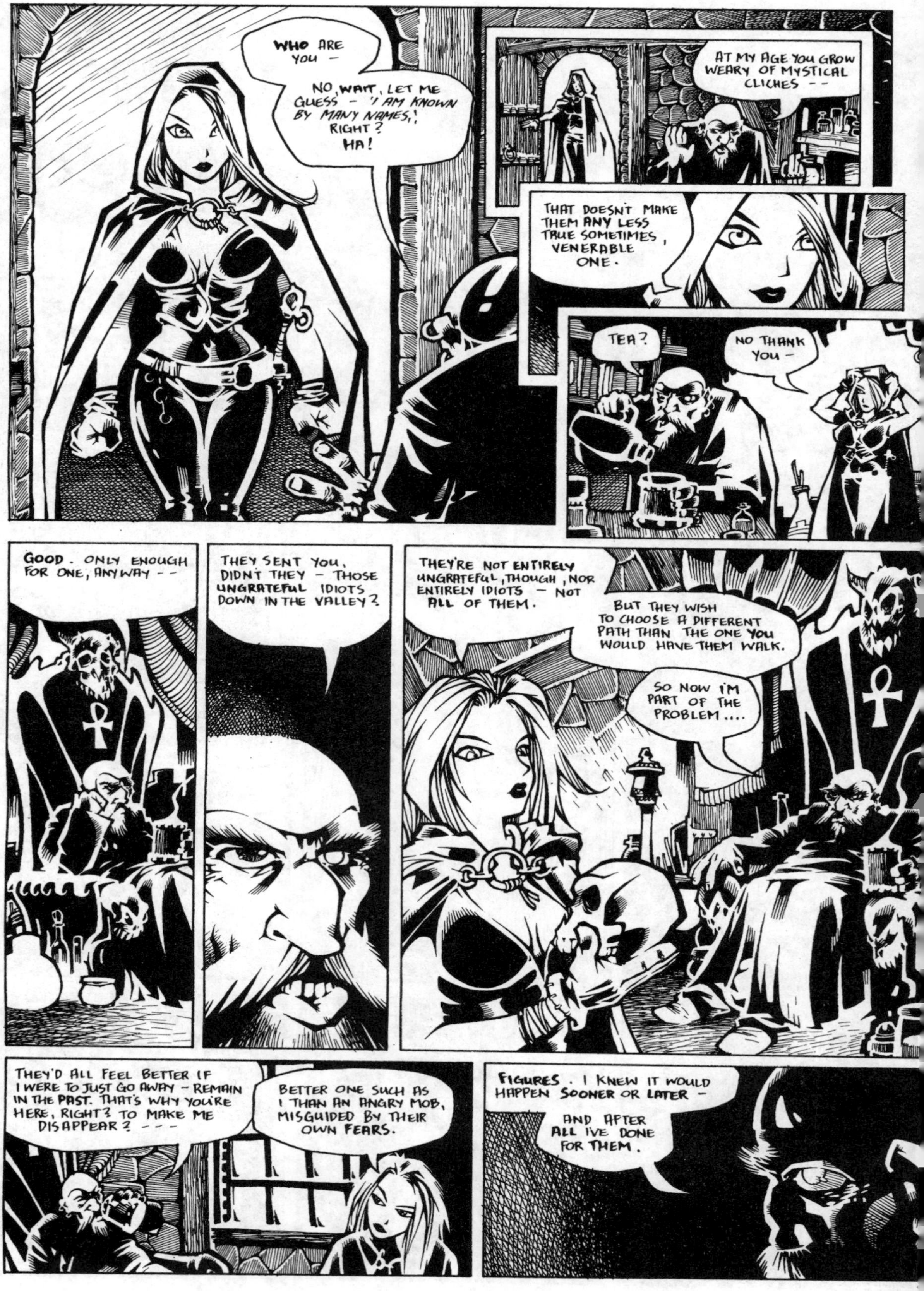
WHO ARE YOU –
NO, WAIT, LET ME GUESS – 'I AM KNOWN BY MANY NAMES,' RIGHT? HA!
AT MY AGE YOU GROW WEARY OF MYSTICAL CLICHES --
THAT DOESN'T MAKE THEM ANY LESS TRUE SOMETIMES, VENERABLE ONE.
TEA?
NO THANK YOU –
GOOD. ONLY ENOUGH FOR ONE, ANYWAY --
THEY SENT YOU, DIDN'T THEY – THOSE UNGRATEFUL IDIOTS DOWN IN THE VALLEY?
THEY'RE NOT ENTIRELY UNGRATEFUL, THOUGH, NOR ENTIRELY IDIOTS – NOT ALL OF THEM.
BUT THEY WISH TO CHOOSE A DIFFERENT PATH THAN THE ONE YOU WOULD HAVE THEM WALK.
SO NOW I'M PART OF THE PROBLEM....
THEY'D ALL FEEL BETTER IF I WERE TO JUST GO AWAY – REMAIN IN THE PAST. THAT'S WHY YOU'RE HERE, RIGHT? TO MAKE ME DISAPPEAR? ---
BETTER ONE SUCH AS I THAN AN ANGRY MOB, MISGUIDED BY THEIR OWN FEARS.
FIGURES. I KNEW IT WOULD HAPPEN SOONER OR LATER –
AND AFTER ALL I'VE DONE FOR THEM.

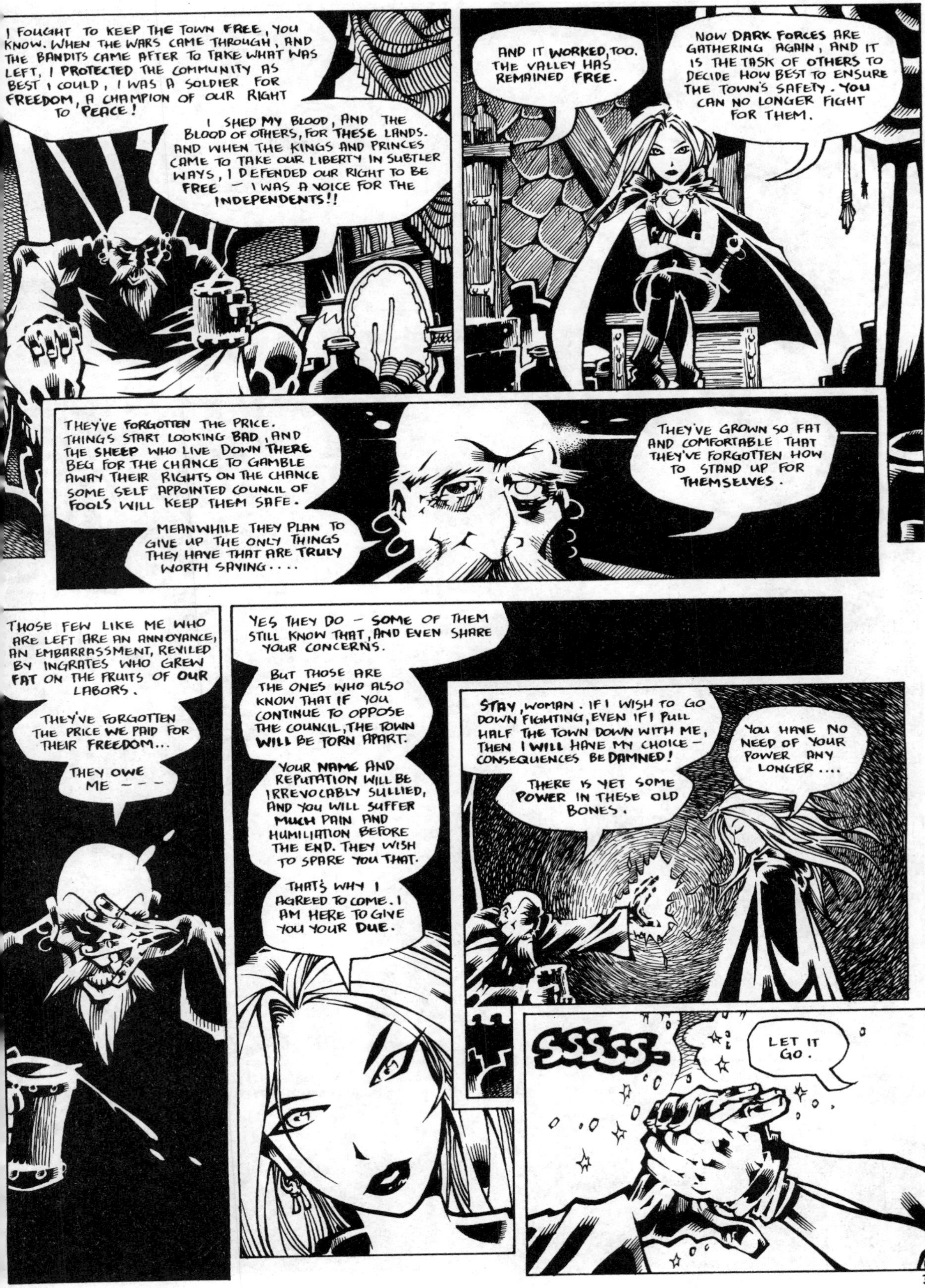
I FOUGHT TO KEEP THE TOWN FREE, YOU KNOW. WHEN THE WARS CAME THROUGH, AND THE BANDITS CAME AFTER TO TAKE WHAT WAS LEFT, I PROTECTED THE COMMUNITY AS BEST I COULD, I WAS A SOLDIER FOR FREEDOM, A CHAMPION OF OUR RIGHT TO PEACE!
I SHED MY BLOOD, AND THE BLOOD OF OTHERS, FOR THESE LANDS. AND WHEN THE KINGS AND PRINCES CAME TO TAKE OUR LIBERTY IN SUBTLER WAYS, I DEFENDED OUR RIGHT TO BE FREE — I WAS A VOICE FOR THE INDEPENDENTS!!
AND IT WORKED, TOO. THE VALLEY HAS REMAINED FREE.
NOW DARK FORCES ARE GATHERING AGAIN, AND IT IS THE TASK OF OTHERS TO DECIDE HOW BEST TO ENSURE THE TOWN'S SAFETY. YOU CAN NO LONGER FIGHT FOR THEM.
THEY'VE FORGOTTEN THE PRICE. THINGS START LOOKING BAD, AND THE SHEEP WHO LIVE DOWN THERE BEG FOR THE CHANCE TO GAMBLE AWAY THEIR RIGHTS ON THE CHANCE SOME SELF APPOINTED COUNCIL OF FOOLS WILL KEEP THEM SAFE.
MEANWHILE THEY PLAN TO GIVE UP THE ONLY THINGS THEY HAVE THAT ARE TRULY WORTH SAVING....
THEY'VE GROWN SO FAT AND COMFORTABLE THAT THEY'VE FORGOTTEN HOW TO STAND UP FOR THEMSELVES.
THOSE FEW LIKE ME WHO ARE LEFT ARE AN ANNOYANCE, AN EMBARRASSMENT, REVILED BY INGRATES WHO GREW FAT ON THE FRUITS OF OUR LABORS.
THEY'VE FORGOTTEN THE PRICE WE PAID FOR THEIR FREEDOM...
THEY OWE ME ---
YES THEY DO — SOME OF THEM STILL KNOW THAT, AND EVEN SHARE YOUR CONCERNS.
BUT THOSE ARE THE ONES WHO ALSO KNOW THAT IF YOU CONTINUE TO OPPOSE THE COUNCIL, THE TOWN WILL BE TORN APART.
YOUR NAME AND REPUTATION WILL BE IRREVOCABLY SULLIED, AND YOU WILL SUFFER MUCH PAIN AND HUMILIATION BEFORE THE END. THEY WISH TO SPARE YOU THAT.
THAT'S WHY I AGREED TO COME. I AM HERE TO GIVE YOU YOUR DUE.
STAY, WOMAN. IF I WISH TO GO DOWN FIGHTING, EVEN IF I PULL HALF THE TOWN DOWN WITH ME, THEN I WILL HAVE MY CHOICE — CONSEQUENCES BE DAMNED!
THERE IS YET SOME POWER IN THESE OLD BONES.
YOU HAVE NO NEED OF YOUR POWER ANY LONGER....
SSSSS-
LET IT GO.
3.

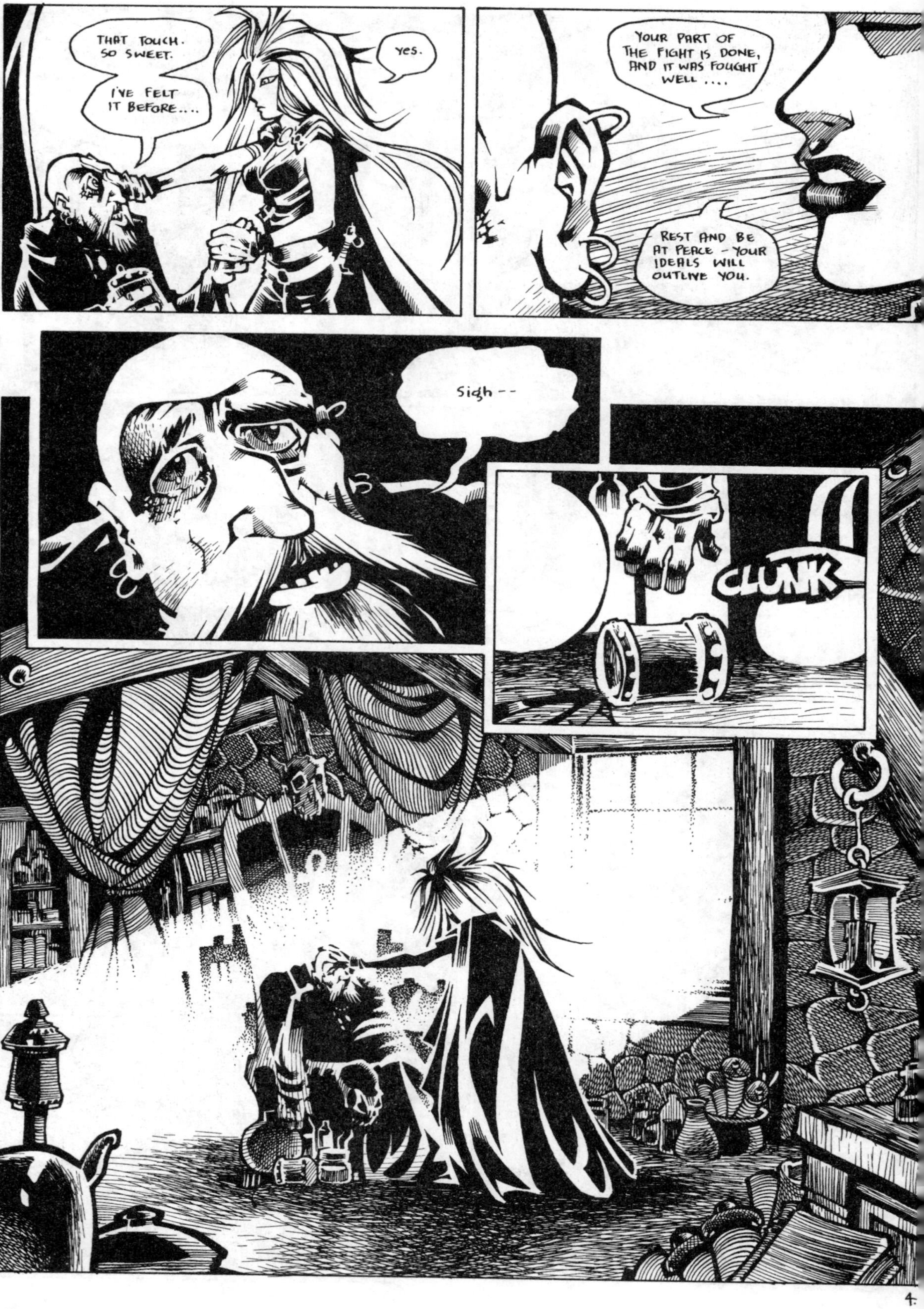
THAT TOUCH. SO SWEET.
I'VE FELT IT BEFORE....
YES.
YOUR PART OF THE FIGHT IS DONE, AND IT WAS FOUGHT WELL....
REST AND BE AT PEACE - YOUR IDEALS WILL OUTLIVE YOU.
Sigh--
CLUNK

4.

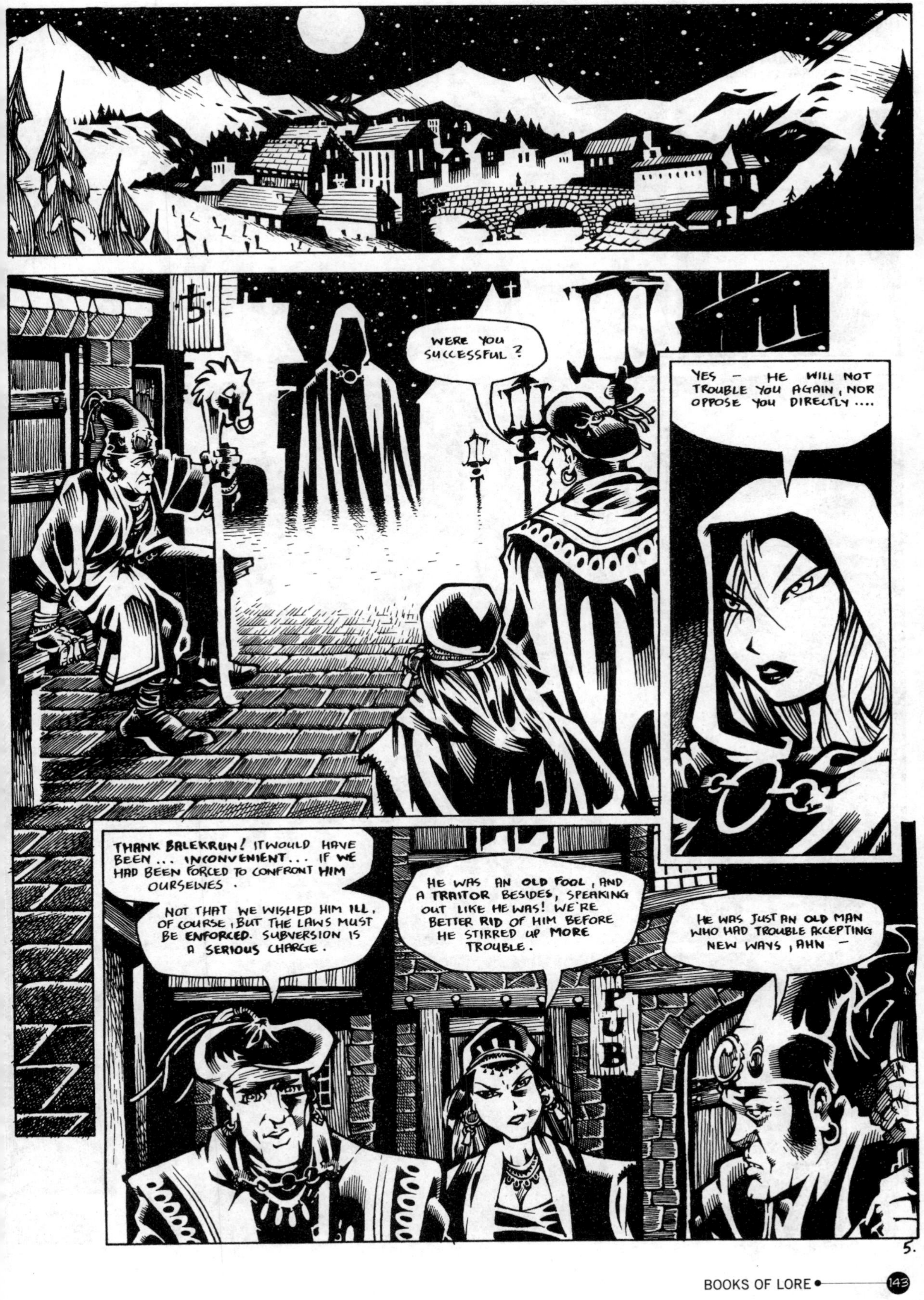
WERE YOU SUCCESSFUL?
YES — HE WILL NOT TROUBLE YOU AGAIN, NOR OPPOSE YOU DIRECTLY....
THANK BALEKRUN! IT WOULD HAVE BEEN... INCONVENIENT... IF WE HAD BEEN FORCED TO CONFRONT HIM OURSELVES.
NOT THAT WE WISHED HIM ILL, OF COURSE, BUT THE LAWS MUST BE ENFORCED. SUBVERSION IS A SERIOUS CHARGE.
HE WAS AN OLD FOOL, AND A TRAITOR BESIDES, SPEAKING OUT LIKE HE WAS! WE'RE BETTER RID OF HIM BEFORE HE STIRRED UP MORE TROUBLE.
HE WAS JUST AN OLD MAN WHO HAD TROUBLE ACCEPTING NEW WAYS, AHN —
PUB

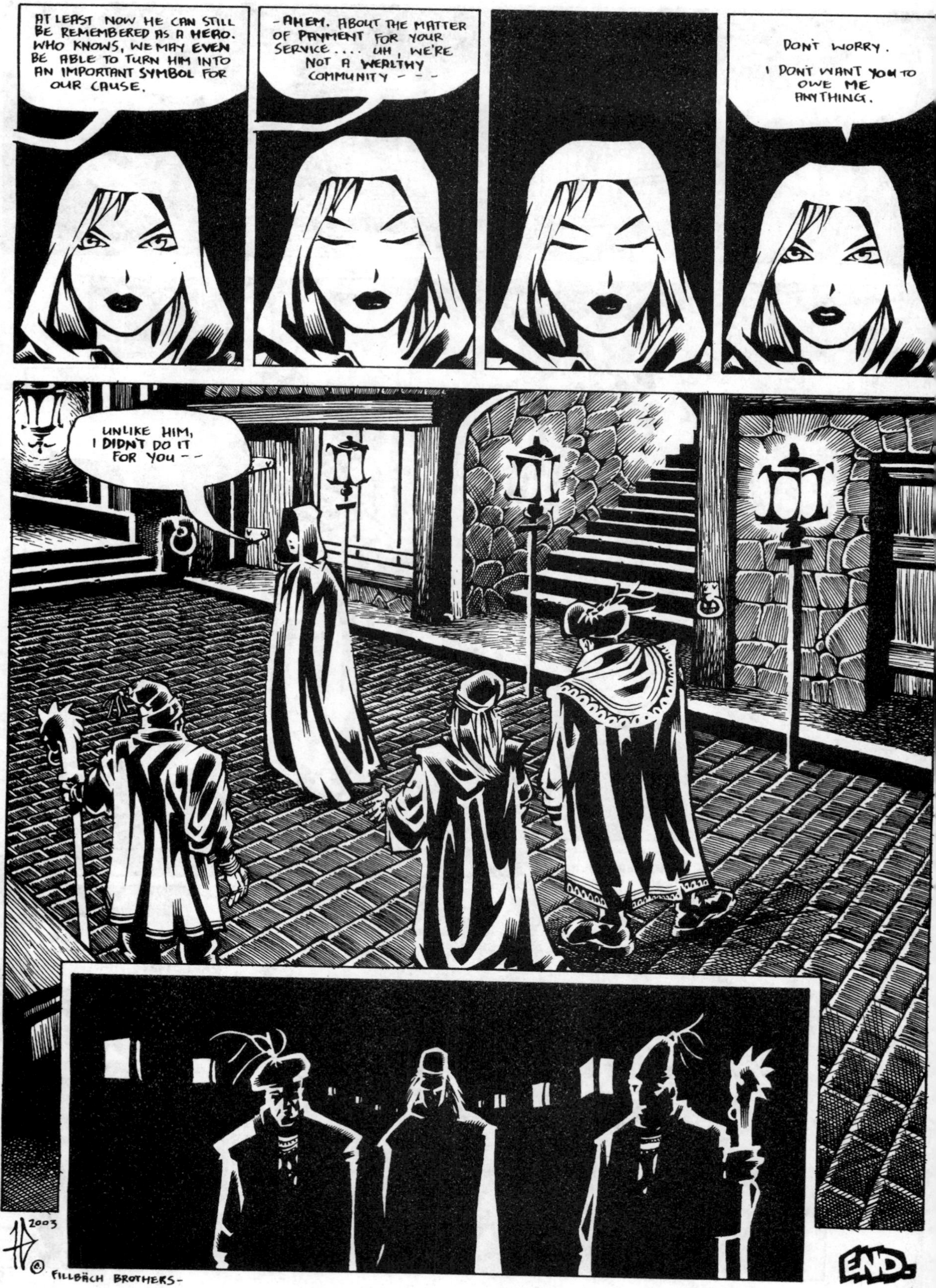
AT LEAST NOW HE CAN STILL BE REMEMBERED AS A HERO. WHO KNOWS, WE MAY EVEN BE ABLE TO TURN HIM INTO AN IMPORTANT SYMBOL FOR OUR CAUSE.
-AHEM. ABOUT THE MATTER OF PAYMENT FOR YOUR SERVICE.... UH, WE'RE NOT A WEALTHY COMMUNITY---
DON'T WORRY.
I DON'T WANT YOU TO OWE ME ANYTHING.
UNLIKE HIM, I DIDN'T DO IT FOR YOU--
2003
©. FILLBÄCH BROTHERS-
END.
6.

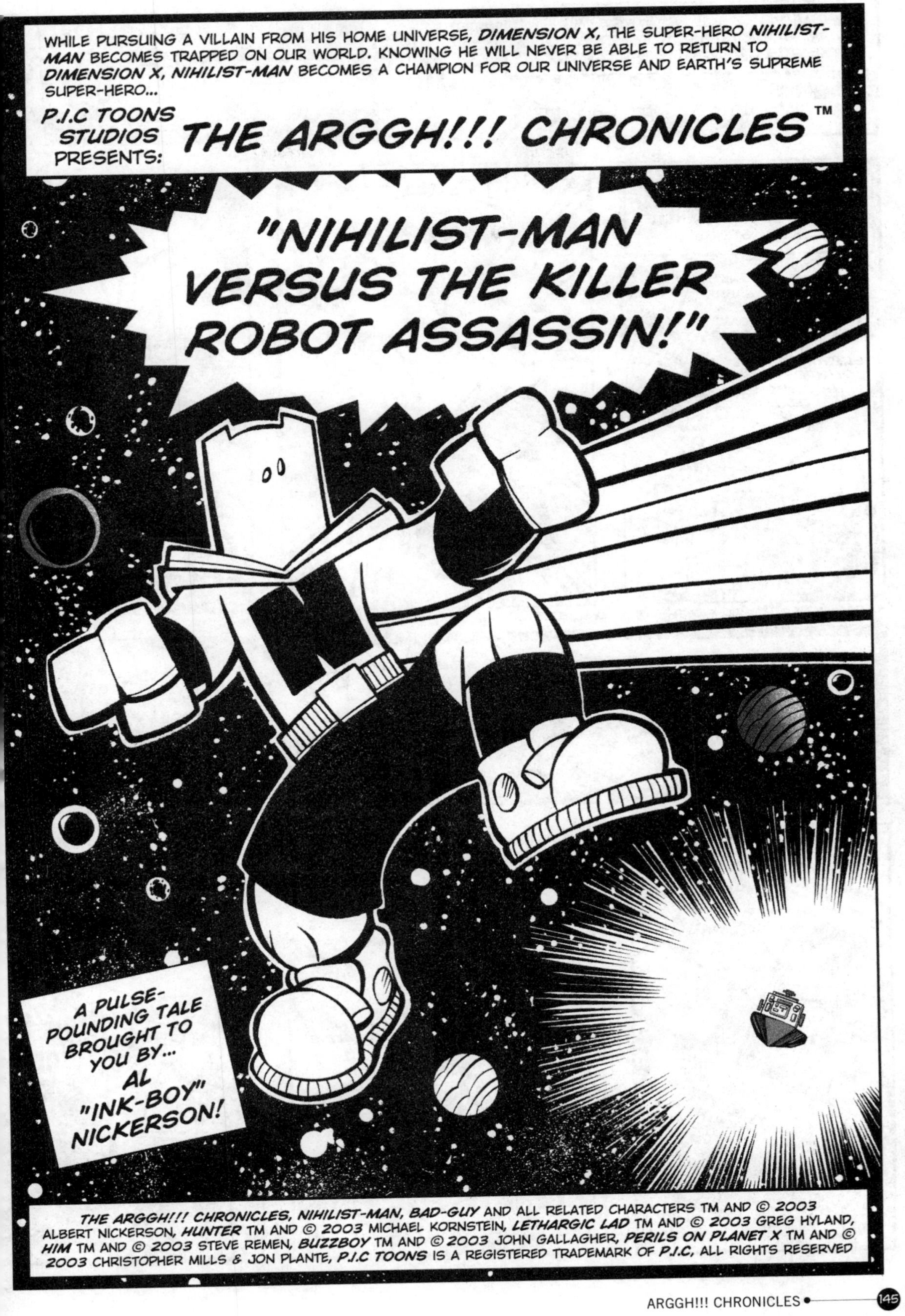
WHILE PURSUING A VILLAIN FROM HIS HOME UNIVERSE, *DIMENSION X*, THE SUPER-HERO *NIHILIST-MAN* BECOMES TRAPPED ON OUR WORLD. KNOWING HE WILL NEVER BE ABLE TO RETURN TO *DIMENSION X*, *NIHILIST-MAN* BECOMES A CHAMPION FOR OUR UNIVERSE AND EARTH'S SUPREME SUPER-HERO...
P.I.C TOONS STUDIOS PRESENTS:
THE ARGGH!!! CHRONICLES™
"NIHILIST-MAN VERSUS THE KILLER ROBOT ASSASSIN!"
A PULSE-POUNDING TALE BROUGHT TO YOU BY... AL "INK-BOY" NICKERSON!
THE ARGGH!!! CHRONICLES, *NIHILIST-MAN*, *BAD-GUY* AND ALL RELATED CHARACTERS TM AND © 2003 ALBERT NICKERSON, *HUNTER* TM AND © 2003 MICHAEL KORNSTEIN, *LETHARGIC LAD* TM AND © 2003 GREG HYLAND, *HIM* TM AND © 2003 STEVE REMEN, *BUZZBOY* TM AND © 2003 JOHN GALLAGHER, *PERILS ON PLANET X* TM AND © 2003 CHRISTOPHER MILLS & JON PLANTE, *P.I.C TOONS* IS A REGISTERED TRADEMARK OF *P.I.C*, ALL RIGHTS RESERVED

URBAN CITY... THE *GREATEST* OF *COMIC BOOK* CITIES! THIS *METROPOLIS* IS THE *HUB* OF ALL THAT IS *UNCANNY*...

CRUSH...

KILL...

Fatty Fan-boy's Comic Book Emporium

INSIDE *FATTY FAN-BOY'S COMIC BOOK EMPORIUM* (*URBAN CITY'S* FAVORITE COMIC BOOK STORE)...

YA SEE, WHEN HE DIED AND CAME BACK, HE WASN'T *SUPPOSED* TO LET HIS *WIFE* KNOW HE CAME BACK FROM THE *DEAD!* HE WAS JUST *SUPPOSED* TO GET A *GLIMPSE* OF *HER!* THAT WAS THE *DEAL!* *

TWO HEADED TALES

BUZZ BOY

SINFEST

ARGGH!!!

MAIM...

BLAM!

...DESTROY NIHILIST-MAN!!!

*I REALLY HEARD A KID SAY THIS IN A COMIC BOOK STORE

URBAN CITY'S SUPREME *SUPER-HERO* IS *NIHILIST-MAN!* HERE, IN HIS *CITADEL*, NIHILIST-MAN CAN KEEP A *WATCHFUL* VIGIL OVER OUR *UNIVERSE*...

LEFT TO RIGHT: HUNTER, HIM, LETHARGIC LAD, BUZZBOY, AND NIAND

SUPERHEROES SAVE UNIVERSE.... AGAIN! PAGE TWO

ALSO THIS ISSUE:
WHO IS JACK STAFF, BRITAIN'S GREATEST HERO?

DIAMOND KING STILL MISSING!

"BAT SPAWN" WHO CARES

WHAT'S WITH THESE *'ULTIMATE SPIDERMAN', 'ULTIMATE X-MEN',* AND *'ULTIMATES'* COMICS!?! DIDN'T *MARVEL COMICS* ALREADY DO THESE STORIES!?! THIS IS ALMOST AS *UNNECESSARY* AS *'HEROES REBORN'!*

NOT WIZARD MAGAZINE!

BEEP! BEEP! BEE

UH-OH! THERE GOES THE *PROXIMITY ALARM!* LOOKS LIKE THERE'S *TROUBLE* DOWN AT *FATTY FAN-BOY'S COMIC BOOK EMPORIUM!*

BEEP!! BEEP!! BEEP!!

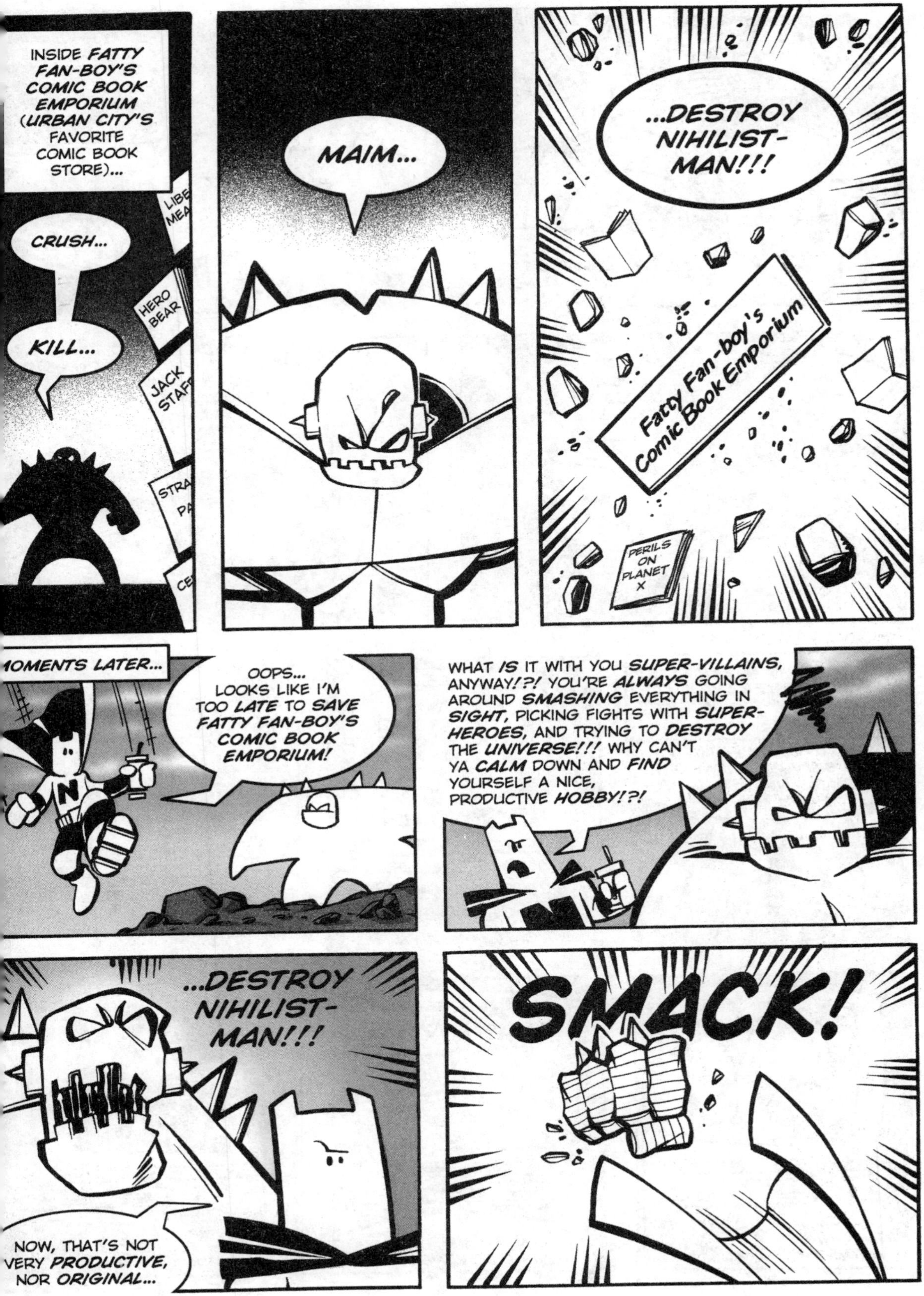
INSIDE FATTY FAN-BOY'S COMIC BOOK EMPORIUM (URBAN CITY'S FAVORITE COMIC BOOK STORE)...
CRUSH...
KILL...
HERO BEAR
JACK STAFF
MAIM...
...DESTROY NIHILIST-MAN!!!
Fatty Fan-boy's Comic Book Emporium
PERILS ON PLANET X
MOMENTS LATER...
OOPS... LOOKS LIKE I'M TOO LATE TO SAVE FATTY FAN-BOY'S COMIC BOOK EMPORIUM!
WHAT IS IT WITH YOU SUPER-VILLAINS, ANYWAY!?! YOU'RE ALWAYS GOING AROUND SMASHING EVERYTHING IN SIGHT, PICKING FIGHTS WITH SUPER-HEROES, AND TRYING TO DESTROY THE UNIVERSE!!! WHY CAN'T YA CALM DOWN AND FIND YOURSELF A NICE, PRODUCTIVE HOBBY!?!
...DESTROY NIHILIST-MAN!!!
NOW, THAT'S NOT VERY PRODUCTIVE, NOR ORIGINAL...
SMACK!

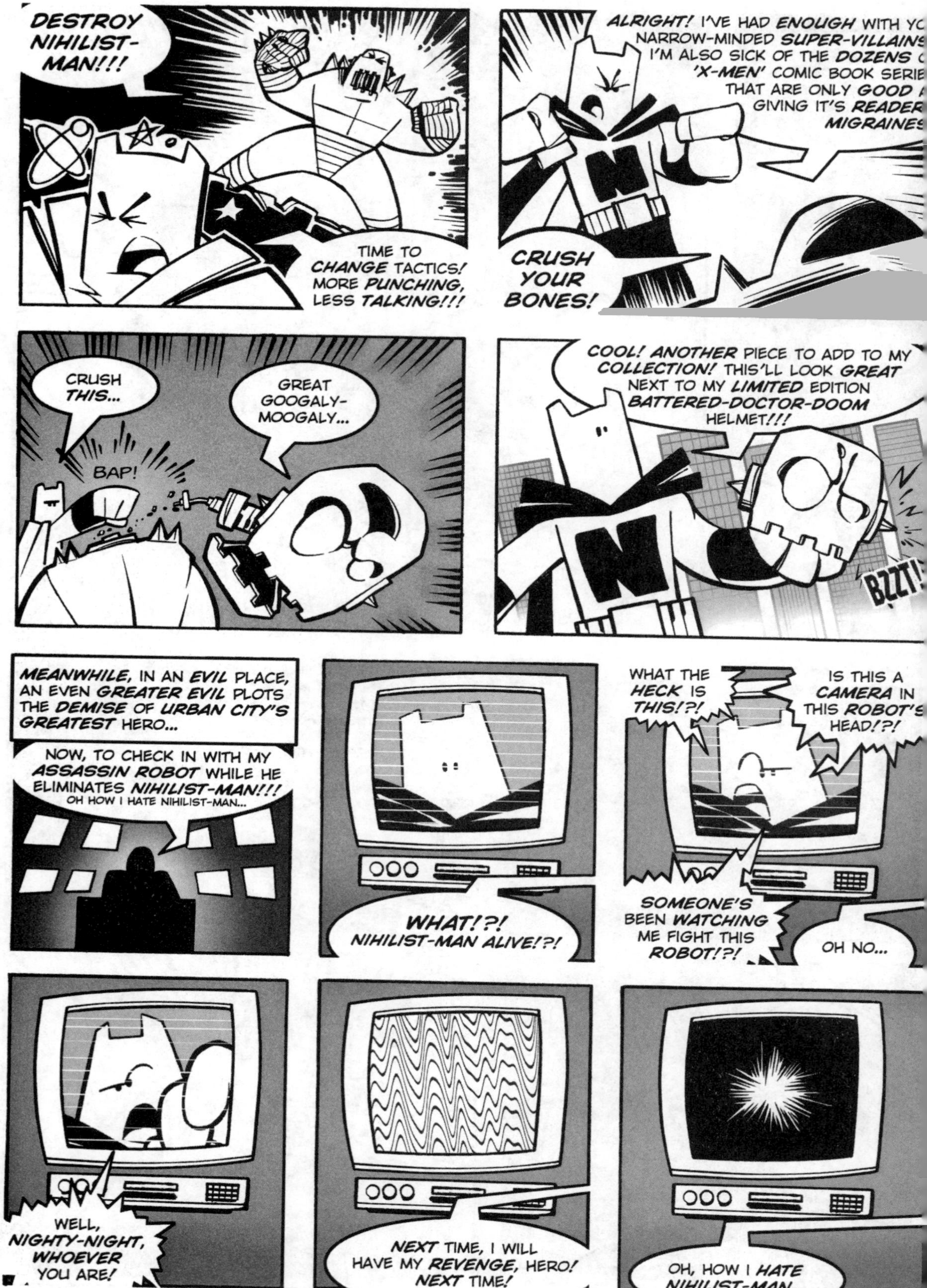
DESTROY NIHILIST-MAN!!!
TIME TO CHANGE TACTICS! MORE PUNCHING, LESS TALKING!!!
ALRIGHT! I'VE HAD ENOUGH WITH YO NARROW-MINDED SUPER-VILLAINS I'M ALSO SICK OF THE DOZENS 'X-MEN' COMIC BOOK SERIE THAT ARE ONLY GOOD GIVING IT'S READER MIGRAINES
CRUSH YOUR BONES!
CRUSH THIS...
BAP!
GREAT GOOGALY-MOOGALY...
COOL! ANOTHER PIECE TO ADD TO MY COLLECTION! THIS'LL LOOK GREAT NEXT TO MY LIMITED EDITION BATTERED-DOCTOR-DOOM HELMET!!!
BZZT!
MEANWHILE, IN AN EVIL PLACE, AN EVEN GREATER EVIL PLOTS THE DEMISE OF URBAN CITY'S GREATEST HERO...
NOW, TO CHECK IN WITH MY ASSASSIN ROBOT WHILE HE ELIMINATES NIHILIST-MAN!!! OH HOW I HATE NIHILIST-MAN...
WHAT!?! NIHILIST-MAN ALIVE!?!
WHAT THE HECK IS THIS!?!
IS THIS A CAMERA IN THIS ROBOT'S HEAD!?!
SOMEONE'S BEEN WATCHING ME FIGHT THIS ROBOT!?!
OH NO...
WELL, NIGHTY-NIGHT, WHOEVER YOU ARE!
NEXT TIME, I WILL HAVE MY REVENGE, HERO! NEXT TIME!
OH, HOW I HATE NIHILIST-MAN...

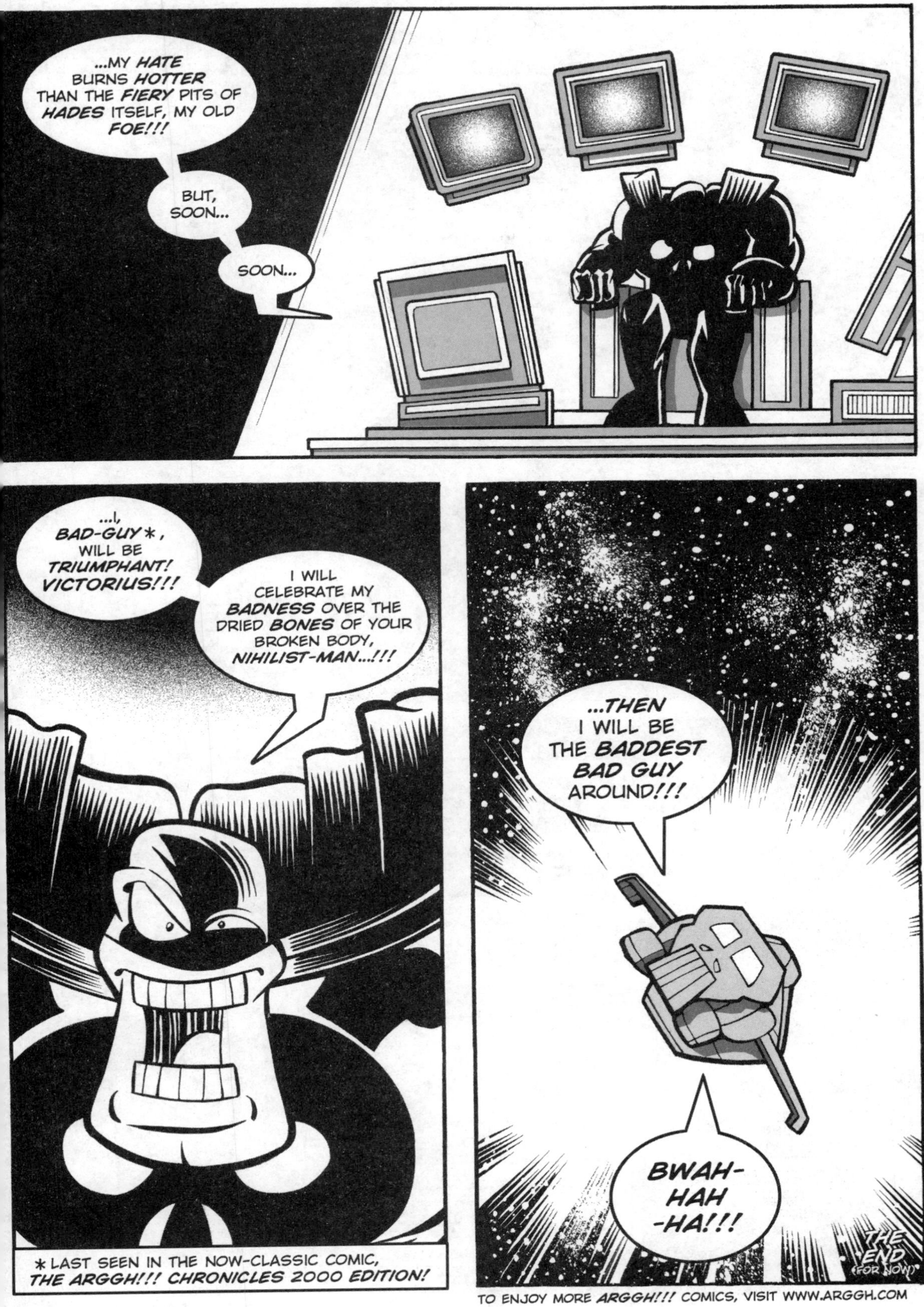
...MY HATE BURNS HOTTER THAN THE FIERY PITS OF HADES ITSELF, MY OLD FOE!!!
BUT, SOON...
SOON...
...I, BAD-GUY*, WILL BE TRIUMPHANT! VICTORIUS!!!
I WILL CELEBRATE MY BADNESS OVER THE DRIED BONES OF YOUR BROKEN BODY, NIHILIST-MAN...!!!
...THEN I WILL BE THE BADDEST BAD GUY AROUND!!!
BWAH-HAH-HA!!!
THE END (FOR NOW)
* LAST SEEN IN THE NOW-CLASSIC COMIC, THE ARGGH!!! CHRONICLES 2000 EDITION!

TO ENJOY MORE *ARGGH!!!* COMICS, VISIT WWW.ARGGH.COM

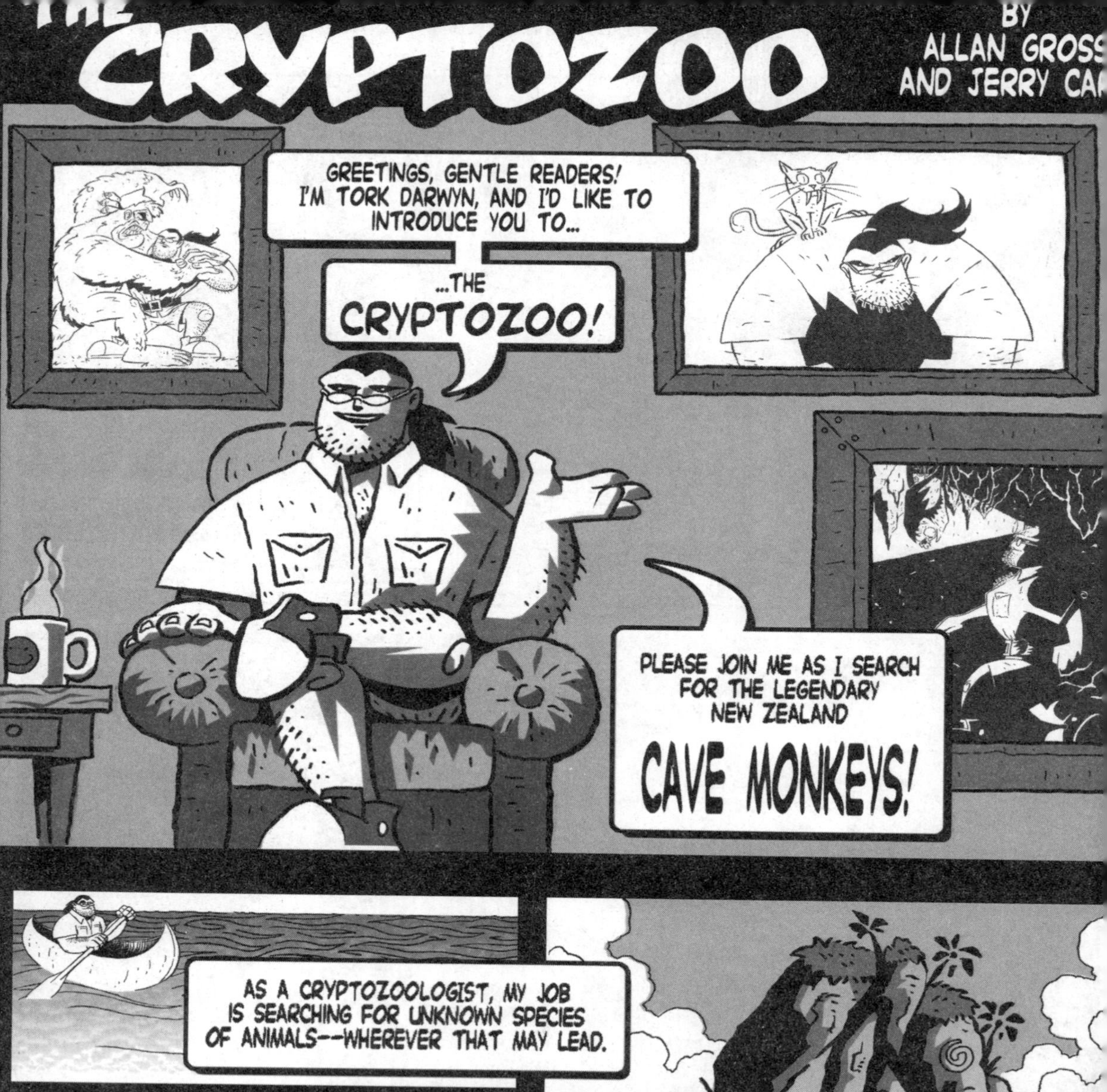
THE CRYPTOZOO
BY ALLAN GROSS AND JERRY CARR
GREETINGS, GENTLE READERS! I'M TORK DARWYN, AND I'D LIKE TO INTRODUCE YOU TO...
...THE CRYPTOZOO!
PLEASE JOIN ME AS I SEARCH FOR THE LEGENDARY NEW ZEALAND CAVE MONKEYS!
AS A CRYPTOZOOLOGIST, MY JOB IS SEARCHING FOR UNKNOWN SPECIES OF ANIMALS--WHEREVER THAT MAY LEAD.
I WAS FOLLOWING A TIP FROM A REPUTABLE TIBETAN DREAMWALKER.
BUT AFTER TWO DAYS OFF THE SOUTHERN TIP OF NEW ZEALAND...
I WAS BEGINNING TO WONDER IF I'D EVER FIND THE STRANGE ISLAND HE HAD DESCRIBED.
FINALLY, ON THE THIRD MORNING AS THE FOG LIFTED, I SAW IT!

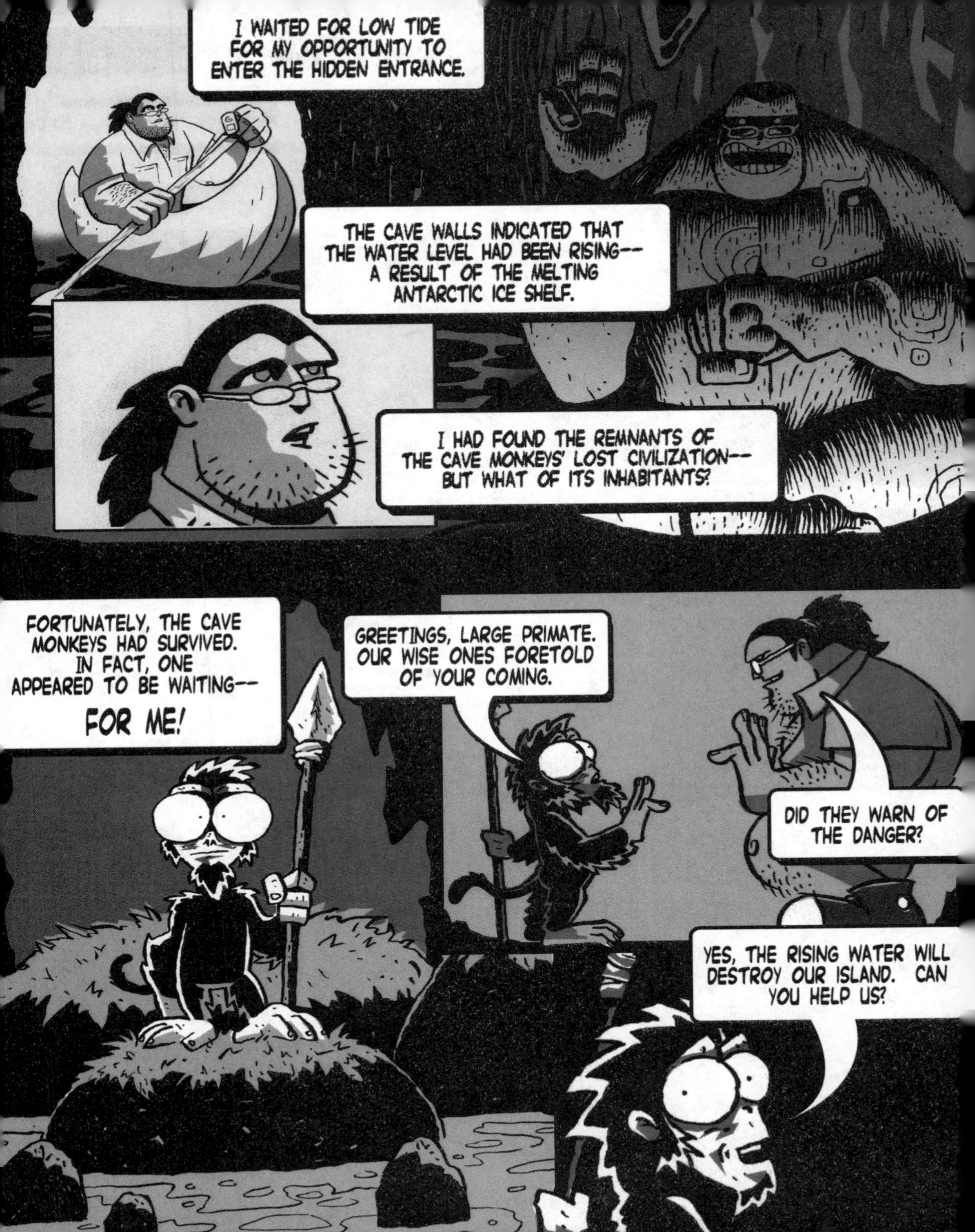
I WAITED FOR LOW TIDE FOR MY OPPORTUNITY TO ENTER THE HIDDEN ENTRANCE.
THE CAVE WALLS INDICATED THAT THE WATER LEVEL HAD BEEN RISING-- A RESULT OF THE MELTING ANTARCTIC ICE SHELF.
I HAD FOUND THE REMNANTS OF THE CAVE MONKEYS' LOST CIVILIZATION-- BUT WHAT OF ITS INHABITANTS?
FORTUNATELY, THE CAVE MONKEYS HAD SURVIVED. IN FACT, ONE APPEARED TO BE WAITING--
FOR ME!
GREETINGS, LARGE PRIMATE. OUR WISE ONES FORETOLD OF YOUR COMING.
DID THEY WARN OF THE DANGER?
YES, THE RISING WATER WILL DESTROY OUR ISLAND. CAN YOU HELP US?

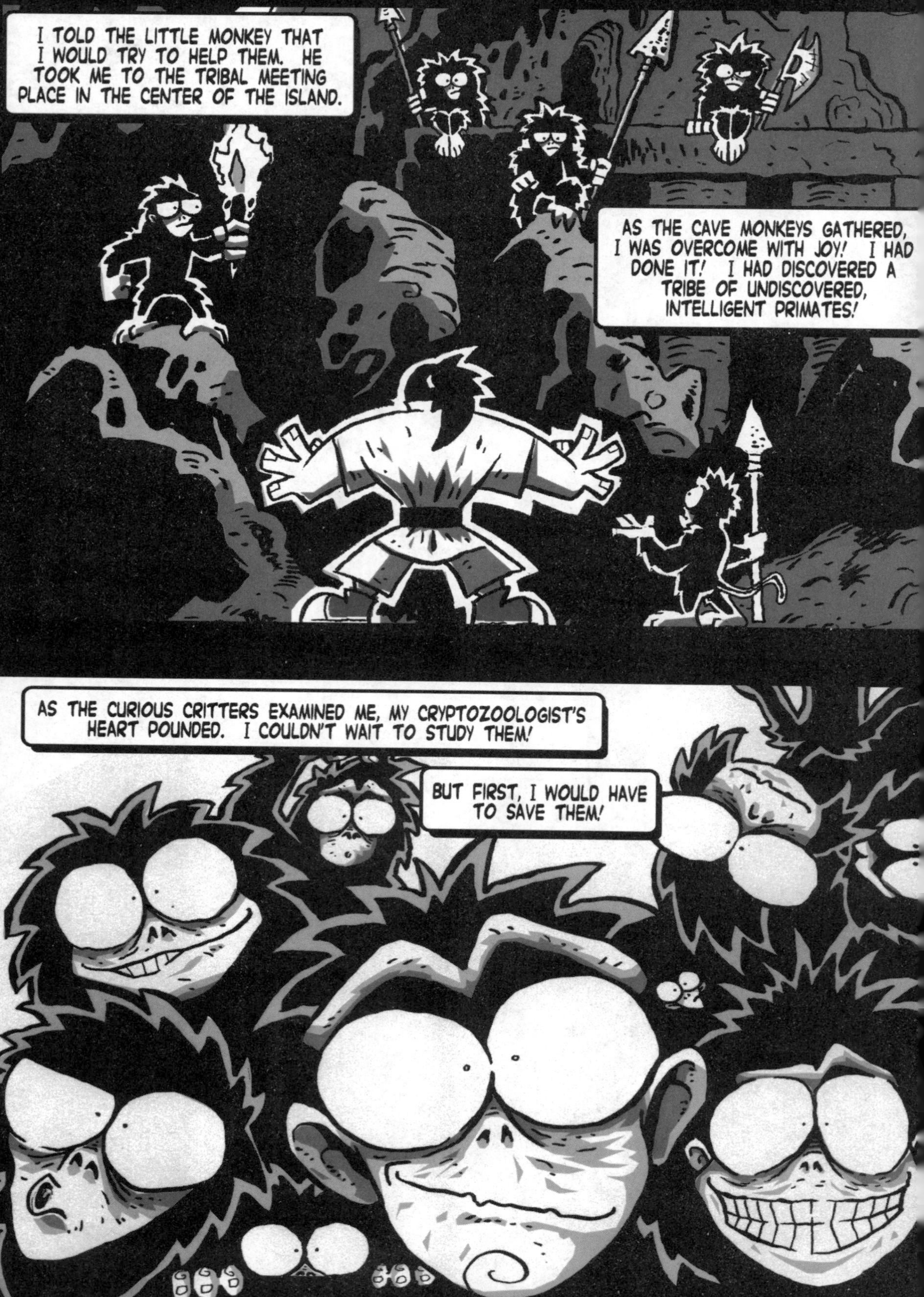

I TOLD THE LITTLE MONKEY THAT I WOULD TRY TO HELP THEM. HE TOOK ME TO THE TRIBAL MEETING PLACE IN THE CENTER OF THE ISLAND.
AS THE CAVE MONKEYS GATHERED, I WAS OVERCOME WITH JOY! I HAD DONE IT! I HAD DISCOVERED A TRIBE OF UNDISCOVERED, INTELLIGENT PRIMATES!
AS THE CURIOUS CRITTERS EXAMINED ME, MY CRYPTOZOOLOGIST'S HEART POUNDED. I COULDN'T WAIT TO STUDY THEM!
BUT FIRST, I WOULD HAVE TO SAVE THEM!

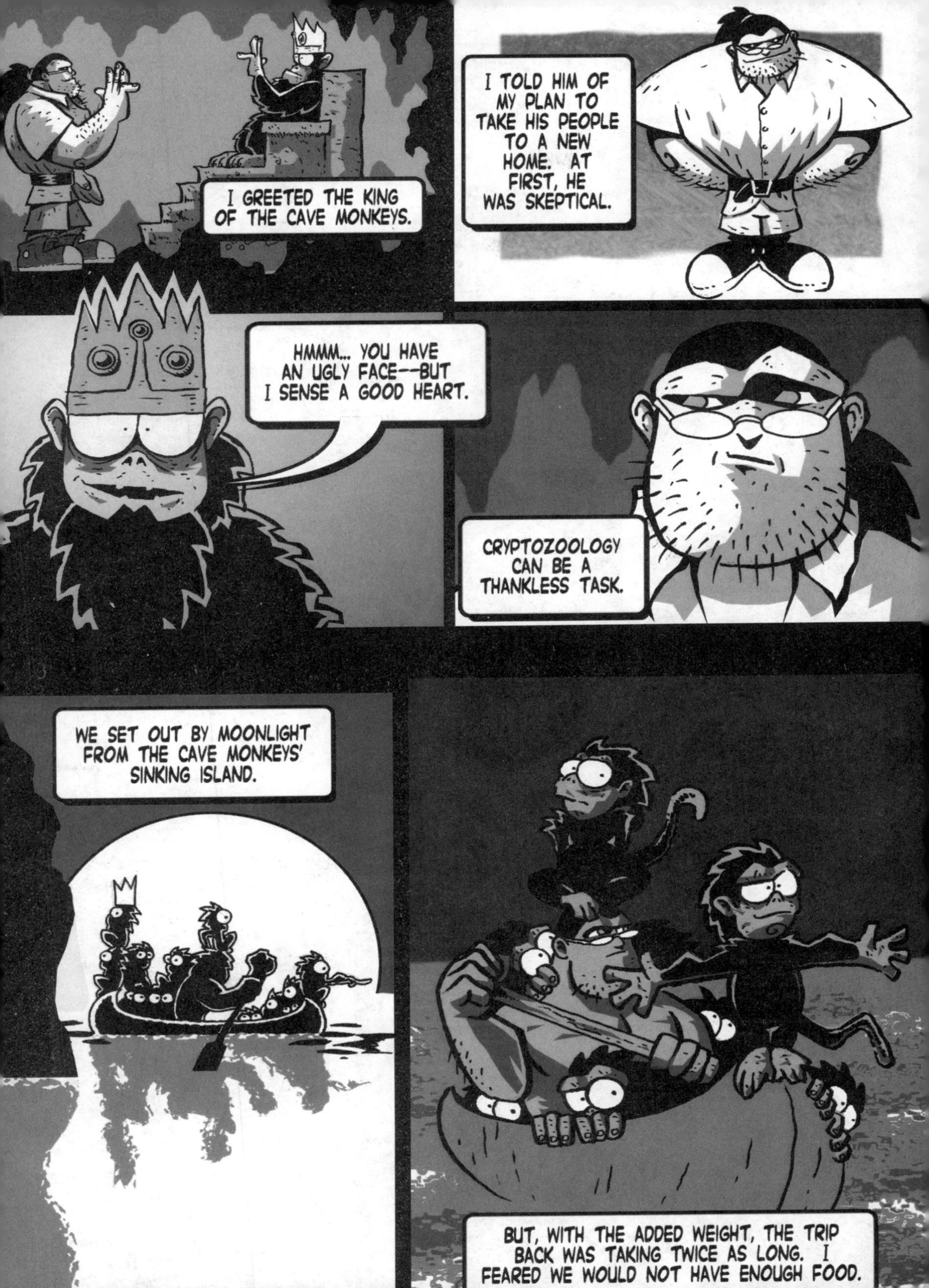

I GREETED THE KING OF THE CAVE MONKEYS.
I TOLD HIM OF MY PLAN TO TAKE HIS PEOPLE TO A NEW HOME. AT FIRST, HE WAS SKEPTICAL.
HMMM... YOU HAVE AN UGLY FACE--BUT I SENSE A GOOD HEART.
CRYPTOZOOLOGY CAN BE A THANKLESS TASK.
WE SET OUT BY MOONLIGHT FROM THE CAVE MONKEYS' SINKING ISLAND.
BUT, WITH THE ADDED WEIGHT, THE TRIP BACK WAS TAKING TWICE AS LONG. I FEARED WE WOULD NOT HAVE ENOUGH FOOD.

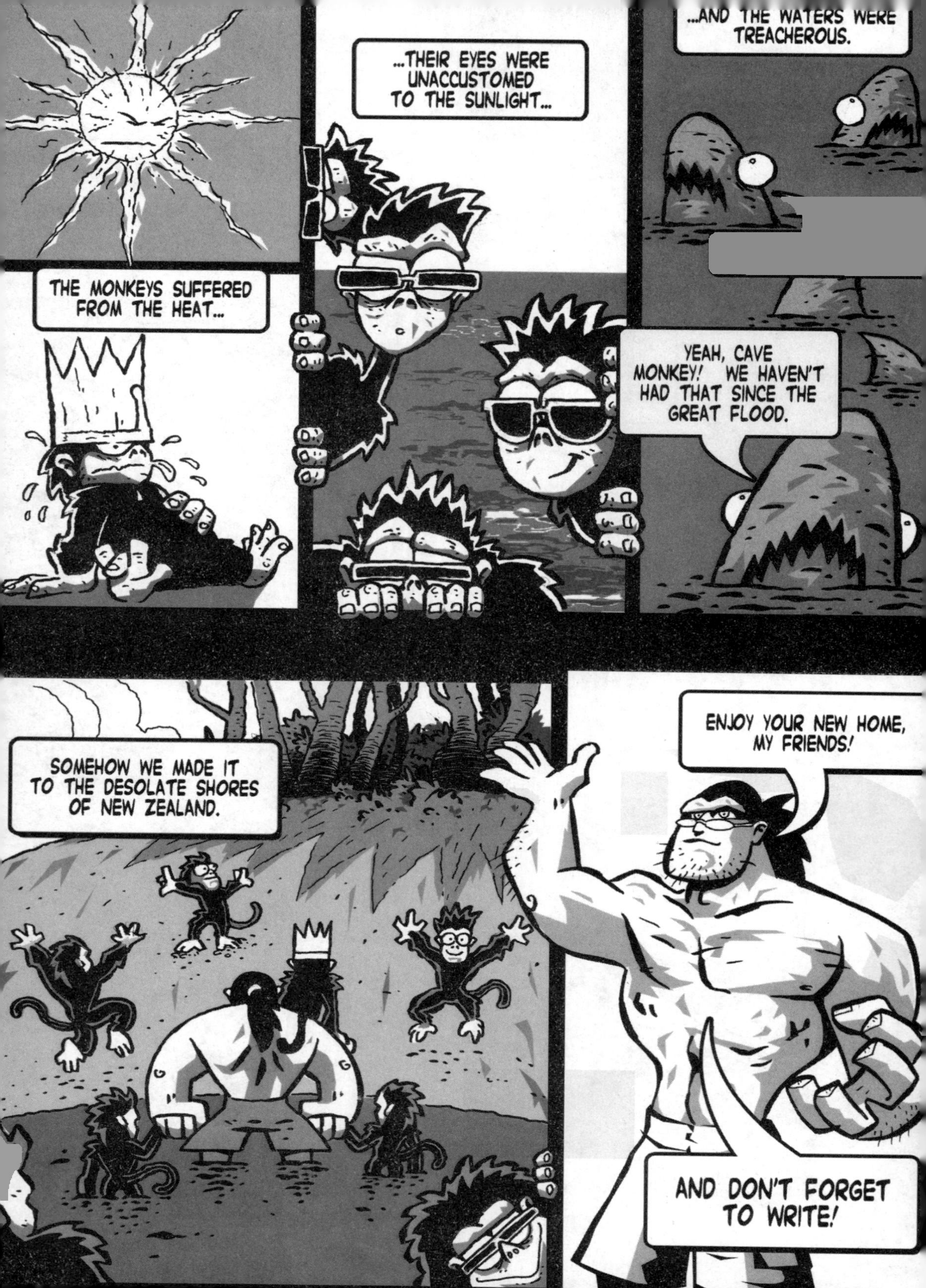
THE MONKEYS SUFFERED FROM THE HEAT...
...THEIR EYES WERE UNACCUSTOMED TO THE SUNLIGHT...
...AND THE WATERS WERE TREACHEROUS.
YEAH, CAVE MONKEY! WE HAVEN'T HAD THAT SINCE THE GREAT FLOOD.
SOMEHOW WE MADE IT TO THE DESOLATE SHORES OF NEW ZEALAND.
ENJOY YOUR NEW HOME, MY FRIENDS!
AND DON'T FORGET TO WRITE!

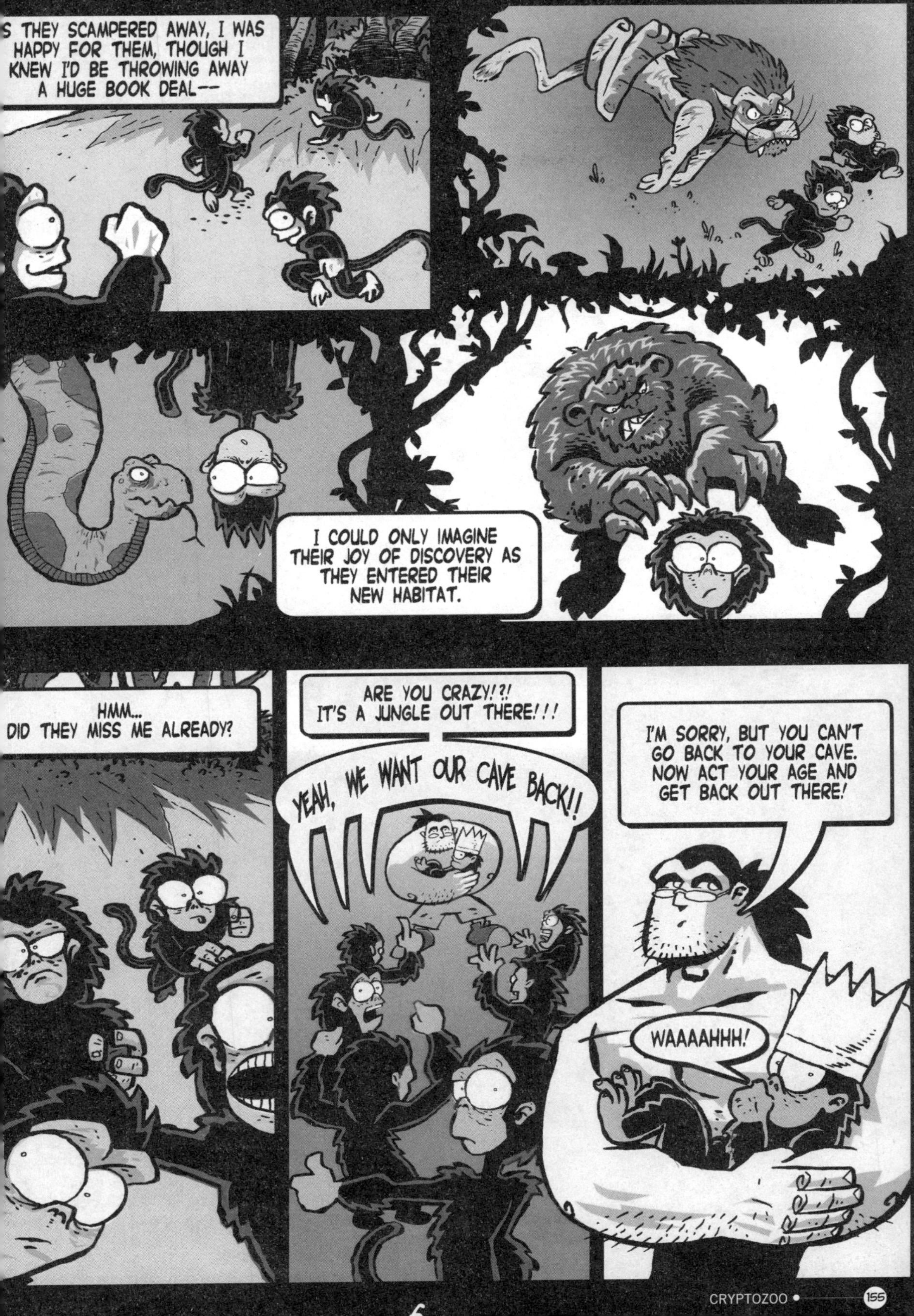
S THEY SCAMPERED AWAY, I WAS HAPPY FOR THEM, THOUGH I KNEW I'D BE THROWING AWAY A HUGE BOOK DEAL--
I COULD ONLY IMAGINE THEIR JOY OF DISCOVERY AS THEY ENTERED THEIR NEW HABITAT.
HMM... DID THEY MISS ME ALREADY?
ARE YOU CRAZY!?! IT'S A JUNGLE OUT THERE!!!
YEAH, WE WANT OUR CAVE BACK!!
I'M SORRY, BUT YOU CAN'T GO BACK TO YOUR CAVE. NOW ACT YOUR AGE AND GET BACK OUT THERE!
WAAAAHHH!

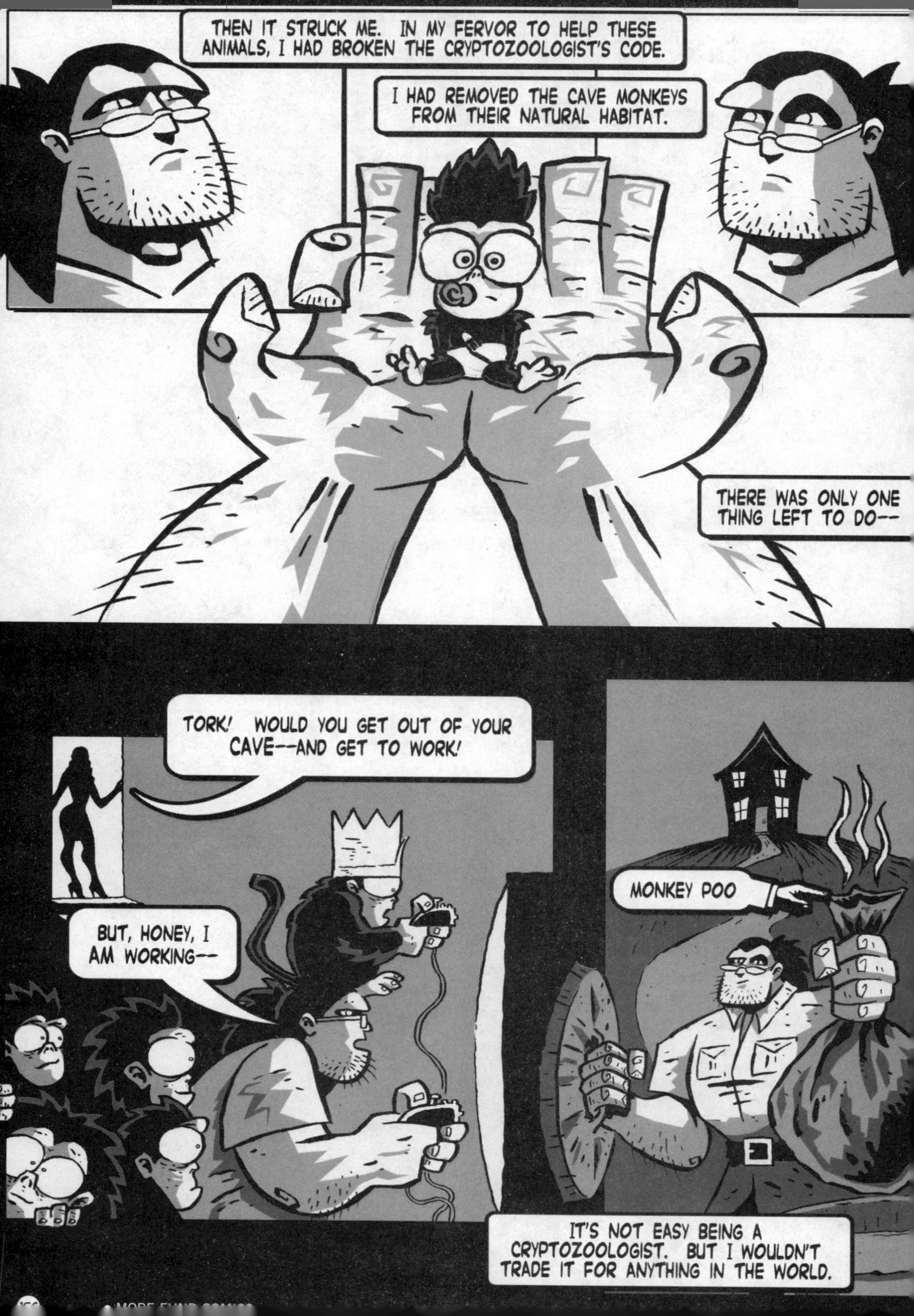

THEN IT STRUCK ME. IN MY FERVOR TO HELP THESE ANIMALS, I HAD BROKEN THE CRYPTOZOOLOGIST'S CODE.
I HAD REMOVED THE CAVE MONKEYS FROM THEIR NATURAL HABITAT.
THERE WAS ONLY ONE THING LEFT TO DO--
TORK! WOULD YOU GET OUT OF YOUR CAVE--AND GET TO WORK!
BUT, HONEY, I AM WORKING--
MONKEY POO
IT'S NOT EASY BEING A CRYPTOZOOLOGIST. BUT I WOULDN'T TRADE IT FOR ANYTHING IN THE WORLD.

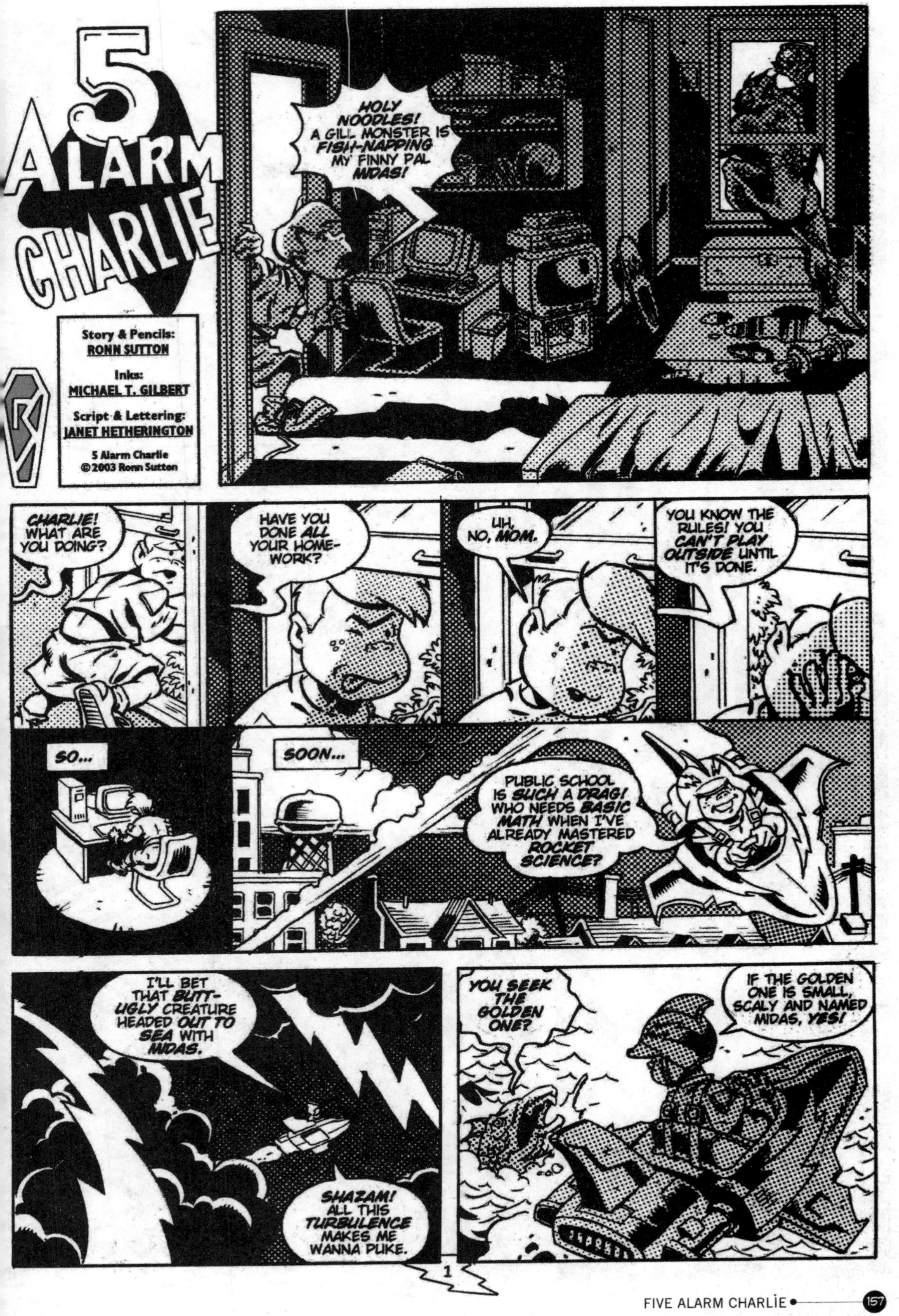
5 ALARM CHARLIE
Story & Pencils: RONN SUTTON
Inks: MICHAEL T. GILBERT
Script & Lettering: JANET HETHERINGTON
5 Alarm Charlie © 2003 Ronn Sutton
HOLY NOODLES! A GILL MONSTER IS FISH-NAPPING MY FINNY PAL MIDAS!
CHARLIE! WHAT ARE YOU DOING?
HAVE YOU DONE ALL YOUR HOME-WORK?
UH, NO, MOM.
YOU KNOW THE RULES! YOU CAN'T PLAY OUTSIDE UNTIL IT'S DONE.
SO...
SOON...
PUBLIC SCHOOL IS SUCH A DRAG! WHO NEEDS BASIC MATH WHEN I'VE ALREADY MASTERED ROCKET SCIENCE?
I'LL BET THAT BUTT-UGLY CREATURE HEADED OUT TO SEA WITH MIDAS.
SHAZAM! ALL THIS TURBULENCE MAKES ME WANNA PUKE.
YOU SEEK THE GOLDEN ONE?
IF THE GOLDEN ONE IS SMALL, SCALY AND NAMED MIDAS, YES!
1

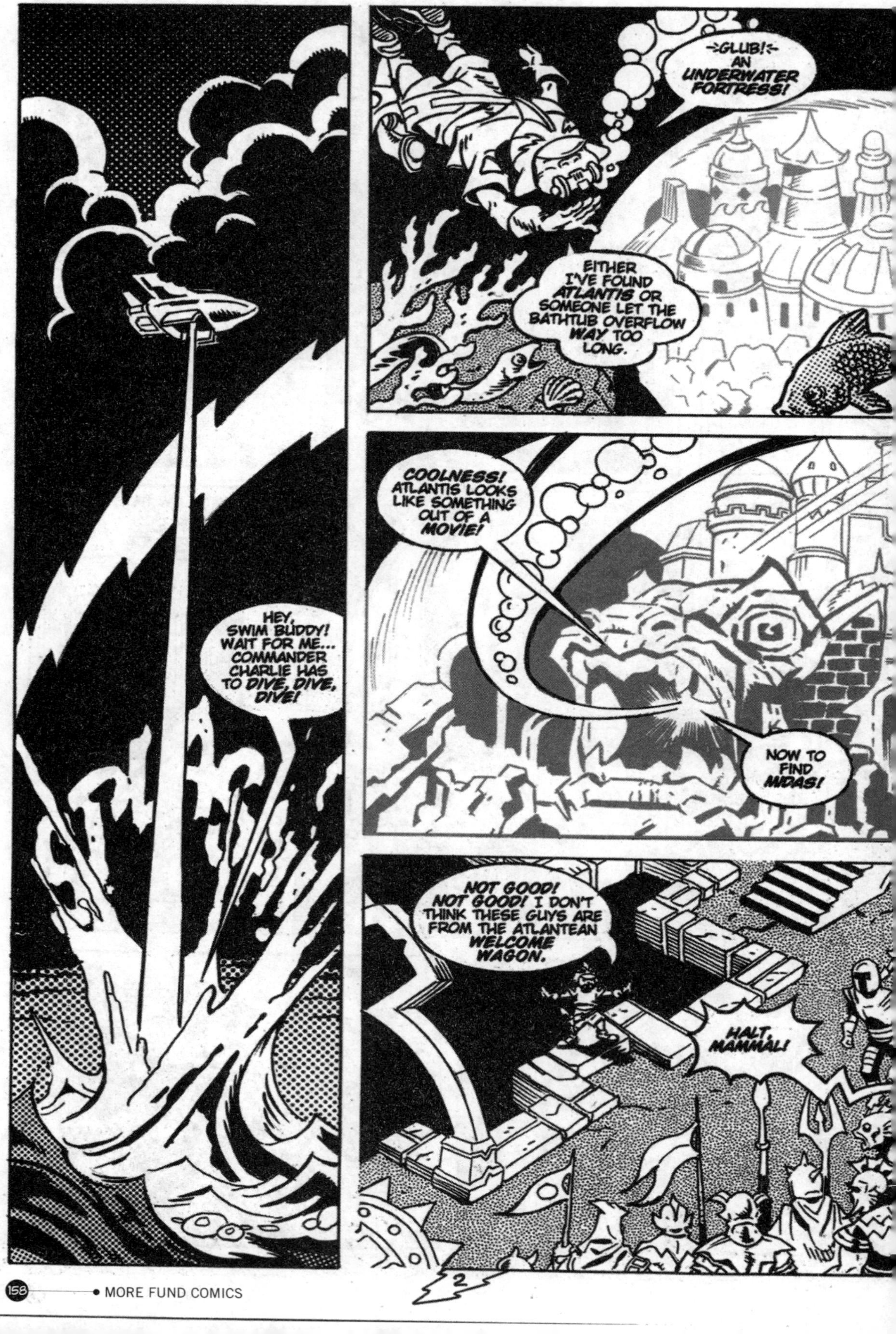
HEY, SWIM BUDDY! WAIT FOR ME... COMMANDER CHARLIE HAS TO DIVE, DIVE, DIVE!
-GLUB!- AN UNDERWATER FORTRESS!
EITHER I'VE FOUND ATLANTIS OR SOMEONE LET THE BATHTUB OVERFLOW WAY TOO LONG.
COOLNESS! ATLANTIS LOOKS LIKE SOMETHING OUT OF A MOVIE!
NOW TO FIND MIDAS!
NOT GOOD! NOT GOOD! I DON'T THINK THESE GUYS ARE FROM THE ATLANTEAN WELCOME WAGON.
HALT, MAMMAL!
2

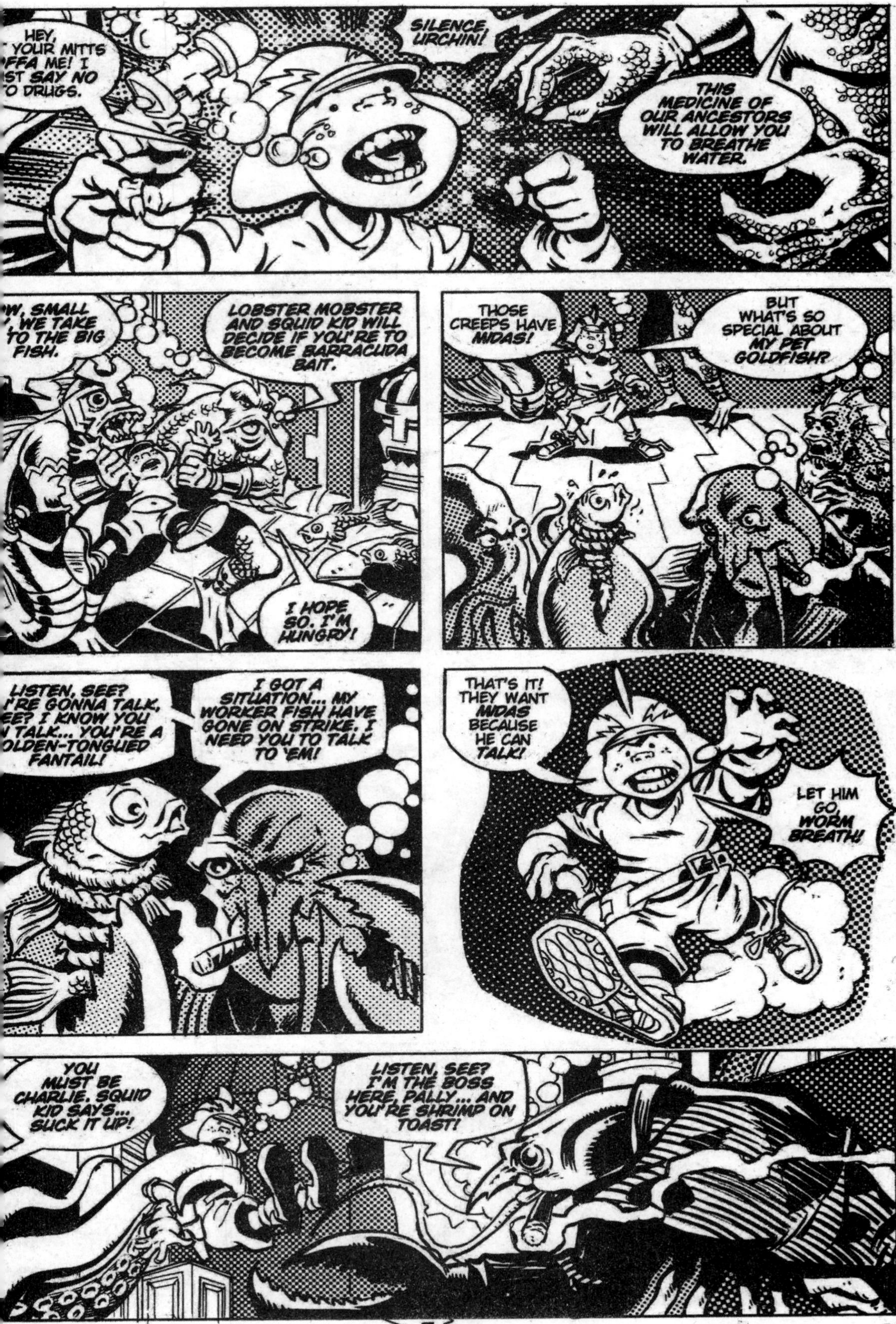
HEY,
T YOUR MITTS FFA ME! I ST SAY NO O DRUGS.
SILENCE, URCHIN!
THIS MEDICINE OF OUR ANCESTORS WILL ALLOW YOU TO BREATHE WATER.
W, SMALL , WE TAKE TO THE BIG FISH.
LOBSTER MOBSTER AND SQUID KID WILL DECIDE IF YOU'RE TO BECOME BARRACUDA BAIT.
I HOPE SO. I'M HUNGRY!
THOSE CREEPS HAVE MIDAS!
BUT WHAT'S SO SPECIAL ABOUT MY PET GOLDFISH?
LISTEN, SEE? 'RE GONNA TALK, EE? I KNOW YOU N TALK... YOU'RE A OLDEN-TONGUED FANTAIL!
I GOT A SITUATION... MY WORKER FISH HAVE GONE ON STRIKE. I NEED YOU TO TALK TO 'EM!
THAT'S IT! THEY WANT MIDAS BECAUSE HE CAN TALK!
LET HIM GO, WORM BREATH!
YOU MUST BE CHARLIE. SQUID KID SAYS... SUCK IT UP!
LISTEN, SEE? I'M THE BOSS HERE, PALLY... AND YOU'RE SHRIMP ON TOAST!

3

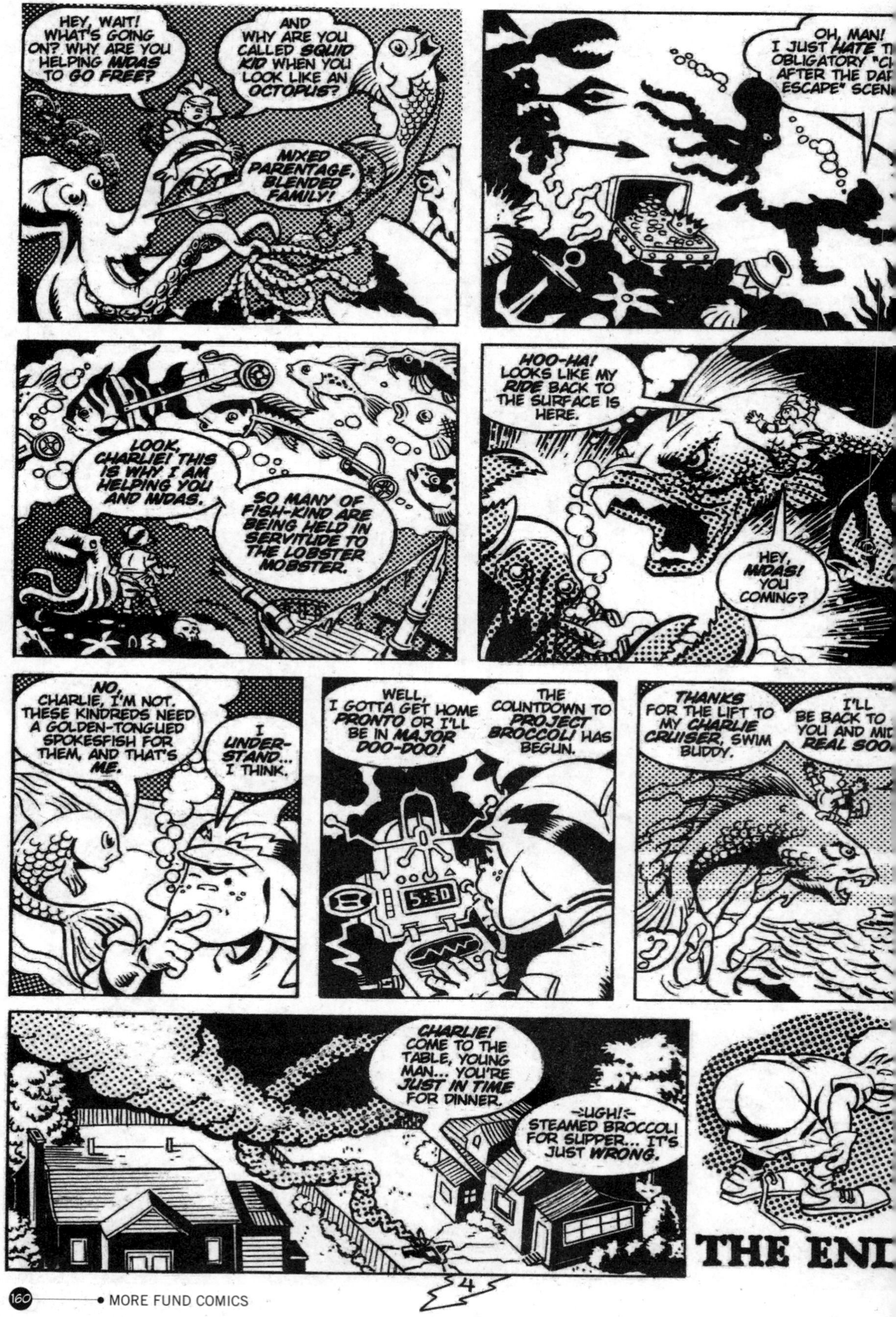
HEY, WAIT! WHAT'S GOING ON? WHY ARE YOU HELPING MIDAS TO GO FREE?
AND WHY ARE YOU CALLED SQUID KID WHEN YOU LOOK LIKE AN OCTOPUS?
MIXED PARENTAGE, BLENDED FAMILY!
OH, MAN! I JUST HATE T
OBLIGATORY "C
AFTER THE DA
ESCAPE" SCEN
LOOK, CHARLIE! THIS IS WHY I AM HELPING YOU AND MIDAS.
SO MANY OF FISH-KIND ARE BEING HELD IN SERVITUDE TO THE LOBSTER MOBSTER.
HOO-HA! LOOKS LIKE MY RIDE BACK TO THE SURFACE IS HERE.
HEY, MIDAS! YOU COMING?
NO, CHARLIE, I'M NOT. THESE KINDREDS NEED A GOLDEN-TONGUED SPOKESFISH FOR THEM, AND THAT'S ME.
I UNDERSTAND... I THINK.
WELL, I GOTTA GET HOME PRONTO OR I'LL BE IN MAJOR DOO-DOO!
THE COUNTDOWN TO PROJECT BROCCOLI HAS BEGUN.
5:30
THANKS FOR THE LIFT TO MY CHARLIE CRUISER, SWIM BUDDY.
I'LL BE BACK TO YOU AND MI
REAL SOO
CHARLIE! COME TO THE TABLE, YOUNG MAN... YOU'RE JUST IN TIME FOR DINNER.
-UGH!- STEAMED BROCCOLI FOR SUPPER... IT'S JUST WRONG.
THE EN
4

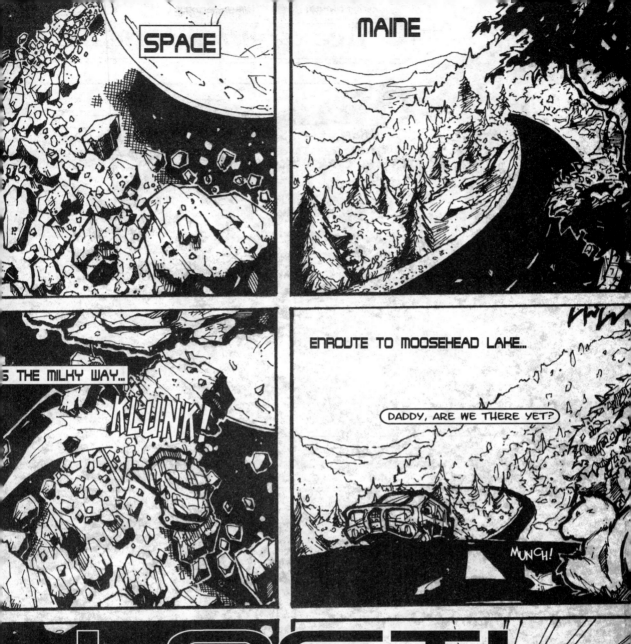

SPACE

MAINE

S THE MILKY WAY...

KLUNK!

ENROUTE TO MOOSEHEAD LAKE...

DADDY, ARE WE THERE YET?

MUNCH!

LOST!

I NEED TO GO TO THE BATHROOM!

1

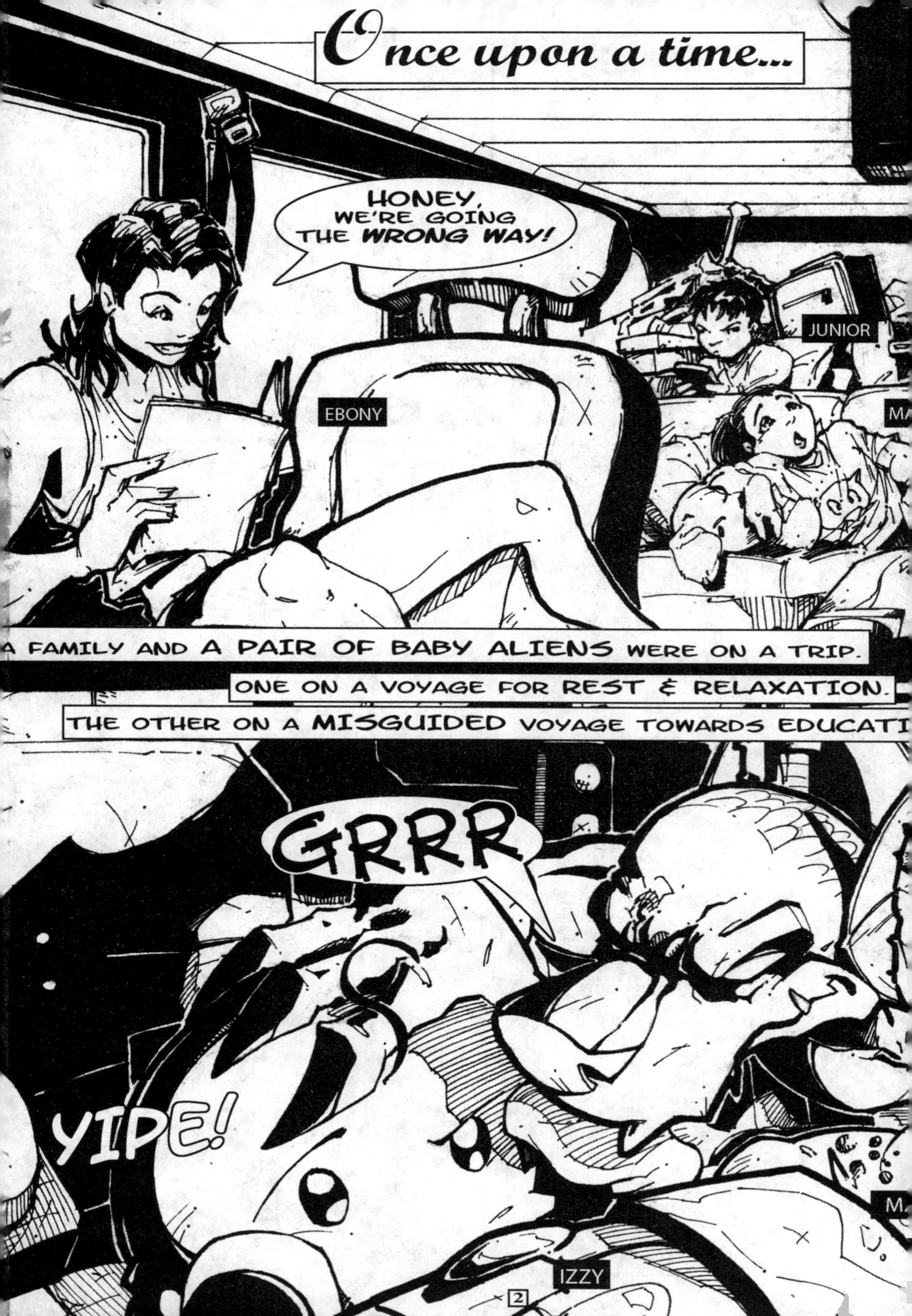

Once upon a time...
HONEY, WE'RE GOING THE WRONG WAY!
JUNIOR
EBONY
A FAMILY AND A PAIR OF BABY ALIENS WERE ON A TRIP.
ONE ON A VOYAGE FOR REST & RELAXATION.
THE OTHER ON A MISGUIDED VOYAGE TOWARDS EDUCATI
GRRR
YIPE!
IZZY

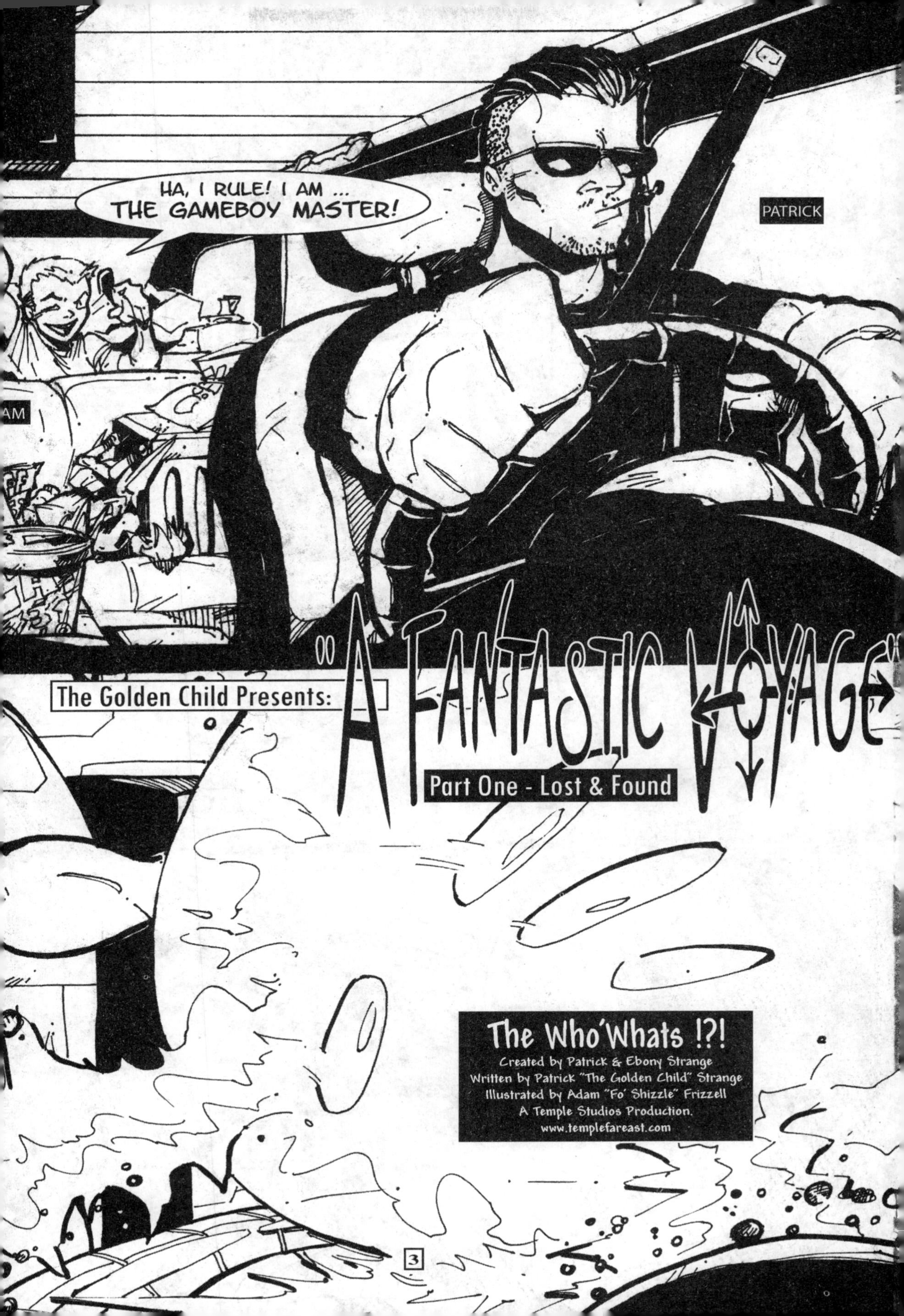

HA, I RULE! I AM ... THE GAMEBOY MASTER!
PATRICK
AM
The Golden Child Presents:
"A FANTASTIC VOYAGE"
Part One - Lost & Found
The Who'Whats !?!
Created by Patrick & Ebony Strange
Written by Patrick "The Golden Child" Strange
Illustrated by Adam "Fo' Shizzle" Frizzell
A Temple Studios Production.
www.templefareast.com

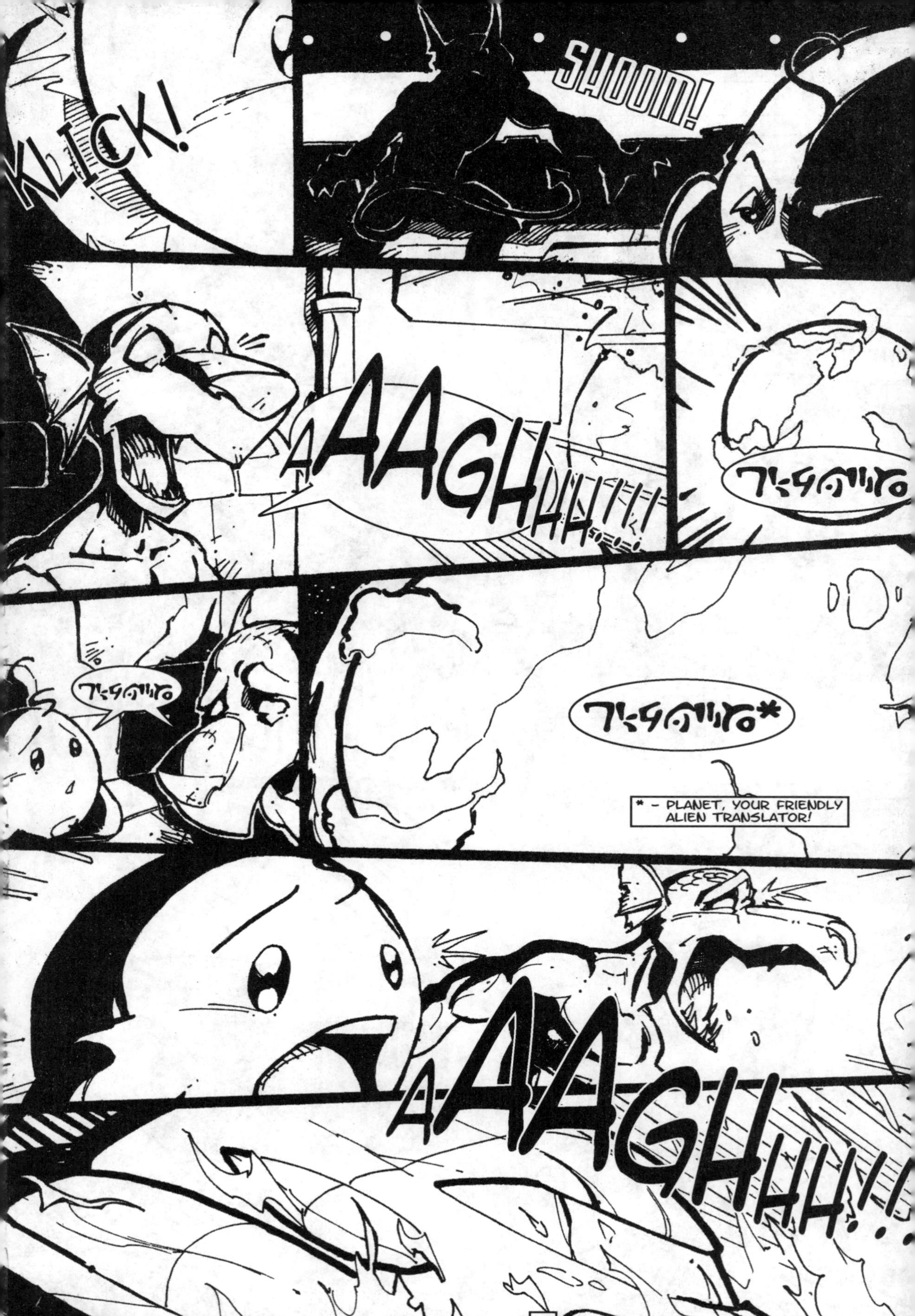
KLICK!
SHOOM!
AAAGHHHH!!!
* - PLANET, YOUR FRIENDLY ALIEN TRANSLATOR!
AAAGHHHH!!!

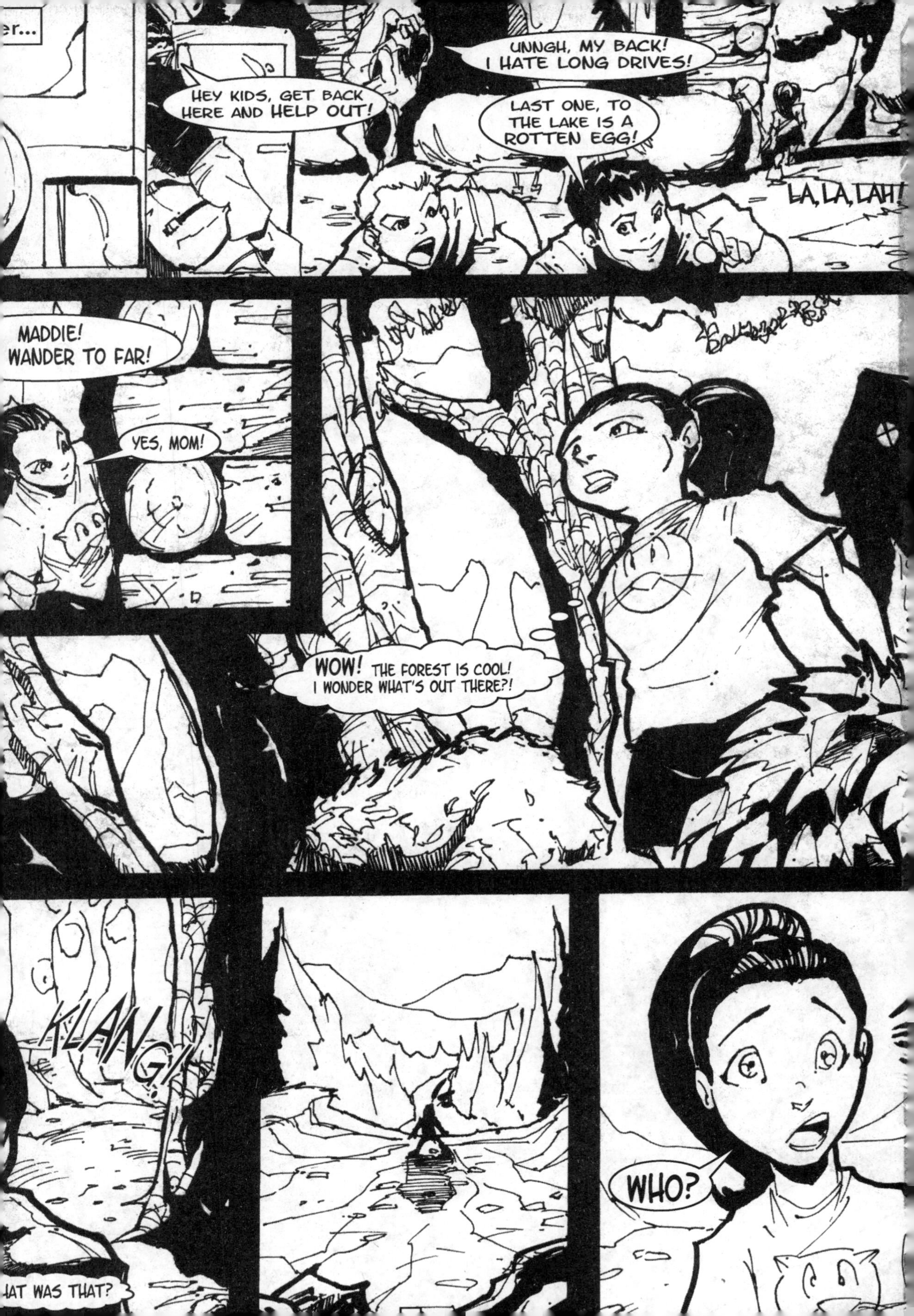

er...
HEY KIDS, GET BACK HERE AND HELP OUT!
UNNGH, MY BACK! I HATE LONG DRIVES!
LAST ONE, TO THE LAKE IS A ROTTEN EGG!
LA, LA, LAH!
MADDIE! WANDER TO FAR!
YES, MOM!
WOW! THE FOREST IS COOL! I WONDER WHAT'S OUT THERE?!
KLANG!
HAT WAS THAT?
WHO?

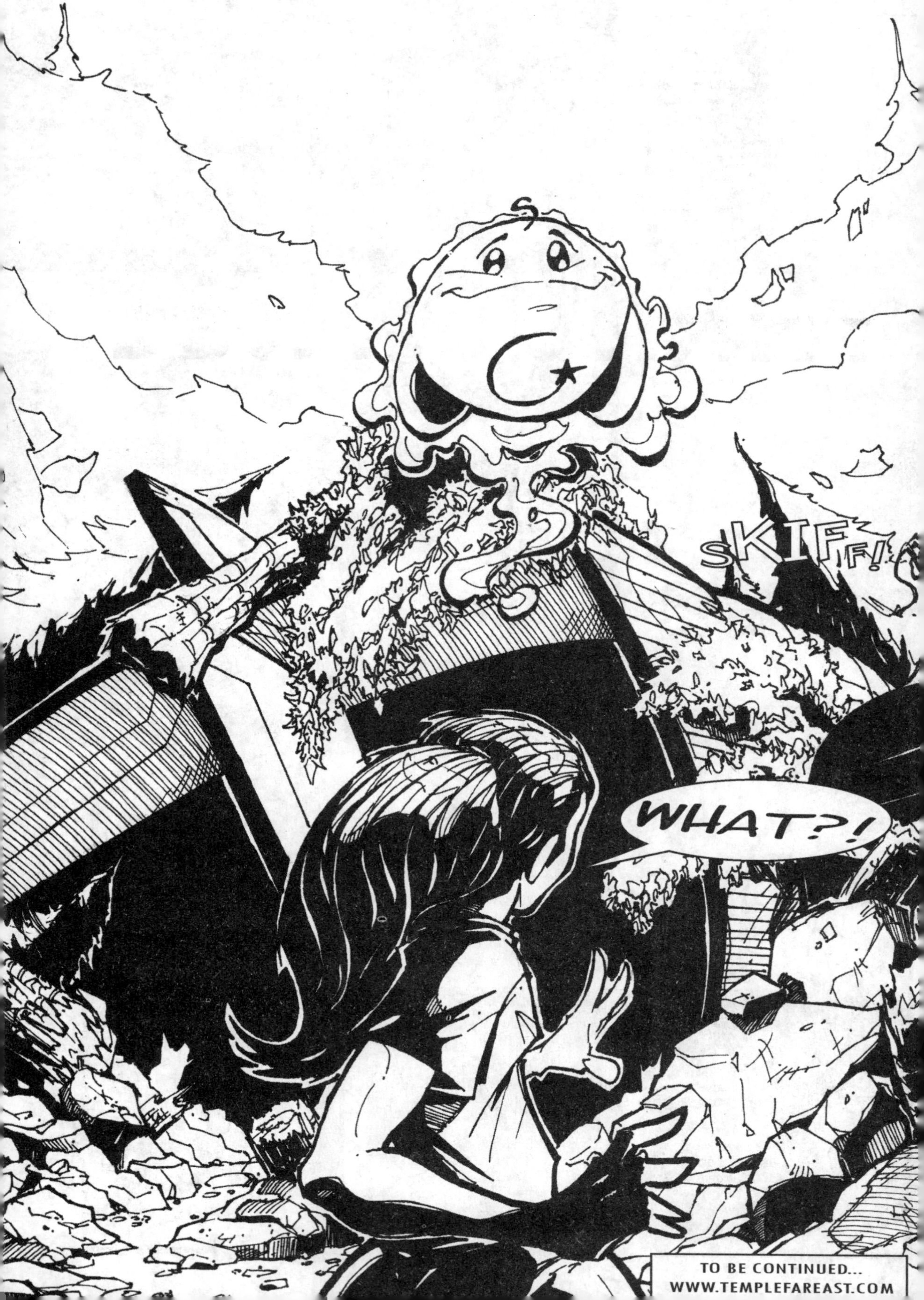
sKIFFF!
WHAT?!
TO BE CONTINUED...
WWW.TEMPLEFAREAST.COM

The Crater Kid™

The planet's basic freedoms are challenged as the Kid discovers one of the great truths of liberty in the shade of...

THE YARNOG TREE

BY MARTY BAUMANN

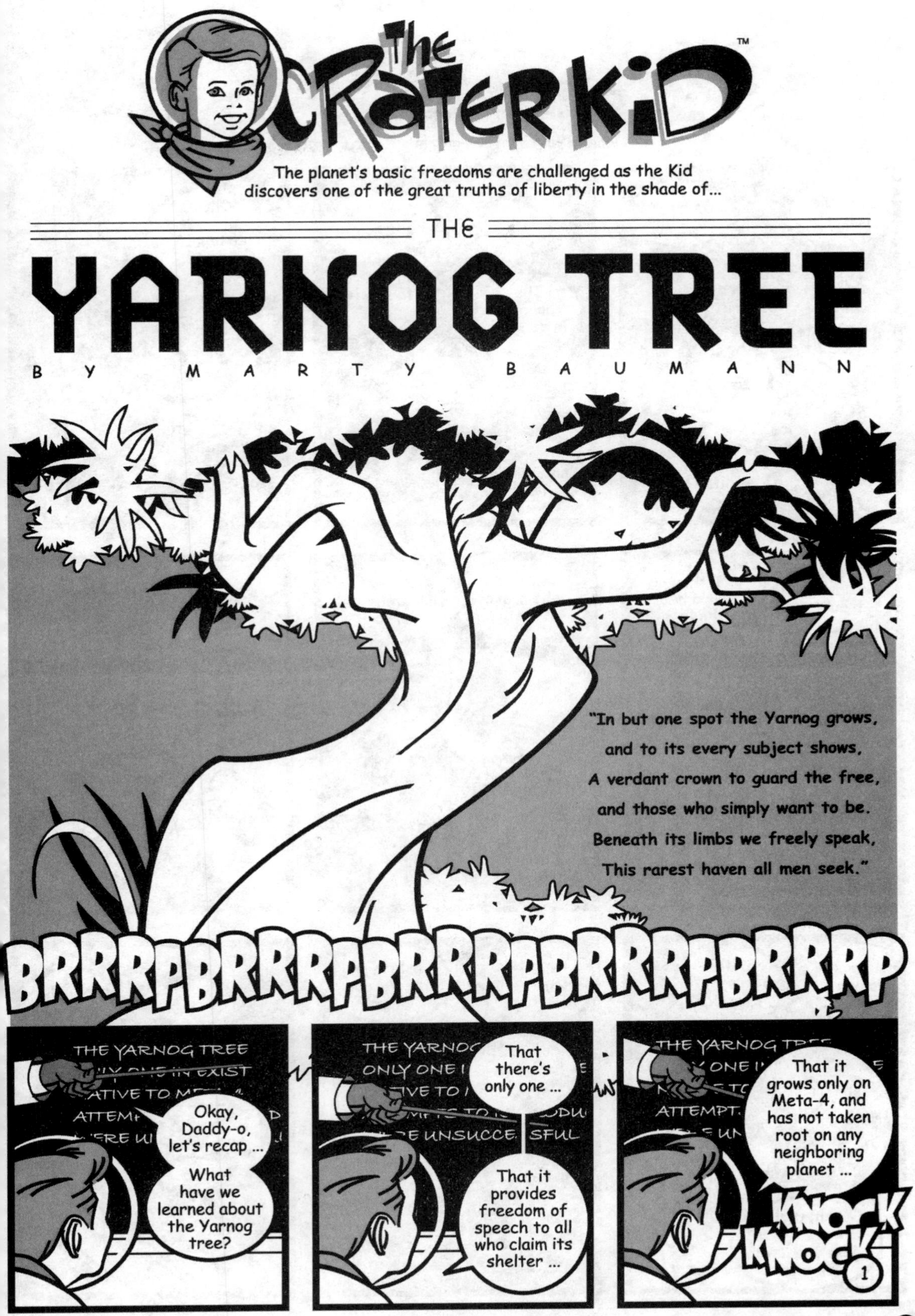

"In but one spot the Yarnog grows,
and to its every subject shows,
A verdant crown to guard the free,
and those who simply want to be.
Beneath its limbs we freely speak,
This rarest haven all men seek."
BRRRPBRRRRPBRRRRPBRRRRPBRRRRP
THE YARNOG TREE
Okay, Daddy-o, let's recap ...
What have we learned about the Yarnog tree?
That there's only one ...
That it provides freedom of speech to all who claim its shelter ...
That it grows only on Meta-4, and has not taken root on any neighboring planet ...
KNOCK KNOCK
1

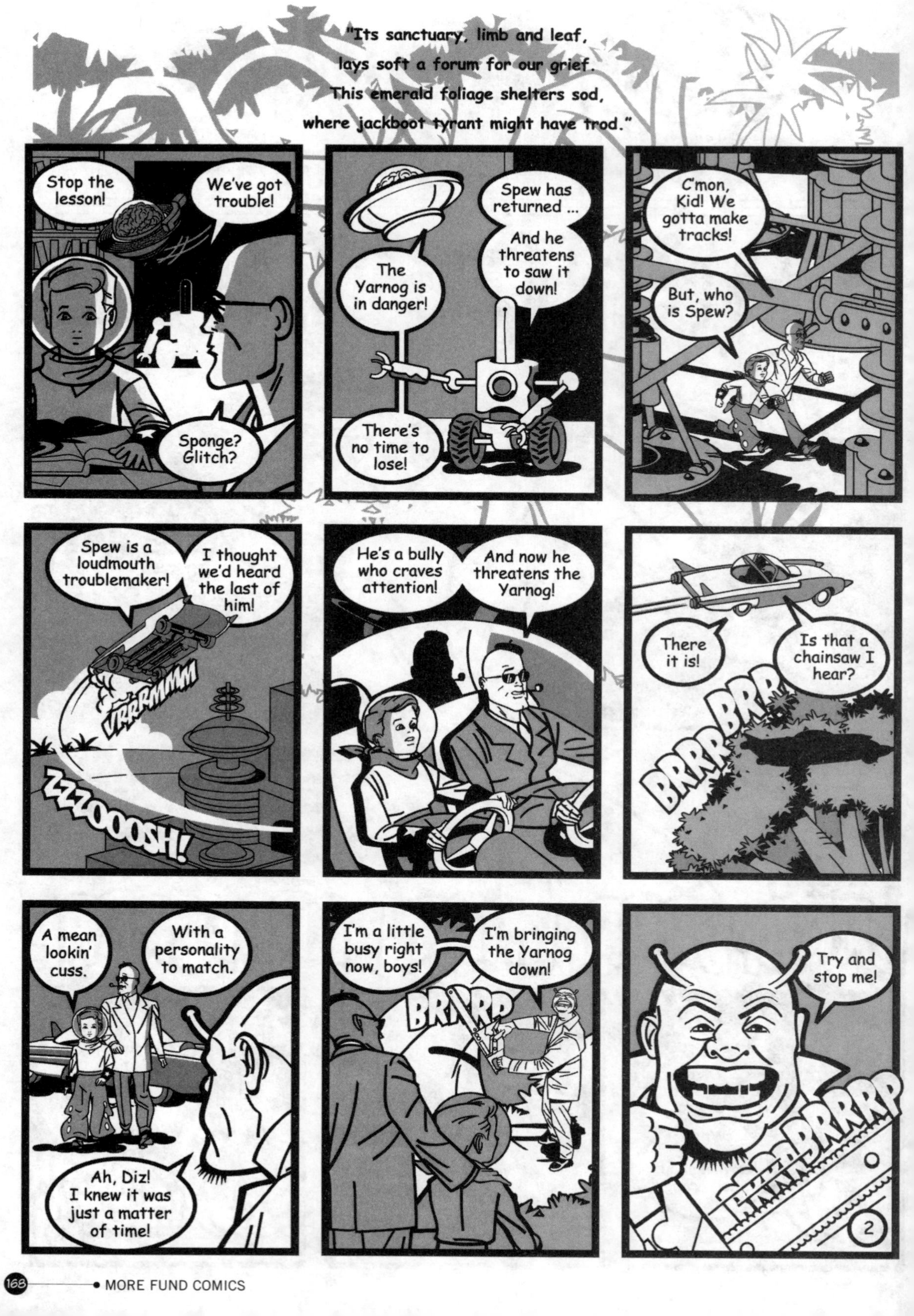
"Its sanctuary, limb and leaf,
lays soft a forum for our grief.
This emerald foliage shelters sod,
where jackboot tyrant might have trod."
Stop the lesson!
We've got trouble!
Sponge? Glitch?
Spew has returned ...
And he threatens to saw it down!
The Yarnog is in danger!
There's no time to lose!
C'mon, Kid! We gotta make tracks!
But, who is Spew?
Spew is a loudmouth troublemaker!
I thought we'd heard the last of him!
VRRRMMM
ZZZOOOOSH!
He's a bully who craves attention!
And now he threatens the Yarnog!
There it is!
Is that a chainsaw I hear?
BRRRBRR
A mean lookin' cuss.
With a personality to match.
Ah, Diz! I knew it was just a matter of time!
I'm a little busy right now, boys!
I'm bringing the Yarnog down!
BRRRP
Try and stop me!
BRRRRP
2

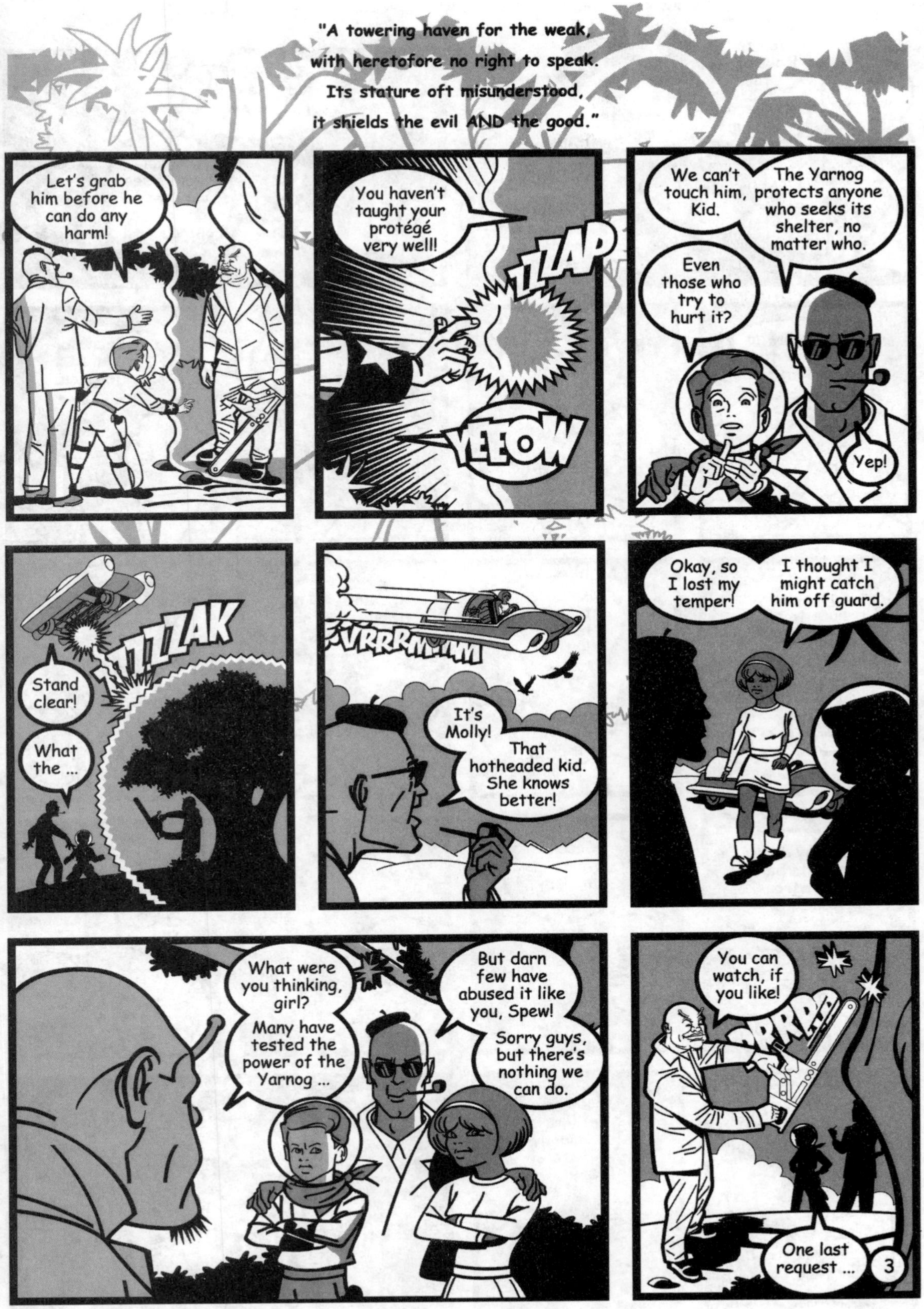
"A towering haven for the weak,
with heretofore no right to speak.
Its stature oft misunderstood,
it shields the evil AND the good."
Let's grab him before he can do any harm!
You haven't taught your protégé very well!
ZZZAP
YEEOW
We can't touch him, Kid.
The Yarnog protects anyone who seeks its shelter, no matter who.
Even those who try to hurt it?
Yep!
ZZZZZAK
Stand clear!
What the ...
VRRRMMMM
It's Molly!
That hotheaded kid. She knows better!
Okay, so I lost my temper!
I thought I might catch him off guard.
What were you thinking, girl?
Many have tested the power of the Yarnog ...
But darn few have abused it like you, Spew!
Sorry guys, but there's nothing we can do.
You can watch, if you like!
One last request ...
3

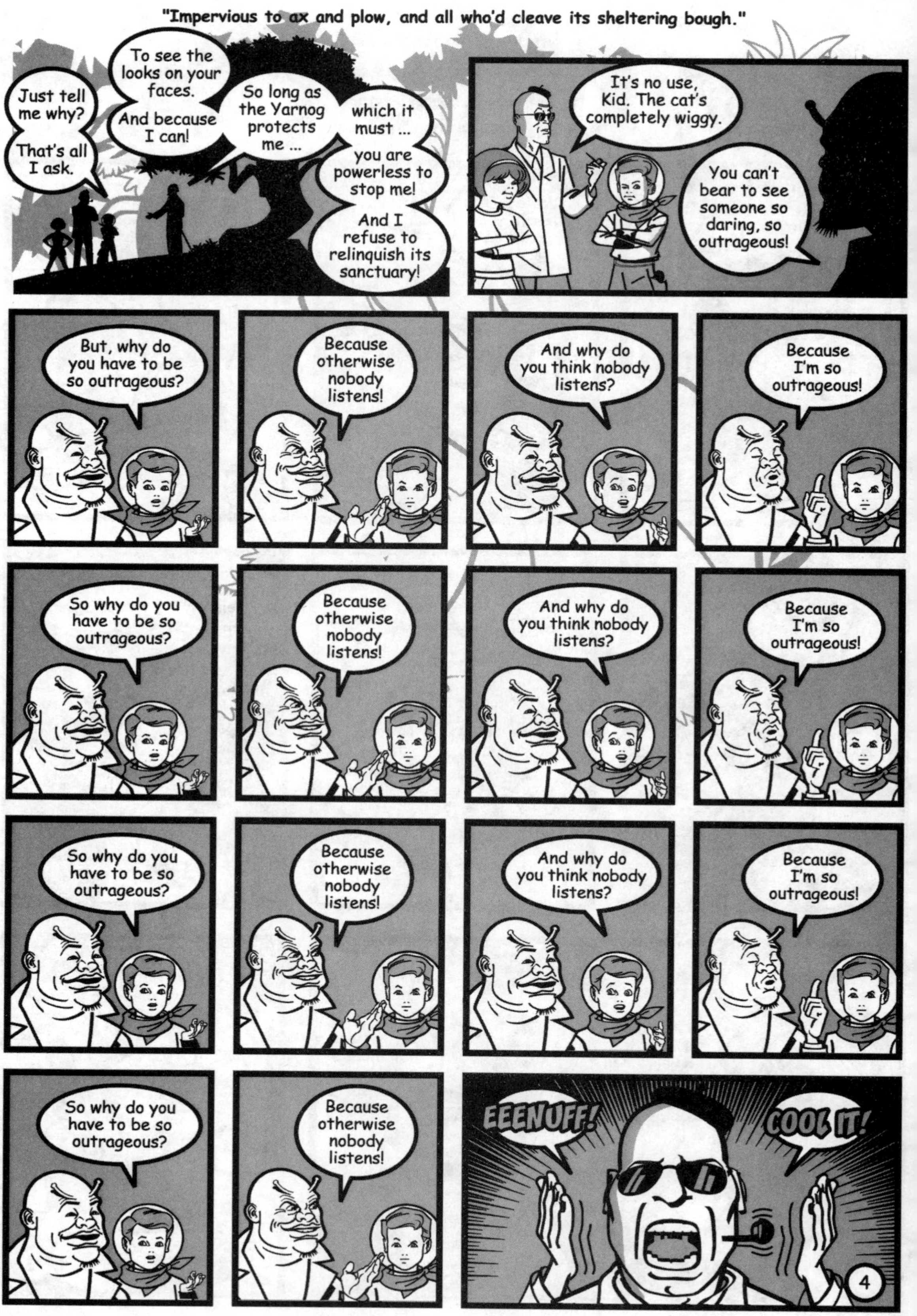
"Impervious to ax and plow, and all who'd cleave its sheltering bough."
Just tell me why?
That's all I ask.
To see the looks on your faces.
And because I can!
So long as the Yarnog protects me ...
which it must ...
you are powerless to stop me!
And I refuse to relinquish its sanctuary!
It's no use, Kid. The cat's completely wiggy.
You can't bear to see someone so daring, so outrageous!
But, why do you have to be so outrageous?
Because otherwise nobody listens!
And why do you think nobody listens?
Because I'm so outrageous!
So why do you have to be so outrageous?
Because otherwise nobody listens!
And why do you think nobody listens?
Because I'm so outrageous!
So why do you have to be so outrageous?
Because otherwise nobody listens!
And why do you think nobody listens?
Because I'm so outrageous!
So why do you have to be so outrageous?
Because otherwise nobody listens!
EEENUFF!
COOL IT!
4

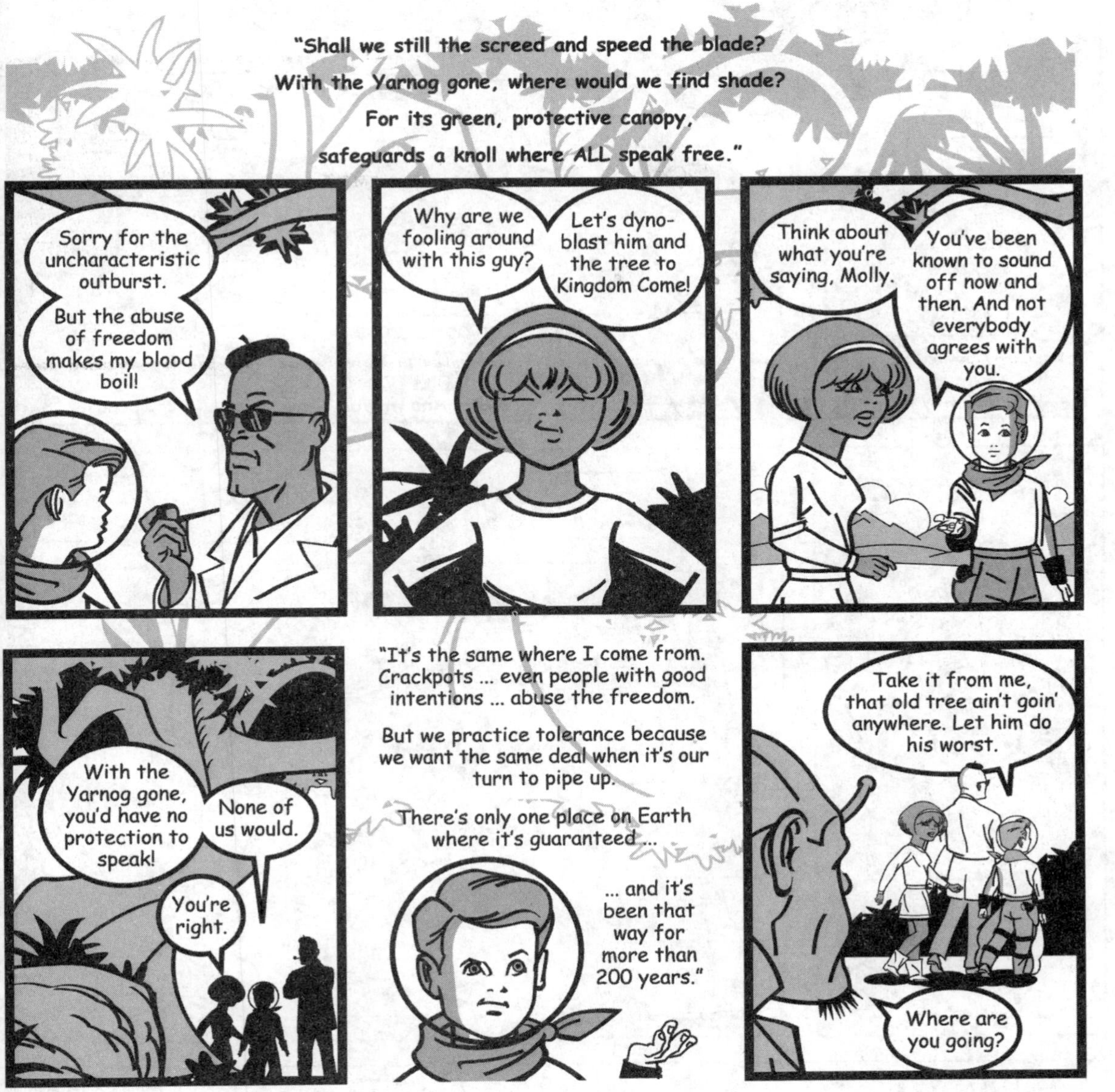
"Shall we still the screed and speed the blade?
With the Yarnog gone, where would we find shade?
For its green, protective canopy,
safeguards a knoll where ALL speak free."
Sorry for the uncharacteristic outburst.
But the abuse of freedom makes my blood boil!
Why are we fooling around with this guy?
Let's dyno-blast him and the tree to Kingdom Come!
Think about what you're saying, Molly.
You've been known to sound off now and then. And not everybody agrees with you.
With the Yarnog gone, you'd have no protection to speak!
None of us would.
You're right.
"It's the same where I come from. Crackpots ... even people with good intentions ... abuse the freedom.
But we practice tolerance because we want the same deal when it's our turn to pipe up.
There's only one place on Earth where it's guaranteed ...
... and it's been that way for more than 200 years."
Take it from me, that old tree ain't goin' anywhere. Let him do his worst.
Where are you going?
ZOOOM
Do you think I won't?
Are you testing me?
BRRRP
But ... you can't leave ...
You have to listen ...
"So let the reckless shout and the evil rave.
For we must suffer fools to protect the brave."
But... I'm so outrageous.
THE END
Visit www.craterkid.com for more fun!

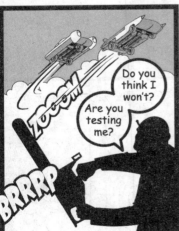

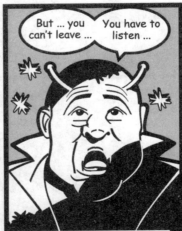

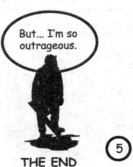

WORKIN' THE BEACH

BY GEOFF JOHNS AND SCOTT KOLINS

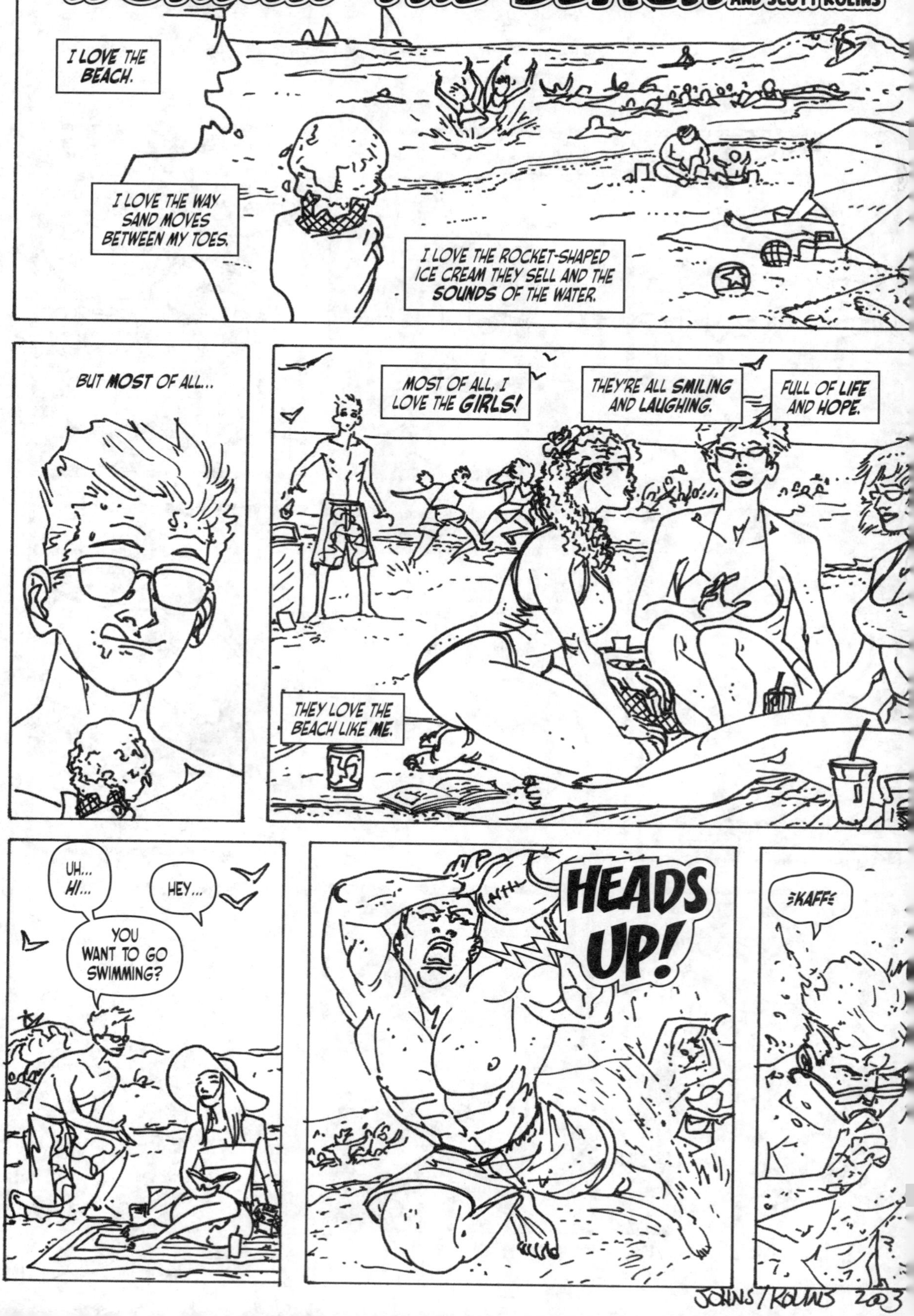

I LOVE THE BEACH.
I LOVE THE WAY SAND MOVES BETWEEN MY TOES.
I LOVE THE ROCKET-SHAPED ICE CREAM THEY SELL AND THE SOUNDS OF THE WATER.
BUT MOST OF ALL...
MOST OF ALL, I LOVE THE GIRLS!
THEY'RE ALL SMILING AND LAUGHING.
FULL OF LIFE AND HOPE.
THEY LOVE THE BEACH LIKE ME.
UH... HI...
HEY...
YOU WANT TO GO SWIMMING?
HEADS UP!
KAFF
JOHNS / KOLINS 2003

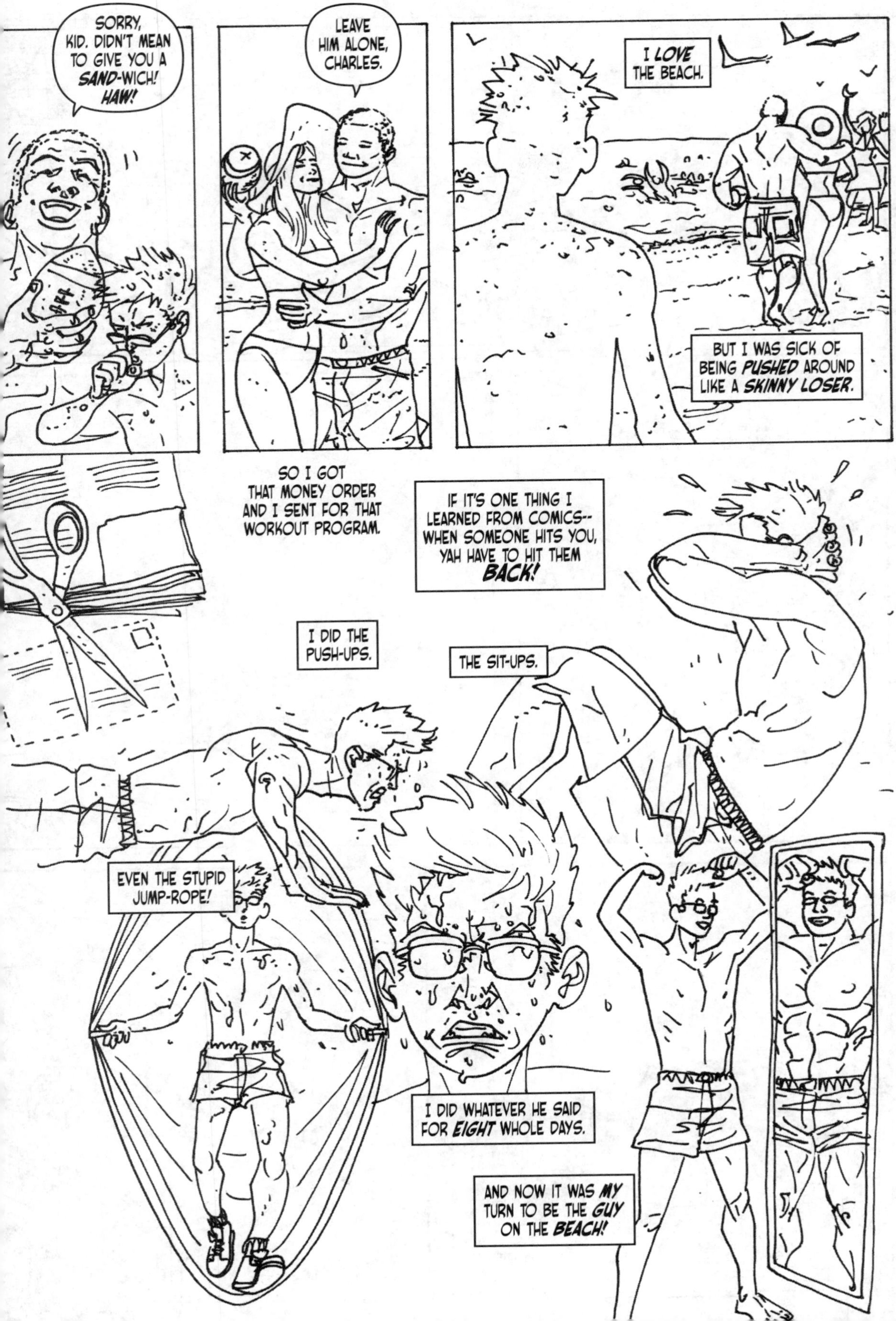
SORRY, KID. DIDN'T MEAN TO GIVE YOU A SAND-WICH! HAW!
LEAVE HIM ALONE, CHARLES.
I LOVE THE BEACH.
BUT I WAS SICK OF BEING PUSHED AROUND LIKE A SKINNY LOSER.
SO I GOT THAT MONEY ORDER AND I SENT FOR THAT WORKOUT PROGRAM.
IF IT'S ONE THING I LEARNED FROM COMICS--WHEN SOMEONE HITS YOU, YAH HAVE TO HIT THEM BACK!
I DID THE PUSH-UPS.
THE SIT-UPS.
EVEN THE STUPID JUMP-ROPE!
I DID WHATEVER HE SAID FOR EIGHT WHOLE DAYS.
AND NOW IT WAS MY TURN TO BE THE GUY ON THE BEACH!

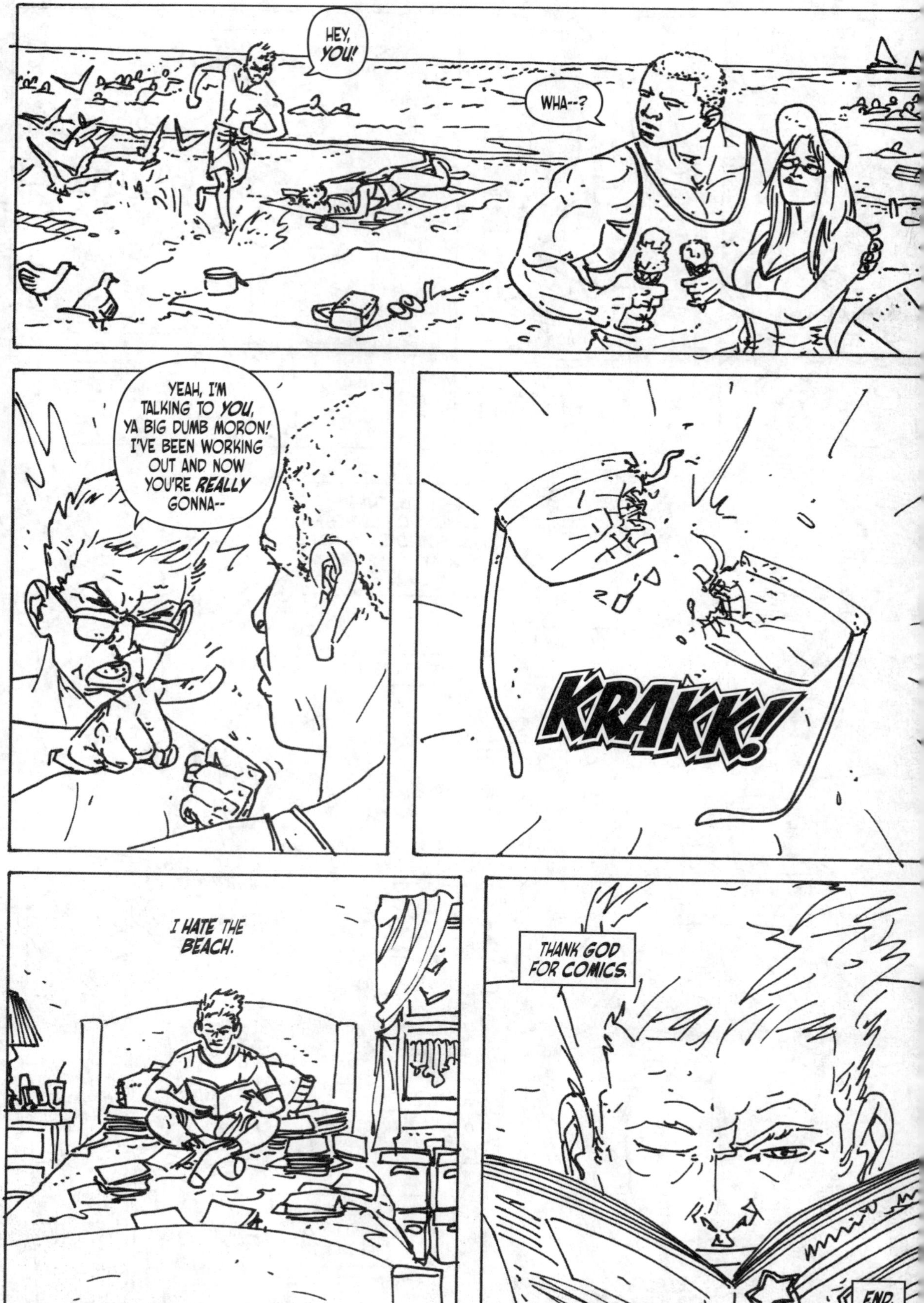
HEY, YOU!
WHA--?
YEAH, I'M TALKING TO YOU, YA BIG DUMB MORON! I'VE BEEN WORKING OUT AND NOW YOU'RE REALLY GONNA--
KRAKK!
I HATE THE BEACH.
THANK GOD FOR COMICS.
END.

LETTERING BY VINCE SNEED

JOHNS / KOLINS 200

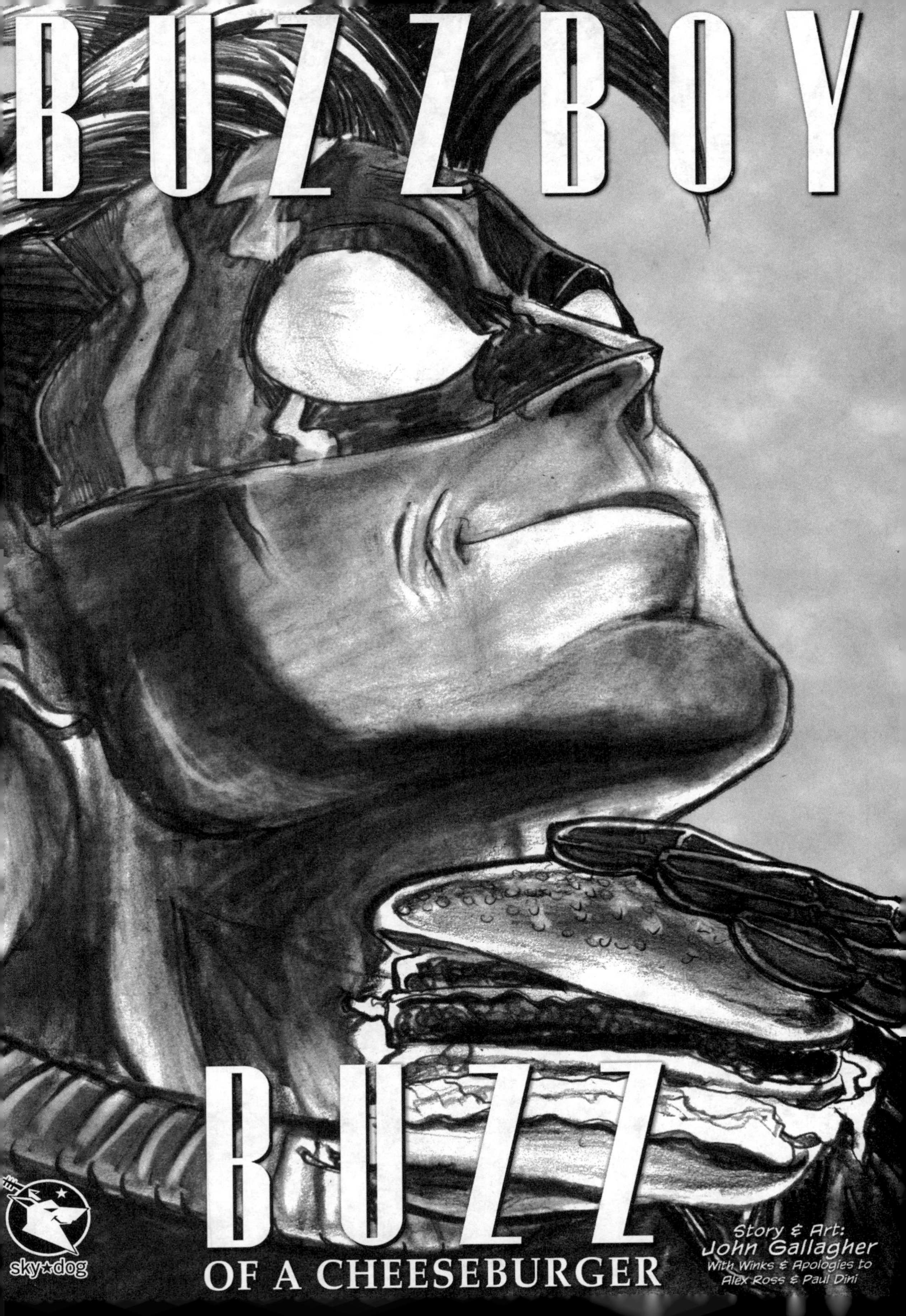
BUZZBOY
BUZZ
OF A CHEESEBURGER
Story & Art:
John Gallagher
With Winks & Apologies to
Alex Ross & Paul Dini
sky★dog

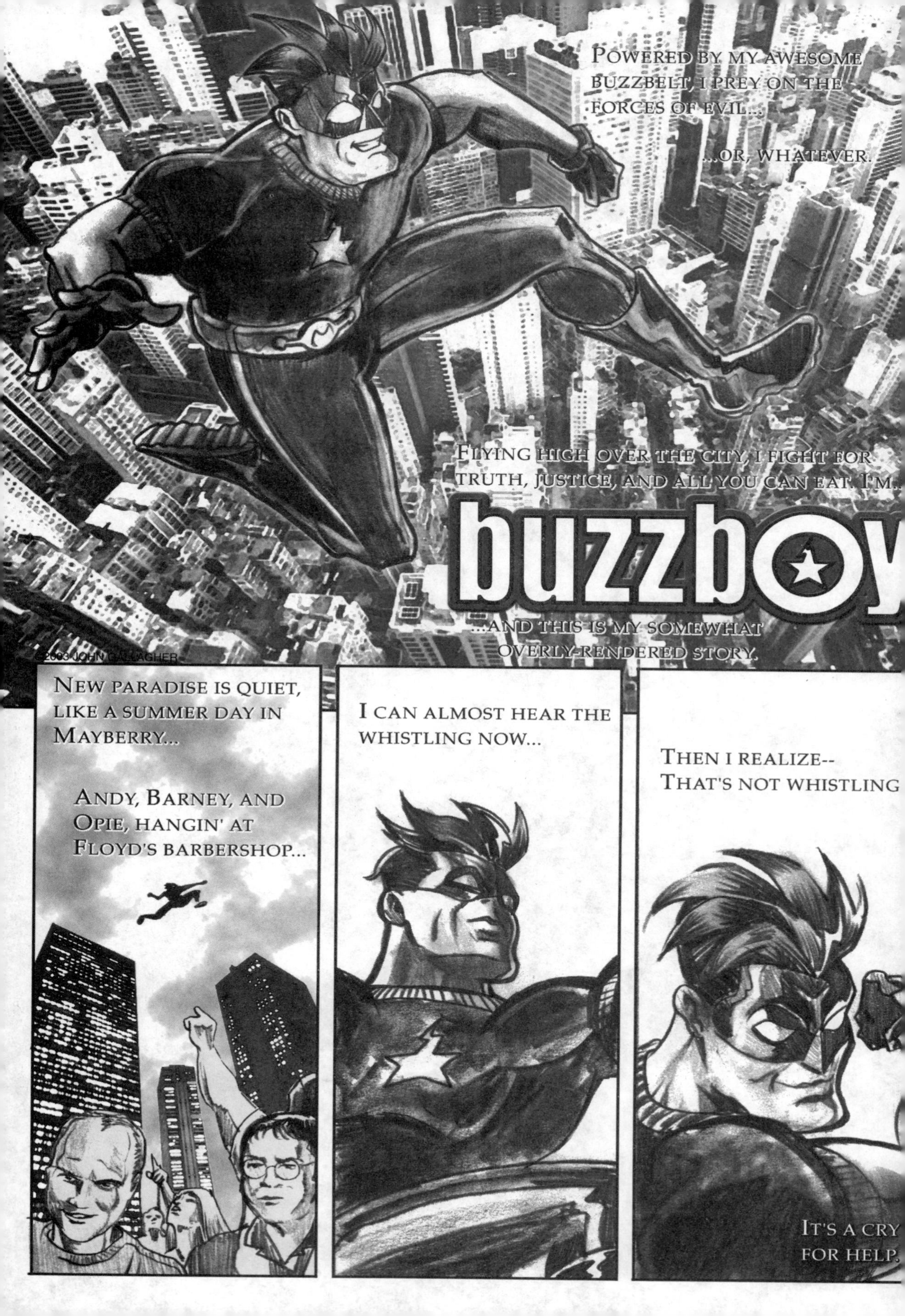
POWERED BY MY AWESOME BUZZBELT, I PREY ON THE FORCES OF EVIL...
...OR, WHATEVER.
FLYING HIGH OVER THE CITY, I FIGHT FOR TRUTH, JUSTICE, AND ALL YOU CAN EAT. I'M...
buzzboy
...AND THIS IS MY SOMEWHAT OVERLY-RENDERED STORY.
©2003 JOHN GALLAGHER
NEW PARADISE IS QUIET, LIKE A SUMMER DAY IN MAYBERRY...
ANDY, BARNEY, AND OPIE, HANGIN' AT FLOYD'S BARBERSHOP...
I CAN ALMOST HEAR THE WHISTLING NOW...
THEN I REALIZE-- THAT'S NOT WHISTLING
IT'S A CRY FOR HELP.

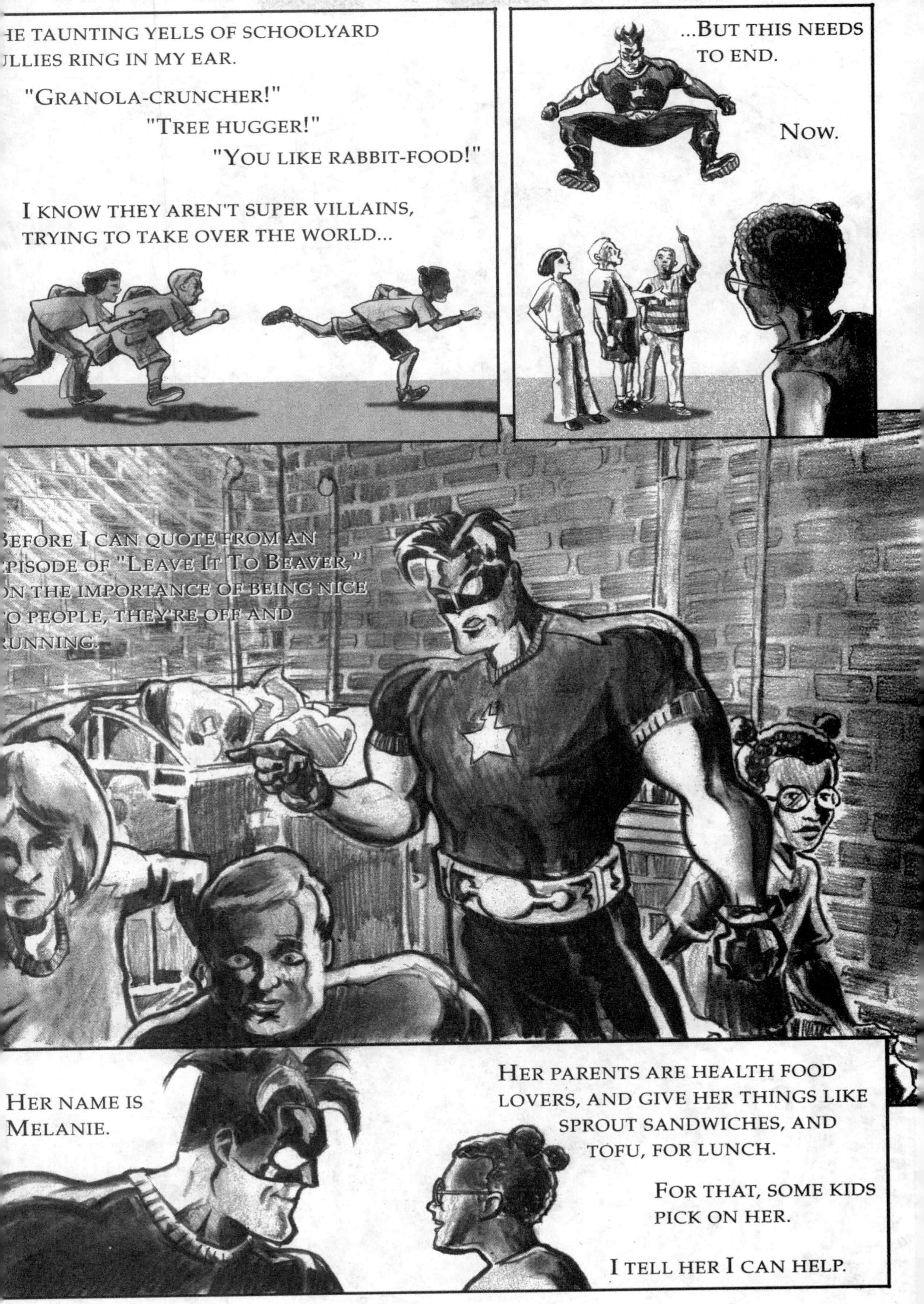

HE TAUNTING YELLS OF SCHOOLYARD
ULLIES RING IN MY EAR.
"GRANOLA-CRUNCHER!"
"TREE HUGGER!"
"YOU LIKE RABBIT-FOOD!"
I KNOW THEY AREN'T SUPER VILLAINS, TRYING TO TAKE OVER THE WORLD...
...BUT THIS NEEDS TO END.
NOW.
EFORE I CAN QUOTE FROM AN PISODE OF "LEAVE IT TO BEAVER," ON THE IMPORTANCE OF BEING NICE O PEOPLE, THEY'RE OFF AND RUNNING.
HER NAME IS MELANIE.
HER PARENTS ARE HEALTH FOOD LOVERS, AND GIVE HER THINGS LIKE SPROUT SANDWICHES, AND TOFU, FOR LUNCH.
FOR THAT, SOME KIDS PICK ON HER.
I TELL HER I CAN HELP.

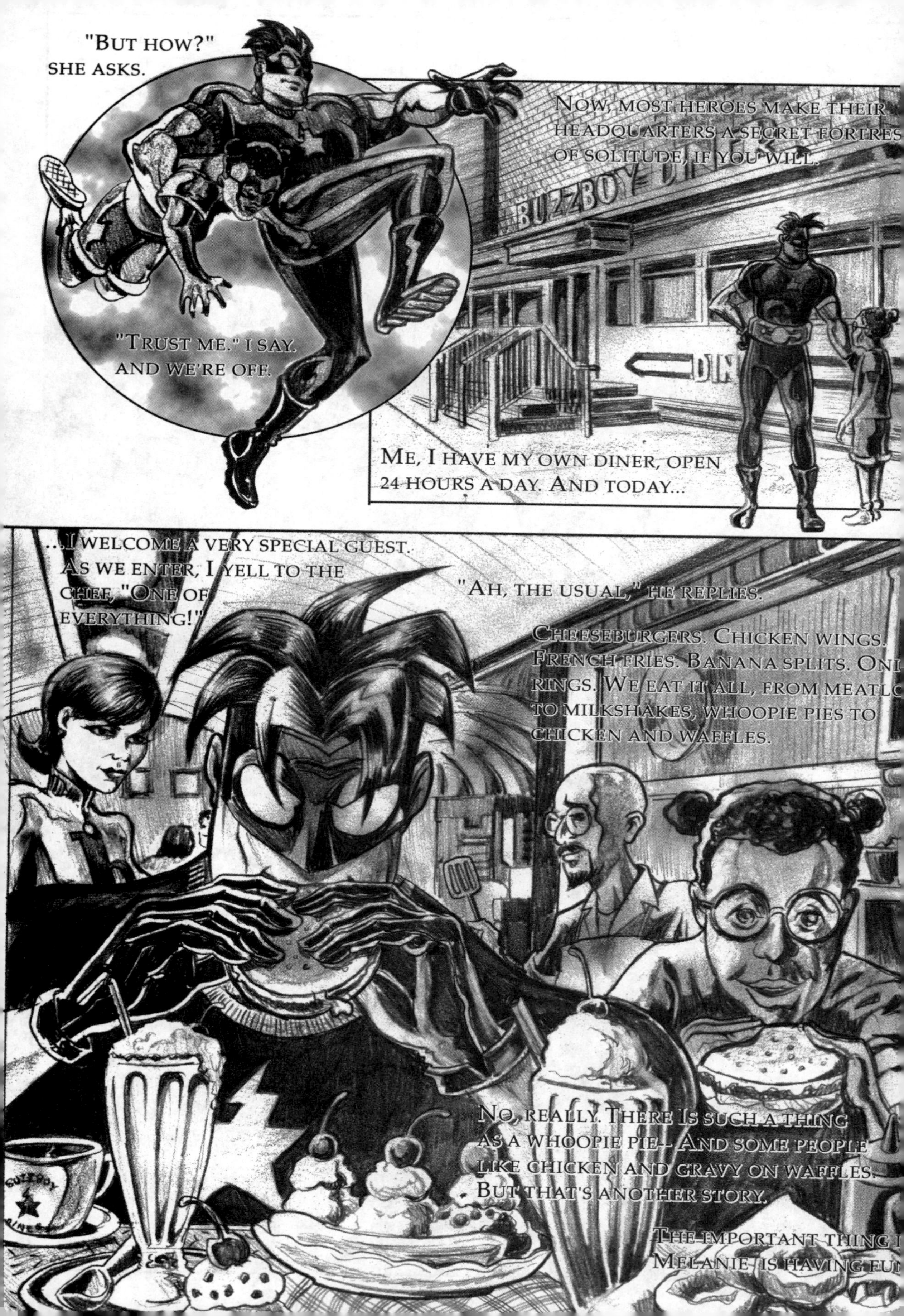
"But how?" she asks.
"Trust me." I say. And we're off.
Now, most heroes make their headquarters a secret fortres of solitude, if you will.
Me, I have my own diner, open 24 hours a day. And today...
...I welcome a very special guest. As we enter, I yell to the chef, "One of everything!"
"Ah, the usual," he replies.
Cheeseburgers. Chicken wings. French fries. Banana splits. Oni rings. We eat it all, from meatlo to milkshakes, whoopie pies to chicken and waffles.
No, really. There is such a thing as a whoopie pie. And some people like chicken and gravy on waffles. But that's another story.
The important thing i Melanie is having fu

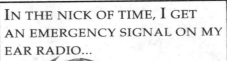

"THANK YOU, MISTER BUZZBOY," SHE SAYS. "BUT HOW WILL THIS HELP WITH THOSE BULLIES?"

"UH..."

IN THE NICK OF TIME, I GET AN EMERGENCY SIGNAL ON MY EAR RADIO...

...JUST AS MELANIE REALIZES SHE'S HAD ENOUGH TO EAT.

WE SAY OUR GOODBYES...

BUT NO SOONER HAVE I LEAPT AWAY, THEN THE JUNIOR HENCHMAN OF AMERICA RETURN.

BRAVELY, MY SMALL, NEAR-SIGHTED FRIEND WALKS UP TO THE LEADER...

..AND THROWS UP ALL OVER HIS SHOES.

...THEY RUN AWAY DEFEATED, AND IN NEED OF A GOOD BATH.

MELANIE LEARNED THAT STANDING UP FOR YOURSELF IS SOMETIMES EASIER THAN YOU THINK.

AND ME? I LEARNED THAT I SHOULD STICK TO SAVING THE WORLD...

AND NEVER, EVER, HAVE THE FRIED CHICKEN ON A THURDAY, AT THE BUZZBOY DINER. ★

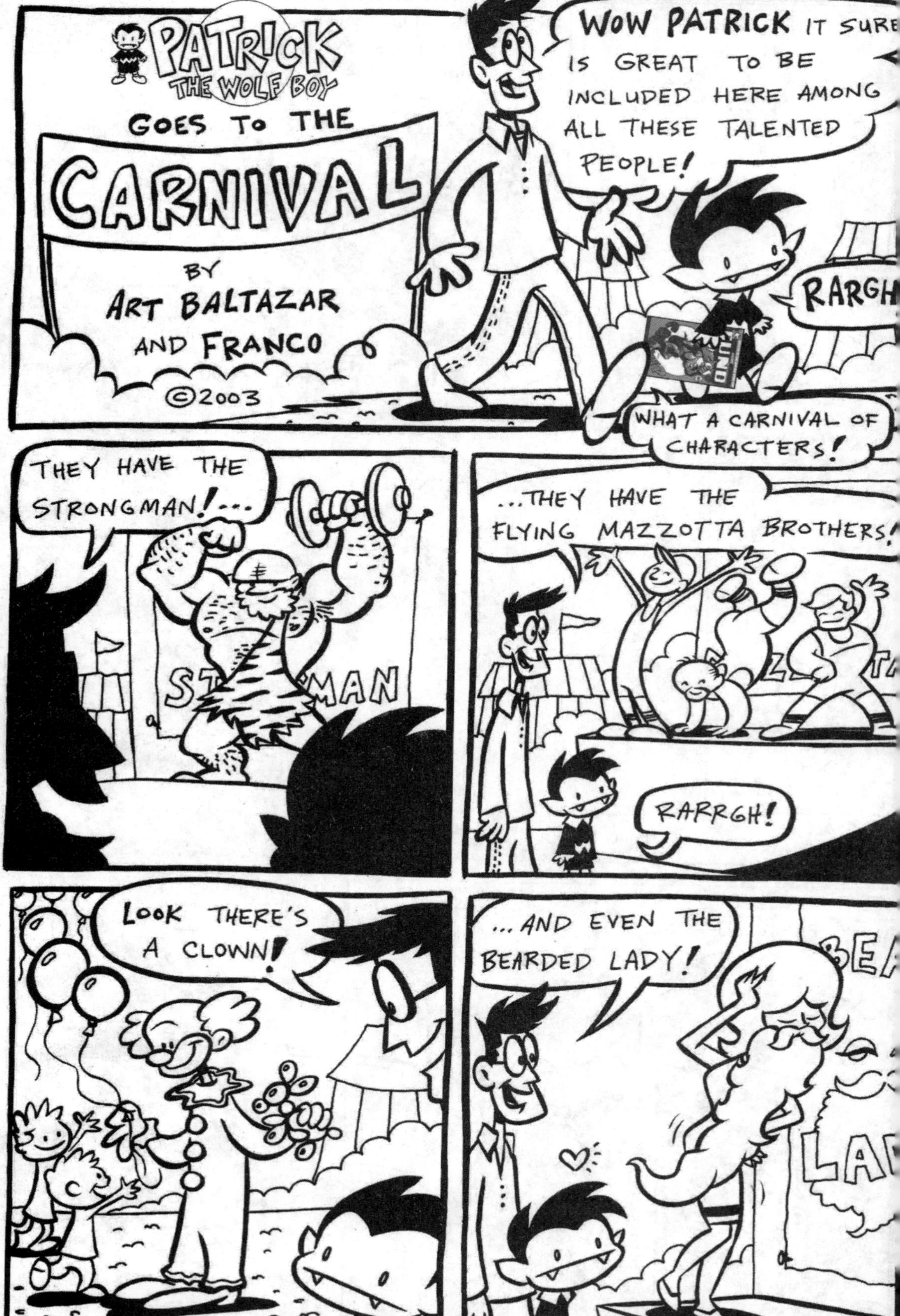
PATRICK THE WOLF BOY
GOES TO THE
CARNIVAL
BY
ART BALTAZAR
AND FRANCO
©2003
WOW PATRICK IT SURE IS GREAT TO BE INCLUDED HERE AMONG ALL THESE TALENTED PEOPLE!
RARGH
WHAT A CARNIVAL OF CHARACTERS!
THEY HAVE THE STRONGMAN!...
ST MAN
...THEY HAVE THE FLYING MAZZOTTA BROTHERS!
RARRGH!
LOOK THERE'S A CLOWN!
...AND EVEN THE BEARDED LADY!

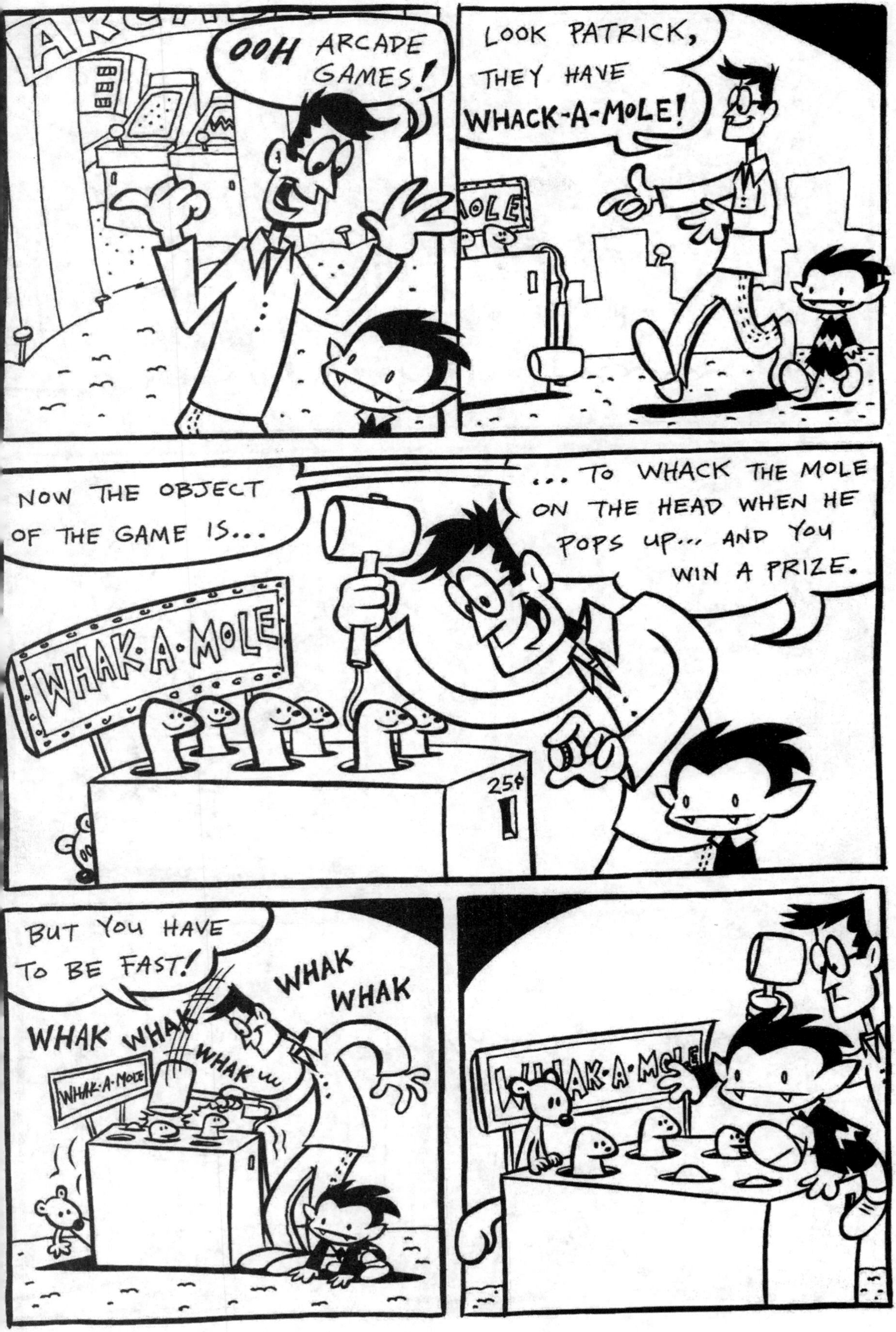
OOH ARCADE GAMES!
LOOK PATRICK, THEY HAVE WHACK-A-MOLE!
NOW THE OBJECT OF THE GAME IS...
... TO WHACK THE MOLE ON THE HEAD WHEN HE POPS UP... AND YOU WIN A PRIZE.
WHAK-A-MOLE
25¢
BUT YOU HAVE TO BE FAST!
WHAK WHAK
WHAK WHAK WHAK WHAK
WHAK-A-MOLE
WHAK-A-MOLE

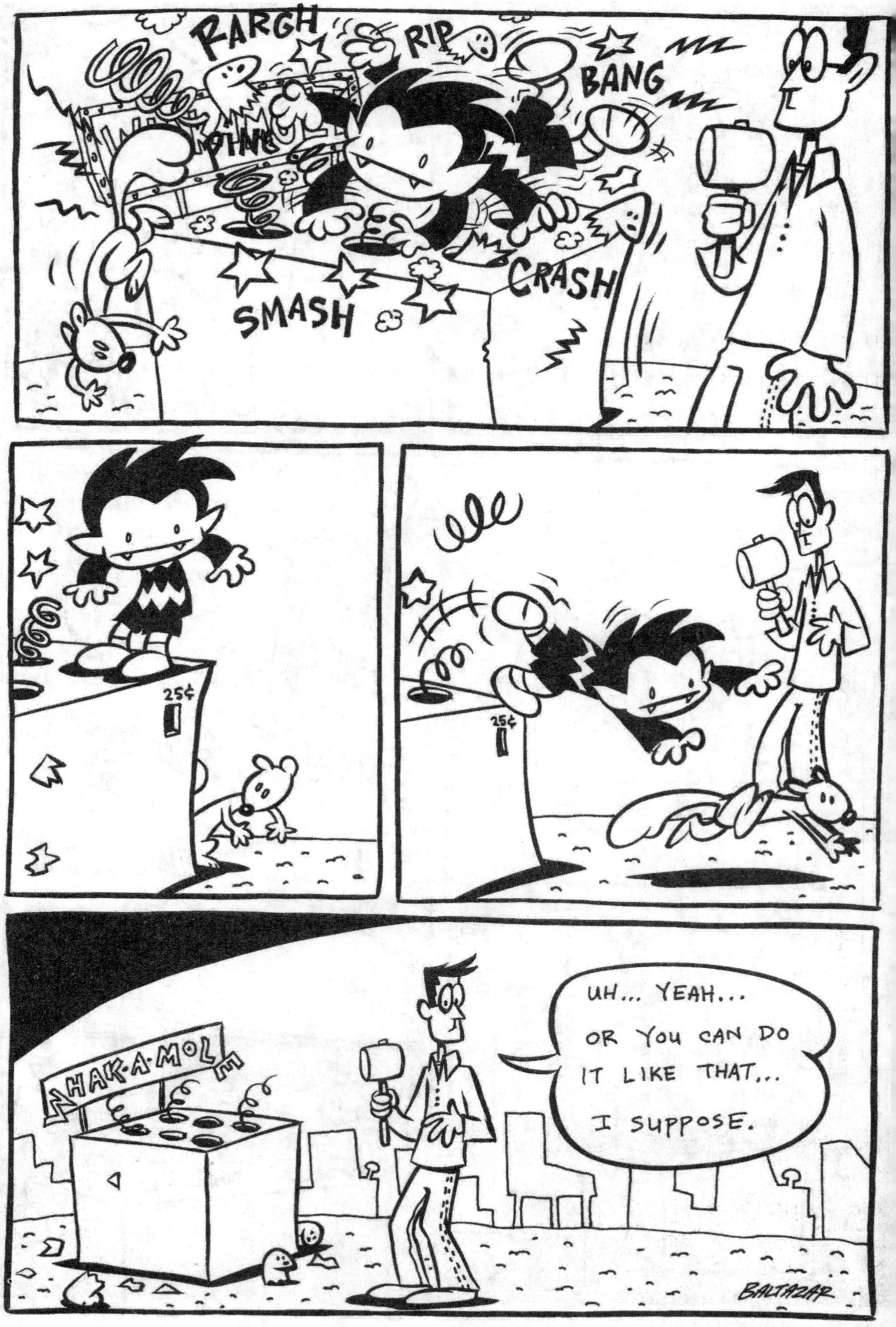

RARGH
RIP
BANG
SMASH
CRASH
25¢
25¢
HAK·A·MOLE
UH... YEAH... OR YOU CAN DO IT LIKE THAT... I SUPPOSE.
BALTAZAR

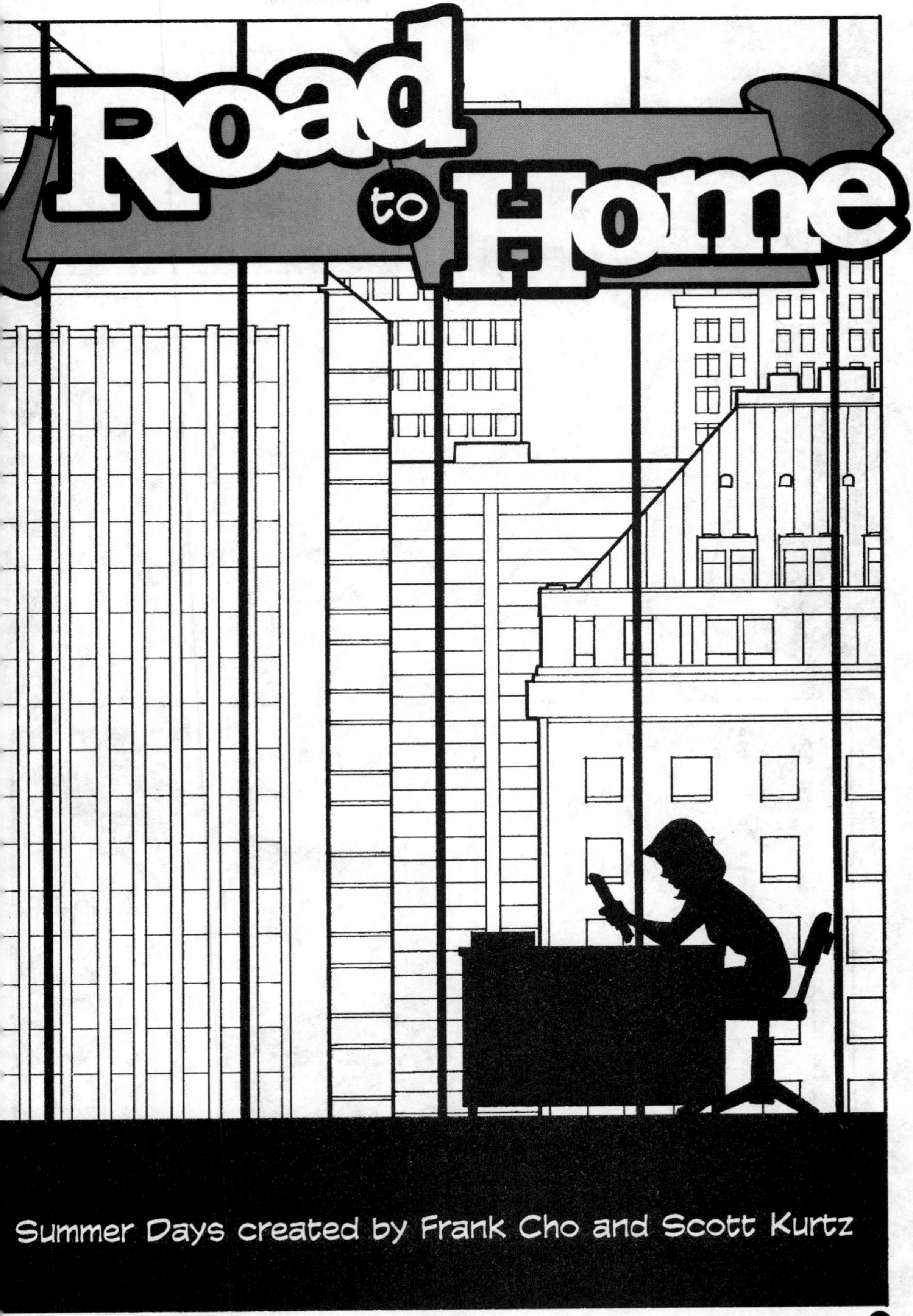
Road to Home
Summer Days created by Frank Cho and Scott Kurtz

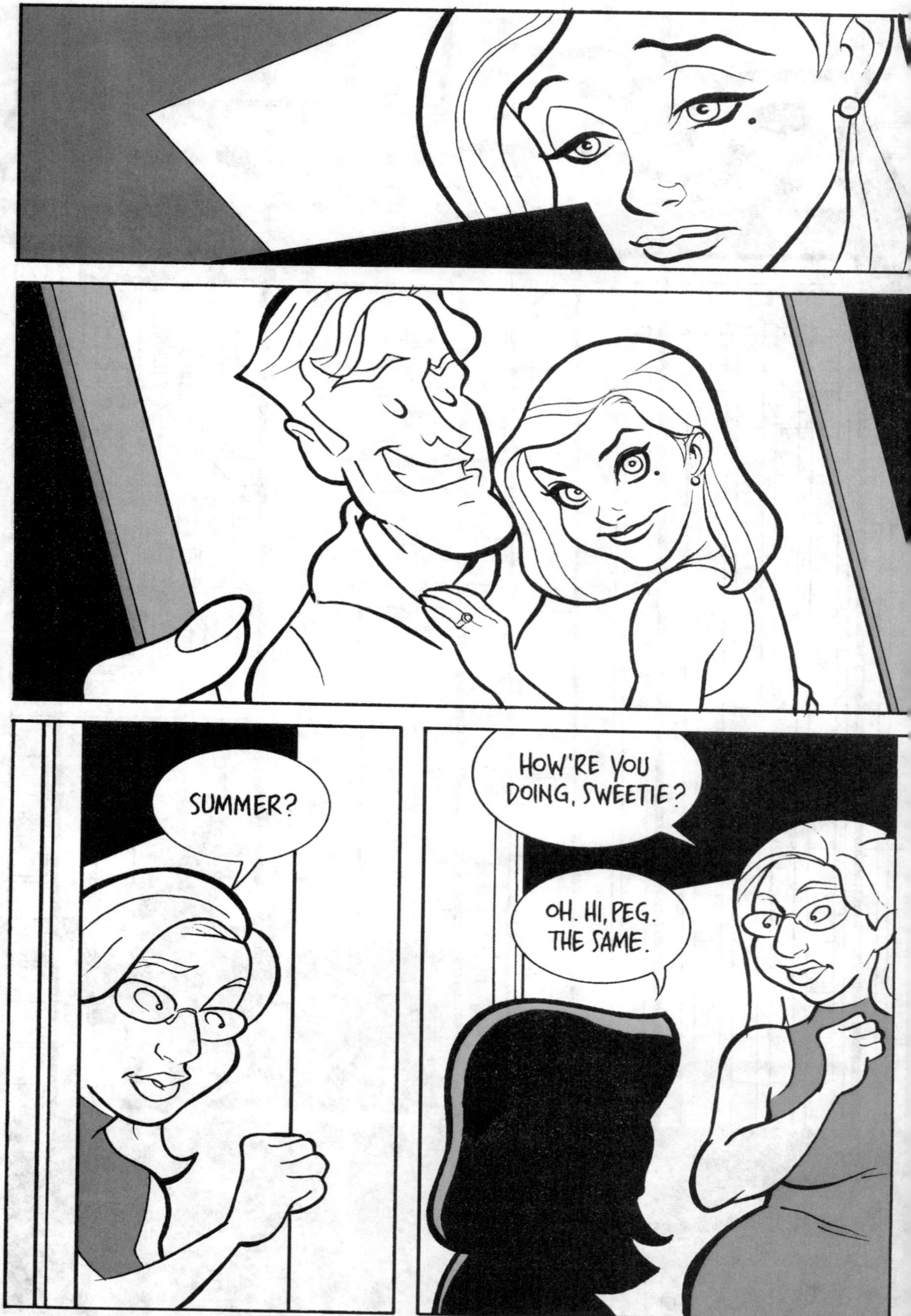
SUMMER?
HOW'RE YOU DOING, SWEETIE?
OH. HI, PEG. THE SAME.

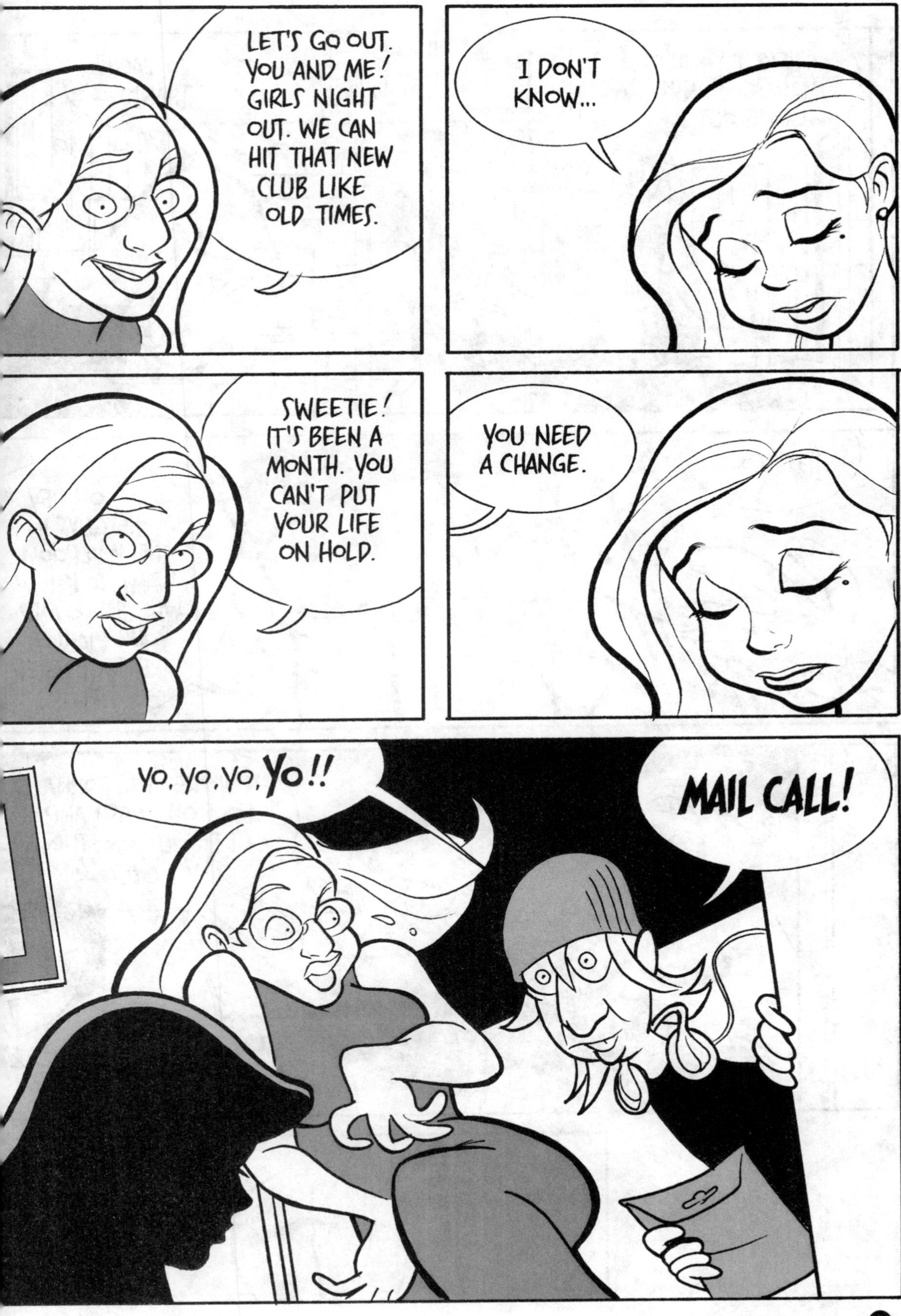
LET'S GO OUT. YOU AND ME! GIRLS NIGHT OUT. WE CAN HIT THAT NEW CLUB LIKE OLD TIMES.
I DON'T KNOW...
SWEETIE! IT'S BEEN A MONTH. YOU CAN'T PUT YOUR LIFE ON HOLD.
YOU NEED A CHANGE.
yo, yo, yo, Yo!!
MAIL CALL!

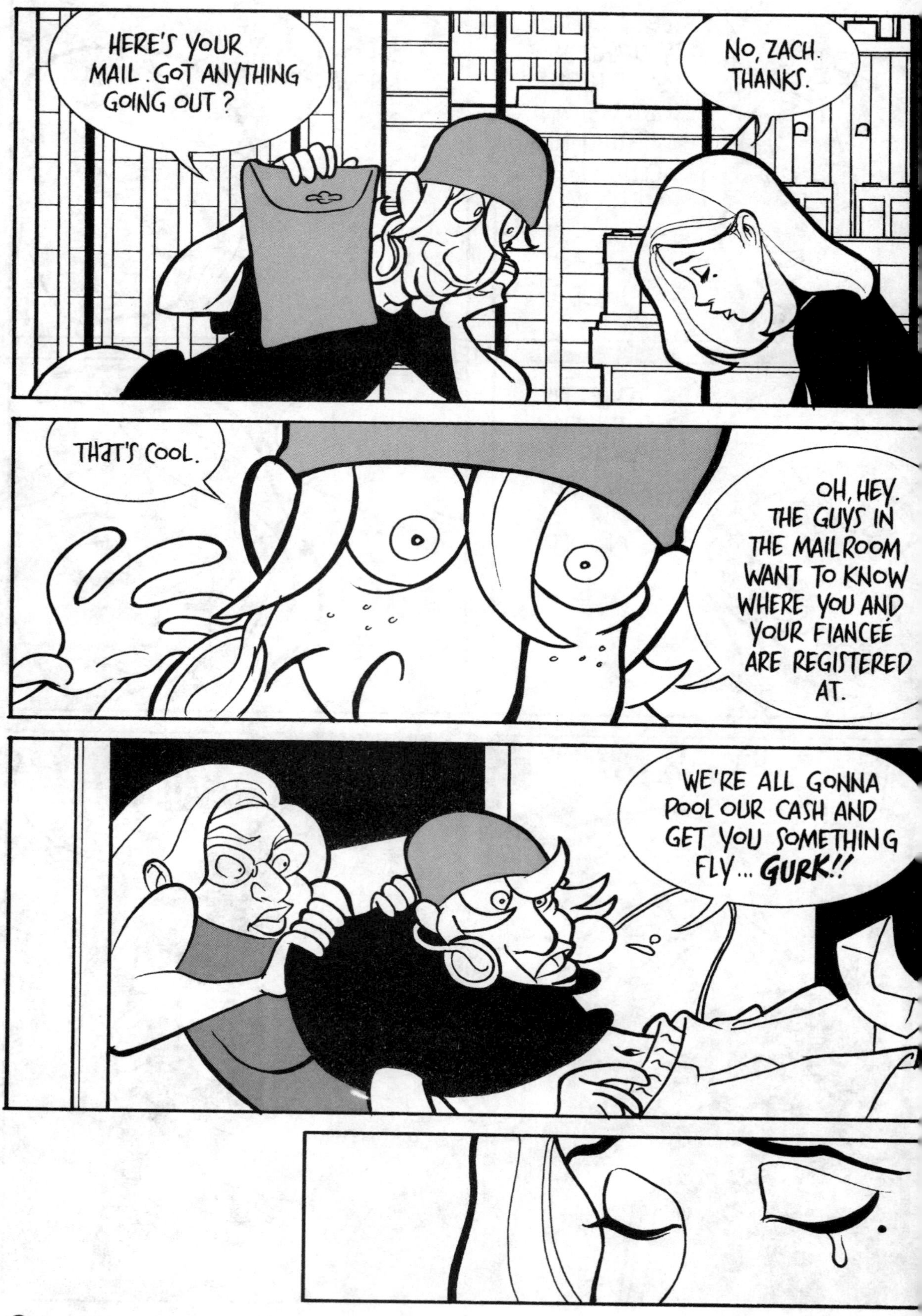
HERE'S YOUR MAIL. GOT ANYTHING GOING OUT?
NO, ZACH. THANKS.
THAT'S COOL.
OH, HEY. THE GUYS IN THE MAILROOM WANT TO KNOW WHERE YOU AND YOUR FIANCEÉ ARE REGISTERED AT.
WE'RE ALL GONNA POOL OUR CASH AND GET YOU SOMETHING FLY... **GURK!!**

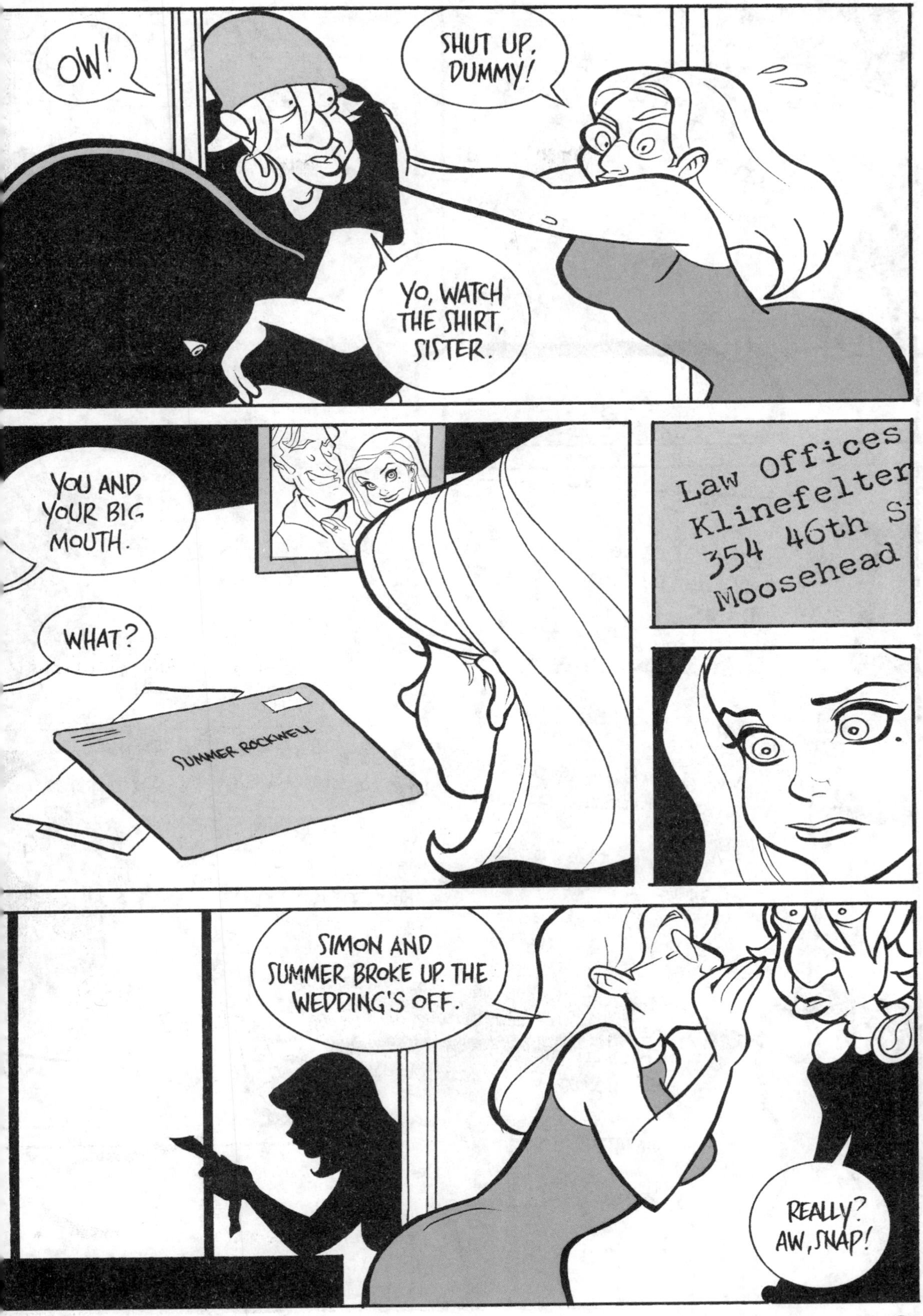
OW!
SHUT UP, DUMMY!
YO, WATCH THE SHIRT, SISTER.
YOU AND YOUR BIG MOUTH.
WHAT?
SUMMER ROCKWELL
Law Offices
Klinefelter
354 46th S
Moosehead
SIMON AND SUMMER BROKE UP. THE WEDDING'S OFF.
REALLY? AW, SNAP!

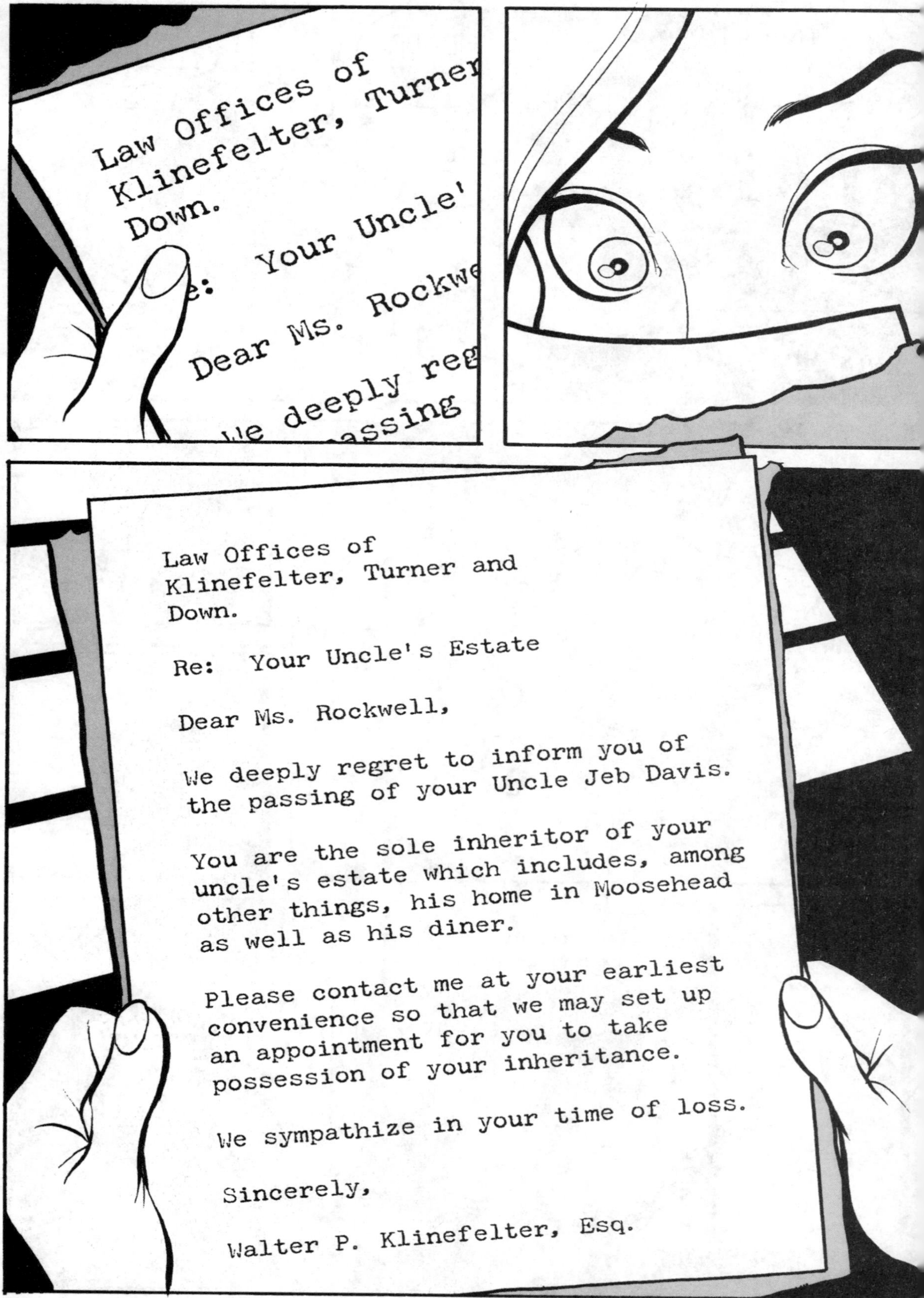
Law Offices of
Klinefelter, Turner
Down.
Your Uncle'
Dear Ms. Rockwe
We deeply reg
passing
Law Offices of
Klinefelter, Turner and
Down.
Re: Your Uncle's Estate
Dear Ms. Rockwell,
We deeply regret to inform you of the passing of your Uncle Jeb Davis.
You are the sole inheritor of your uncle's estate which includes, among other things, his home in Moosehead as well as his diner.
Please contact me at your earliest convenience so that we may set up an appointment for you to take possession of your inheritance.
We sympathize in your time of loss.
Sincerely,
Walter P. Klinefelter, Esq.

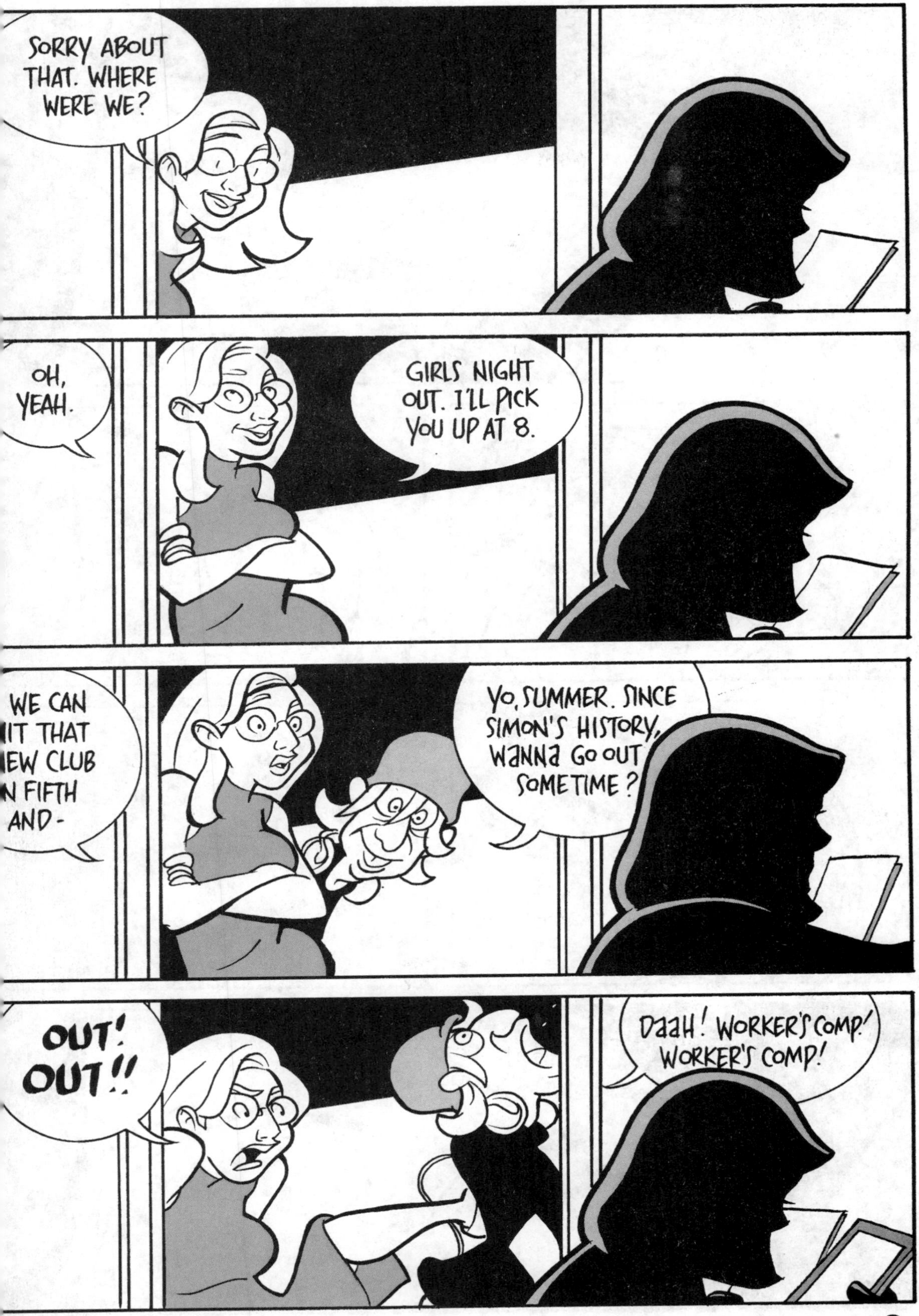
SORRY ABOUT THAT. WHERE WERE WE?
OH, YEAH.
GIRLS NIGHT OUT. I'LL PICK YOU UP AT 8.
WE CAN
IT THAT
EW CLUB
N FIFTH
AND-
YO, SUMMER. SINCE SIMON'S HISTORY, WANNA GO OUT SOMETIME?
OUT! OUT!!
DAAH! WORKER'S COMP! WORKER'S COMP!

...s Estate

Ms. Rockwell,

We deeply regret to inform you of
the passing of your Uncle Jeb Davis.

...u are the sole inheritor of your
...cle's estate which includes, among
other things, his home in Moosehead
as well as his diner.

Please contact me at your earliest
convenience so that we may set up
an appointment for you to t...
possession of your in...

We sympat...

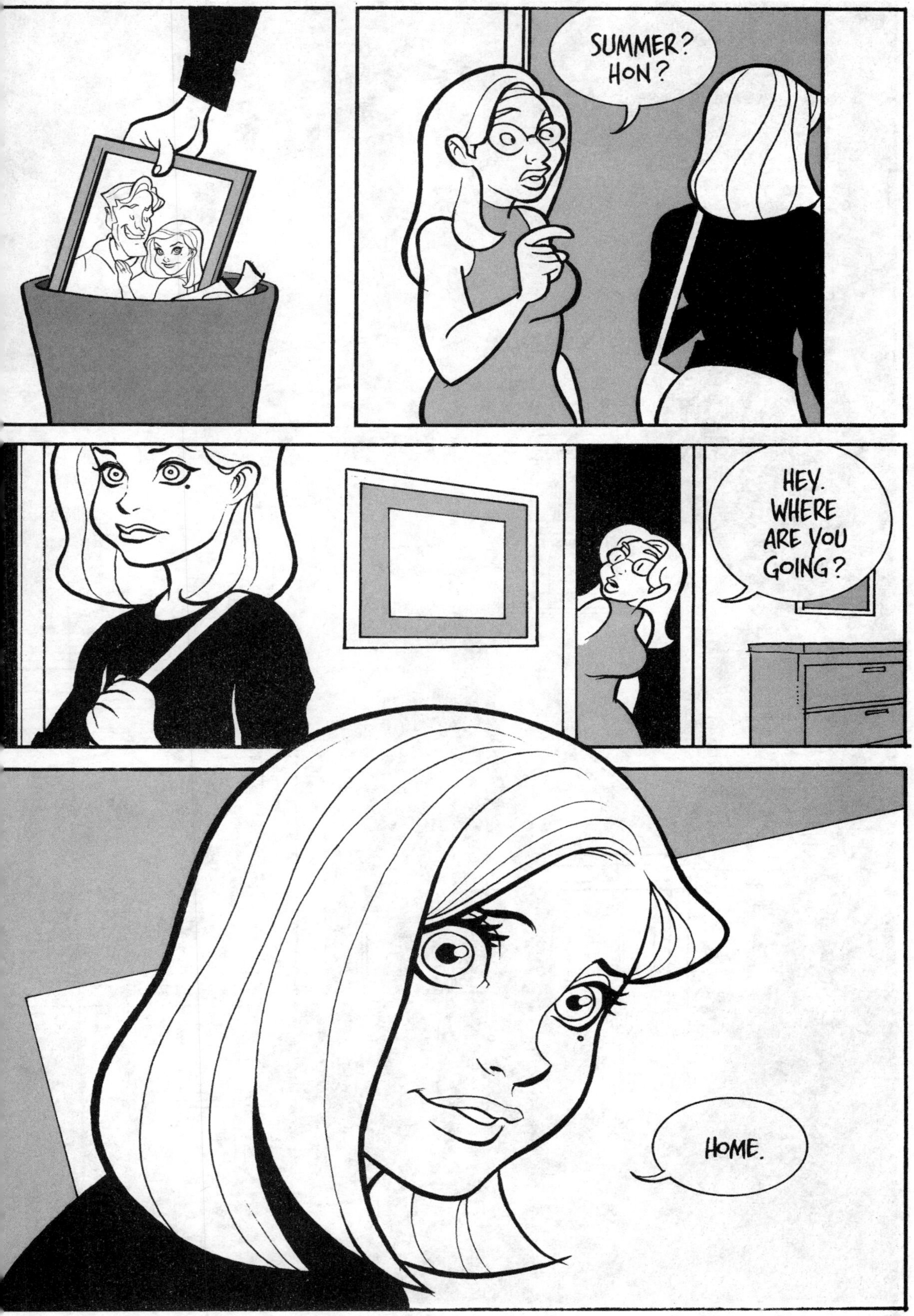
SUMMER? HON?
HEY. WHERE ARE YOU GOING?
HOME.

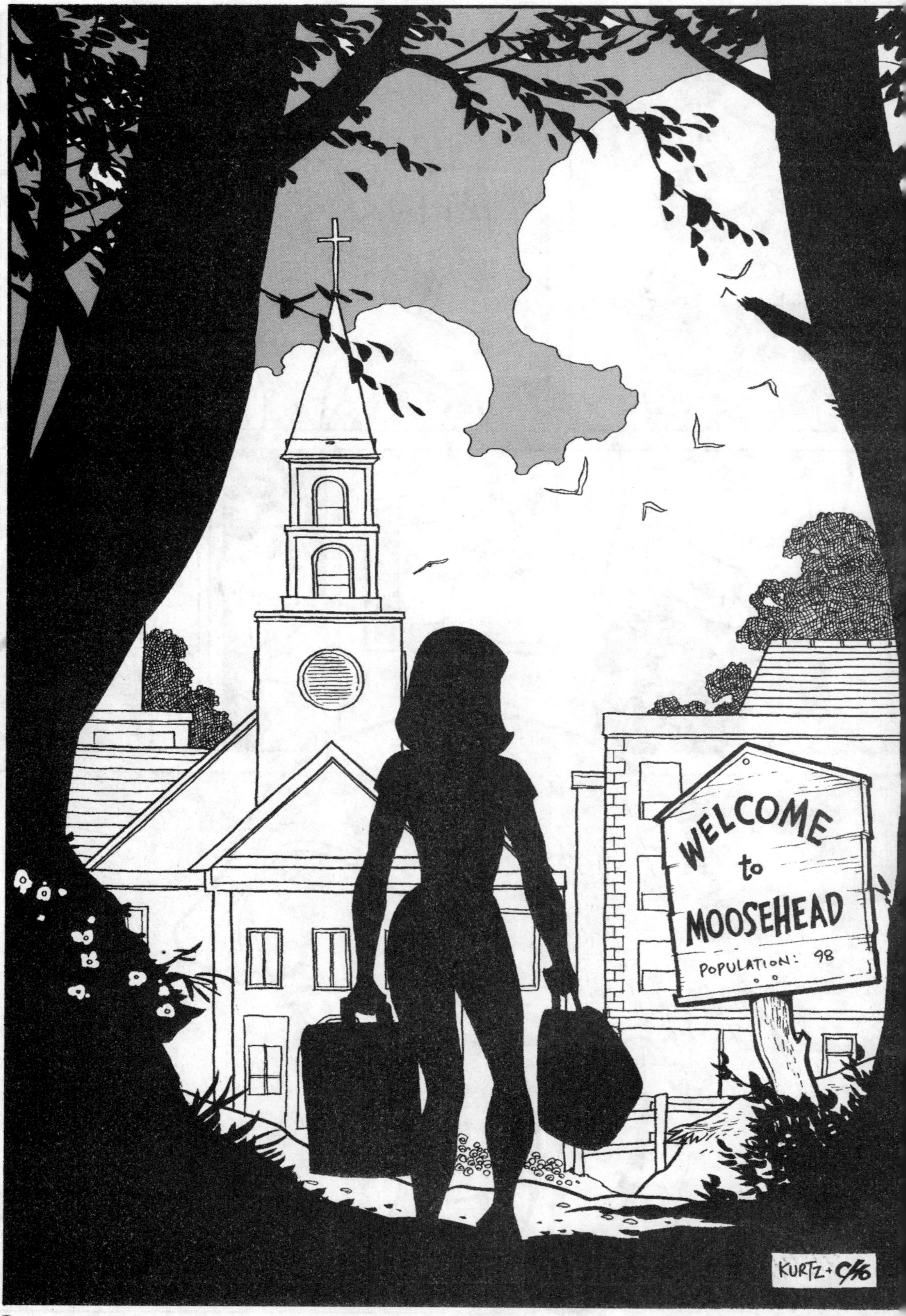
WELCOME to MOOSEHEAD
POPULATION: 98
KURTZ + C/SG